Darwinism as Religion

What Literature Tells Us About Evolution

MICHAEL RUSE

OXFORD
UNIVERSITY PRESS

Oxford University Press is a department of the University of Oxford. It furthers
the University's objective of excellence in research, scholarship, and education
by publishing worldwide. Oxford is a registered trade mark of Oxford University
Press in the UK and certain other countries.

Published in the United States of America by Oxford University Press
198 Madison Avenue, New York, NY 10016, United States of America.

Library of Congress Cataloging-in-Publication Data
Names: Ruse, Michael.
Title: Darwinism as religion : what literature tells us about evolution / Michael Ruse.
Description: [Oxford]; New York : Oxford University Press, 2016. | Includes
bibliographical references and index.
Identifiers: LCCN 2015048181 | ISBN 9780190241025 (hardcover : alk. paper)
Subjects: LCSH: English literature-19th century-History and criticism. |
Literature and science-Great Britain-History. | Religion and
literature-Great Britain-History. | Evolution (Biology) in literature. |
Nature in literature. | Religion in literature. | Religion and science. |
Darwin, Charles, 1809–1882-Influence.
Classification: LCC PR878.E95 R87 2016 | DDC 820.9/356-dc23 LC record available at
http://lccn.loc.gov/2015048181

1 3 5 7 9 8 6 4 2
Printed by Sheridan Books, Inc., United States of America

For my children:
Nigel
Rebecca
Emily
Oliver
Edward

"Happy is the man who hath his quiver full of them."

"In all civilised countries man accumulates property and bequeaths it to his children."

CONTENTS

PREFACE

In 1873, some fourteen years after Charles Darwin had published his *Origin of Species* and two years after the *Descent of Man* appeared, a perceptive if unsympathetic critic wrote of Thomas Henry Huxley, Darwin's self-styled "bulldog":

> He has the moral earnestness, the volitional energy, the absolute conviction in his own opinions, the desire and determination to impress them upon all mankind, which are the essential characteristics of the Puritan character. His whole temper and spirit is essentially dogmatic of the Presbyterian or Independent type, and he might fairly be described as a Roundhead who had lost his faith. He himself shows the truest instinct of this in calling his republished essays 'Lay Sermons.' They abound, in fact, with the hortatory passages, the solemn personal experiences, the heart-searchings and personal appeals that are found in Puritan literature. (Baynes 1873, 502)

That insight is one end of the Thread of Ariadne that leads to the center of this book. I argue that evolutionary thinking generally over the past 300 years of its existence, and Darwinian thinking in particular since the publication of the two great works mentioned above, has taken on the form and role of a religion. One in opposition to the world system, Christianity, from which in major respects it emerged. "Religion" is a somewhat elastic term, and I do not claim that evolutionists are committed to a god-hypothesis, or to a formal hierarchical system—although amusingly and perhaps revealingly in the popular press Darwin's supporter was known as "Pope" Huxley. But I shall argue that in the way that evolution tries to speak to the nature of humans and their place in the scheme of things, we have a religion, or if you want to speak a little more cautiously a "secular religious perspective."

I am very much NOT saying that this is all there is to be said about evolutionary thinking. An important part of my story is that today there is a professional science of Darwin-indebted evolutionary studies that is in no sense a religion. I am saying that there was and is another side to the story, about what I shall call "evolutionism" or "Darwinism," and here religious talk is appropriate. I shall also argue that Charles Darwin is the key figure in my story and thus, in this respect, there was absolutely, totally, and completely a "Darwinian Revolution." He was building on things that had gone before, but he changed our world—for those who agreed with him fully, for those who agreed with him but partially, and for those who rejected his thinking in various ways.

Nigh a decade into the twentieth century, the novelist Mrs. Humphry Ward (the former Mary Augusta Arnold), looking back forty years to her early years in Oxford, wrote:

> In addition to Christ Church, Balliol, and Lincoln, with the literary and philosophical culture for which they stood, there was, of course, Science, camped around the University Museum, in the background. As far as my own personal recollection goes, the men of science entered but little into the struggle of ideas that was going on. The main Darwinian battle had been won long before 1870; science was quietly verifying and exploring along the new lines; it was in literature, history, and theology that evolutionary conceptions were most visibly and dramatically at work. (Ward 1909, xxii)

Mrs. Ward's recollection frames the approach of this book. For forty years, piece by piece, I have been pasting together my collage. Starting with straight history of science, in *The Darwinian Revolution: Science Red in Tooth and Claw* (1979) I gave an overview of Darwin's thinking, its sources, and its consequences. I followed this with *Monad to Man: The Concept of Progress in Evolutionary Biology* (1996) and *Mystery of Mysteries: Is Evolution a Social Construction?* (1999), looking at the story as a history of ideas, focusing on the ways in which values can get into (or out of) scientific thinking. *Darwinism Defended: A Guide to the Evolution Controversies* (1982) and *Darwinism and Its Discontents* (2006) looked more at the science itself. In *Taking Darwin Seriously: A Naturalistic Approach to Philosophy* (1986) and *Philosophy After Darwin* (2009) I took up the philosophical issues. And in *Darwin and Design: Does Nature Have a Purpose?* (2003) and *The Evolution-Creation Struggle* (2005) and other works I looked at religious factors and their histories. Now I want to do this one more time, from (what is for me) a totally new perspective: evolution including Darwin as seen through the lens of literature, fiction and poetry. Note that I am not using evolutionary thinking to analyze literature but seeing the influence of evolutionary thinking on literature and from this drawing conclusions. I say simply that in equal measures I have confirmed much that was believed and discovered much that was new. I say humbly that I am absolutely staggered at the amount of material I have found pertinent to my inquiry and hugely impressed at the sophistication and sensitivity of the massive corpus of secondary material. Again and again, to modify a famous metaphor of Newton, I found myself holding but a small mug while standing at the shore of a great ocean, into which I dipped and came up always with a catch teeming with unknown, brilliant life.

I tell the story chronologically from the beginnings in the early eighteenth century to the ongoing present in the twenty-first century. With regret, apart from a couple of early exceptions, I write only of material in the English language. There is much to say about work in other languages, but not here. Again with one or two obvious exceptions, I have avoided science fiction. I wanted to stay with culture at a more general level, rather than getting into a specialized field where perhaps there might be a bias toward the sorts of things I want to discuss. Also, apart from a couple of brief references, I decided that the theatre and cinema were beyond my scope. Even so, worried that I might end with little more than a catalogue, I have had to be severely selective. I have tried to be balanced and fair, but I have had to leave out more than I could include, and so I apologize now and leave things at that. I will say that I am incredibly lucky. I am well into the decade past my allotted biblical span of years. I have never, ever, had such an exciting project and if I can infect you with some of my enthusiasm that will be justification enough and more. If you do not sense that this has been a labor of great love, paying respect and thanks to writings that have filled my life with joy and inspiration since I was a small child, then I have failed both the topic and you, the reader. I had long hesitated to take on such a task as this precisely because literature was my world away from my professional interests and I did not want to mix the two. Now I have done so and I think at last the time was ripe.

So to the best part of all. First let me thank my editor, Peter Ohlin. He saw, what is true, that this is not really a work of literary criticism but a history of ideas that is used, in the tradition of Arthur Lovejoy and Isaiah Berlin, to throw light on philosophical issues, in this case the nature of evolutionary theorizing. I am very grateful both for his insight and for his support. As with the choice of topic, I am incredibly lucky in the people with whom, as one does, I have shared my thinking as I have worked on this project. I am much aware of the difficulties in trying to think in an interdisciplinary fashion, but I can only say that the students of English literature with whom I have interacted and begged advice have, to an exemplary degree, been thoughtful and helpful and totally nonthreatened by a presumptuous stranger. Above all, mention must be made on the American side of the Atlantic to John Glendening, who has shared with me his deep knowledge of evolution in fiction, and on the British side of the Atlantic to John Robert Holmes, who has shared with me his equally deep knowledge of evolution in poetry. I regard Holmes's *Darwin's Bards: British and American Poetry in the Age of Evolution* as one of the landmark works in recent scholarship. Ian Hesketh in Australia has been both reader and critic, and as important an enthusiastic supporter of the very idea of my project. My friendship with Philip Appleman goes back forty years since I was a visiting professor at Indiana University. I am grateful to Anne DeWitt for the wonderful quote from Mrs. Ward. The antiquarian bookseller Jeremy Parrott has recently acquired a set of Charles Dickens's weekly magazine, *All the Year Round*, with marginalia (probably by Dickens himself) identifying the anonymous authors. He has very generously shared with me information about the authorship of the pieces on the *Origin* in 1860 and 1861. Jeff O'Connell tracked down more articles and books than morally I had any right to ask him to find. It goes without saying that no one could tackle such a project as mine without the nigh-transcendentalist aura of those pioneers Gillian Beer and George Levine. The generous bequest of William and Lucyle Werkmeister funds both my professorship at Florida State University and my research expenses. Very great thanks are due to the Stellenbosch Institute for Advanced Study in South Africa that provided a home while I worked on the background for this study. The warmth and support of Hendrik Geyer and his staff made the four months I spent there the most productive time in my whole academic career.

In *Our Mutual Friend*, the little schoolmistress, hopelessly in love with the unresponsive schoolmaster, learns the name of her hated rival.

"I wonder," said Miss Peecher, as she sat making up her weekly report on a half-holiday afternoon, "what they call Hexam's sister?"

Mary Anne, at her needlework, attendant and attentive, held her arm up.

"Well, Mary Anne?"

"She is named Lizzie, ma'am."

"She can hardly be named Lizzie, I think, Mary Anne," returned Miss Peecher, in a tunefully instructive voice. "Is Lizzie a Christian name, Mary Anne?"

Mary Anne laid down her work, rose, hooked herself behind, as being under catechization, and replied: "No, it is a corruption, Miss Peecher."

"Who gave her that name?" Miss Peecher was going on, from the mere force of habit, when she checked herself; on Mary Anne's evincing theological impatience to strike in with her godfathers and her godmothers, and said: "I mean of what name is it a corruption?"

"Elizabeth, or Eliza, Miss Peecher."

"Right, Mary Anne. Whether there were any Lizzies in the early Christian Church must be considered very doubtful, very doubtful." Miss Peecher was exceedingly sage here. "Speaking correctly, we say, then, that Hexam's sister is called Lizzie; not that she is named so. Do we not, Mary Anne?"

"We do, Miss Peecher." (Dickens [1865] 1948, 339)

Called or named, I too love a Lizzie and through this project, as always, she has been there to support and to encourage.

Finally, for having let me live into the age of the Internet, let me give thanks to whatever deity it is that Darwinians worship. Twenty years ago this project would not have been possible. Now within seconds one can track down an obscure poem or interesting reference and keep working as though one had labored all day, as in the past, in the bowels of a great library. Some change really is Progress.

PROLOGUE

Charles Robert Darwin (1809–1882), the great English scientist, spent from 1831 through to 1836 going around the globe on board HMS *Beagle* (Browne 1995). The ship's mandate was to map the coastline of South America. Although Darwin was, at least informally, the ship's naturalist, he was not officially part of the crew. He was a gentleman, paying his own way. He was independent. Hence, partly because he was a terrible sailor much afflicted by seasickness and partly because his real scientific interests back then lay in geologizing, Darwin spent as much time as possible on dry land, leaving it to his shipmates to get on with their surveying tasks. Wherever he went, he made sure to include in his baggage his copy of *Paradise Lost* by John Milton, for—as he recorded in his *Autobiography*, written many years later—this was his "chief favourite," the work for inspiration and relaxation after the day's labors (Darwin 1958, 85).

In 1859, Charles Darwin published his *Origin of Species*, where he argued that organisms are the products of a process of gradual natural change—evolution— fueled mainly by a mechanism that he called "natural selection." Darwin changed our world. He changed his own world, the one that thirty years earlier he had encountered and seen through the glorious visions of the great Puritan poet.

> God said,
> 'Be gathered now ye waters under Heaven
> Into one place, and let dry land appear.'
> Immediately the mountains huge appear
> Emergent, and their broad bare backs upheave
> Into the clouds; their tops ascend the sky:
> So high as heaved the tumid hills, so low
> Down sunk a hollow bottom broad and deep,
> Capacious bed of waters
> (Milton [1667] 2000, 7.282–290)

Next, the creation of organisms, numbers without limit, throbbing with life.

> And God created the great whales, and each
> Soul living, each that crept, which plenteously
> The waters generated by their kinds;
> And every bird of wing after his kind;
> And saw that it was good, and blessed them, saying.
> 'Be fruitful, multiply, and in the seas,
> And lakes, and running streams, the waters fill;
> And let the fowl be multiplied, on the Earth.'
>
> (7.391–398)

Finally, the climax:

> 'Let us make now Man in our image, Man
> In our similitude, and let them rule
> Over the fish and fowl of sea and air,
> Beast of the field, and over all the earth,
> And every creeping thing that creeps the ground!'
> This said, he formed thee, Adam, thee, O Man,
> Dust of the ground, and in thy nostrils breathed
> The breath of life; in his own image he
> Created thee, in the image of God
> Express, and thou becam'st a living Soul.
> Male he created thee, but thy consort
> Female, for race; then blessed mankind, and said,
> 'Be fruitful, multiply, and fill the Earth.'
>
> (7.519–531)

When Darwin started the *Beagle* voyage he was a fairly conventional Christian. Then, Darwin's religion transmuted into a form of deism, seeing God as unmoved mover, one who had started the process but then let things unfurl according to unbroken law. But Darwin never forgot, and nor should we, that it was the Miltonian world vision that set the challenge to which he rose so magnificently. The challenge that the philosopher-scientist John Herschel called the "mystery of mysteries"—a scientific understanding of the world and the life teaming upon it (Cannon 1961). This is at the center of our story—the coming of evolution and its implications for the old Judeo-Christian story of origins—and we begin not that long after Milton lived and wrote, as the old verities started to crumble and people sought new ways and new ideas.

1

The Eighteenth Century

The Sicilian philosopher Empedocles (c490–c430 B.C.) was a proto-evolutionist, thinking that the elements come together randomly and sometimes form parts of animals and plants—a head here and a leg there—and that in turn these sometimes combine to make functioning organisms (Bowler 1984). This thinking found little favor with the great Greek philosophers, Plato and Aristotle. They did not reject evolution out of prejudice—certainly not out of religious prejudice. It was simply that a story that put everything down to blind chance could not account for the most distinctive aspect of organisms—what we would call their "teleological" nature, what Aristotle would speak of in terms of "final cause." Organisms, plants, and animals are not just hodge-podges; they are complex, functioning entities, with parts that seem as if they were designed—Plato thought they were designed—for intended ends. The eye is for seeing; the hand is for grasping; the pretty, fragrant flower is to attract pollinating insects (Ruse 2003).

With the coming of Christianity, bringing in its wake what the nineteenth-century Scottish essayist Thomas Carlyle was to call "Hebrew old clothes"— starting with the creation story of Genesis—the Western world was even more set against evolutionary thinking, something that lasted up to and through the sixteenth and seventeenth centuries, covering the main events of the Scientific Revolution. What then was to change people's thinking? What was it that was so powerful that the grip of final-cause thinking and of Jewish-creation thinking could be loosened and people could start contemplating a natural story of origins? It was not that these two factors simply collapsed and died. It is true that the Scientific Revolution broke the hold of final-cause thinking in the physical world—Francis Bacon famously referred to them as Vestal Virgins, decorative but sterile. But in the world of animals and plants, such teleological thinking had even greater force, especially in Britain. Above all, what made possible speculation about natural origins was the new philosophy of Progress, the idea that somehow and for some reason or reasons things are and can continue to improve, and that this can come about through human (rather than divine) effort

(Ruse 1996). This was not an idea that was really known to the Greeks. By the beginning of the eighteenth century, however, what we now call the beginnings of the Enlightenment, successes and advances in science and technology, combined with political improvements as occurred in Britain when the autocratic monarch James the Second was overthrown, were starting to engender hope and confidence that it was possible that there was, and might be, change for the good. And with the coming of this world vision, it was almost natural—at least it was almost natural for some people—to take this thinking from the world of humans and to apply it to the world of organisms. Often, having found this kind of moving-upward progress in the living world, people were happy in a kind of circular fashion to apply it to confirmation of Progress in the human world![1]

We start our story with Progress, move then to evolution, and end by looking at the implications for religious thinking.

Progress

The most distinguished historian of the concept of Progress defined the notion thus: "The idea of human Progress, then, is a theory which involves a synthesis of the past and a prophecy of the future. It is based on an interpretation of history, which regards men as slowly advancing—*pedetemtim progredietes*—in a definite and desirable direction, and infers that this progress will continue indefinitely" (Bury 1920, 5). Taken in this sense, we can distinguish three basic forms or interpretations.

First, there were the French, living (until the Revolution) under a religion-infused repressive monarchy, the *ancien régime*. Fermenting and writing against this were the public intellectuals, the *philosophes*, the best known of whom was Voltaire. For them, hopes of Progress were all-absorbing and inspiring, something illustrated by history and made possible by ever-increasing advances in technology, in medicine and education, and in general thinking about society and culture. Most famous was the Marquis de Condorcet, who wrote (in the early 1790s) even as he was imprisoned and about to die due to misfortunes in the Revolution: "No one can doubt that, as preventative medicine improves, and food and housing becomes healthier, as a way of life is established that develops our physical powers by exercise without ruining them by excess, as the two most virulent causes of deterioration, misery and excess wealth, are eliminated, the average length of human life will be increased and a better health and stronger physical constitution will be ensured" (Condorcet [1795] 1956, 199).

---

[1] Following convention, I use the capitalized "Progress" for the cultural notion and the uncapitalized "progress" for the biological notion.

Particularly interesting to us is Denis Diderot (1713–1784), general man of letters and cofounder of the *Encyclopédie* (1751–1772), a characteristically revealing attempt to bring all of human knowledge together into one overarching work. He made explicit the extent to which he saw Progress as something showing itself in human societies today, from the most primitive to the most sophisticated, and his own being very much toward the latter end of the scale rather than the former. "The Tahitian is at a primary stage in the development of the world, the European is at its old age. The interval separating us is greater than that between the new-born child and the decrepit old man" (Diderot 1943, 152). Note the analogy with human individual growth.

Second we have a more German-based notion of Progress. This is an upward growth that is less physical and more something perceived or apprehended by the mind—a perspective central to the philosophy of the greatest of all the German thinkers, Immanuel Kant, who argued that all understanding is a function of mind-imposed categories or restraints on empirical experience. It is to be found in many others, notably the poet Johann Wolfgang von Goethe and those following him, the so-called nature philosophers or *Naturphilosophen* like the philosopher Friedrich Schelling and the anatomist Lorenz Oken. Although writing a little after our time, the philosopher G. W. F. Hegel gives perfect expression to the idea: "Nature is to be regarded as a system of stages, one arising necessarily from the other and being a proximate truth of the stage from which it results; but it is not generated naturally out of the other, but only in the inner Idea which constitutes the ground of Nature" (Hegel [1817] 1970, 20). Such Progress (in many respects an outgrowth of the Romantic movement, which put such emphasis on apprehension) is above all organic, developing like a plant, and spiritual or soulful in the sense of set off against the material world.

And third we have the British notions of Progress, understandably tending more to pragmatic, political, and economic themes. This was a country at the cutting edge of science, leading the way in the development of industry and of political and economic thinking to match and control the advent of so societally transforming a phenomenon. Much of the really innovative thinking came from north of the Border, notably in the philosophical thinking of David Hume (1711–1776) and the economic thinking of Adam Smith (1723–1790). The former—trying to do for philosophy what Newton had done for physics—articulated the most profound empiricist worldview ever seen before or since. The latter, trying to speak to the needs of a society where business interests were now becoming paramount, expressed an idea that we shall encounter again, arguing that self-interest is at the heart of the human psyche and any efforts to control and manage society must take this first and foremost. "It is not from the benevolence of the butcher, the brewer, or the baker that we expect our dinner, but from their regard to their own interest" (Smith [1776] 1994, 15).

William Godwin

Most famous of all the British writers on Progress is William Godwin (1756–1836) who expressed his ideas first in a work of theory and then in fiction. His *Enquiry Concerning Political Justice, and Its Influence on General Virtue and Happiness* was published in 1793, provocatively at the height of the French Revolution. With reason considered a strong statement in favor of a form of anarchism—Godwin thought society should never interfere with individual judgment—the work offered trenchant attacks on existing institutions from those affecting the public domain like the law courts to those affecting the private domain of family life—"marriage, as now understood, is a monopoly, and the worst of monopolies. So long as two human beings are forbidden, by positive institution, to follow the dictates of their own mind, prejudice will be alive and vigorous. So long as I seek, by despotic and artificial means, to maintain my possession of a woman, I am guilty of the most odious selfishness" (Godwin [1793] 1976, 762).[2] At the same time, a positive message to balance the negative attacks, there was an almost-fanatical belief in human perfectibility and consequent progressive improvement of society. Vices and moral weaknesses can be overcome. This apparently is a function of our receptivity to truth. "Every truth that is capable of being communicated is capable of being brought home to the conviction of the mind. Every principle which can be brought home to the conviction of the mind will infallibly produce a correspondent effect upon the conduct" (145). You may worry that we will simply have a body of perfect human beings, sitting around in isolation. Fortunately this will not be so. Because we are all fundamentally the same, a sentiment in favor of ourselves will extend to the favors of others. "We are partakers of a common nature, and the same causes that contribute to the benefit of one will contribute to the benefit of another" (183).

Against this background, we have Godwin's novel—written immediately after the *Enquiry* and published a mere fifteen months later—*Things as They Are; or, The Adventures of Caleb Williams*. It is an odd work, combining strong social criticism with thrilling adventure, explicit detective investigations with implicit psychosexual relationships that have given twentieth-century Freudians many happy hours of analysis. It tells the story of a young servant, Caleb Williams, and his master, Ferdinando Falkland, and their often tortured interactions, manifesting love and hate in nigh equal quantities. Falkland is a man who is wise and generous but given to atypical outbursts of temper. Apparently these outbursts

---

[2] This passage actually comes from an appendix, "Of Cooperation, Cohabitation and Marriage" added to the second edition of 1786. Godwin was worse than Henry James when it came to messing with his texts.

date back to a conflict with a tyrannical neighbor, Barnabas Tyrrel, who (hardly surprisingly given his appalling nature and behavior) gets himself murdered by person or persons unknown. Because of his interfering with Tyrrel's bad behavior, suspicion falls on Falkland. However, not only does he deny this but tenants of Tyrrel are arrested and then hanged for the murder.[3]

It is this course of events that has unnerved Falkland, and Williams, who is given to poking his nose into the business of others, suspects Falkland of the deed. He confronts his master, forces a confession, but also is bound never to reveal this fact. Naturally finding himself somewhat uncomfortable with his situation, Williams flees but then is induced to return to face the (false) accusation that he has stolen from his master. Offered the chance of a fair trial before Falkland's brother-in-law, it turns out that this is but a weak promise, and Williams ends up convicted and thrown in jail, where fortunately one of Falkland's servants takes pity on him and gives him tools to make his escape.

Now Williams starts a life of hiding, of deception, of discovery, of misery, and of constant motion, hounded as he is by a fiend called Gines (Jones in some versions), who in a much-imitated-later mode—notably the American television series *The Fugitive*—is always on his track trying to call him in and return him to his punishment. In one instance, Falkland and Williams come face to face, but the meeting leads to no resolutions other than that now Falkland sends Williams money to support him! Finally, with his former master cornered, Williams is able to get Falkland brought to court to face his accuser, and to establish Falkland's guilt once and for all. At this point, rather like *Great Expectations*, we are offered a choice of endings. In an unpublished version, the magistrate ridicules Williams's charges and the unfortunate man ends up back in prison, fairly clearly now unhinged and mentally unstable. In the published version, written because Godwin was not satisfied with the first version, Williams succeeds in his efforts, Falkland and he are reconciled, but then not only does Falkland die (he dies in the unpublished version too) but Williams is consumed with guilt at what he has done to a man who is essentially good.

As I say, it is an odd work, not the least because of the love-hate relationship between Williams and Falkland. But what really counts is that Caleb Williams is a vehicle for Godwin's political philosophy and psychology of humankind (Graham 1990). Again and again, Godwin hammers away at the inequity of the laws against the poor—the game laws particularly come in for vicious critique—and the oppression of the weak and powerless—especially given the way that trials and tribunals (of which there are many in the novel) are always stacked against them. Tyrrel quarreled with one of his tenants by the name of Hawkins.

---

[3] The novel of Godwin's daughter, Mary Shelley's *Frankenstein*, likewise has someone hanged for a crime she (in this case a woman) did not commit.

He therefore barred the man's usual path to his own home. The son got up in the night and broke the padlocks. What a mistake! The son was sent to jail and the father was broken. "He had trusted to persevering industry and skill, to save the wreck of his little property from the vulgar spite of his landlord. But he had now no longer any spirit to exert those efforts which his situation more than ever required" (Godwin [1794] 1982, 75). It was this that sparked the quarrel with Falkland and led to Tyrrel's death. Not that this ended with much consolation for Hawkins and his son, for it was they who were falsely accused of the murder and ended their lives in the hangman's noose.

In the world described by Godwin, given the oppressive nature of society's laws and their mode of enforcement, there was not much more joy for women. Adding to Tyrrel's inequities, we have the story of poor Emily, his niece. This is not a novel that Charles Darwin would have liked—he demanded a pretty woman and a happy ending—for first the poor girl is threatened with rape by the man whom her supposed protector had arbitrarily chosen for her husband and then she is imprisoned for nonpayment of her room and board over the past years. Expectedly, she falls sick. "Her fever became more violent; her delirium was stronger; and the tortures of her imagination were proportioned to the unfavourableness of the state in which the removal had been effected. It was highly improbable that she could recover" (85). She doesn't.

This unfairness of the judicial system—something that apparently spawned countless imitators—is the ongoing theme of the novel. Not one of the many trials throughout the novel turns out as it should. But intertwined through all is the more positive theme about human nature, namely, that doing ill is not a function of some innate human depravity but of the oppressive nature of circumstances. As Williams said, speaking of himself and trying to understand why he shows such a lack of generosity to his master: "I was born free: I was born healthy, vigorous, and active, complete in all the lineaments and members of a human body. I was not born indeed to the possession of hereditary wealth; but I had a better inheritance, an enterprising mind, an inquisitive spirit, a liberal ambition" (135). What is striking—and perhaps more explicable by the demands of the philosophy than by unspoken sexual desires—is the extent to which Williams constantly emphasizes the overall worth of his oppressor, Falkland. Even at the end—and remember our subject is a man who has not only committed one murder but who has let two innocent people hang in his stead—we find Williams saying: "Mr. Falkland is of a noble nature. Yes; in spite of the catastrophe of Tyrrel, of the miserable end of the Hawkinses, and of all that I have myself suffered, I affirm that he has qualities of the most admirable kind" (323).

The point being made is that had it not been for the unjust laws that allowed Tyrrel to oppress Emily and the Hawkinses and thus led to the murder of Tyrrel by Falkland, a sin compounded by relief at the Hawkinses getting the blame and subsequently being punished for the murder, Falkland would not have then opened himself to Williams's inquisitiveness and all that followed afterward, namely, the master's hounding of a former servant for whom he clearly felt deep affection. But there is more than this. A key element of Godwin's thinking is that the truth sets us free, or rather the truth leads to good moral behavior. All agree that dramatically the second ending to the novel is better than the first, but the real reason for the revision is the urge to express Godwin's philosophy and psychology. Had Williams only been willing to rely on the truth and its effect on Falkland's nature, rather than recourse to the evil of the law, all would have been well. "I am sure that if I had opened my heart to Mr. Falkland, if I had told to him privately the tale that I have now been telling, he could not have resisted my reasonable demand" (323). And if this had happened, Falkland would not have collapsed and died of shame, and Williams would not have ended the novel wracked by guilt.

Enough! The point to be made is that Progress as a philosophy is firmly on the scene. A novel can present ideas in a way more dramatic, engaging, and hence threatening than countless nonfictional volumes of political philosophy. Revealingly, the Prime Minister of the day thought, because no one was going to read the work anyway, there was little point in prosecuting Godwin for his subversive ideas as expressed in his *Enquiry*. It is not the first, nor will it be the last, time that a British leader has made a mistake. Thanks to *Caleb Williams*—a great commercial success from the moment of its appearance, praised and hated in equal measures—Progress was now part of the general discourse.

Evolution

In retrospect, it is hard to keep count of the factors in the eighteenth century that point to the coming of evolution. For a start, people were starting to push back the age of the Earth (Rudwick 2005). Even conservatives happily took refuge in such biblical notions as 1,000 years being but a day in the eyes of the Lord. The French naturalist Georges Buffon thought that the Earth was about 70,000 years old—not much by modern standards, 4.5 billion years, but a lot more than 6,000 years, the figure calculated in the seventeenth century by Archbishop Ussher and embraced by today's American Creationists. With the extension of Earth's age came speculations about how the Earth was formed. One group, the Neptunists, put it all down to water and sediments settling out and forming the strata that so characterize the Earth's surface. Naturally, this more and more promoted study of the fossils as evidence of events of the past. Another group, the Vulcanists, put all down to fire and its effects. Most interesting is the Scottish geologist James Hutton (1788). Clearly influenced by the Newcomen engine, which fueled by fire went round and round as it drove the pumps that emptied the mines of water, Hutton saw the Earth as a kind of machine, forever going round and round bringing rocks to the surface and in turn being sucked down again (Ruse 2013). Famously he extended life's history to virtual eternity—"no vestige of a beginning, no prospect of an end."

Another factor pointing toward evolution came from the physical sciences. Newton's universe just keeps circling around without essential change. But, before long, people started speculating on possible beginnings. In the eighteenth century a number of figures—Immanuel Kant, Pierre Laplace, William Herschel—began to speculate about the gas clouds that one sees about the universe (Bush 1996). Could these "nebulae" be the parents of solar systems, as the matter collapses into itself thanks to gravity? Is it possible that at the center we get solid masses, generating heat from the condensation, and then around them smaller bodies forever circulating? More than one person found this a suggestive analogy, pointing to the possibility of a natural origin of organisms. Related to these physical speculations were what we today would call biological speculations. A long-held belief was that different organisms form no random pattern. In his wisdom, God has created life so that it can be put in a continuous chain from the most humble forms to the most sophisticated. In the natural world this upper point is filled by humankind, although most supporters of the "chain of being" extended it to include higher forms of being, the orders of angels right up to the top. The poet Alexander Pope (in 1734) captured this idea in verse.

> Vast chain of being, which from God began,
> Natures ethereal, human, angel, man,
> Beast, bird, fish, insect! what no eye can see,
> No glass can reach! from infinite to thee,
> From thee to nothing!—On superior pow'rs
> Were we to press, inferior might on ours:
> Or in the full creation leave a void,
> Where, one step broken, the great scale's destroy'd:
> From nature's chain whatever link you strike,
> Tenth or ten thousandth, breaks the chain alike.
> *An Essay on Man*, Epistle I, section VIII

Note that this was a static world picture, but as the century went on there were certainly hints by some of the enthusiasts that it could be made to move, in an escalator-type fashion.

The work of the great classifier Carl Linnaeus was clearly going to be crucial in some sense to the coming of evolution (Frangsmyr 1983). He set about putting all organisms into one coherent, connected system—a hierarchy of nested sets. Thus, for instance, dogs and wolves are separate species, but individuals are clearly more similar to each other than they are to cats and lions. Following this insight, Linnaeus put the members of the dog and wolf species into a higher grouping, the genus, that included all of them and excluded others, like members of the cat and lion species. None of this in itself implies evolution, as such, although there is some evidence that toward the end Linnaeus was thinking that some species might form naturally. But the greater the success of the system, the more it called for an explanation and the more evolution seemed a plausible candidate. More immediately, what was important and to some shocking was the way in which Linnaeus grouped humans together with higher apes. He was not alone in being fascinated by the similarities between us and the apes. For instance, the Scottish judge James Burnet, Lord Mondboddo, was much interested in the origins of language, and this led him to think that possibly the higher apes were primitive forms of humanity. No more than Linnaeus was Mondboddo a full-blown evolutionist, however. He denied that there are links between humans and apes and other lower forms of humanity (Burnett 1773–1792).

Expectedly, Buffon was also making a contribution to the debate about origins (Roger 1997). He speculated at times that some groups of species had common ancestors, from which—thanks to the effects of the environment—today's forms "degenerated." The ancestral cat form gave rise to tigers and lions and domestic cats, and so forth. He did not publicly take this thinking back to its logical conclusions and roots, although privately he may have thought this way. Not that he was ever really committed to the idea—sometimes he pictured life's history as a tree and at other times used different metaphors, like maps or nets. Complicating any final assessment, Buffon ran into trouble with the religious authorities and smartly stepped back into line, although whether from conviction or expediency is still debated.

The Evolutionists

Against this background, what of genuine transmutationists or evolutionists? Denis Diderot staked an early claim. And it was clear that it was Progress that was fueling his thinking. As in the human societal case, also drawing analogy with the growth of the individual, he wrote:

> Just as in the animal and vegetable kingdoms, an individual begins, so to speak, grows, subsists, decays and passes away, could it not be the same with the whole species? . . . would not the philosopher, left free to speculate, suspect that animality had from all eternity its particular elements scattered in and mingled with the mass of matter; that it has happened

to these elements to reunite, because it was possible for this to be done; that the embryo formed from these elements had passed through an infinity of different organizations and developments . . . that it has perhaps still other developments to undergo, and other increases to taken on, which are unknown to us; that it has had or will have a stationary condition; . . . that it will disappear for ever from nature, or rather it will continue to exist in it, but in a form, and with faculties, quite different from those observed in it at this moment of time. (Diderot 1943, 48)

Most thorough was the grandfather of Charles Darwin, Erasmus Darwin (1731–1802). A prominent figure in the British Midlands—physician, inventor, educational theorist, friend of many (including Ben Franklin), member of the Lunar Society (a Birmingham-based club of industrialists and scientists including Josiah Wedgwood, Matthew Boulton, James Watt, and Joseph Priestly)—Darwin was also a poet, much given to discussing scientific ideas in verse. Linnaeus had based a lot of plant classification on their sexual organs, opening an opportunity for Darwin (who had three children with his first wife, two with a mistress in the interregnum, and then seven with a second wife, and probably more to boot) to hymn the botanic world in somewhat racy terms.

> —Fair CHUNDA smiles amid the burning waste,
>   Her brow unturban'd, and her zone unbrac'd;
>   *Ten* brother-youths with light umbrella's shade,
>   Or fan with busy hands the panting maid;
>   Loose wave her locks, disclosing, as they break,
>   The rising bosom and averted cheek;
> Clasp'd round her ivory neck with studs of gold
>   Flows her thin vest in many a gauzy fold;
>   O'er her light limbs the dim transparence plays,
> And the fair form, it seems to hide, betrays.
>   (Darwin 1789, 331–340)

Published around the same time as Godwin's works, in *Zoonomia*, a medical work that at once attracted attention and respect—it was soon translated into German and read by the elderly Immanuel Kant—Erasmus Darwin wrote unambiguously in favor of evolution.

From thus meditating on the great similarity of the structure of the warm-blooded animals, and at the same time of the great changes they undergo both before and after their nativity; and by considering in how minute a portion of time many of the changes of animals above described have been produced; would it be too bold to imagine, that in the great length of time, since the earth began to exist, perhaps millions of ages before the commencement of the history of mankind, would it be too bold to imagine, that all warm-blooded animals have arisen from one living filament, which THE GREAT FIRST CAUSE endued with animality, with the power of acquiring new parts, attended with new propensities, directed by irritations, sensations, volitions, and associations; and thus possessing the faculty of continuing to improve by its own inherent activity, and of delivering down those improvements by generation to its posterity, world without end! (Darwin 1794–1796, 2, 240)

Then a little later (actually published posthumously) he turned to verse.

> Organic Life beneath the shoreless waves
> Was born and nurs'd in Ocean's pearly caves;
> First forms minute, unseen by spheric glass,
> Move on the mud, or pierce the watery mass;
> These, as successive generations bloom,
> New powers acquire, and larger limbs assume;
> Whence countless groups of vegetation spring,
> And breathing realms of fin, and feet, and wing.
>
>   Thus the tall Oak, the giant of the wood,
> Which bears Britannia's thunders on the flood;
> The Whale, unmeasured monster of the main,
> The lordly Lion, monarch of the plain,
> The Eagle soaring in the realms of air,
> Whose eye undazzled drinks the solar glare,
> Imperious man, who rules the bestial crowd,
> Of language, reason, and reflection proud,
> With brow erect who scorns this earthy sod,
> And styles himself the image of his God;
> Arose from rudiments of form and sense,
> An embryon point, or microscopic ens!
>   (Darwin 1803, Canto I, lines 295–314)

Notions of biological progress, from the blob to the human, are the very backbone (to use an apt metaphor) of this vision, and Darwin explicitly tied his biology into his philosophy. The idea of organic progressive evolution "is analogous to the improving excellence observable in every part of the creation; such as the progressive increase of the wisdom and happiness of its inhabitants" (Darwin

1794–1796, 2, 247–248). Indeed, it wasn't just Progress in general that he endorsed but a form with very significant similarities (and probably debts) to that of Godwin. In particular, as in science, it is all very much a matter of starting with the individual and finding the truth, about others and about the world.

> Immortal Guide! O, now with accents kind
> Give to my ear the progress of the Mind.
> How loves, and tastes, and sympathies commence
> From evanescent notices of sense?
> How from the yielding touch and rolling eyes
> The piles immense of human science rise?—
> With mind gigantic steps the puny Elf,
> And weighs and measures all things but himself!"
> > (Darwin 1803, Canto III, lines 41–48)

Then with knowledge accumulating, a form of sympathy for others takes over and makes for harmonious society. For Darwin, as for Godwin, Progress is all very much a matter of something stemming from the individual rather than something imposed.

The Anti-Jacobin Attack

It was during the first part of the last decade of the eighteenth century that the French Revolution started to go badly wrong. The early receptions of *Zoonomia* basically passed over the evolutionary speculations without comment. But it was not long before conservative critics started to panic at the subversive thoughts of Progress. No good could come of them. One of the most effective weapons forged by the opponents of Progress, who included notably George Canning— then Under Secretary of State for Foreign Affairs and, some years later, the Prime Minister—was the satirical weekly *The Anti-Jacobin*. Some of its best squibs were devastating parodies of Darwin's poetry—parodies that not only named Darwin explicitly but for good measure included Godwin's name too. No one had any doubt that this was a package deal. In the "Progress of Man," human bloodlust is made our defining character and woe to any unfortunate mammal that gets in our way.

> Ah, hapless porker! what can now avail,
> Thy back's stiff bristles, or thy curly tail?
> Ah! what avail those eyes so small and round,
> Long pendant ears, and snout that loves the ground?

Not unreveng'd thou diest!—in after times
From thy spilt blood shall spring unnumber'd crimes.
Soon shall the slaught'rous arms that wrought thy woe,
Improved by malice, deal a deadlier blow;
When social man shall pant for nobler game,
And 'gainst his fellow man the vengeful weapon aim.
(Canning, Frere, and Ellis [1798] 1854, 90–91)

Note not just that evolution came into this world as a function of—an epi-phenomenon on—thoughts of human Progress, and how its reception therefore was going to be very much a matter of how people regarded Progress as an idea, but what this meant for the status—certainly the perceived status—of the idea of evolution itself. If you want to support or counter a regular scientific claim—for instance, about the nature of the double helix—then you turn to the empiri-cal evidence, for and against. There was no question of doing that here. At least in part this was because there really wasn't that much empirical evidence. But also in part—a bigger part—because people saw that value commitments were what was really at stake. In this sense, then, what we have is less something strictly scientific—certainly not something scientific like the real sciences of the day, physics and chemistry—but more something that fell into a category already recognized (the French king had set up a commission that found just this of mesmerism) and that was soon to be labeled a "pseudoscience." One means here something of a pretender—something backed by and promoting values rather than empirical evidence. It is also something that tends to set up tensions in the conventional and staid, a bit of a threat to the status quo. In this respect, then, it is something that bears some similarities to a religion, a suspicion strengthened if one finds that it sets out to challenge existing, conventional religions. It is to this issue that we turn now.

Religion and Its Critics

At the beginning of the eighteenth century, both in Catholic countries like France and in Protestant countries like England, religion was very much part of the state—endorsed by authorities and in turn offering support and ground-ing for such authorities (Evans 2001; Hilton 2006). Expectedly, therefore, those wanting change had religion and its institutions in their sights. Famously, he who has been described as God's greatest gift to the infidel, David Hume, tore into the foundations of Christianity with a vigor that has yet to be equaled, even by those dubbed the "New Atheists." He denied the plausibility of miracles and he was scathing about some of the traditional arguments for God's existence. The argument from design was subjected to detailed and withering critical discussion. Across the Channel, Voltaire was playing his part, in his farce *Candide* ripping to shreds those who would argue (as did the philosopher Leibniz) that evil can be explained away in the cause of the greater good in the ultimate effects. Meeting his old teacher, the philosopher Dr. Pangloss, Candide is appalled to see his dreadful state. He had become "a beggar all covered with scabs, his eyes diseased, the end of his nose eaten away, his mouth distorted, his teeth black, choking in his throat, tormented with a violent cough, and spitting out a tooth at each effort." How could this have happened?

> "My dear Candide," replied Pangloss, "you remember Paquette, that pretty girl who used to wait on our noble lady. In her arms I tasted the delights of Paradise, and they produced these hellish torments by which you now see me devoured. She was infected, and now perhaps she is dead. Paquette was given this present by a learned Franciscan, who had traced it back to its source. He had had it from an old countess, who had had it from a cavalry officer, who was indebted for it to a marchioness. She took it from her page, and he had received it from a Jesuit who, while still a novice, had had it in direct line from one of the companions of Christopher Columbus. As for me, I shall not give it to anyone, for I am a dying man."
>
> "What a strange genealogy, Pangloss!" exclaimed Candide. "Isn't the devil at the root of it?"
>
> "Certainly not," replied the great man. "It is indispensible in this best of worlds. It is a necessary ingredient. For if Columbus, when visiting the West Indies, had not caught this disease, which poisons the source of generation, which frequently even hinders generation, and is clearly opposed to the great end of Nature, we should have neither chocolate nor cochineal." (Voltaire [1759] 1947, 29–30)

Little wonder that so few take philosophy seriously.

Or religion for that matter. Although there were atheists, Voltaire was no atheist and neither was David Hume (Ruse 2015a). Nor for that matter was Erasmus Darwin. They tended as did many at that time to a form of deism, seeing God as the unmoved mover who has set the world in motion and who now stands back and lets the laws of nature do all, giving Jesus (at most) the status of a great teacher and moral ideal. But what truly drove the critics was reform of society, and that meant breaking the hold of the Church. Someone like Godwin—who incidentally started life as a nonconformist minister (and hence outside the corridors of power)—obviously wanted to destroy the status of the established Anglican Church. The same was true of those under the Catholic suzerainty.

Diderot more than anyone illustrates the links we are trying to draw—endorsing social and cultural Progress, linking this with evolution, and at the same time attacking the rival world picture of Christianity. His novel *The Nun* started out as a joke on a friend but turned into one of the most anti-Catholic diatribes of all time. Supposedly it is the story of a young girl who is forced into joining a religious order and of what happens to her when she does. Predictably it is not long before she is beaten up, stripped naked, and put in solitary in a cell. When she expresses a desire to leave, she is treated as one dead. "I was made to lie in a coffin in the centre of the choir, candles were placed on either side with a holy-water stoup, I was covered with a shroud and the prayers for the dead were recited, after which each nun, as she went out, sprinkled me with holy water and said *Requiescat in pace*" (Diderot [1796] 1972, 81). She is made to pick up red-hot tongs and to walk on broken glass. She is made to eat bread and water while sitting on the floor and wearing a hair shirt. She is made to scourge herself while naked before the Mother Superior; although this has consequences that one might not have foreseen—or perhaps one would! The abbess is so moved that she kisses the sore spots better, and this is but a preliminary.

> By now she had raised her collar and put one of my hands on her bosom. She fell silent, and so did I. She seemed to be experiencing the most exquisite pleasure. She invited me to kiss her forehead, cheeks, eyes and mouth, and I obeyed. I don't think there was any harm in that, but her pleasure increased, and as I was only too glad to add to her happiness in any innocent way, I kissed her again on forehead, cheeks, eyes and lips. The hand she had rested on my knee wandered all over my clothing from my feet to my girdle, pressing here and there, and she gasped as she urged me in a strange, low voice to redouble my caresses, which I did. Eventually a moment came, whether of pleasure or of pain I cannot say, when she went as pale as death, closed her eyes, and her whole body tautened violently, her lips were first pressed together and moistened with a sort of foam, then they parted and she seemed to expire with a deep sigh. (Diderot [1796] 1972, 137–138)

And so it goes. You cannot trust anyone, not even a nice young Benedictine, her confessor. It is almost a relief to end up working in a brothel.

I won't say that this is all good, clean fun because it isn't. But it is certainly a bit of a tongue-in-cheek romp, very much in the style of the then-popular gothic novels, not to mention a series of like tales of the appalling practices of the Catholic priesthood. Although written more for entertainment than instruction, published in the same year as *The Nun* (1796), *The Monk: A Romance* by the English writer Matthew Gregory Lewis ([1796] 2008) is typical—sex, rape, imprisonment, murder, and a bit of incest thrown in as a spice. Whatever the intent, however, the effect is the same, to pour scorn and ridicule on a system that is as corrupt as it is powerful—a system that needs to be abolished and re-placed by a more enlightened regime governed by principles of reason and with aspirations of Progress.

What of the Church?

In England, the two universities Oxford and Cambridge were Church establish-ments. You had to be a professing Anglican to attend, and you had to be ordained if you were to teach at one of them. William Paley (1743–1805), Archdeacon of Carlisle, was the writer of texts for the undergraduates who, along with a bit of mathematics and classics, were all fed a diet of theology—the solid, empiricist theology of the Anglican middle way.

> There is a book, who runs may read,
> which heavenly truth imparts,
> and all the lore its scholars need,
> pure eyes and Christian hearts.

> The works of God above, below,
> within us and around,
> are pages in that book, to shew
> how God himself is found.[4]

In this mode, writing thirty years after Hume, Paley blithely ignored all of the counterarguments. In his *Evidences of Christianity* ([1794] 1819), he made the biblical miracles the keystone of faith—if people were prepared to die before denying them, can one not assume that we have here a bit more than a fabrication, more than a story made up to deceive 2,000 years of followers? In his *Natural Theology* ([1802] 1819)—which actually even mentions Hume—the argument from design is trotted out and made the centerpiece. The eye is like a telescope. Telescopes have telescope makers. Therefore the eye must have an eye maker— the Great Optician in the Sky. Theology in short—both revealed and natural—begins in nature and points up from there. That was just the sort of God appreciated by the British—making their way through science and technology, harnessing the forces of nature. Nothing showy but solid and dependable.

---

[4] By John Keble, published in 1827.

It is against this background that we can understand the thinking of Thomas Robert Malthus (1766–1834), another parson of the Church of England. He was worried by what was becoming a national obsession, the rising population rate brought on by industrialization. (In the country, there was reason to limit one's family, at least until one inherited the family farm. In the town, in factories, children were much needed for agile tasks difficult for adults. Hence there was reason to start on a large family earlier.) Relatedly, Malthus was appalled by what he took to be the naïve optimism of Condorcet in France and Godwin in Britain. Thus he penned his *Essay on the Principle of Population* (1798) in counterresponse. In one of the most famous calculations of all time, he argued that food supplies can only increase arithmetically whereas population potentially increases geometrically. Because the latter is much stronger than the former, we are doomed to inevitable struggles for existence. Hopes of Godwin-like Progress are chimerical. "This natural inequality of the two powers of population and of production in the earth, and that great law of our nature which must constantly keep their effects equal, form the great difficulty that to me appears insurmountable in the way to the perfectibility of society. All other arguments are of slight and subordinate consideration in comparison of this" (Malthus [1798] 1959, 6). If the premises are just, the argument is conclusive against the improvement of the nature or lot of the mass of mankind.

One cannot overstress that Malthus was arguing within what he took to be a Christian, natural-theological context (Mayhew 2014). He was not Voltaire-like, arguing that this is such a horrible world that the problem of evil is beyond solution within a Christian context. To the contrary, he saw the clash between population potentials and food actualities as something put in place by a good god to motivate us, to get us up on our legs and working for a living. If everything were handed to us on a plate, we would do little or nothing. God in His wisdom saw this danger and so put in place a remedy before we even started. The consequence, however, is that whole wonderful dream of Godwin-like Progress fades before our eyes. Its hopes are not realized and never can be. And with that rather gloomy—or if you prefer, realistic—conclusion, we can leave the eighteenth century and move into the next.

2

Before Darwin

Evolution arrived on the back of the social doctrine of Progress. It was therefore at once plunged into the battle against religion. Progress, with good reason, was seen as opposed to the societal status quo, and in both Britain and France a major support of the societal status quo was organized religion. This is not to downplay theological issues. Crude literalism was no longer really the issue. In 1823, William Buckland, professor of geology at Oxford, published a work supporting a supposed world-wide flood. Even conservative Christians laughed at him. Time had moved on. What was troublesome, however (especially for Protestants), was the opposition between Progress and Providence, where the latter is taken to be the claim that we sinners can do nothing save through the Blood of the Lamb (Ruse 2005). Our own efforts count for naught.

> When I survey the wondrous cross
> On which the Prince of glory died,
> My richest gain I count but loss,
> And pour contempt on all my pride.[1]

If evolution is to move forward, it must speak to both the social and the theological, in its own support and in critique of the opposition.

Progress Revives

Until 1815 and the end of the Napoleonic Wars, lifting the fear of invasion, times were tense in Britain. Thoughts of Progress and of its corollary evolution were not much in favor. One can never speak absolutely. In 1808 that strange visionary William Blake, as part of a long work on Milton (probably begun in 1804),

---

[1] By the Congregationalist minister Isaac Watts, published in 1707.

published the poem (that we now call) "Jerusalem." Making reference to Jesus's supposed visit to England and to the grim aspects of the Industrial Revolution, it urges us to action.

> And did those feet in ancient time
> Walk upon England's mountains green:
> And was the holy Lamb of God,
> On England's pleasant pastures seen!
>
> And did the Countenance Divine,
> Shine forth upon our clouded hills?
> And was Jerusalem builded here,
> Among these dark Satanic Mills?
>
> Bring me my Bow of burning gold;
> Bring me my Arrows of desire:
> Bring me my Spear: O clouds unfold!
> Bring me my Chariot of fire!
>
> I will not cease from Mental Fight,
> Nor shall my Sword sleep in my hand:
> Till we have built Jerusalem,
> In England's green & pleasant Land

This poem, turned into a hymn by being set to the music of Hubert Parry, is always sung at the closing of the annual conference of the British Labor Party. To be candid, for all the references to the need of our effort, what with the talk of the Savior and what He has already done and the fact that Jerusalem is not the physical city in Palestine but the heavenly city where true believers will live for eternity with Him—"And I John saw the holy city, new Jerusalem, coming down from God out of heaven, prepared as a bride adorned for her husband" (Revelation 21:2)—one can make a case for saying that the work is as much about Providence as about (a somewhat Romantic notion of) Progress. Certainly, generally in British society, the emphasis was on the virtues of stability and the need to preserve the old and tried and trusted ways of life. But the wars did come to an end and before long it became clear that the spirit of the eighteenth century may have been battered and subdued but it was far from extinguished. The young poet Percy Bysshe Shelley sounded the clarion call loud and clear. The past was a time of suppression and superstition. The future beckons.

> Joy to the Spirit came.
> Through the wide rent in Time's eternal veil,

> Hope was seen beaming through the mists of fear;
>> Earth was no longer hell;
>> Love, freedom, health had given
> Their ripeness to the manhood of its prime,
>> And all its pulses beat
> Symphonious to the planetary spheres;
>> Then dulcet music swelled
> Concordant with the life-strings of the soul;
> It throbbed in sweet and languid beatings there,
> Catching new life from transitory death;
> Like the vague sighings of a wind at even
> That wakes the wavelets of the slumbering sea
> And dies on the creation of its breath,
> And sinks and rises, falls and swells by fits,
>> Was the pure stream of feeling
>> That sprung from these sweet notes,
> And o'er the Spirit's human sympathies
> With mild and gentle motion calmly flowed.

In fact, these particular sentiments—from Shelley's poem "Queen Mab"—were (in 1813) published privately and only started to become well-known when some ten years later existing copies were bound up and sold and—this never hurts sales—the bookseller was prosecuted for its inflammatory themes.

But we don't really need radical poets to make our point. Even to the most conservative members of society, it was increasingly clear that things could not stand still. In *Mansfield Park,* Jane Austen depicts social stability (Levine 1998). Yet, she raises the issue of slavery in the West Indies (White 2006). We are talking of a time when the independent country of Eire was but a dream, and a third of the population was Irish. Catholics and others had to be brought somewhat into the fold, allowed to vote, and allowed to enter parliament. This happened at the end of the third decade of the century, and then shortly thereafter in 1832 came the First Reform Act, something fueled by pressures from growing urban areas (like Birmingham and Manchester) that tended to have little or no parliamentary representation, contrasting with rural areas with an overabundance of representation, often thanks to "rotten boroughs" with just a handful of electors (who would vote just as their powerful patron dictated). One must keep these things in perspective. Although redistributed somewhat, the electorate still only rose from about half a million to just over three-quarters of a million—meaning in a total population of about 14 million about one in five adult males could vote. Working-class men were going to have to wait. The same was true of women, who it turned out were going to have to wait until the twentieth century for their vote.

One humorous (if at times a little strained) contribution to the debate came from the pen of the satirist Thomas Love Peacock. His novel *Melincourt* (1817) draws heavily on the ideas of Lord Mondboddo, having as its central character an orangutan that is given a baronetcy and put forward as a member of parliament. For this reason, it is often characterized as an early excursion into the world of evolution, but this is not really so. Mondboddo was no full-blooded evolutionist and neither was Peacock. Rather, Mondboddo thought that the higher apes are primitive humans and Peacock followed him in this. "Sir Oran Haut-ton was caught very young in the woods of Angola . . . He is a specimen of the natural and original man—the wild man of the woods. . . . Some presumptuous naturalists have refused his species the honours of humanity; but the most enlightened and illustrious philosophers agree in considering him in his true light as the natural and original man" ([1817] 1891, 1, 54). It is true that we regular humans have progressed beyond this form, but not so far as to take us to a new species.

Peacock was scathing about institutions in his society, and expectedly the Church was right in his sights. The Reverend Mr. Grovelgrub (I told you the humor was a bit strained) lives right up to—or down to—his name. Meeting a pretty girl, "he sate down to calculate the probability of Miss Melincourt's fortune on the one hand, and the certainty of church preferment through the patronage of the Marquis of Algaric, on the other" (1, 86). Fortunately for the girl, he thinks the second option the safer strategy. But it is the political system and the buying and selling of seats in the house of commons that really raises Peacock's ire.

> With a view of ensuring him the respect of society which always attends on rank and fortune, I have purchased him a baronetcy, and made over to him an estate. I have also purchased of the Duke of Rottenburgh one half of the electoral franchise vested in the body of Mr Christopher Corporate, the free, fat, and dependent burgess of the ancient and honourable borough of Onevote who returns two members to parliament, one of whom will shortly be Sir Oran. (1, 62)

In due course, the baronet is elected, although shortly thereafter things go dreadfully wrong when the new member mistakes friendliness for aggression and destroys much of the borough he now represents. Fortunately the town was "rebuilt a few days afterwards, at the joint expense of its two representatives, and his grace the Duke of Rottenburgh" who owns the seats (2, 29).

Thomas Carlyle and Charles Dickens

All a good joke, but closer to the truth than many felt comfortable acknowledging. Yet, moving forward, be not mistaken that the "Reform" Bill meant sweetness and light for all of his majesty's subjects. The newly constituted parliament contained a fair representation of the business class whose members had their own ends. They wanted the working classes to have spurs to accept the lowest paying of jobs. Thus, one of the first moves was to pass draconian poor laws, condemning the indigent to workhouses of so miserable a ferocity that, to avoid them, people would do anything—laboring for pitiful returns and getting off the Malthusian carousel by practicing what he called "prudential restraint." For critics, this whole politicoeconomic approach to society was altogether too formulaic and soulless. Even in 1829, in a noted essay "Signs of the Times," the up-and-coming Thomas Carlyle (1795–1881) was inveighing against the "mechanical" nature and philosophy of society. While agreeing that it led to cheap and plentiful goods, he worried that it was being applied too readily to human beings without thought of the consequences.

> It is no longer the moral, religious, spiritual condition of the people that is our concern, but their physical, practical, economical condition, as regulated by public laws. Thus is the Body-politic more than ever worshipped and tendered; but the Soul-politic less than ever. Love of country, in any high or generous sense, in any other than an almost animal sense, or mere habit, has little importance attached to it in such reforms, or in the opposition shown them. Men are to be guided only by their self-interests. Good government is a good balancing of these; and, except a keen eye and appetite for self-interest, requires no virtue in any quarter. To both parties it is emphatically a machine: to the discontented, a "taxing-machine"; to the contented, a "machine for securing property." (Carlyle [1829] 1864, 191)

Adding: "But though Mechanism, wisely contrived, has done much for man in a social and moral point of view, we cannot be persuaded that it has ever been the chief source of his worth or happiness" (191). We lose out on poetry and love and religion and fear and wonder and enthusiasm, all of which make for fulfilled and truly happy living.

Then in his rather strange novel, *Sartor Resartus* ([1834] 1987), about a German philosopher Diogenes Teufelsdröckh ("God-born devil-dung"), who had written a tome on the origin and influence of clothes—a metaphor for the practices and customs of society that have to be cast off to see the true nature of things—Carlyle continued on these themes, showing the great influence of German idealism or (what came to be known in America as) "transcendentalism."[2] Notice in the following passage the organic metaphor—one speaking of natural growth rather than human mechanical design and suggesting that in some sense everything is alive. Spirit in some sense infuses the whole of existence. "Cast forth thy Act, thy Word, into the ever-living, ever-working Universe: it is a seed-grain that cannot die; unnoticed to-day (says one), it will be found flourishing as a Banyan-grove (perhaps, alas, as a Hemlock-forest!) after a thousand years" (31).[3] We must break from the purely mechanical and strive for genuine freedom. " 'Satisfy yourselves,' he says, 'by universal, indubitable experiment, even as ye are now doing or will do, whether FREEDOM, heaven-born and leading heavenward, and so vitally essential for us all, cannot peradventure be mechanically hatched and brought to light in that same Ballot-Box of yours; or at worst, in some other discoverable or devisable Box, Edifice, or Steam-mechanism' " (Carlyle [1834] 1987, 189). This is not to say that Carlyle and his many enthusiastic readers (which included Charles Dickens as well as the biologists Richard Owen and a little later Thomas Henry Huxley) were against change or Progress—it was just that it had to be of a more idealistic nature—one that spoke to the free soul of human beings.

We all know how Dickens loathed the new poor laws—has there ever been a novel so emotionally directed against a social position as was *Oliver Twist* (1837), with its devastating picture of the new workhouses and those like Mr. Bumble who ran them? Later, he promoted Carlyle's thinking more generally in *Hard Times* (1854), so much so that at times it is less a novel and more a tract—"Signs of the Times" "might be regarded as an ideological prospectus to the novel" (Goldberg 1972, 79)—something you are rather flagged to when (apart from the echo in the title) you learn that one of the main characters named his children Adam Smith and Malthus!

> So many hundred Hands in this Mill; so many hundred horse Steam Power. It is known, to the force of a single pound weight, what the engine will do; but, not all the calculators of the National Debt can tell

---

[2] As German thinking about Progress entered into the Anglophone world, so also did French thinking, particularly through the so-called Positivist movement headed by Auguste Comte, to have a great influence on many British intellectuals, notably George Henry Lewes, the common-law husband of George Eliot, the novelist.

[3] Spirit but not necessarily thinking spirit. "The choice of plant metaphors rather than, say, animal metaphors makes acceptance of the role of the unconscious unavoidable, since plants are distinguished by lack of volition" (Tennyson 1965, 163, n.6). We shall later see wrestling with this notion of spirit and whether at some point it can achieve consciousness.

me the capacity for good or evil, for love or hatred, for patriotism or discontent, for the decomposition of virtue into vice, or the reverse, at any single moment in the soul of one of these its quiet servants, with the composed faces and the regulated actions. (Dickens [1854] 1948, 69)

And then: "'I beg your pardon for interrupting you, sir,' returned Bitzer; 'but I am sure you know that the whole social system is a question of self-interest. What you must always appeal to, is a person's self-interest. It's your only hold. We are so constituted'" (288).

Not that one should think that Dickens any more than Carlyle was against change as such. *Bleak House* (1853) is a powerful attack on the legal system of his day. The man from Shropshire—"My whole estate, left to me in that will of my father's, has gone in costs. The suit, still undecided, has fallen into rack, and ruin, and despair, with everything else—and here I stand, this day!" (Dickens [1853] 1948, 214)—is but one of the unfortunates. It is rather that Dickens is looking for change that will free and promote the human spirit rather than bind and crush it—in *Bleak House* as much as *Oliver Twist* and *Hard Times*.

Wrestling with Industrialism

The late 1830s and 1840s saw the rise of Chartism, an essentially working-class movement, sparked by hatred of the new poor laws, aimed at universal suffrage (for men). In the end—although it pointed to further reforms in the 1860s and 1870s—after violent strikes and savage repressions, it all rather petered out. Naturally the Church was a target of the would-be reformers. In general, it was unresponsive. Indeed, the 1840s saw the classic hymnal testament to the status quo.

> The rich man in his castle,
> The poor man at his gate,
> God made them high and lowly,
> And ordered their estate.[4]

But there were those who sympathized with the masses, including the novelist, naturalist, and so-called Christian Socialist Charles Kingsley (1819–1875). His second novel, *Alton Locke*, tells the tale of a poor lad from a repressively narrow Christian background who becomes a tailor and of what befalls him. He meets Chartists and is attracted to them and to their philosophy, even getting

---

[4] By Cecil F. Alexander, published in 1848.

himself involved in a strike and getting himself put in prison. There is not much love of Malthusian ideas—"I believe them to be an infernal lie" ([1848] 1983, 112)—and even less of the new poor laws. Yet, Kingsley was and always was to be a clergyman, a believing Christian, and in respects rather conservative and committed to the structure of the land. (He was a favorite of the Royal Family.) In the end, the solution lies not in ourselves but in our Lord. "Claim your share in national life, only because the nation is a spiritual body, whose king is the Son of God; whose work, whose national character and powers, are allotted to it by the Spirit of Christ" (364).

Complementing Kingsley, almost at the end of our period (1855), more interesting and more radical (and a far superior novel) is *North and South* by Mrs. Elizabeth Gaskell (1810–1865), the wife of a Unitarian minister in Manchester. Telling the story of the daughter of a clergyman who loses his faith, Margaret Hale is moved from the rural south of England to Milton (Manchester), a grim city in the north. There she meets and clashes with John Thornton, a self-made mill owner with a rough, nigh-contemptuous attitude to his workers. Margaret is his equal. She too turns out to be as tough as nails. Others are crushed by misfortune and die. Not she. Others run from threats and challenges. Again, not she. When Thornton is threated by strikers, it is Margaret who stands up to them.

> Even while she looked, she saw lads in the back-ground stooping to take off their heavy wooden clogs—the readiest missile they could find; she saw it was the spark to the gunpowder, and, with a cry, which no one heard, she rushed out of the room, down stairs,—she had lifted the great iron bar of the door with an imperious force—had thrown the door open wide—and was there, in face of that angry sea of men, her eyes smiting them with flaming arrows of reproach. The clogs were arrested in the hands that held them—the countenances, so fell not a moment before, now looked irresolute, and as if asking what this meant. For she stood between them and their enemy. ([1855] 2011, 230)

This is the world of Malthus. Thornton speaking of his early life:

> Week by week our income came to fifteen shillings, out of which three people had to be kept. My mother managed so that I put by three out of these fifteen shillings regularly. This made the beginning; this taught me self-denial. Now that I am able to afford my mother such comforts as her age, rather than her own wish, requires, I thank her silently on each occasion for the early training she gave me. Now when I feel that in my own case it is no good luck, nor merit, nor talent,— but simply the habits of life which taught me to despise indulgences

not thoroughly earned,—indeed, never to think twice about them,—
I believe that this suffering, which Miss Hale says is impressed on
the countenances of the people of Milton, is but the natural punishment of dishonestly-enjoyed pleasure, at some former period of their
lives. I do not look on self-indulgent, sensual people as worthy of my
hatred; I simply look upon them with contempt for their poorness of
character. (108)

Does this mean that Gaskell has turned her face on Progress? Far from it, nor
indeed would Malthus have thought that she should. He was not against Progress
and at the end of his *Essay* spoke enthusiastically of it. Rather it was that he was
against naïve hopes of Progress as he found in Condorcet and Godwin. Gaskell
would have agreed with him. Life is tough but the best survive and triumph.[5] As
the relationship between Margaret and Thornton develops and matures—yes,
this is a novel that Charles Darwin would have liked[6]—she comes to see that
morality and trade are not enemies but indeed are or should be one. And rub-
bing in the moral, before the story ends Margaret returns to her old home in
the South, where she hears an appalling story of cat roasting—a poor feline is
burned alive to get favors from the powers of darkness. Even she who lost her
pet accepts the efficacy of such a course of action: "it were very cruel for sure,
and she should not like to do it; but that there were nothing like it for giving a
person what they wished for; she had heard it all her life; but it were very cruel
for all that" (505). It is not just that Margaret is a person facing the future; she is
also a person leaving the past. And although Gaskell would have been shocked
at the suggestion that she was writing in a materialistic or atheistic context—she
was not—in respects we are already in a world light years away from, light years
ahead of, the world of Kingsley and *Alton Locke*. Hers is a world that has embraced the factors transforming Britain (Martin 1983).[7]

---

[5] Note the sharp division between Progress and Providence is starting to crumble. Just as, at
the end of this book, we shall see a Calvinist wrestling with reconciling human free will against the
background of an all-powerful, determining God, so here we have Christians who believe in God's
Providence nevertheless having to recognize a place for human-driven Progress.

[6] "He could not enjoy any story with a tragical end, for this reason he did not keenly appreciate
George Eliot, though he often spoke warmly in praise of 'Silas Marner.' Walter Scott, Miss Austen, and
Mrs. Gaskell, were read and re-read till they could be read no more" (F. Darwin 1887, 1, 124–125).

[7] The novel is more complex than this brief sketch implies. Stressing that Malthusianism does
not mean the end of morality, Thornton refuses to speculate wildly, risking the money of others.
Eventually he is bailed out by an unexpected inheritance of Margaret. There is more than a hint in
the novel that his misfortunes make Thornton sympathetic to a more Carlyle-like philosophy of life.
What we do see is Gaskell's deep respect for people with vitality and guts, much as we shall see in
post-*Origin* writers like George Gissing and Edith Wharton.

Evolution

Two great French scientists dominate our period—the sometime Chevalier (later Citoyen) Jean-Baptiste de Lamarck and Georges Cuvier (Ruse 1979). Lamarck was the first to offer a fully articulated theory of evolution—notably in his *Philosophie Zoologique* (1809). Although today Lamarck is known for the supposed inheritance of acquired characteristics, an idea not in fact new with him, the main force of his theory was one of continuous spontaneous combustion followed by an almost vitalistic climb up the chain of being, disrupted occasionally by external factors. Cuvier was the father of comparative anatomy, founding paleontologist, and strong opponent of evolution. Expectedly, Lamarck was strongly in favor of Progress—How else would a minor aristocrat thrive through the French Revolution?—and Cuvier was not—he was the ultimate civil servant, appalled at the Revolution and its disruption of stability. Lamarck is important for our story, especially after, in the second volume of the *Principles of Geology* (1830–1833), the Scottish geologist Charles Lyell gave a full exposition of his theory—an exposition that, although critical, was sufficiently detailed to convince more than one, notably Herbert Spencer (1820–1903), of the truth of the evolutionary story. But in respects it is Cuvier (1813) who sets the scene against which all else plays out. He saw the Earth as developmental, with a series of deluges (what the British were to call "catastrophes") wiping out most or all of the then-existent organisms, and then new ones being (certainly in the opinion of the British) created miraculously to fill the gaps. Using his anatomical skills on fossil remains, it was Cuvier who (for all his opposition to social Progress) started us on the road to seeing the fossil record as roughly progressive, with primitive forms oldest (as judged from being further down the strata) and complex and more familiar forms the newest.

Among the poets, Byron (around 1820) was quick to pick up on this:

> But let it go:—it will one day be found
>   With other relics of "a former World,"
> When this World shall be former, underground,
>   Thrown topsy-turvy, twisted, crisped, and curled,
> Baked, fried, or burnt, turned inside-out, or drowned,
>   Like all the worlds before, which have been hurled
> First out of, and then back again to chaos—
> The superstratum which will overlay us.
>
> So Cuvier says; —and then shall come again
>   Unto the new creation, rising out
> From our old crash, some mystic, ancient strain

Of things destroyed and left in airy doubt;
Like to the notions we now entertain
Of Titans, giants, fellows of about
Some hundred feet in height, not to say miles,
And mammoths, and your winged crocodiles.
(*Don Juan*, 9, 37–38; in Byron 1847, 700)

Apart from its great industrial significance—knowing the fossils could
yield significant clues to commercially important strata—geology as a healthy
outdoor activity became a very popular science in the first half of the nineteenth century, not the least because spectacular remains—including the first
dinosaurs—were now being unearthed. Immensely popular were the models of
extinct giant forms created for the park when the Crystal Palace building (of the
Great Exhibition of 1851) was moved to South London (Shatto 1976). At once
Dickens picked up on them. Opening *Bleak House* ([1853] 1948):

London. Michaelmas term lately over, and the Lord Chancellor sitting
in Lincoln's Inn Hall. Implacable November weather. As much mud in
the streets as if the waters had but newly retired from the face of the
earth, and it would not be wonderful to meet a Megalosaurus, forty feet
long or so, waddling like an elephantine lizard up Holborn Hill. (1)

Adding to the interest in geology was the whiff of controversy, when Lyell in
his *Principles* challenged British catastrophism, arguing in an updated version of
James Hutton's philosophy that the whole of the past can be explained as a function of laws operating incessantly at the same intensities. Although Lyell was
sure that Lamarckian evolution is not the solution, his "uniformitarianism"—
stressing that everything must be the result of unbroken law—intensified the
problem of the origins of species. Even though biblical literalism was no real
barrier to a solution, there was still the problem highlighted by the Greeks and
reemphasized by Cuvier (1817), who (influenced by Kant and beyond that
Aristotle) argued that the intricate functioning nature of organisms—what he
called the "conditions of existence"—made change from one form to another
impossible (because transitional forms would be nonfunctional).

Lamarckism speaks somewhat to this issue, but with as yet no real answer
those who were going to promote evolution had to be so enamored of Progress
that it was going to ride roughshod over philosophical objections. One who felt
this way was the Scottish anatomist (and mentor of the young Charles Darwin)
Robert Grant (Desmond 1984). Then spectacularly and notoriously came the
Scottish publisher (writing anonymously) Robert Chambers (Secord 2000). In
his *Vestiges of the Natural History of Creation* (1844), he argued for a full-blown

evolutionary theory, drawing eclectically on the support of the nebular hypothesis, on the similarities between frost patterns (ferns) on windows and real plants, on our growing knowledge of the fossil record, on analogies between the individual's growth and that of the group, on Lamarckian views of upward change, on increasing understanding of monstrosities and their causes, and—fortified by a total disdain for the kinds of functional issues raised by Cuvier and his followers—all wrapped up with (as one might expect of a very successful businessman) an enthusiasm for Progress and its implications in the biological world.

> A progression resembling development may be traced in human nature, both in the individual and in large groups of men. . . . Now all of this is in conformity with what we have seen of the progress of organic creation. It seems but the minute hand of a watch, of which the hour hand is the transition from species to species. Knowing what we do of that latter transition, the possibility of a decided and general retrogression of the highest species towards a meaner type is scarce admissible, but a forward movement seems anything but unlikely. (Chambers 1846, 401–402)

There were also happy speculations about the future. "Is our race but the initial of the grand crowning type? Are there yet to be species superior to us in organization, purer in feeling, more powerful in device and act, and who shall take a rule over us!" (Chambers 1844, 276). Chambers was happy to assure his readers that: "There may then be occasion for a nobler type of humanity, which shall complete the zoological circle on this planet, and realize some of the dreams of the purest spirits of the present race" (276).

As you might suppose, none of this went down well with the staid and established in the scientific community, especially if (necessarily if they were at Oxford or Cambridge) they were ordained members of the Church of England, and hence themselves under some pressure from yet more conservative members of their Church for agreeing that the Earth is very old and that some forms of organism are now extinct—apparently thereby implying that God scrapped some of his creations before his favored organisms, humans, appeared on the scene. Both on the epistemological grounds that *Vestiges* was bad science and on the sociological grounds that *Vestiges* was personally threatening, these scientific leaders had little doubt that evolutionary theorizing is pseudoscientific (Ruse 2013). Benjamin Disraeli, the future conservative Prime Minister, picked up on this and in one of his novels parodied *Vestiges* through one of his ditzy female characters.

> First there was nothing, then there was something; then, I forget the next, I think there were shells, then fishes; then we came, let me see, did

we come next? Never mind that; we came at last. And the next change
there will be something very superior to us, something with wings.
Oh! that's it; we were fishes, and I believe we shall be crows. (Disraeli
[1847] 1871, 38)

Fortunately, the English anatomist and paleontologist Richard Owen (1804–
1892) was by then articulating an alternative position, one that owed much to
Cuvier with its stress on function, but that in respects owed more to Germanic
thinking, stressing neoplatonic forms linking organisms—what Owen (1849)
was to call "archetypes"—that reveal themselves in ever more complex organisms as one moves up the fossil record. As with someone like Hegel, this was
not necessarily physically evolutionary—and certainly made important the role
of a creative God—but in its idealistic way was as Progressive as anything to be
found in Erasmus Darwin or Chambers.

Genuine Evolution?

Expectedly, given the downplay of Progress, there is not much evolution from
the creative writers in the first part of our period, although some of the lines of
Shelley do echo those of Erasmus Darwin.
    On war and violent conflict:

> And one great Slaughter-house the warring world!
>   (Darwin 1803, 4, 66)
> Making the earth a slaughter house!
>   (Shelley 1821, 7, 48)

And more amusingly:

> HENCE when a Monarch or mushroom dies,
> Awhile extinct the organic matter lies;
> But, as a few short hours or years resolve,
> Alchemic powers the changing mass dissolve. . .
>   (Darwin 1803, 4, 383–386)
> Yon monarch, in his solitary pomp,
> Was but the mushroom of a summer day.
>   (Shelley 1821, 9, 31–32)

We have to wait until the 1830s to get what is often taken to be the first explicit
use of evolution, by Robert Browning (1812–1889) in his poem "Paracelsus."

> Thus he dwells in all,
> From life's minute beginnings, up at last
> To man — the consummation of this scheme
> Of being, the completion of this sphere
> Of life: whose attributes had here and there
> Been scattered o'er the visible world before,
> Asking to be combined, dim fragments meant
> To be united in some wondrous whole,
> Imperfect qualities throughout creation,
> Suggesting some one creature yet to make,
> Some point where all those scattered rays should meet
> Convergent in the faculties of man.
>
> (Browning 1981, 2, 56–67)

But although later, after Darwin, Browning rather claimed that he was expressing full-blooded evolutionary ideas here, I suspect they were as likely more idealistic than physical (Beach [1936] 1966, 440). Just before this passage, the poet says: "God renews His ancient rapture," suggesting that the deity may have been more directly involved in the process than Erasmus Darwin (or Lamarck) would have allowed.

I am unsure whether we get even this in another potential candidate, Arthur Hugh Clough's celebrated "Natura Naturans" (1849)—nature doing its own thing—that celebrates the growing sexual attraction between a couple in a railway carriage, tying it to a rise through the ladder of life. We start at the bottom with low plant life.

> Yet owned we, fused in one,
> The Power which e'en in stones and earths
> By blind elections felt, in forms
> Organic breeds to myriad births;
> By lichen small on granite wall
> Approved, its faintest feeblest stir
> Slow-spreading, strengthening long, at last
> Vibrated full in me and her.

The emotion builds and builds—one suspects that the vibrations have less to do with mechanical sex aids and more with the rough and shaky nature of early rail travel. It takes the couple up through animal forms to the climax.

> Their shells did slow crustacea build,
> Their gilded skins did snakes renew,

While mightier spines for loftier kind
  Their types in amplest limbs outgrew;
Yea, close comprest in human breast,
  What moss, and tree, and livelier thing,
What Earth, Sun, Star of force possest,
  Lay budding, burgeoning forth for Spring.

Such sweet preluding sense of old
  Led on in Eden's sinless place
The hour when bodies human first
  Combined the primal prime embrace,
Such genial heat the blissful seat
  In man and woman owned unblamed,
When, naked both, its garden paths
  They walked unconscious, unashamed:
                              (Clough 2003, 43–44)

The final lines rather suggest that the reference is to the creation story of Genesis, although clearly in a way Clough is pushing toward drawn-out sequential change and there is a raw eroticism not found in the biblical account. One is not entirely surprised that the future Mrs. Arthur Hugh Clough nearly broke off their engagement when she discovered this little number—"I did hardly know that good men were so rough and coarse" (Kenny 2005, 263).

What of another popular candidate for pre–Charles Darwin evolution—a rather strange dream sequence in *Alton Locke*? The sleeping hero is told: "He who falls from the golden ladder must climb through ages to its top. He who tears himself in pieces by his lusts, ages only can make him one again. The madrepore [coral] shall become a shell, and the shell a fish, and the fish a bird, and the bird a beast; and then he shall become a man again, and see the glory of the latter days" (Kingsley [1848] 1983, 336–337). Sure enough he goes through the sequence of crab, remora, ostrich, mylodon, ape, man. Yet here we can be fairly certain that we are not dealing with physical evolution, because five years later Kingsley wrote a popular little book (*Glaucus*) about the spiritual, moral, and physical benefits of naturalizing at the seashore where he firmly put in the boot to *Vestiges* and as firmly endorsed Owen's transcendentalist visions, which the anatomist had now laid out firmly at the lecture podium and in print.

Not (understand well) that they have any "transmutation" or "development of species" (of individuals, as it ought honestly to be called, if the notion is intended to represent a supposed fact,) — a theory as unsupported by experiment and induction, as it is by a priori reason: but that there has been, in the Creative Mind, as it gave life to new species, a development of the idea on which older species were created, in order that every mesh of the great net might gradually be supplied, and there should be no gaps in the perfect variety of Nature's forms. (Kingsley 1855, 70)

Alfred Tennyson

Who then might be taken as expressing genuine evolutionary thoughts? Remarkably the man at the very center of Victorian literary culture, the poet Alfred Tennyson (1809–1892) (Stevenson 1932). Even more remarkably, he did not do this just casually or quietly, but as the theme making full sense of the message in his central and most famous poem, *In Memoriam* (1850), that which was to gain him the Poet Laureate's position and was to be so beloved of the Victorians and such a great comfort to the queen on her bereavement. Evolution was not some new enthusiasm—like Spencer, Tennyson was probably moved (in a way unintended by the author) by Lyell's arguments against Lamarckian evolution—although even before he read Lyell he was toying with developmental ideas (where the stages of history are recapitulated in the life of the individual) that may or may not have been fully physically evolutionary.

> "From change to change four times within the womb
>   The brain is moulded," she began,
> "So through all phases of all thought I come
>   Into the perfect man.
> "All nature widens upward: evermore
>   The simpler essence lower lies.
> More complex is more perfect, owning more
>   Discourse, more widely wise."

("The Palace of Art," written 1833. These stanzas do not appear in the published version of 1842.)

Tennyson was also deeply committed to the idea of change, although within a Christian context. This is said by the dying King Arthur about the dissolution of the Round Table.

> The old order changeth, yielding place to new,
> And God fulfils himself in many ways,
> Lest one good custom should corrupt the world.
>   ("Morte D'Arthur," [1842] 1994, 131)

And thoughts of Progress—industry, trade and the rule of law—were ever present.

> For I dipt into the future, far as human eye could see,
> Saw the Vision of the world, and all the wonder that would be;
>
> Saw the heavens fill with commerce, argosies of magic sails,
> Pilots of the purple twilight dropping down with costly bales;
>
> Heard the heavens fill with shouting, and there rain'd a ghastly dew
> From the nations' airy navies grappling in the central blue;
>
> Far along the world-wide whisper of the south-wind rushing warm,
> With the standards of the peoples plunging thro' the thunder-storm;
>
> Till the war-drum throbb'd no longer, and the battle-flags were furl'd
> In the Parliament of man, the Federation of the world.
>
> There the common sense of most shall hold a fretful realm in awe,
> And the kindly earth shall slumber, lapt in universal law.
>   (*Locksley Hall*, written mid-1830s,
>   published 1842, in Tennyson 1994, 167–168)

It was however *Vestiges* that confirmed and spurred on Tennyson's thinking. *In Memoriam* (1850) was written over some twenty years as a tribute to a close friend, Arthur Hallam, who died young. Always interested in science, Tennyson found the underlying message of Lyell's *Principles* profoundly depressing. Lyell had argued that nature is going nowhere, just simply bound by unbroken stern laws, and that there is no end in prospect, nor any progress in view. Life comes and life goes without meaning as expressed in the following famous passages:

> Are God and Nature then at strife,
>   That Nature lends such evil dreams?
>   So careful of the type she seems,
> So careless of the single life;
> . . .
> So careful of the type? but no.
>   From scaped cliff and quarried stone
>   She cries, 'A thousand types are gone:
> I care for nothing, all shall go.'
>   (Tennyson 1850, 78, 80)

Given Nature "red in tooth and claw"—this is the source of this famous phrase—nothing seems to make any sense. Not only are individuals pointless mortals, but so also are groups. We are born, we live, and then we die—usually painfully. Nothing makes sense or has meaning. There are just endless Lyellian cycles. Then toward the end of the 1840s Tennyson read Chambers, or at least he read a very detailed review of Chambers's *Vestiges* (Killham 1958, 85). Finding that Chambers argued for an organic evolution which was unambiguously progressionist—that is, moving up from simple forms up to humans, and then perhaps beyond, Tennyson picked up pen and finished his poem. He argued in the final lines that, despite a Lyellian uniformitarianism, perhaps there is meaning after all: that life is progressing upward, and that perhaps will go on beyond the human form that we have at present. Could it not be that Hallam represented some anticipation of the more-developed life to come, cut short as it were in its prime? There is therefore hope for us all and a meaning for the life of Hallam.

> A soul shall strike from out the vast
> And strike his being into bounds,
>
> And moved thro' life of lower phase,
>   Result in man, be born and think,
>   And act and love, a closer link
> Betwixt us and the crowning race
> . . .
> Whereof the man, that with me trod
>   This planet, was a noble type
>   Appearing ere the times were ripe,
> That friend of mine who lives in God.
> (Tennyson 1850, 209, 210)

This is not a materialist view of life. It is not really even a deistic view akin to that endorsed by Erasmus Darwin, for one senses that Tennyson's God is not about to leave anything to chance or blind law. His was basically the Christian God.

> O YET we trust that somehow good
>   Will be the final goal of ill,
>   To pangs of nature, sins of will,
> Defects of doubt, and taints of blood;
>
> That nothing walks with aimless feet;
>   That not one life shall be destroyed,
>   Or cast as rubbish to the void,
> When God hath made the pile complete;
> (Tennyson 1850, 76)

Yet it is unambiguously an evolutionary view and one that clearly owes at least something to Chambers. Note the echo of Chambers's "crowning type" in

Tennyson's "crowning race," a phrase to which incidentally he seems to have
been rather partial because he used in *The Princess* (1847)—"Then springs the
crowning race of humankind./May these things be!"—and then later in *Maud*
(1855), expressing the same hopes as in *In Memoriam*:

> And he felt himself in his force to be Nature's crowning race.
> As nine months go to the shaping an infant ripe for his birth,
> So many a million of ages have gone to the making of man:
> He now is first, but is he the last? is he not too base?
> (Tennyson 1994, 386)

Evolution is right there in Victorian culture in the middle of the nineteenth century and—as often is the case with pseudosciences—the elite may have loathed
it, but the public was lapping it up.

Religion

This is a story about evolution in opposition to religion, the Christian religion.
We have already seen some of this: the push of Progress against the establishment and the clash between Progress and Providence. Tennyson, who was in respects the most successful evolutionist, succeeded precisely because he did not
want to take up the battle against religion. There is more to say than this. Thomas
Kuhn (1962) makes the important point that you don't take up with a new paradigm unless there are good reasons to drop the old one. Kuhn is talking about
science, but his point applies to our story.[8] For now, leave the troubles of religion in relation to evolution and ask about religion in its own right. There were
those who were unambiguously Christian, whether they were for or against evolution. Charles Kingsley was one. Charles Dickens was another. No one could
read *A Christmas Carol* without seeing that here was a man who took absolutely
and completely seriously Jesus's message of love and care for our fellow human
beings. This is not to say that these people saw no faults in the religion. Kingsley
would hardly have written *Alton Locke* if he were entirely happy at the ways in
which things were going. Dickens was often far more critical than he was positive. He loathed and detested the unctuous hypocrisy of so much evangelical

---

[8] I take it that this discussion ties in with the crumbling of the Providence-Progress dichotomy.
The problem was how far you could bring Progress into your Providential world picture and think
of it still as Providential. Although I refer favorably here to Kuhn's thinking, this should not be taken
as an endorsement of his radical view of revolutions, where the world literally changes. In this book,
I am talking of a very great change in perspective, but as this very note implies I see such change as
messy and overlapping and in respects gradual. One is not surprised to find hybrids like Tennyson.

religion—with its humorless condemnation of human urges. There is no funnier or more ridiculous figure in the whole of fiction than the Reverend Mr. Stiggins, in *Pickwick Papers*. He was also more than capable of poking fun at notions of Providence. Sam and Toby Weller are talking of the death of Toby's wife.

> "Vell," said Sam, venturing to offer a little homely consolation, after the lapse of three or four minutes, consumed by the old gentleman in slowly shaking his head from side to side, and solemnly smoking, "vell, gov'nor, ve must all come to it, one day or another."
>
> "So we must, Sammy," said Mr. Weller the elder.
>
> "There's a Providence in it all," said Sam.
>
> "O' course there is," replied his father, with a nod of grave approval. "Wot 'ud become of the undertakers vithout it, Sammy?" (Dickens [1837] 1948, 733)

Most significantly, Dickens saw that one of the biggest problems of contemporary Christianity lay in its inability to reach out to the urban masses. In *Hard Times*, with acid tongue in cheek, he wrote of the churches of Coketown, the industrial city in which his story occurs, that:

> [T]he perplexing mystery of the place was, Who belonged to the eighteen denominations? Because, whoever did, the labouring people did not. It was very strange to walk through the streets on a Sunday morning, and note how few of *them* the barbarous jangling of bells that was driving the sick and nervous mad, called away from their own quarter, from their own close rooms, from the corners of their own streets, where they lounged listlessly, gazing at all the church and chapel going, as at a thing with which they had no manner of concern. (Dickens [1854] 1948, 23)[9]

It wasn't just the growing social irrelevance of Christianity. It was that the story was failing to engage. Some, like Shelley, went all of the way to nonbelief.

> the name of God
> Has fenced about all crime with holiness,

---

[9] In his essay on the mechanical age, Carlyle had written: "the Bible-Society, professing a far higher and heavenly structure, is found, on inquiry, to be altogether an earthly contrivance: supported by collection of moneys, by fomenting of vanities, by puffing, intrigue and chicane; a machine for converting the Heathen . . ." (Carlyle [1829] 1864, 189). Dickens echoes this in *Bleak House*, writing of one of the would-be converters of life's unfortunates (Mrs. Pardiggle) that she "would have got on infinitely better if she had not had such a mechanical way of taking possession of people" ([1853] 1948, 107).

Himself the creature of his worshippers,
Whose names and attributes and passions change,
Seeva, Buddh, Foh, Jehovah, God, or Lord,
Even with the human dupes who build his shrines,
Still serving o'er the war-polluted world
For desolation's watchword; whether hosts
Stain his death-blushing chariot-wheels, as on
Triumphantly they roll, whilst Brahmins raise
A sacred hymn to mingle with the groans;
Or countless partners of his power divide
His tyranny to weakness; or the smoke
Of burning towns, the cries of female helplessness,
Unarmed old age, and youth, and infancy,
Horribly massacred, ascend to heaven
In honor of his name; . . .

(Shelley 1821, 7, 26–42)

Notice—and this is important—that nonbelief is rarely if ever purely epistemological (Ruse 2015a). Does God exist? It is a moral issue. Should we believe in a
God who justifies such awful behavior? God is not just nonexistent. He and his
followers are immoral.

Transcendentalism

Was there an escape, an alternative? As Carlyle showed us, from Germany were
various transcendental ideas and themes, making God a less ethereal figure and
bringing him more into the world, as a kind of living force. Back in 1798 the poet
Wordsworth had been trying out these ideas.

And I have felt
A presence that disturbs me with the joy
Of elevated thoughts; a sense sublime
Of something far more deeply interfused,
Whose dwelling is the light of setting suns,
And the round ocean and the living air,
And the blue sky, and in the mind of man;
A motion and a spirit, that impels
All thinking things, all objects of all thought,
And rolls through all things.

("Tintern Abbey," written in 1798. In Wordsworth 1994, 207)

It is this kind of thinking that infuses *Sartor Resartus*. Arguing for what he called "natural supernaturalism," Carlyle proposed a kind of pantheism where the world of God and the world of nature are collapsed down into one.

> "But is not a real Miracle simply a violation of the Laws of Nature?" ask several. Whom I answer by this new question: What are the Laws of Nature? To me perhaps the rising of one from the dead were no violation of these Laws, but a confirmation; were some far deeper Law, now first penetrated into, and by Spiritual Force, even as the rest have all been, brought to bear on us with its Material Force. (Carlyle [1834] 1987, 194)

We can but scratch at the surface of true understanding. "Nature remains of quite *infinite* depth, of quite infinite expansion; and all Experience thereof limits itself to some few computed centuries and measured square-miles." Not that this deprives us of obligations. We must move from the "Everlasting No" to the "Everlasting Yes." "On the roaring billows of Time, thou art not engulfed, but borne aloft into the azure of Eternity. Love not Pleasure; love God. This is the EVERLASTING YEA, wherein all contradiction is solved: wherein whoso walks and works, it is well with him" (146).

Similar thinking was tremendously influential, particularly in the New World, where the New England transcendentalists like Ralph Waldo Emerson and Henry Thoreau embraced it with enthusiasm. It is right there in the poetry of the great American poet Walt Whitman (1819–1892), who—combining everything with a kind of Malthusian struggle—goes so far as to give the world's life force an evolutionary twist.[10]

The world below the brine,

Forests at the bottom of the sea, the branches and leaves,

Sea-lettuce, vast lichens, strange flowers and seeds, the thick tangle, openings, and pink turf,

Different colors, pale gray and green, purple, white, and gold, the play of light through the water,

Dumb swimmers there among the rocks, coral, gluten, grass, rushes, and the aliment of the swimmers,

---

[10] Beach (1936) links Whitman to Emerson. Whitman always expressed a huge admiration for Charles Darwin: "Of this old theory, evolution, as broach'd anew, trebled, with indeed all-devouring claims, by Darwin, it has so much in it, and is so needed as a counterpoise to yet widely prevailing and unspeakably tenacious, enfeebling, superstitions" (Whitman 1892, 326). It seems though that an earlier, and perhaps deeper, influence was the evolutionary theory of Robert Chambers. This poem is from the much-expanded edition of "Leaves of Grass," published in 1860 (Blake 2010).

Sluggish existences grazing there suspended, or slowly crawling
close to the bottom,

The sperm-whale at the surface blowing air and spray, or disporting
with his flukes,

The leaden-eyed shark, the walrus, the turtle, the hairy
sea-leopard, and the sting-ray,

Passions there, wars, pursuits, tribes, sight in those ocean-depths,
breathing that thick-breathing air, as so many do,

The change thence to the sight here, and to the subtle air breathed by beings
like us who walk this sphere,

The change onward from ours to that of beings who walk other spheres.

                                        (Whitman 2004, 287–288)

"Nemesis of Faith"

Yet, although obviously all this sort of stuff resonated with thinking like Owen's
archetypal vision of life's history—hardly surprising given the similar Germanic
sources—for many it was not enough.[11] It could not fill the gap created by the
other dropped shoe of German scholarship—"higher criticism." People were now
in full flight looking at the bible as a human document and finding that much
simply did not withstand the glare of critical scrutiny. Works like David Strauss's
Life of Jesus struck right at the heart of the Christian story, arguing that the miracles
were simply natural events gussied up to make plausible the claims about Jesus
being the Messiah. Hated and praised in equal terms, the controversial tome could
not be ignored. In 1846, Marion Evans (1819–1880)—the future novelist George
Eliot—published an English translation and the fat was in the fire. The flames shot
up dangerously with the publication of *Nemesis of Faith* (1849), a semiautobio-
graphical novel by James Anthony Froude, whose brother Richard Hurrell Froude
had been a close associate of John Henry Newman, one of the founders of the
Oxford Movement—the very high church party within the Church of England. It
tells the story of an Anglican priest, Markham Sutherland, ordained under family
pressure despite significant doubts, and of his unhappy life thereafter.

---

[11] The attraction of Owen's archetypal theory was that it did not have to be interpreted as evolutionary. It could be taken in an idealist form as simply showing the conceptual links. Obviously,
though, it did lend itself to an evolutionary interpretation and many took it that way. Where Owen
himself stood on evolution was ambiguous (Rupke 1994). Later in life he clearly endorsed some kind
of actual change. He may well have done so earlier as well, but owing to his need to satisfy conservative patrons, like the fellows of Cambridge colleges, strategically he said nothing.

Brotherly sentiment did not extend to the future cardinal of the Church of Rome. "Newman talked much to us of the surrender of reason. Reason, first of every thing, must be swept away, so daily more and more unreasonable appeared to modern eyes so many of the doctrines to which the Church was committed. As I began to look into what he said about it, the more difficult it seemed to me. What did it mean? Reason could only be surrendered by an act of reason" (157). Biblical literalism was out now that the Germans had shown its fallibility. In any case, the message of Christianity is very dubious.

> I will not, I must not, believe that the all-just, all-merciful, all-good God can be such a Being as I find him there described. He! He! to have created mankind liable to fall — to have laid them in the way of a temptation under which He knew they would fall, and then curse them and all who were to come of them, and all the world, for their sakes; jealous, passionate, capricious, revengeful, punishing children for their fathers' sins, tempting men, or at least permitting them to be tempted into blindness and folly, and then destroying them. (11)

And Carlyle—whom in fact Froude much admired—is no true substitute. "Carlyle! Carlyle only raises questions he cannot answer, and seems best contented if he can make the rest of us as discontented as himself . . ." (35). That was a nasty crack although one suspects more than one reader chortled at the sentiment.[12]

But why did Markham care so much, apart from the fact that—inevitably— he lost his job? Simply because of the moral issues. He feared that without religion there can be no morality. After he leaves the priesthood, he meets a married woman and they fall in love, in good part because her husband spends no time at all at home and virtually turns down the bed sheets for them. But should they consummate their relationship? Can one have morality without God? They remain apart physically. "His conscience was satisfied with what he had done. Unsteady as it was, and without the support of a strongly believed religious faith had once provided for it, he experienced at last what so long he had denied, that to attempt to separate religion from morality is madness; that religion resisting only on internal emotion, is like a dissolving view which will change its image as the passions shift their focal distances; . . ." (180–181).

Unfortunately, this does not prevent God or the fates from drowning her child, leaving them both consumed with guilt. They end up in Roman Catholic monastic institutions. She interestingly dies happy, regretting her marriage but

---

[12] Samuel Butler quipped: "It was very good of God to let Carlyle and Mrs Carlyle marry one another, and so make only two people miserable and not four" (Butler 1935, 349).

not her relationship. Markham, having been converted to Roman Catholicism by a Newman-type figure from the past, also proves not to have staying power and dies wracked with guilt about his affair tinged with regret that he did not make a proper meal out of it. If there is no God, he might as well have enjoyed the fruits on offer in this life.

> [A]midst the wasted ruins of his life, where the bare bleak soil was strewed with wrecked purposes and shattered creeds; with no hope to stay him, with no fear to raise the most dreary phantom beyond the grave, he sank down into the barren waste, and the dry sands rolled over him where he lay; and no living being was left behind him upon earth, who would not mourn over the day which brought life to Markham Sutherland. (226–227)

And on that somber note let us end our pre-Darwinian survey and move the story forward.

3

The Darwinian Theory

Charles Darwin's father, Dr. Robert Darwin, was the oldest son of Dr. Erasmus Darwin (Browne 1995, 2002). His mother was the daughter of Josiah Wedgwood, the founder of the famous pottery works. He married a first cousin, Emma Wedgwood, and they raised seven children to maturity. Darwin was a great revolutionary, but he was no rebel. He was born into a comfortable, upper-middle-class family and accepted and absorbed the beliefs and ideologies of his background. His genius was to take these beliefs and ideologies and, breaking them down, reassemble them into a whole new way of looking at the world (Richards and Ruse 2016).

Becoming an Evolutionist

Teenage years at one of England's famous public schools (in reality, private schools) were followed by two years at Edinburgh University, studying to be a physician like his father and grandfather before him. This did not take and so Darwin was packed off to the University of Cambridge, intending after his studies to become an Anglican priest. This intention faded and was dropped after Darwin on graduation accepted the offer to be ship's naturalist on HMS *Beagle*—a trip that eventually lasted five years (1831–1836) and took the crew all the way around the globe. As noted, at some point on this journey, Darwin's Christian beliefs metamorphosed into a kind of deism, primarily because he could not accept the biblical miracles—remember how Paley had made these the keystone for the faith—and this lasted right through until the final years of his life, when he became somewhat of an agnostic (never an atheist).

Darwin knew about evolution, having read his grandfather's *Zoonomia* and having been mentored by Grant when at Edinburgh—as well as reading about Lamarck's theory in Lyell's *Principles of Geology*, a work he read on the voyage. These early readings obviously primed but did not convert him. A number of factors on the trip spurred his thinking—these included fossils in South America and (particularly) the distributions of the birds and reptiles on the Galapagos Archipelago in the Pacific. But Darwin did not slip over into being an evolutionist until he got home and his collections were being classified. Early 1837 is the almost-certain date. Then for some eighteen months Darwin pursued a cause, until at the end of September 1838, reading Malthus's *Essay* sparked understanding, and he grasped the principle of natural selection brought on by the struggle for existence.

He wrote up his ideas in the early 1840s, but for reasons we still do not fully understand, he then sat on his theory for fifteen years. Finally, in the summer of 1858, a young collector in the Malay Archipelago, Alfred Russel Wallace (1823–1913), sent to Darwin an essay with essentially the same ideas as Darwin himself had discovered some twenty years previously (Darwin and Wallace 1858). Quickly, Darwin prepared a manuscript and the *Origin of Species* appeared late in 1859. Apart from a provocative comment at the end of the book, there is nothing on our own species, *Homo sapiens*. This was not because Darwin did not think his theory applied to us. His first clear statement of natural selection in a private notebook toward the end of 1838 talks of natural selection applied to our brains and intelligence. It was rather that Darwin wanted first to get his main theory out in public. But of course it was the "monkey theory" that everyone wanted to talk about and through the 1860s this was the main topic of discussion. Somewhat reluctantly, after Wallace started to argue that human evolution demands spirit forces to get the full effects, Darwin turned to humankind, and the *Descent of Man* appeared in 1871, with somewhat of a supplemental volume, the *Expression of the Emotions,* in 1872. Then Darwin had had enough and for the final ten years of his life turned to issues in botany and the like.

Let us start by laying out the theory of the *Origin* and the extension in the *Descent*. Then, after discussing some of the reactions by the scientific community and the implications of these, I will turn to the reception of Darwin's theory by the writers, novelists and poets. In this chapter and the next I will be concerned with the general reception of the theory and then later will turn to the main theme of this book, the ways in which it became a form of secular religion challenging Christianity. The period being covered goes from 1859 to roughly around the late 1920s, when Mendelian genetics was incorporated into evolutionary thinking.

The Origin of Species

Darwin referred to his book as "one, long argument" and that is the right way to approach it (Ruse 1975a, 1975b). He had (in 1831) read the *Preliminary Discourse on the Study of Natural Philosophy*, a little text on the philosophy of science by John

Herschel, and both as undergraduate and on the *Beagle's* return he had been close to the polymath William Whewell, and read (twice in 1837) his *History of the Inductive Sciences* and (in 1841) a long review by Herschel of Whewell's *Philosophy of the Inductive Sciences*. Darwin knew that the best science—the best Newtonian science—is hypothetico-deductive (a body of laws) and that it has at its heart a central cause or force, a *vera causa* ("true cause"). Herschel, more an empiricist, stressed that the mark of a *vera causa* is that one have analogical, experienced evidence—we know that a force keeps the moon in orbit around the Earth because we have experienced the tug along a piece of string when we use it to whirl a stone in orbit around our hand. Whewell, more a rationalist, stressed that a *vera causa* unites different areas of study into one whole—it lies at the center of a "consilience of inductions." We infer the cause, rather than experience it, even analogically.

Darwin set out to do everything by the book or books. He opened the *Origin* by talking of artificial selection by fanciers and farmers, an analogy that had probably led him to natural selection in the first place. Pigeons today would probably be put in different genera let alone species, and yet we know that they have all come from the same original stock. We have therefore the makings of an empiricist *vera causa*. Then, he gave a pair of quasi-deductive arguments to establish first the struggle for existence and second natural selection.

> A struggle for existence inevitably follows from the high rate at which all organic beings tend to increase. Every being, which during its natural lifetime produces several eggs or seeds, must suffer destruction during some period of its life, and during some season or occasional year, otherwise, on the principle of geometrical increase, its numbers would quickly become so inordinately great that no country could support the product. Hence, as more individuals are produced than can possibly survive, there must in every case be a struggle for existence, either one individual with another of the same species, or with the individuals of distinct species, or with the physical conditions of life. (Darwin 1859, 63–64)

Next, drawing on the fact that whenever you have a population of organisms, you find that there are differences between them and that every now and then something new seems to pop up into being, Darwin speculated that in the struggle, some types or forms are likely to prove more successful than others, simply because these types or forms will help their possessors against others. Given enough time, these types will spread through the group and eventually there will be full-blooded change.

> Let it be borne in mind how infinitely complex and close-fitting are the mutual relations of all organic beings to each other and to their physical

conditions of life. Can it, then, be thought improbable, seeing that variations useful to man have undoubtedly occurred, that other variations useful in some way to each being in the great and complex battle of life, should sometimes occur in the course of thousands of generations? If such do occur, can we doubt (remembering that many more individuals are born than can possibly survive) that individuals having any advantage, however slight, over others, would have the best chance of surviving and of procreating their kind? On the other hand, we may feel sure that any variation in the least degree injurious would be rigidly destroyed. This preservation of favourable variations and the rejection of injurious variations, I call Natural Selection. (80–81)

It is important to note that, for Darwin, change was not random. It was a matter of having features that lead to success. In other words, having features like the hand and the eye that are "as if" designed for their ends—they are "adaptations." Natural selection gives a scientific explanation of final causes. Darwin always stressed that it was the influence of Paley's *Natural Theology*, bolstered undoubtedly by Cuvier's thinking (taking us back to Kant and then to Aristotle), that was crucial here. As also was Adam Smith. The Scotsman's theory of the division of labor—you get much more done if you divide the jobs among specialists—fed right into what Darwin was to call his "principle of divergence." We have many different forms of organism, because they do better in the struggle for existence if they are specialized for certain niches and lifestyles and do not try to do everything. This led to his metaphor of the tree of life.

> The affinities of all the beings of the same class have sometimes been represented by a great tree. I believe this simile largely speaks the truth. The green and budding twigs may represent existing species; and those produced during each former year may represent the long succession of extinct species. . . . As buds give rise by growth to fresh buds, and these, if vigorous, branch out and overtop on all sides many a feebler branch, so by generation I believe it has been with the great Tree of Life, which fills with its dead and broken branches the crust of the earth, and covers the surface with its ever branching and beautiful ramifications. (129–130)

The third section of the *Origin* is devoted to applying natural selection qua rationalist *vera causa* to a wide range of biological phenomena—instinct and behavior, paleontology and the fossil record, biogeography and the distributions of organisms around the globe, systematics and the relationships between groups, anatomy and particularly the similarities (homologies) between organisms of different species, and then embryology and the links shown by developing forms. All the time, note, Darwin uses his cause, his mechanism, as the explanatory power. It is not just a matter of evolution but of evolution through natural selection. Thus, for instance, to explain why it is that the embryos of organisms very different are frequently similar, he argues that this is because selection only really gets to work on the adult forms—the embryos protected in the womb feel no such forces. It is important to note also another Adam Smith influence. For Darwin, selection is always a matter of one organism against another—we are all self-regarding if you like. No one puts themselves out for anyone else unless there is return—like help or passing on one's heredity (as with children), and so forth. Here Darwin differed from Wallace. The latter, much influenced by the socialism of the 1840s reformer Robert Owen, always found a place for selection aiding the group even at the expense of the individual.

Concluding, Darwin wrote the most famous lines in the whole of biology if not science.

> It is interesting to contemplate an entangled bank, clothed with many plants of many kinds, with birds singing on the bushes, with various insects flitting about, and with worms crawling through the damp earth, and to reflect that these elaborately constructed forms, so different from each other, and dependent on each other in so complex a manner, have all been produced by laws acting around us . . . Thus, from the war of nature, from famine and death, the most exalted object which we are capable of conceiving, namely, the production of the higher animals, directly follows. There is grandeur in this view of life, with its several powers, having been originally breathed into a few forms or into one; and that, whilst this planet has gone cycling on according to the fixed law of gravity, from so simple a beginning endless forms most beautiful and most wonderful have been, and are being, evolved. (489–490)

Do note that Darwin was fully committed to biological progress and this was a reflection of his belief in social and cultural Progress—what other philosophy would be embraced by the grandchild of one of the greatest successes in the Industrial Revolution? In the third edition of the *Origin* (1861) he suggested that biological progress might come from what today we would call arms races, where lines of organisms compete—predator and prey, for instance—thus perfecting their adaptations.

> If we look at the differentiation and specialisation of the several organs of each being when adult (and this will include the advancement of the brain for intellectual purposes) as the best standard of highness

of organisation, natural selection clearly leads towards highness; for all physiologists admit that the specialisation of organs, inasmuch as they perform in this state their functions better, is an advantage to each being; and hence the accumulation of variations tending towards specialisation is within the scope of natural selection. (134)

Note, however, that Darwin is not (unlike his predecessors) putting forward his theory of evolution based on his belief in human Progress. He didn't need to because with selection he had a naturalistic explanation of final causes. Rather, his belief in biological progress is based on his theory. Thus we expect to see a shift away from evolution-as-pseudoscience. More on this shortly, but note that even though Darwin is not supporting evolution through his philosophy, one might still argue that the philosophy makes the theory attractive and that there is as much wishing as solid science in making the science support the philosophy. What is important to stress is that—even though he was still at this point a deist—he was not like Tennyson or his own friend, the American botanist Asa Gray (1876), in wanting to involve God directly in the upward direction of change. Darwin had little real idea about where and why the variations for change originate (he had many unreal suggestions), but he was always certain that they were not directed. In this sense, variation is "random."[1]

The Descent of Man

Turn now to the *Descent of Man and Selection in Relation to Sex* (1871). As the subtitle flags you, it is an odd book for most of it is not about the descent of man! It is rather about Darwin's secondary mechanism of sexual selection. This is a notion that goes back to the earliest formulation of the theory and makes a brief appearance in the *Origin*. Clearly based on the analogy with the domestic world, Darwin argued that along with natural selection—analogous (with its focus on existence) to such features prized by the breeder as size (the beefiness of the steer) and coat covering (the fleece of sheep)—there is sexual selection—analogous (with its focus on reproduction) to such features prized

---

[1] This matter of heredity, what today we call "genetics," was an ongoing problem for Darwin. In a work published between the *Origin* and the *Descent*—*The Variation of Animals and Plants Under Domestication* (1868)—he introduced what he called his "provisional theory of pangenesis," arguing that particles are given off from all over the body and then collected in the sex cells. Apart from anything else, this gave Darwin a material basis for a kind of Lamarckism, the inheritance of acquired characteristics, something to which he always subscribed along with selection. No one was very impressed, but no one had any other suggestions (Olby 1963).

by the breeder as weapons (the spurs of the cock) and attractiveness (tail of the peacock). Indeed, impressed by such examples, Darwin divided sexual selection into male combat—the stag fighting for the harem of hinds—and female choice—the male birds on display in a lek before the females.

Why this newfound interest in sexual selection? Simply that this was the naturalistic response to Wallace (Ruse 2015b). Darwin agreed with the younger naturalist that there are human features like skin color and hairlessness and probably great intelligence that do not seem to have their origin in natural selection. Savages (as they both thought of native people), for instance, rarely use all of their available brain power. It was here that sexual selection was brought into play as Darwin argued that much of human evolution resulted from such a process—something that he stressed was no less natural than natural selection. Nevertheless, despite the somewhat distorting discussion of the secondary mechanism, overall it must be understood to be secondary. The main cause of human evolution, as for all other organisms, is natural selection. And to this end, the first part of the *Descent* trots out familiar sorts of facts and analyses, showing how morphologically and in all other ways we humans may be special but we are not different. Our ancestors do not exist today, but we are primates and it is clear that the higher apes are our closest relatives.

Particularly significant are Darwin's discussions of religion and of morality. His treatment of the former showed a heavy debt to David Hume, whose *Natural History of Religion* (1757) Darwin read around the time that he discovered natural selection. For Hume, religion was all a big mistake. "We find human faces in the moon, armies in the clouds; and by a natural propensity, if not corrected by experience and reflection, ascribe malice and good will to everything that hurts or pleases us." Darwin basically took the same tack: "my dog, a full-grown and very sensible animal, was lying on the lawn during a hot and still day; but at a little distance a slight breeze occasionally moved an open parasol, which would have been wholly disregarded by the dog, had any one stood near it. As it was, every time that the parasol slightly moved, the dog growled fiercely and barked. He must, I think, have reasoned to himself in a rapid and unconscious manner, that movement without any apparent cause indicated the presence of some strange living agent, and no stranger had a right to be on his territory" (1, 67). Adding: "The belief in spiritual agencies would easily pass into the belief in the existence of one or more gods."

Morality took more care and imagination. However, the basic idea is simple—morality pays off because the moral person does better in the struggle than the immoral person. "It must not be forgotten that although a high standard of morality gives but a slight or no advantage to each individual man and his children over the other men of the same tribe, yet that an advancement in the standard of morality and an increase in the number of well-endowed men will certainly give an immense advantage to one tribe over another" (1, 166). Darwin doesn't mince words about what this means: "There can be no doubt that a tribe including many members who, from possessing in a high degree the spirit of patriotism, fidelity, obedience, courage, and sympathy, were always ready to give aid to each other and to sacrifice themselves for the common good, would be victorious over most other tribes; and this would be natural selection." And so we get the consequence. "At all times throughout the world tribes have supplanted other tribes; and as morality is one element in their success, the standard of morality and the number of well-endowed men will thus everywhere tend to rise and increase." Parenthetically, this might seem as though Darwin is here appealing to the good of the group over the good of the individual. He made it clear that he regarded tribes as inter-related families, and the family he took to be one individual, a kind of super organism. In other words, with respect to morality, humans are parts of a whole rather than individuals in their own right.

What does Darwin get out of sexual selection? A lot of fairly standard views on human beings, especially human beings as seen by the mid-Victorians.

> Man is more courageous, pugnacious, and energetic than woman, and has a more inventive genius. His brain is absolutely larger, but whether relatively to the larger size of his body, in comparison with that of woman, has not, I believe been fully ascertained. In woman the face is rounder; the jaws and the base of the skull smaller; the outlines of her body rounder, in parts more prominent; and her pelvis is broader than in man; but this latter character may perhaps be considered rather as a primary than a secondary sexual character. She comes to maturity at an earlier age than man.
>
> Male and female children resemble each other closely, like the young of so many other animals in which the adult sexes differ; they likewise resemble the mature female much more closely, than the mature male. The female, however, ultimately assumes certain distinctive characters, and in the formation of her skull, is said to be intermediate between the child and the man. (2, 316–317)

Darwin was always a great ferreter, looking for facts that he could carry off and use. He looked upon this as a strength of his approach rather than a weakness. The whole point of his theorizing was to take information that was known already and to put it in a new context, giving it a new meaning. Expectedly, a great deal of what he had to say about humankind was secondary, sometimes depressingly so. "It is well known that with many Hottentot women the posterior part of the body projects in a wonderful manner; they are steatopygous; and Sir Andrew Smith is certain that this peculiarity is greatly admired by the men." Adding: "Some of the women in various negro tribes are similarly characterised; and, according to Burton, the Somal men 'are said to choose their wives by ranging them in a line, and by picking her out who projects farthest *a tergo,* Nothing can be more hateful to a negro than the opposite form'" (2, 345–346). Complementing this, there isn't much love of European features. "With respect to colour, the negroes rallied Mungo Park on the whiteness of his skin and the prominence of his nose, both of which they considered as "unsightly and unnatural conformations" (2, 346). In the same vein: "On the western coast, as Mr. Winwood Reade informs me, the negroes admire a very black skin more than one of a lighter tint." And so it goes. Both male combat and female choice seem to be active in human affairs and sometimes probably other factors outweigh sexual selection. But in the end, we are animals, and that is all there is to it.

First Reactions

At the British Association meeting in Oxford in 1860, Thomas Henry Huxley (1825–1895) squared off against the leader of the Church of England high church faction, "Soapy Sam" Wilberforce (son of William), Bishop of Oxford (Desmond 1997). Supposedly the bishop asked Huxley if he was descended from monkeys on his grandfather's side or his grandmother's side. Supposedly Huxley responded that he would rather be descended from a monkey than from a bishop of the Church of England! All a good lark, with the combatants going off to supper together later. Probably mythological, although a myth with a purpose, like Moses leading his people out of Egypt and to the Promised Land. There were real quarrels with undertones of bitterness. Huxley and Richard Owen differed over whether or not humans were unique in having a brain part, the hippocampus minor. Yes, said Owen. No, said Huxley, who proved to be right. Charles Kingsley had great fun parodying this in his *Water Babies* (1863). Owen and Huxley are hybridized into Professor Ptthmllnsprts—"Put them all in spirits."

> Now it befell that, on the very shore, and over the very rocks, where Tom was sitting with his friend the lobster, there walked one day the little white lady, Ellie herself, and with her a very wise man indeed – Professor Ptthmllnsprts... He held very strange theories about a good many things. He had even got up once at the British Association, and declared that apes had hippopotamus majors in their brains just as men have. Which was a shocking thing to say; for, if it were so, what would become of the faith, hope, and charity of immortal millions? You may think that there are other more important differences between you and an ape, such as

being able to speak, and make machines, and know right from wrong, and say your prayers, and other little matters of that kind; but that is a child's fancy, my dear. Nothing is to be depended on but the great hippopotamus test. If you have a hippopotamus major in your brain, you are no ape, though you had four hands, no feet, and were more apish than the apes of all aperies. But if a hippopotamus major is ever discovered in one single ape's brain, nothing will save your great-great-great-great-great-great-great-great-great-great-great-greater-greatest-grandmother from having been an ape too. (Kingsley [1863] 2008, 85)

Joking apart, two things are clear. Although Darwin had rather run together the fact of evolution and the cause of evolution, people had little trouble in pulling them apart. As far as the fact of evolution is concerned, of course, there were those who opposed it. Apart from Wilberforce, many of Darwin's old teachers at Cambridge—famously Professor of Geology Adam Sedgwick and the by now Master of Trinity William Whewell—for all that they were major influences on Darwin (Sedgwick gave Darwin a crash course on geology before he set off on the *Beagle* and Whewell's importance has been noted already) were strong against the message of the *Origin*. Across the Atlantic, Swiss-born Louis Agassiz (discoverer of ice ages) at Harvard and Charles Hodge, Principal of Princeton Theological College, never accepted evolution. At less exalted levels it was also opposed. Mrs. Alfred Gatty—editor of *Aunt Judy's Magazine*, a family publication for children—hit the ground running in 1861 with a somewhat labored story—explicitly intended to combat "the Darwinian presumption as far as I could in a small way"—about rooks expounding (in a fashion intended to reduce the ideas to risible absurdity) on their degenerate offspring, humans. "My friends, man is not our superior, was never so, for he is neither more nor less than a degenerated brother of our own race! Yes, I venture confidently to look back on thousands on thousands of generations, and I see that *men* were once *rooks*!" (Gatty 1862, 146–147). What led to our decline and fall? "Alas! indolence and a fatal tendency to yield to the ease of the moment are the causes of our own conduct; and so they were, I have no doubt whatever, of the degradation of our ancestors." Apparently, those of us who go down coal mines and end the day with black faces are truly doing their bit to get us back to our longed-for earlier rook-like state. Far better, however, that we aspire to a true transformation. "Except ye become as little children, ye shall not enter into the kingdom of Heaven."

Whatever the immediate effect on infant minds, this kind of stuff seems not to have had a lasting effect. Naysayers notwithstanding, evolution as fact was accepted almost immediately and almost universally, especially by the younger generation. With the exception of the American South, this is true even in religious circles (Roberts 1988). Like the emperor's new clothes, as soon as the respectable Charles Darwin said "but we did evolve," people said they had known it all along. A good guide is the final exam of the honors biology program at Cambridge (Ruse 1979). In 1851, the first year there was such a degree, students were asked to give a refutation of evolutionary thinking. By the mid-1860s, students were told not to bother with defending evolution but to discuss the causes! Given that Frank Darwin, Charles's son, got a First, one assumes that being a chip off the old block was no handicap.

What of natural selection? Talk now about the scientific community. There was some good work done using selection and this continued right down through our period (Kimler and Ruse 2013; Ruse 1996). Soon after the *Origin* was published, Henry Walter Bates, a collector who had traveled with Wallace in South America, came up with a finding and an explanation that still rightly bears his name. Some nonpoisonous butterflies mimic poisonous forms, even though there is no close relationship. Bates showed that this is a function of natural selection with the nonpoisonous forms, as it were, piggybacking on the poisonous butterflies (Bates 1862, 1863). There was more work of this ilk—that is, work on fast-breeding organisms with readily identifiable adaptations. The German-born naturalist Fritz Müller who had emigrated to Brazil was also much interested in selection as a mechanism and he too came up with a Darwinian explanation of mimicry, this time of different species of poisonous butterflies who grow to look alike (and have strong, distinctive coloration) so that predators will more quickly learn that that form is not for good eating.[2] In the same vein, pioneering investigations were done in the 1870s by the German biologist August Weismann, perhaps better known for his ferocious attacks in the 1880s on Lamarckian inheritance. In a major study on the markings of caterpillars, translated into English by 1882 and published in a collection with an appreciative preface by Charles Darwin no less, he was categorical in assigning importance to the Darwinian mechanism: "it has been established that each of the elements of marking occurring in the larvae of the Sphingidae originally possessed a decided biological significance, which was produced by natural selection" (Weismann 1882, 388). This kind of thinking was used and endorsed by British scientists, notably including Wallace, who from the 1860s picked up on mimicry and through the years wrote overview articles (Wallace 1866, 1889, 1891). Then, from the next generation, Edward B. Poulton (1890, 1908), professor of zoology at Oxford, made significant selection-based contributions to problems of animal coloration. Also (especially among collectors of butterflies and moths) there

---

[2] Darwin was appreciative of this work using selection. He praised Bates's work in reviews, was instrumental in getting Bates's work published by his own publisher, John Murray, and then through Murray's good offices getting the lower-middle-class Bates a good job as secretary of the Royal Geographical Society. Darwin also arranged at his own expense for a little book by Müller, *Für Darwin*, to be translated and published in English, *Facts and Arguments for Darwin* (1869).

was considerable interest in industrial melanism, where insects take on darker forms as camouflage in response to the blackening of trees because of industrial pollution. "I believe . . . that Lancashire and Yorkshire melanism is the result of the combined action of the 'smoke,' etc., plus humidity [thus making bark darker], and that the intensity of Yorkshire and Lancashire melanism produced by humidity and smoke, is intensified by 'natural selection' and 'hereditary tendency'" (Tutt 1890, 56). One enthusiast even told Darwin about this, although he seems not to have taken it up.[3] Then at the end of the century, W. F. R. Weldon (1898) began doing groundbreaking studies on crab adaptations. In this he was supported by the mathematical genius of Karl Pearson (1900)—who made his name as a statistician devising the chi-squared test, among other innovations.

But generally it cannot be denied that, starting with Huxley himself, many of the better-known professional biologists as professional biologists were not overly committed to the power of natural selection. In part, this was because they could not see its full force. Huxley kept stressing that no one had yet artificially made two different species. And in combination with this, no one seemed to have set out to prove the critics wrong. Darwin himself seemed always to have thought that the action of selection was too weak to show itself in human time. You need thousands of years to see it in full action.[4] In part, though—and this

---

[3] My dear Sir,

The belief that I am about to relate something which may be of interest to you, must be my excuse for troubling you with a letter.

Perhaps among the whole of the British Lepidoptera, no species varies more, according to the locality in which it is found, than does that Geometer, Gnophos obscurata. They are almost black on the New Forest peat; grey on limestone; almost white on the chalk near Lewes; and brown on clay, and on the red soil of Herefordshire.

Do these variations point to the "survival of the fittest"? I think so. It was, therefore, with some surprise that I took specimens as dark as any of those in the New Forest on a chalk slope; and I have pondered for a solution. Can this be it?

It is a curious fact, in connexion with these dark specimens, that for the last quarter of a century the chalk slope, on which they occur, has been swept by volumes of black smoke from some lime-kilns situated at the bottom: the herbage, although growing luxuriantly, is blackened by it.

I am told, too, that the very light specimens are now much less common at Lewes than formerly, and that, for some few years, lime-kilns have been in use there.

These are the facts I desire to bring to your notice.

I am, Dear Sir, Yours very faithfully,

A. B. Farn

Letter from Albert Brydges Farn on November 18, 1878 (Darwin Correspondence Project, 11747).

[4] Darwin introduced a full discussion of Bates's work into the fourth edition of the *Origin* (1866), although interestingly towards the end of the book. Perhaps this was a function of his Lyellian beliefs

is the bigger part—selection was a solution in search of a problem. The direction of science before Darwin and after Darwin was just not in the Darwinian direction, meaning something that made adaptation fundamental and central.[5] It was homology—the foundation of Germanic biology with its neoplatonic resonances—that was central. By looking at isomorphisms one could discern relationships. This is what Darwin himself used in a massive study of barnacles that he performed between discovering natural selection and publishing on it. This is what was central to the work of both Owen and Huxley—in respects, their quarrels were a classic case of what Freud was to call the "narcissism of small differences." And it was what was central to biology after Darwin, especially when people like the German biologist Ernst Haeckel got involved (Richards 2008). It wasn't that people weren't doing professional evolutionary biology but that it wasn't Darwinian biology. Especially after the huge numbers of spectacular fossils started to flood in from excavations in the American West, the focus was less on causes and more on patterns and paths, on what were known as "phylogenies"—what was related to what, as in: "Are the birds descended from the dinosaurs?" (Bowler 1996) Haeckel's "biogenetic law" – ontogeny recapitulates phylogeny – was a great help here. [6]

Causes therefore were something of a luxury item, but fortunately no one was going to use them very much. They would be more tacked on after the work was done. Huxley favored some kind of evolution by jumps, "saltationism." Others, particularly those who thought there was something to adaptation, were more inclined to the Lamarckian inheritance of acquired characteristics. And yet a third

---

in the necessity of huge amounts of time for significant change, so even he was not entirely convinced of the power of selection to have rapid and important effects. Also, paradoxically, as a professional biologist, he himself was not very Darwinian.

[5] Amusingly but significantly Huxley (1893) actually denied that butterfly coloration could have any biological significance.

[6] It is tempting therefore to say that the paradox is that while the professional scientists often belittled natural selection, at first it was hobbyists—amateur lepidopterists—who were most aware of and ready to turn to natural selection for explanations. This is true in part. Farn was a minor civil servant, mainly notable as a sportsman, having shot thirty birds in thirty shots on the estate of Lord Walsingham, thus establishing a record "which has probably never been equaled" (Salmon 2000, 176). Wallace was appreciated for his contributions, and in the 1870s for his work on geographical distributions, but particularly thanks to his enthusiasm for spiritualism, he was always a bit of a fringe figure. No one was prepared to give him a proper job and his entry to the Royal Society came late (1893). Bates was now more a servant of the scientific community than a leading member. But this characterization of those actually using natural selection in a scientific manner to explain change as outside the central professional loop is only partially true. Given the appreciation of Weismann's work, not to mention home-grown studies of people like Poulton and of Weismann's translator, the London-based professor of organic chemistry and keen entomologist Raphael Meldola, it is better to say that there were professional, selection-based evolutionary studies but that they were a minority interest in the general professional biological world, even in that (especially that) which was understanding classifications and lines of descent in an evolutionary manner.

group, particularly in America and particularly in the paleontological realm, favored a kind of momentum—orthogenesis—that carried organisms along, even
sometimes taking them over into nonadaptive dead ends. The bizarre snouts of
the titanotheres were thought to be a prime example. All of this meant that, with
the speculations about causes and the fact that too often phylogenetic speculation collapsed into ignorance and contradiction, even putting selection on one
side, judged as professional science, evolutionary studies did not have very high
status and ambitious young biologists turned to other fields like cytology and
then a bit later genetics (Bateson 1922).

Darwinism as Popular Science

All of this has led some students of the period to speak of the "myth" of the
Darwinian Revolution (Bowler 1988)—itself an egregious myth of the worst
kind.[7] This is clear even before we turn to the world of the creative writer, the
novelist, and the poet. Take Thomas Henry Huxley, who in respects is the key
player in our period, even more than Charles Darwin (Desmond 1997). He is
the man with energy, who is a brilliant teacher and administrator, creating and
working at the Royal School of Mines, plotting the move (in 1872) to the new
science complex in South Kensington. He is also collaborating with others
trying to bring Great Britain right into the nineteenth century—for instance,
his students were much involved in medical education—and called upon and
respected for his abilities and his general passion to improve the lot of his fellow
country men and women. It is true that, as a professional scientist and educator,
he was not much of a Darwinian. Apart from not being able to use selection very
much in his own science, he could not really see how to use it practically. He

---

[7] All-too-typical is Lightman (2010) who argues that, as far as the general public in Britain and
America was concerned, when it came to evolution, "Darwin was just one author among many competing for their attention and patronage" (20). To make his case, seeking things that separate off general opinion from that of Darwin, Lightman picks out Lamarckian inheritance, biological progress,
and a desire to see evolution in a God-infused manner. Reinforcing his conclusion, Lightman argues
that natural selection is basically absent from the general view. To which one can only respond to all
of these charges, read this book. Darwin was far more a man of his age than Lightman realizes, and
natural selection was known to all and sexual selection even more. Remember, there was no film or
television in the nineteenth century. Emma Darwin read fiction aloud to Charles after lunch every
day. They were not alone. If you want popular opinion, that is where you should look (Holmes 2012).
In a way, more interesting than refuting the false vision is trying to understand the popularity of such
misconceptions. One suspects that, even today, many find the Darwinian story unsettling. This is
certainly true in the philosophical world, with deniers both religious, Alvin Plantinga (2011), and
non-religious, Thomas Nagel (2012). As we shall see, this is true in the literary world also. So why
not historians of science?

realized that if you are going to get science supported and let it flourish you have got to find customers prepared to pay good cash—that was his interest in medical education (doctors) and why he sat on the London School Board (teachers)—and that was why he could push anatomy and embryology. That was also why in his huge course on biology of 165 lectures there was less than one lecture on evolution and less than ten minutes on natural selection.

But it didn't mean that he thought that natural selection was irrelevant to human nature and even less did he think it was not worth talking about. In the public realm, night after night he spoke to working men's clubs and the like, or debated with other intellectuals (including bishops and cardinals), and wrote essay after essay for the popular press or the solid, middle-class journals that throve in that literate society. And natural selection was right there. From the start: "How far 'natural selection' suffices for the production of species remains to be seen. Few can doubt that, if not the whole cause, it is a very important factor in that operation; and that it must play a great part in the sorting out of varieties into those which are transitory and those which are permanent" (Huxley [1859] 1893).

Most revealing is the talk Huxley gave right at the end of his career, a decade after the death of Darwin and but a couple of years before he himself died. He was discussing ethics and why it is that we cannot simply deduce right and wrong from the processes of nature. But to get to this point in the discussion, he had to admit that organisms—humans in particular—are faced with a struggle for existence and that there is a consequent selection for various adaptations.

> Man, the animal, in fact, has worked his way to the headship of the sentient world, and has become the superb animal which he is, in virtue of his success in the struggle for existence. The conditions having been of a certain order, man's organization has adjusted itself to them better than that of his competitors in the cosmic strife. In the case of mankind, the self-assertion, the unscrupulous seizing upon all that can be grasped, the tenacious holding of all that can be kept, which constitute the essence of the struggle for existence, have answered. For his successful progress, throughout the savage state, man has been largely indebted to those qualities which he shares with the ape and the tiger; his exceptional physical organization; his cunning, his sociability, his curiosity, and his imitativeness; his ruthless and ferocious destructiveness when his anger is roused by opposition. (Huxley 1893, 51–52)

Huxley now wanted to argue that ruthlessness and the like are not particularly moral qualities and that we must learn to control them, but this is not the writing of a man who has turned his back on the struggle for existence and natural selection in human evolution. The whole point is that that is what did cause us and now we show the effects.

Charles Darwin was faced with evolution as a pseudoscience. He wanted to upgrade it, I very much suspect, to the status of a professional science like physics and chemistry. He did not succeed in doing this, at least not a universally practiced, professional evolutionary science in the Darwinian mode, meaning one that made natural selection central. But if Huxley is anything to go on, he did make for a Darwinian evolutionary popular science—one of the public domain.[8] Do note, though, unlike pre-*Origin* evolutionary thinking, it was not rejected and despised and found threatening by the scientific elite. They may not have wanted to use selection as a tool, but they certainly accepted it for what they thought it was. Do note also that as something in the public domain, although evolutionary thinking was no longer simply the epiphenomenon of a particular philosophy or world view (Progress), it was still perfectly legitimate to introduce social and other values and link them to the discussion. That is what a popular science is all about. Darwin himself realized all this and in respects took what was on offer. Certainly, compared to the *Origin of Species*—almost painfully forced in its exclusion of social or cultural values—the *Descent of Man* is written in a more popular way with greater willingness to introduce social values. Dealing with humans, of course, this is bound to happen to a certain extent, but Darwin saw the opportunity and embraced it.[9]

---

[8] We shall see later that having an adequate theory of heredity was a key factor in making evolutionary studies into professional science. But without getting into counterfactual history, which is always dicey, my sense is that (as noted) its absence at the time of the *Origin* and the *Descent* was not the key to the indifference towards and sometimes rejection of selection in the professional world and the consequent move to popular science. It is true that some astute critics pointed out that without an adequate theory of heredity, it was hard to see how selection could be effective (Hull 1973). One suspects, however, that while this may have reinforced the doubts of those inclined to turn away from selection anyway, no one turned from selection purely on this account. Later in the century, Weldon started to do very sophisticated selection studies without a proper understanding of heredity. The fact is that most professional scientists were just not looking for a selection-based professional science. They were keen on a selection-based popular science.

[9] Although people like Huxley were pushing a popular-professional science division, and basically won, many at the time (being excluded from the professional ranks) denied entirely that there was or could be such a division (Lightman 2009, 1, 4). Others were contesting the very idea (and consequent authority) of professional science (DeWitt 2013). This reinforces my point about being uncomfortable with simply saying that selection was taken up as a tool of science only by or mainly by amateurs. Where do you put someone like James W. Tutt, writer of popular books like *A Natural History of the British Lepidoptera. A Text-book for Students and Collectors* (1908) and founder of the *Entomologist's Record and Journal of Variation*? Many of the contributors to the journal make their livings in other fields, as did someone like Meldola who was a professor of chemistry, and yet the sophisticated understanding of Tutt and his contributors makes one uncomfortable with simply labeling them amateurs, any more than one would so type Darwin who never held a paid post in his life.

4

Reception

Thomas Hardy (1840–1928), writing of "this strange message Darwin brings," summed it up nicely.

> We all are one with creeping things;
> And apes and men
> Blood-brethren,
> And likewise reptile forms with stings.
>   (Hardy 1994, 842, written in the 1920s)

So turn now to the creative writers. How did they react to Darwinism? Was Hardy the exception or the norm? Did the poets and novelists accept it? Did they understand it? Did they modify it? Did they clarify it? In what sense did they contribute to the status of Darwinism as a popular science and make us very wary of sloshing around terms like "myth"?

Reception: Natural Selection

Charles Darwin himself was a known figure, the author of the popular *Voyage of the Beagle,* and even though by the time of the *Origin* he had for many years been tucked away in the Kent village of Downe, folk were aware that for long he had labored over the classification of barnacles. To such an extent that a popular novelist (Edward Bulwer Lytton, in *What Will He Do with It?* published a year before the *Origin*) could make fun of Darwin's efforts: thus an announcement in the window of a shopkeeper in a provincial town.

> GATESBORO' ATHENIEUM
> AND LITERARY INSTITUTE.
> LECTURE ON CONCHOLOGY.
> BY PROFESSOR LONG.
> Author of "Researches into the Natural History of Limpets."

One fears that the professor's audience was mainly a captive group of girls from the local school. The mayor, wanting to improve the literary standards of his town, has presented to the local library the professor's two-volume tome on the subject. The shopkeeper, having conveyed this information to a curious customer, "mechanically resumed the task of cutting those leaves, which, had the volumes reached the shelves of the library uncut, would have so remained to the crack of doom." Even thus prepared for readers, their wait will be long and lonely.

After the *Origin*, the tone changes. Mrs. Gaskell's *Wives and Daughters* (1866), set around 1830, has a thoroughly attractive naturalist hero, Roger Hamley, by the author's own account modeled on Darwin (Litvack 2004). The novelist knows her science, although her Darwin-held views are diametrically opposed to the real Darwin. Roger is invited to meet "M. Geoffroi St. H—, whose views on certain subjects Roger had been advocating" (301). For background, Geoffroy St. Hilaire (as we would spell it) was a French comparative anatomist, supporter of evolution and opponent of Cuvier, albeit inclined to Germanic-type thinking about archetypes and hence opposed to the adaptationism of Cuvier and, of course, Darwin. Mrs. Gaskell knew Darwin and was distantly related to him, so this might have been an in-joke. The important thing is that in her story Mrs. Gaskell made Roger a serious and appreciated supporter of evolution, long before it was fashionable in England.[1]

What of evolution through natural selection? It is there, through the whole period. Expectedly, Dickens is immediately sensitive, having Pip the hero of *Great Expectations* say of his five dead siblings, that they "gave up trying to get a living, exceedingly early in that universal struggle" ([1860] 1948, 1).[2] Just an aside comment, but it was published first in December 1860, showing that the Malthus-Darwin theme is right up there in popular consciousness. Dickens himself would have known all about Darwin's theory because in the weekly magazine he edited, *All the Year Round* (circulation c100,000), he carried two articles

---

[1] Debrabant (2002) perceptively suggests that there is change of tone also from Gaskell's earlier novels. In this post-*Origin* world, the superintendence of a benevolent deity is entirely gone and the thoroughly amoral but more forceful—although, to be fair, wonderfully dreadful—heroine's stepmother, Mrs. Gibson, thrives to the end of the novel without divine retribution. Henson (2003) suggests that Gaskell was already on the way to a Darwinian world before the *Origin* was published. This is obviously true in some senses—*North and South* showed that—but there is in *Wives and Daughters* a new sense of social change, a move to the world of Thomas Henry Huxley. Roger starts the novel as the unappreciated, second son of a country squire but ends on his own merits as a respected London scientist (Hughes 2007). Although set in early times, the novel reflects a power shift in the 1860s back from the North—the setting of the earlier novels *Mary Barton* (1848) and *North and South* (1855)—to London (Uglow 1993, 586).

[2] Dickens probably drew on Darwin's work on barnacles as inspiration for his savage attack on the British civil service in *Little Dorrit*, starting serialization in 1855. Like real crustacea, the Barnacle family, running the Circumlocution Office, fasten themselves parasitically on the ship of state, benefiting themselves only and slowing down the proper functioning of everything else (Smith 1999).

in mid-1860 and another early in 1861 that discussed the *Origin* and natural selection carefully (Anon. 1860a, 1860b, 1861).[3]

> How, asks Mr. Darwin, . . . have all these exquisite adaptations of one part
> of the organisation to another part, and to the conditions of life, and of one
> distinct organic being to another, been perfected? He answers, they are so
> perfected by what he terms Natural Selection — the better chance which a
> better organised creature has of surviving its fellows — so termed in order
> to mark its relation to Man's power of selection. Man, by selection in the
> breeds of his domestic animals and the seedlings of his horticultural pro-
> ductions, can certainly effect great results, and can adapt organic beings to
> his own uses, through the accumulation of slight but useful variations given
> to him by the hand of Nature. But Natural Selection is a power incessantly
> ready for action, and is as immeasurably superior to man's feeble efforts, as
> the works of Nature are to those of Art. Natural Selection, therefore, accord-
> ing to Mr. Darwin — not independent creations — is the method through
> which the Author of Nature has elaborated the providential fitness of His
> works to themselves and to all surrounding circumstances. (Anon. 1860a)

The author, David Thomas Ansted (1814–1880), was a professional geologist and long-time acquaintance of Darwin. It is stressed that there is nothing
to cause worry for the religious, and the status of Darwin as a scientist and his
worth as a human being are likewise strongly underlined. Although the pieces
are ostensibly agnostic about Darwin's work, opponents are referred to as
"timid" and overall the sentiment is very positive. "We are no longer to look at
an organic being as a savage looks at a ship—as at something wholly beyond his
comprehension; we are to regard every production of nature as one which has
had a history; we are to contemplate every complex structure and instinct as the
summing up of many contrivances, each useful to the possessor, nearly in the
same way as when we look at any great mechanical invention as the summing
up of the labour, the experience, the reason, and even the blunders, of numerous
workmen" (1860b, 299). One doubts that Dickens was surprised by any of this
for it was not a one-off by the author. In a book Ansted published later in 1860,
Geological Gossip, the treatment is even more favorable.[4]

---

[3] Even as early as 1848 Dickens was showing enthusiasm for the *Vestiges* of Chambers (Fielding
1996). He hovered over every word written in *All the Year Round,* and so it is interesting that although
he was a good friend of Richard Owen (Sage 1999), he did not prevent the author from being very
critical of Owen's thinking on the species question.

[4] Darwin was a little disappointed in the first, brief piece. "There is notice of me in penultimate
no' of 'All the Year Round', but not worth consulting; chiefly a well-done hash of my own words.—"
(Darwin 1985–, 8, 254, letter to Charles Lyell, June 14, 1860). He was much more positive about the
treatment in *Geological Gossip*. "I want to express my admiration at the clear and correct manner in
which you have given a sketch of natural selection" (8, 446, letter to D. T. Ansted, October 27, 1860).

And so the coverage continued, in the popular press and in journals like *Punch*, with its well-known cartoons.[5] Taking an early example of Darwin's ideas in fiction, the *Cornhill Magazine* rivaled *All the Year Round* as *the* literary magazine of the 1860s and 1870s—the first issue sold over 100,000 copies. Edited initially by the novelist William Thackeray, it published (among others) *Framley Parsonage* by Anthony Trollope, *Wives and Daughters* by Mrs. Gaskell, *Romola* by George Eliot, and *Far from the Madding Crowd* by Thomas Hardy. It was read widely. In 1862 it carried a little skit by one E. S. Dixon,[6] *A Vision of Animal Existences*, about a man who goes off to the zoo one hot summer's day and who meets up with a couple of very strange people, a woman by the name of "Natural Selection," with the occupation "Originator of Species"—"Was the woman mad? Yours is a bold assumption, madam!"—and a boy, presumably her son, "Struggle for Existence"—"As he looked me in the face, I saw that his eyes were luminous, like a cat's in the dark; his canine teeth were short strong tusks; his fingernails were retractile talons; his tunic was the colour of arterial blood" (313).

They take him round the zoo, showing him that talk of miraculous origins of species is simply false and that there is clear evidence of descent with modification. "The swimming-bladder of the fish is the first sketch of the apparatus that was gradually perfected into lungs. There are fish with gills which breathe the air dissolved in the water at the same time that they also breathe free air in their swim-bladders. Believe me, sir, all vertebrate animals having true lungs have descended, by ordinary generation, from an ancient prototype furnished with a swimming-bladder" (314). And don't be conned into thinking that the Earth is but 6,000 years old. "Read Sir Charles Lyell, and make your mind easy that the world is considerably older than that." What of causes?

> "See, now, *how* we work!" she continued, with less calmness than was habitual to her. She walked through a herd of antelopes: every individual that was not agile to escape the lion, swift to travel to fresh pastures

Ansted was in Darwin's debt, literally, for help given to an unsuccessful business venture, but there is no reason to think his scientific appreciation was other than genuine. That said, especially given that a year or two later Darwin basically forgave Ansted his debt—a few hundred pounds, nothing to Darwin but enough for a middle-class family to live on for a year—it is a lovely example of how the Darwinians furthered their cause. The examples of Ansted and Bates and Müller show that Darwin himself did his bit.

[5] Ellegård (1958), still in major respects the best introduction to the reception of the *Origin* by the general public, makes the point about how quickly word about the *Origin* and its contents was spread about. The pieces in *All the Year Round* were not unique. Ellegård also makes the point, made in the last chapter, that in respects it was the general public who grabbed onto Darwin's ideas before the professionals; although, as you have seen, I would qualify this.

[6] Edmund Saul Dixon, born the same year as Darwin, was a parson in Norfolk from 1842–1893. He was an expert on the breeding of poultry. Darwin had read one of his books and in 1848 they had

when the old ones were exhausted, robust to endure the perpendicular rays of the sun, and the scorching wind of the desert — she touched with her golden weapon, and it fell dead! All that she left surviving were the very few most agile, swiftest, and robustest antelopes, to represent that numerous herd. (317)

The son does much the same. He deprives the wolves of their food. "As the pangs of hunger became sharper and sharper, the ravenous brutes set to devouring each other, the vigorous destroying the old, the healthy tearing the feeble limb from limb, till none were left but a single pair, male and female, the gauntest, savagest, and most powerful of all that savage group" (317). Get on now with reproducing, says this horrible child. Have offspring as "wolfish" as you.

Madame Selection recognizes that what she is offering is a cold and heartless view of nature. But if that is the way things are, then that is the way things are. "Nature is relentless and inflexible," she said, returning toward the refreshment room. "She will not change her laws to humour the preconceived ideas, the caprices, the blunders, and the follies of men" (317). And if that means that strength is to prevail in the future, rather than more desirable attributes, then so be it. Of course, this is all as Darwin says it is. Who can say he is absolutely right? "Still the book has given me more comprehensive views than I had before . . . Here we are offered a rational and a logical explanation of many things which hitherto have been explained very unsatisfactorily, if at all. It is conscientiously reasoned and has been patiently written. If it be not the truth, I cannot help respecting it as sincere effort after truth" (318).

This is all a little bit silly, but perhaps that is the point. Here we are, a couple of years after the *Origin*, in a very popular magazine that is going to fall into the hands of literally hundreds of thousands of good respectable Victorians, and there are Darwin's ideas—unforced, unambiguous, no special pleading. Darwin may not have the whole truth, but this folks is basically where we are at today, and you had better get used to it.[7] Obviously at least part of what was important here was that

a brief, friendly exchange as Darwin sought information on the workings of artificial selection. Dixon wrote often for periodicals on a variety of subjects, including many pieces for *Household Words*, the predecessor of *All the Year Round*.

[7] Even earlier, in May 1861 appearing in another popular magazine (*Blackwood's Edinburgh Magazine*—later to serialize Joseph Conrad's *The Heart of Darkness*), is a much-reprinted poem by a Scottish Judge, Lord (Charles) Neave, a parody of a popular song ("For He's a Jolly Good Fellow"). It links Erasmus Darwin with Charles Darwin. First the grandfather:

> The original Monad, our great-great-grandsire,
> To little or nothing at first did aspire;
> But at last to have offspring it took a desire,
> Which nobody can deny.

Darwin and Lyell were very respectable members of their society—the sort of men whose ideas could be brought into the drawing room and that your wives and daughters could discuss and understand. This was not the stuff of French novels. You can laugh all you like about limpets, but Charles Darwin was a man of real substance—an exciting explorer in his youth and a dedicated man of science in his prime. The Victorians recognized and appreciated quality when they saw it, and Darwin and Lyell were men of quality. Even Huxley, though he loved to shock and ride the edge, was seen as both brilliant and of massive social conscience. It all paid off.

Exploring the Implications

Evolution as such became a given. Natural selection as a force of nature continued to be a theme of interest and importance right down through the century

Then the grandson:

> From reptiles and fishes to birds we ascend,
> And quadrupeds next their dimensions extend,
> Till we rise up to monkeys and men—where we end,
>   Which nobody can deny.

> Some creatures are bulky, some creatures are small,
> As nature sends food for the few or for all;
> And the weakest, we know, ever go to the wall,
>   Which nobody can deny.

Although there are certainly hints here of natural selection, the poem stresses Lamarckian inheritance.

> A deer with a neck that is longer by half
> Than the rest of its family (try not to laugh),
> By stretching and stretching, becomes a Giraffe,
>   Which nobody can deny.

Interestingly, it anticipates what we shall see was a worry later in the nineteenth century, that bad behavior is playing with fire.

> But I'm sadly afraid if we do not take care,
> A relapse to low life may our prospects impair;
> So of beastly propensities let us beware,
>   Which nobody can deny.

There is the possibility that we might decline back to the primitive origins from whence we came.

> Their lofty position our children might lose,
> And, reduced to all-fours, must then narrow their views;
> Which would wholly unfit them for filling our shoes,
>   Which nobody can deny.

We could end up as Monads all over again.

and into the next. Expectedly and satisfyingly some of the great creative thinkers took up the idea and worked with it—in ways that were in Darwin's theorizing but that were not developed fully by him or by others around him. For instance, although Darwin realized that selection is a comparative process—it is not a question of absolute speed when running from the bear but of being faster than the chap next to you—he never really came to grips with this in his thinking about humans. Winners for him really were better in some external sense. In his powerful novel, *New Grub Street*, published about ten years after Darwin's death, George Gissing (1857–1903) dealt with selection in a really illuminating and sensitive fashion. He tells the story of two young men—Edwin Reardon and Jasper Milvain—trying to make their ways in the London literary world around 1880. Edwin is a really gifted writer but will make no compromises to vulgar taste. Things do not go well, externally or at home with his wife. Jasper—well, let him speak for himself.

> "You have no faith. But just understand the difference between a man like Reardon and a man like me. He is the old type of unpractical artist; I am the literary man of 1882. He won't make concessions, or rather, he can't make them; he can't supply the market. I—well, you may say that at present I do nothing; but that's a great mistake, I am learning my business. Literature nowadays is a trade. Putting aside men of genius, who may succeed by mere cosmic force, your successful man of letters is your skillful tradesman. He thinks first and foremost of the markets; when one kind of goods begins to go off slackly, he is ready with something new and appetising. He knows perfectly all the possible sources of income." (Gissing [1891] 1976, 38–39)

In the end, Edwin dies—as people are wont to do in Victorian novels—and Jasper gets Edwin's wife and the editorship of a prized journal. They are both pretty pleased with the outcome. "Amy sprang up and threw her arms about her husband's neck, uttering a cry of delight." Jasper is appreciative. "I owe my fortune to you, dear girl. Now the way is smooth!" (549)

From afar, it is difficult not to write with humorous condescension about this sort of stuff. But the story is a lot more subtle than one might think on first reading. For a start, Gissing is fully aware of the nature of selection. There is a tendency to think that selection is always "red in tooth and claw," and it is true that there is some celebrated fiction of this ilk.

> His teeth closed on Spitz's left fore leg. There was a crunch of breaking bone, and the white dog faced him on three legs. Thrice he tried to knock him over, then repeated the trick and broke the right fore leg.

Despite the pain and helplessness, Spitz struggled madly to keep up. He saw the silent circle, with gleaming eyes, lolling tongues, and silvery breaths drifting upward, closing in upon him as he had seen similar circles close in upon beaten antagonists in the past. Only this time he was the one who was beaten.

There was no hope for him. Buck was inexorable. Mercy was a thing reserved for gentler climes. (London [1903] 1990, 24)

I do not give this example to mock it. The writing is incredibly powerful. I am not at all surprised that there are over thirty—thirty!—editions of Jack London's *Call of the Wild* available today. But subtle it is not.[8] Gissing is more discerning. He knew that Darwin had stressed that the struggle is not necessarily one competing organism directly against another but rather with the environment. "Two canine animals in a time of dearth, may be truly said to struggle with each other which shall get food and live. But a plant on the edge of a desert is said to struggle for life against the drought, though more properly it should be said to be dependent on the moisture" (Darwin 1859, 62). One plant is being selected rather than another, but because it does better in the environment and not because it beats out the other directly. So with our two writers. Gissing also saw that in many respects Edwin is better than Jasper—certainly when it comes to literary talent. So Gissing saw that success is not a matter of climbing some absolute chain of perfection.[9] At the same time, however, Gissing was not about to sell Jasper short. There are hints that success is amoral, and that in the Darwinian world it is all a matter of being tougher and pushier than the competitor, for people as for books.

Speaking seriously, we know that a really good book will more likely than not receive fair treatment from two or three reviewers; yes, but also more likely than not it will be swamped in the flood of literature that pours forth week after week, and won't have attention fixed long enough upon it to establish its repute. The struggle for existence among books is nowadays as severe as among men. If a writer has friends connected with the press, it is the plain duty of those friends to do their

---

[8] London (1876–1916) read the *Origin* and Herbert Spencer's *First Principles* in high school, carried a copy of the *Origin* with him on his travels, and always spoke favorably of Darwin (Berkove 2004).

[9] American author Edith Wharton (1862–1937) makes the same point in a delightful short story, "The Descent of Man," published in 1904. A learned biology professor writes a pastiche of his discipline, filled chock-a-block full of heavy-duty reflections and pseudoscientific speculations. Naturally, it becomes a bestseller and, seduced by the fame and money, our professor turns full time to this kind of literary activity.

utmost to help him. What matter if they exaggerate, or even lie? The simple, sober truth has no chance whatever of being listened to, and it's only by volume of shouting that the ear of the public is held. What use is it to [an author] if his work struggles to slow recognition ten years hence? Besides, as I say, the growing flood of literature swamps everything but works of primary genius. If a clever and conscientious book does not spring to success at once, there's precious small chance that it will survive. (493)

But there is more to the story than that. Jasper may not be as gifted as Edwin, but he has a vitality that Edwin does not have—more than some of his girlfriends too.

"You hear?"

Marian had just caught the far-off sound of the train. She looked eagerly, and in a few moments saw it approaching. The front of the engine blackened nearer and nearer, coming on with dread force and speed. A blinding rush, and there burst against the bridge a great volley of sunlit steam. Milvain and his companion ran to the opposite parapet, but already the whole train had emerged, and in a few seconds it had disappeared round a sharp curve. The leafy branches that grew out over the line swayed violently backwards and forwards in the perturbed air.

"If I were ten years younger," said Jasper, laughing, "I should say that was jolly! It enspirits me. It makes me feel eager to go back and plunge into the fight again."

"Upon me it has just the opposite effect," fell from Marian, in very low tones. (63)

As we know, Edwin was to find marital happiness elsewhere.[10]

Reception: Lamarckism

Expectedly, not everyone was strictly Darwinian. I stress again that this does not make for a non-Darwinian Revolution or a Darwinian non-Revolution. Everyone is thinking and arguing within a framework set by Darwin—questions posed by Darwin—even though they may explicitly or implicitly disagree with

---

[10] I thus agree with Cleto (1992) against many who write on Gissing, uneasy with the nature of his "winners" and his "losers," feeling that he favors dross over gold. The critics miss the point. In Gissing's post-Darwinian world—"intellectual powers and energy"—vitality is a virtue. Not the only one, but significant.

Darwin's own thinking—with Darwin's answers. Early Christianity housed a variety of opinions, for instance, about the relationship between God and Jesus, and these were resolved only at the Council of Nicaea, in A.D. 325, and followed up with further meetings like the Council of Chalcedon, A.D. 451. It would be ludicrous to say that before these meetings there was no Christian Revolution, as one might say. Likewise with Darwin. And this is not just evolution but natural selection also. Apart from the fact that just about everyone accepted some degree of natural selection (and perhaps even more of sexual selection), natural selection was as it were the default position, the null hypothesis. If you wanted to get more than Darwin gave, perhaps some kind of built-in progression as Asa Gray wanted, then you had to work against and beyond what Darwin had given you. Natural selection always loomed there in the background.

Mrs. Gatty, although opposed to evolution and thinking (if it were true) that it is all a matter of Lamarckian inheritance, shows that something big is going on. She is part of the revolution because she is reacting against it. Analogously and more positively we see this move into a Darwinian world perfectly in the case of someone like Charles Kingsley. It would be as ludicrous as the Christian case to say that he was not an ardent Darwinian, or to deny that it was Darwin who changed him—as incidentally was also true of Huxley—from a strong opposition to evolution in the mid-1850s to great enthusiasm. He wrote to Darwin and he went around telling everybody that you could be an even better Christian if you were a Darwinian! A point gratefully noted by the author of the *Origin of Species*. "A celebrated author and divine has written to me that 'he has gradually learnt to see that it is just as noble a conception of the Deity to believe that He created a few original forms capable of self-development into other and needful forms, as to believe that He required a fresh act of creation to supply the voids caused by the action of His laws'" (Darwin 1861, 515).

So grant the general case about there being a Darwinian Revolution. This said, although he made a big thing about his conversion to Darwinism, in the *Water Babies* Charles Kingsley (like Mrs. Gatty) sounds as Lamarckian as he does Darwinian (meaning selection).[11] Reverting to Kingsley, Mrs. Bedonebyasyoudid shows Tom the history of the degeneration of humans into gorillas. Some of it sounds Darwinian. Living up in trees to escape lions, both natural and sexual selection come into play. "Yes, they are getting very strong

---

[11] Remember, while he always thought selection by far the most important agent of change, Darwin accepted the inheritance of acquired characteristics. With few exceptions—perhaps Alfred Russel Wallace, later the already-mentioned, German selection-enthusiast August Weismann—for most people it was a question of trade-off between selection and Lamarckism and assigning proportionate importance, so Kingsley was not so very out of line here.

now; for the ladies will not marry any but the very strongest and fiercest gentle-men, who can help them up the trees out of the lions' way." But other factors also come into play.

> "Why," said Tom, "they are growing no better than savages."
> "And look how ugly they are all getting," said Ellie.
> "Yes; when people live on poor vegetables instead of roast beef and plum-pudding, their jaws grow large, and their lips grow coarse, like the poor Paddies who eat potatoes." (Kingsley [1863] 2008, 133)

Then later:

> "They are grown so stupid now, that they can hardly think: for none of them have used their wits for many hundred years. They have almost forgotten, too, how to talk. For each stupid child forgot some of the words it heard from its stupid parents, and had not wits enough to make fresh words for itself. Beside, they are grown so fierce and suspicious and brutal that they keep out of each other's way, and mope and sulk in the dark forests, never hearing each other's voice, till they have forgotten almost what speech is like. I am afraid they will all be apes very soon, and all by doing only what they liked." (134–135)

Later in the century we have Rudyard Kipling (1865–1936) in the *Second Jungle Book* (1895). There is a good dash of recapitulation—"'Mowgli the Frog have I been,' said he to himself; 'Mowgli the Wolf have I said that I am. Now Mowgli the Ape must I be before I am Mowgli the Buck. At the end I shall be Mowgli the Man. Ho!'" ([1895] 2000, 332)—and then Lamarckism (MacDuffie 2014). The wolf pack is being threatened by the Red Dogs. Mowgli is up a tree baiting the leader. The dog leaps and Mowgli grabs him by the scruff of his neck. Everything shakes and Mowgli almost falls. "But he never loosed his grip, and inch by inch he hauled the beast, hanging like a drowned jackal, up on the branch. With his left hand he reached for his knife and cut off the red, bushy tail, flinging the dhole back to earth again" (334–335). This, apparently, is going to have lasting effects. "'Nay, but consider, wise rat of the Dekkan. There will now be many litters of little tailless red dogs, yea, with raw red stumps that sting when the sand is hot. Go home, Red Dog, and cry that an ape has done this. Ye will not go? Come, then, with me, and I will make you very wise!'" (335) Kipling wrote of Darwin's writings. "I've been trying once more to plough through the *Descent of Man* and every fiber . . . of my body revolted against it" (Kipling 2009, 114). Apparently so.

The most detailed and influential writer in this mode was the novelist Samuel Butler (1835–1902). Initially he was a huge Darwin fan. His satire *Erewhon* (1872)—more or less "nowhere" spelled backward—has a clever take on natural selection applied to machines (this was written around 1862)—something that has led to some rather ponderous philosophizing about anticipating the age of computers. The tale of a land where everything is topsy-turvy—sick people are sent to jail and criminals are treated as if unwell—a visitor (who is the narrator) sees that there are no machines. Apparently they have all been destroyed lest they take over the world. "How many men at this hour are living in a state of bondage to the machines? How many spend their whole lives, from the cradle to the grave, in tending them by night and day? Is it not plain that the machines are gaining ground upon us, when we reflect on the increasing number of those who are bound down to them as slaves, and of those who devote their whole souls to the advancement of the mechanical kingdom?" (202) They may even end up with consciousness and where would we be then? "Assume for the sake of argument that conscious beings have existed for some twenty million years: see what strides machines have made in the last thousand! May not the world last twenty million years longer? If so, what will they not in the end become? Is it not safer to nip the mischief in the bud and to forbid them further progress?" (192)

There were those who thought Butler was ribbing Darwin, but he insisted (truthfully) that he was paying homage and seeing where the ideas led. However, then in the 1870s he turned against Darwin and took up with some vehemence a form of Lamarckian evolution through acquired characteristics, especially a form where inherited memory pays a key role. He wrote several books on the topic. Apparently, you can only change incrementally, bit by bit. Too much change—beyond 2 or 3%—takes you out of focus. However:

> As long as no change exceeds this percentage, and as long, also, as fresh change does not supervene till the preceding one is well established, there seems no limit to the amount of modification which may be accumulated in the course of generations—provided, of course, always, that the modification continues to be in conformity with the instinctive habits and physical development of the organism in their collective capacity. (Butler [1887] 1920, 72–73)

Butler then tried out these ideas fictionally, combining a deeply proto-Freudian view of his own very dysfunctional family—his father was a sanctimonious brute—with his Lamarckian evolutionism. *The Way of All Flesh* did not appear in print until 1903 (after Butler's death), but apparently it was written in the decade after *Erewhon* appeared. Telling the story of the Pontifex family through five generations, we see the gradual rise up to the third-generation Theobald, a

(Church of England) clergyman. An appalling father—"He had had no idea how great a nuisance a baby was" (77)—the son, Ernest, is the hero of the book. He too becomes a clergyman, but loses his faith, ends up in prison for assaulting a woman whom he mistakenly thought was a prostitute, then makes his way as a tailor—shades of *Sartor Resartus* and/or *Alton Locke?*—marries a former house-maid, who turns out to be married already, fathers two children, the wonder being that they do not both suffer from extreme fetal alcohol syndrome given the mother's drinking, and then conveniently inherits a fortune on his twenty-eighth birthday.

The main theme is that the trip to prison had no lasting bad effects. It jolted him out of his complacency, helped him break entirely from his father—"There are orphanages," he exclaimed to himself, "for children who have lost their parents—oh! why, why, why, are there no harbours of refuge for grown men who have not yet lost them?" (257)—and then the positive features acquired by his ancestors came to the fore and Ernest was a far better man than would have been expected given the negativity of the father.

> If a man is to enter into the Kingdom of Heaven, he must do so, not only as a little child, but as a little embryo, or rather as a little zoosperm—and not only this, but as one that has come of zoosperms which have entered into the Kingdom of Heaven before him for many generations. Accidents which occur for the first time, and belong to the period since a man's last birth, are not, as a general rule, so permanent in their effects, though of course they may sometimes be so. (241)

Interestingly, although perceptively—"Of course he read Mr. Darwin's books as fast as they came out and adopted evolution as an article of faith" (317)—Ernest realizes that, like his forefathers, he is more a man of action (starting a successful clothes shop) than a man of the intellect. The same is true of his own son, who becomes the owner-operator of a river steamer—"he has a fair sense of humour and abundance of common sense, but his instinct is clearly a practical one" (349).

For the first half of the twentieth century, Butler was incredibly highly regarded—in part obviously because like Lytton Strachey (1918) he was de-bunking the Victorians—but also because people liked the nonreligious direc-tion they found in his evolutionizing. William Bateson (1909), first professor of genetics at Cambridge, praised him (probably more to irritate the Darwinians with whom he had ongoing battles), Karl Popper (1974), who had his own dif-ficulties with accepting natural selection, was also given to praise, and George Bernard Shaw was an enthusiast. The playwright absolutely loathed what he saw as the blind, uncaring materialism of Darwin and his acolytes like Thomas Henry

Huxley. "What damns Darwinian Natural Selection as a creed is that it takes hope out of evolution, and substitutes a paralyzing fatalism which is utterly discouraging. As Butler put it, it banishes Mind from the universe" (Shaw 1921, c).

Reception: Spencerianism

Samuel Butler's reputation has not lasted, unlike that of George Eliot, whose *Middlemarch* is considered by many to be the greatest novel in the English language.[12] As it happens, she and her consort, George Lewes, were a little grumpy when the *Origin* appeared, rather putting it down: "We began Darwin's work on "The Origin of Species" tonight. It seems to be not well written: though full of interesting matter, it is not impressive, from want of luminous and orderly presentation" (Harris and Johnson 1998, 82). Whatever she may have thought, Henry James (1873) said: "*Middlemarch* is too often an echo of Messrs. Darwin and Huxley" (428).[13] And it is true that evolution is a major structuring theme and this is the world opened by Darwin and Huxley. The story is of the characters in an English provincial town, Middlemarch, between about 1830 and 1832 (with a postscript on the futures of the main actors). There are seven or eight major characters and about the same number of minor figures. Dorothea Brooke, around twenty when we meet her, beautiful and idealistic, fairly well off in her own right, is the leading character and the story traces her marriage to a dry old clergyman Mr. Casaubon, who is engaged in a work of scholarship that we learn in fairly short order is hopelessly outdated before it is finished. Will Ladislaw, a young artist distantly related to Casaubon, becomes the main rival for Dorothea's affections, and they end up married after Casaubon dies. The second main couple is the doctor, Tertius Lydgate, who married Rosamond Vincy, not a happy marriage because he wants to make his name as a medical scientist and she only wants the conventional trappings of a middle-class wife and mother. Then there is Rosamond's brother, Fred, who is a bit of a layabout, but because of his love for Mary Garth is prepared to take a step down socially and go to work for Mary's father, Caleb, who is a builder and estate manager. Fleshing out the story we have Dorothea's sister, Celia, married to Sir James Chettam (who first wanted Dorothea), the sisters' uncle, Mr. Brooke, a local businessman, Mr.

---

[12] I am sure I am not alone in finding her last major novel, *Daniel Deronda*, more interesting and challenging. In part, this is because it is wrestling more deeply with the Darwinian challenge. *Middlemarch* is perhaps the most perfectly integrated novel ever written, and we are about to learn the story behind this.

[13] Better than James's assessment of Dickens. "*Bleak House* was forced; *Little Dorrit* was labored; [*Our Mutual Friend*] is dug out as with a spade and pickaxe" (James 1865, 786).

Bulstrode, who is very religious but with a bit of a shady past, the local vicar, Mr. Farebrother, and others.

James was right. The novel is all very Darwinian. Certain characters move forward and succeed—Dorothea matures and gets greater control of herself and her emotions, Will also grows and shows character in refusing easy money (when Bulstrode tries to assuage his own conscience), and above all Fred goes from a lazy charmer to a serious worker at a real job. Some go backward or fail to move forward—Casaubon, Lydgate, and Bulstrode to name three. And some basically stay in place—Mary and her father are good from start to finish, others, including one Raffles who is into the blackmail business, begin and end bad, and yet others like Brooke and Farebrother (in hopeless love with Mary) are basically ineffectual throughout. However, this is only part of the story, because as all commentators note what is striking is the extent to which Eliot is describing an interwoven net or web of relationships, binding the characters together in an ever more complex whole or organic unity (Shuttleworth 1984). These are not people just doing their own thing as in Gissing's novel, where the success or failure of Edwin and Jasper is really quite independent of the other. Sir James is employing Caleb, Caleb is employing Fred, first Bulstrode and then Dorothea are lending money to Lydgate, Rosamond, married to Lydgate, is also Fred's sister, Casaubon is (to his regret) related to Will and somewhat reluctantly supporting Will because Will was a bit unlucky when it came to getting family money, Bulstrode also has a connection with Will, and so it goes. Sir James is married to Celia and hence brother-in-law to Dorothea and concerned for her welfare and upset when she does what he thinks is wrong. Dorothea gives to Mr. Farebrother the incumbency held by Casaubon. Caleb has an interest in Fred because the lad is in love with his daughter Mary, and Mary is clearly in love with Fred.

Eliot cleverly shows that the whole town is bound together by social arrangements and the like. When Raffles conveniently dies, word gets out and about very quickly.

"Did any doctor attend him?" said Mr. Hawley.

"Yes. Mr. Lydgate. Mr. Bulstrode sat up with him one night. He died the third morning."

"Go on, Bambridge," said Mr. Hawley, insistently. "What did this fellow say about Bulstrode?"

The group had already become larger, the town-clerk's presence being a guarantee that something worth listening to was going on there; and Mr. Bambridge delivered his narrative in the hearing of seven. . . .

But this gossip about Bulstrode spread through Middlemarch like the smell of fire. Mr. Frank Hawley followed up his information by sending a clerk whom he could trust to Stone Court on a pretext of

inquiring about hay, but really to gather all that could be learned about
Raffles and his illness from Mrs. Abel [a servant who unknowingly gave
Raffles a shot of alcohol that proved fatal]. (Eliot [1874] 2011, 821)

It is all rather like ants in the nest passing foodstuffs around from one to the
other. But more than this. To continue with the organic metaphor, it is clear that
Eliot sees ongoing change.[14] The organism evolves, to use a word. In the novel, a
major theme is how—"begetting new consciousness of interdependence" (Eliot
[1874] 2011, 105)—the old eighteenth-century system of lords and squires
living in a rural setting is giving way to the new nineteenth-century system of
educated experts living in an urban setting (Dolin 2008). "Municipal town
and rural parish gradually made fresh threads of connection—gradually, as the
old stocking gave way to the savings-bank, and the worship of the solar guinea
became extinct; while squires and baronets, and even lords who had once lived
blamelessly afar from the civic mind, gathered the faultiness of closer acquain-
tanceship" (106). Externally, there are the debates over the Reform Bill going on
and more immediately the coming of the railway that is going to change England
so very drastically—Progress! This will happen, whether the good people of
Middlemarch want it or not.

> Caleb was a powerful man and knew little of any fear except the fear of
> hurting others and the fear of having to speechify. But he felt it his duty
> at this moment to try and give a little harangue.. . . .
>
> "Why, my lads, how's this?" he began, taking as usual to brief phrases,
> which seemed pregnant to himself, because he had many thoughts
> lying under them, like the abundant roots of a plant that just manages
> to peep above the water. "How come you to make such a mistake as
> this? Somebody has been telling you lies. You thought those men up
> there wanted to do mischief."
>
> "Aw!" was the answer, dropped at intervals by each according to his
> degree of uneasiness.
>
> "Nonsense! No such thing! They're looking out to see which way the
> railroad is to take. Now, my lads, you can't hinder the railroad: it will be
> made whether you like it or not. And if you go fighting against it, you'll
> get yourselves into trouble. The law gives those men leave to come here
> on the land. The owner has nothing to say against it, and if you meddle
> with them you'll have to do with the constable and Justice Blakesley,

---

[14] Critics have noted that there is more change in the later novels than in the earliest, pre-*Origin*
work, *Adam Bede*.

and with the handcuffs and Middlemarch jail. And you might be in for it now, if anybody informed against you." (640–641)

Get used to the idea. In any case, "the railway's a good thing."

Some of the change comes from within. Sir James is a minor figure and not always as quick as others. But basically, unlike Mr. Brooke, he knows the score and that a major part of the score is upkeep and improvement of his property. It is the same with Fred.[15] He "surprised his neighbors in various ways. He became rather distinguished in his side of the county as a theoretic and practical farmer, and produced a work on the *Cultivation of Green Crops and the Economy of Cattle-Feeding* which won him high congratulations at agricultural meetings" (952–953). That is what real change is about. Few of us are going to make the big discoveries—Lydgate did not—but clover and lucerne (alfalfa), now that is solid change and improvement. Dorothea too—she becomes a wife and mother and there are those who regret that she did not aim higher. But change and improvement and Progress are there.

> Her finely touched spirit had still its fine issues, though they were not widely visible. Her full nature, like that river of which Cyrus broke the strength, spent itself in channels which had no great name on the earth. But the effect of her being on those around her was incalculably diffusive: for the growing good of the world is partly dependent on unhistoric acts; and that things are not so ill with you and me as they might have been, is half owing to the number who lived faithfully a hidden life, and rest in unvisited tombs. (959)

"Spent itself in channels." "Incalculably diffusive." "Growing good." This is an organic view of society. Cyrus in fact broke the river Gyndes into 360 channels. One doubts that even Dorothea is affecting quite that many people, but the point is made. Society is an organism, slowly but surely improving, and (to use Eliot's own word) getting ever more interdependent. Now it is true that Darwin does argue that "plants and animals, most remote in the scale of nature, are bound together by a web of complex relations," but this was never an organism. There is too much intergroup tension for this. So Darwinian yes, but not quite Darwinian in the bones as with Gissing. There was, however, another candidate for the job, and even if one was not aware that George Eliot knew Herbert Spencer very well and had studied his writings with great care and sympathy, one might think him

---

[15] Deresiewicz (1998) makes the important point that Eliot is not a blind determinist but sees free choice as an essential element in growth, particularly moral growth. Fred does choose. Lydgate goes under mainly because he does not have the strength to impose his own will on the circumstances within which he finds himself.

a good candidate.[16] From the nonconformist side to the British Midlands—as was Eliot—Spencer broke onto the scene in the 1850s. With some reason, he has a reputation as a stern advocate of a *laissez faire* view of society, and some of his early writings particularly back this up. Any attempt to coddle the poor "absolutely encourages the multiplication of the reckless and incompetent by offering them an unfailing provision, and *discourages* the multiplication of the competent and provident by heightening the prospective difficulty of maintaining a family" (Spencer 1851, 323–324). However, apart from the fact that this was written before Spencer became an evolutionist, one should see that the use he made of such ideas as these are not simple Darwinism, extended to society (Richards 1987). He was less into the idea of struggle to eliminate the weak and inadequate and more into the struggle to make people work and thus improve themselves and, through a Lamarckian process, thereby improve society generally (Spencer 1852). He was totally committed to an organic view of society (Spencer 1860), thinking that we are all part of one great whole—one getting more and more complex ("homogeneity" transforms to "heterogeneity")—and he was as equally committed to Progress. "Whether it be in the development of the Earth, in the development of Life upon its surface, in the development of Society, of Government, of Manufactures, of Commerce, of Language, Literature, Science, Art, this same evolution of the simple into the complex, through successive differentiations, hold throughout" (Spencer 1857, 2–3). This theory of "dynamic equilibrium" describes Middlemarch and its inhabitants to a tee. Fred and Dorothea and Ladislaw improve through effort and in a sad way in converse Lydgate and Casaubon and Bulstrode decline.[17] Contrast with the characters in *New Grub Street*. Edwin and Jasper do not change. Nor do Marion and Amy.[18]

---

[16] Lewes, an early follower of Positivism, would have been another influence. His reading of Comte had ever inclined him toward organicism. Robert J. Richards would challenge my reading of Darwin, arguing that organicism is a central theme of the *Origin* and extends to all groups, not just (as I allow) interrelated tribes or families (Richards and Ruse 2016). Overall, though, Spencer was the key and immediate influence. Again, do not take this as denying that the revolution overall was Darwinian, even if you put to one side that James was right in seeing Darwin in the mix that produced *Middlemarch*. It was Darwin and his status as a scientist who opened it up for the others. Spencer was hugely important. So was St. Paul. Yet it is rightly called the *Christian* religion, for all that the differences between the message of Jesus and the message of Paul were at least as great as those between Darwin and Spencer.

[17] Graver (1984) sees the tensions as negating the organicist model. But the whole point of the Spencerian model is that one does get tensions and struggle. It is through these that improvement comes. Thanks to her suffering in her dysfunctional marriage to Casaubon, Dorothea emerges a better, stronger person. Lydgate goes under through his marriage to Rosamond.

[18] In her strange final work, *The Impressions of Theophrastus Such*, Eliot gets explicitly Darwinian, floating the idea that machines might get more and more sophisticated until "one sees that the process of natural selection must drive men altogether out of the field" (Eliot [1879] 2016, 102). Samuel Butler was not the only one to suggest that this was cribbed from *Erewhon* (Jones 1919, 1, 310).

Reception: The Religious

Thus far we have looked at the secular thinkers and writers. Darwin had supporters who wanted to blend his thinking with Christian doctrine. Mention has
been made of Asa Gray. Tennyson was one who continued on this path, basically
unchanged from before (Stevenson 1932). In "Locksley Hall" (written in 1835,
published in 1842) he is optimistic about progress. By 1886, when he published
"Locksley Hall Sixty Years After," he was a lot less optimistic, and Darwinian
evolution was part of the problem.

> All diseases quench'd by Science, no man halt, or deaf or blind;
> Stronger ever born of weaker, lustier body, larger mind?
> Earth at last a warless world, a single race, a single tongue,
> I have seen her far away—for is not Earth as yet so young?—
> (Tennyson 1886, 23–24)

So far, so good. But:

> Warless? when her tens are thousands, and her thousands millions, then—
> All her harvest all too narrow—who can fancy warless men?
>
> Warless? war will die out late then. Will it ever? late or soon?
> Can it, till this outworn earth be dead as yon dead world the moon?
> (24–25)

Evolution seems to be as much the problem as the solution:

> *Is* there evil but on earth? or pain in every peopled sphere?
> Well be grateful for the sounding watchword, 'Evolution' here.
>
> Evolution ever climbing after some ideal good,
> And Reversion ever dragging Evolution in the mud.
> (28)

Yet, at the end, Tennyson's old faith seems to have returned, as though the fifty
years previously had never occurred.

> Where is one that, born of woman, altogether can escape
> From the lower world within him, moods of tiger, or of ape?
>   Man as yet is being made, and ere the crowning Age of ages,
> Shall not aeon after aeon pass and touch him into shape?

All about him shadow still, but, while the races flower and fade,
Prophet-eyes may catch a glory slowly gaining on the shade,
   Till the peoples all are one, and all their voices blend in choric
Hallelujah to the Maker "It is finish'd. Man is made."
                              ("The Making of Man," Tennyson 1892, 85–86)

For all there is a failure of "chiliastic concretion," there is "incessant effort to in-
tegrate existence into a spiritual Cosmos" (Roppen 1956, 111).

   Charles Dickens—another for whom Christianity was always fundamental—wrestled with these issues in fiction. In *Our Mutual Friend* (1865) he is, as
always, interestingly complex. There are two main threads, one centering on a
working-class girl, whose father is a waterman; the other on a girl taken from her
relatively improvident family to live with a rich old couple. In the one thread, the
conflict between the two suitors for Lizzie Hexam's hand, the indolent lawyer
Eugene Wrayburn and the oversensitive schoolteacher Bradley Headstone, is
one of the most powerful depictions of sexual selection through male combat in
the whole of fiction—even though it may not owe that much to Darwin because
the novel appeared before the extended treatment of the topic in the *Descent of
Man*.[19] In the other thread, the whole tenor of the novel is absolutely and completely against a Darwinian reading of society and human nature—everyone
worthwhile in the novel is so because they reject Darwinian motives and give
through disinterested love (Fulweiler 1994). Bella Wilfer is supposed to gain a
fortune by marrying the son (now presumed dead) of the man who made all of
the money the old couple now possesses. Explicitly, she refers to her own selfishness. "If ever there was a mercenary plotter whose thoughts and designs were
always in her mean occupation, I am the amiable creature. But I don't care. I hate
and detest being poor, and I won't be poor if I can marry money" (321). But then,
there is a transformation and to the rich old couple (the Boffins) who are testing
her—Mr. Boffin (acting the role of a miser) mouths a parody of Darwinism telling Bella that we must "scrunch or be scrunched" (475)—when she meets the
man of her love (unknown to her, the son who is not in fact dead), she acts in a

---

[19] The brutal description of the schoolteacher owes a lot to Carlyle: "Bradley Headstone, in his
decent black coat and waistcoat, and decent white shirt, and decent formal black tie, and decent pan-
taloons of pepper and salt, with his decent silver watch in his pocket and its decent hair-guard round
his neck, looked a thoroughly decent young man of six-and-twenty. He was never seen in any other
dress, and yet there was a certain stiffness in his manner of wearing this, as if there were a want of
adaptation between him and it, recalling some mechanics in their holiday clothes. He had acquired
mechanically a great store of teacher's knowledge. He could do mental arithmetic mechanically,
sing at sight mechanically, blow various wind instruments mechanically, even play the great church
organ mechanically. From his early childhood up, his mind had been a place of mechanical stowage"
(Dickens [1865] 1948, 217).

way that makes a mockery of sexual selection through female choice. She wants no part of the money or the misers whose memory is revered. "'I shall never more think well of *you*,' cried Bella, cutting him short, with intense defiance in her expressive little eyebrows, and championship of the late Secretary [the son who has been employed by the old couple] in every dimple. 'No! Never again! Your money has changed you to marble. You are a hard-hearted Miser. You are worse than Dancer, worse than Hopkins, worse than Blackberry Jones, worse than any of the wretches'" (599). She turns her back on the money and marries a poor man for love. Who of course fortunately turns out not to be so poor after all!

The point to be made here is not that everyone becomes a Darwinian, even if they are not fully aware of the fact. Not everyone became a Christian. It is rather that even if someone like Dickens rejects pure Darwinism, he knows that he is working in a Darwinian environment and his rejection has to be conscious (Bown 2010). "Scrunch or be scrunched" gives that game away.[20] The same is true of those who declared Darwin irrelevant. The Jesuit poet Gerard Manley Hopkins (1844–1889) knew about Darwinism and—as did other prominent Catholics like John Henry Newman—at least in a more directed sense promoted by the Catholic biologist St. George Mivart (1871) seems to have accepted some form of evolutionism (Zaniello 1988). But it was not about to threaten or replace his Christianity. The well-known poem "That nature is a Heraclitean fire and the comfort of the Resurrection" (written in 1888) is perhaps more about meteorology than biology, but the constant turmoil and struggle come through—especially that humans get wiped out.

Cloud-puffball, torn tufts, tossed pillows | flaunt forth, then chevy on an air-
Built thoroughfare: heaven-roysterers, in gay-gangs | they throng;
    they glitter in marches.
Down roughcast, down dazzling whitewash, | wherever an elm arches,

---

[20] Fontana (2005) argues that the Wrayburn-Headstone rivalry is explicitly Darwin-influenced, but he offers no external evidence to support this claim. However, as already shown, Dickens was sufficiently well disposed to Darwinism to allow quite favorable treatment in *All the Year Round*, so one cannot rule out all possible influence. What is interesting is that although readers today (including this author) regard *Our Mutual Friend* as one of Dickens's supreme achievements—not only the sexual themes but the brilliant use of metaphor, the Thames dominating everything giving life and bringing death and the refuse-based source (dust piles, cinders and ash, of value for brick making) of the controlling money, as well as the host of minor figures, including Bella's appalling (and incredibly amusing) mother and sister—at the time, critics were much less enthused. This was because in a Darwinian world already Dickens was dated. Henry James, who was to contribute to the post-Darwinian fiction we consider in this and later chapters, made it clear that this was the source of his discontent. Dickens did not capture human nature as was now understood.

Shivelights and shadowtackle ín long | lashes lace, lance, and pair.
Delightfully the bright wind boisterous | ropes, wrestles, beats earth bare
Of yestertempest's creases; | in pool and rut peel parches
Squandering ooze to squeezed | dough, crust, dust; stanches, starches
Squadroned masks and manmarks | treadmire toil there
Footfretted in it. Million-fuelèd, | nature's bonfire burns on.
But quench her bonniest, dearest | to her, her clearest-selvèd spark
Man, how fast his firedint, | his mark on mind, is gone!
Both are in an unfathomable, all is in an enormous dark
Drowned.

But the Christian story is there to trump it.

Enough! the Resurrection,

A heart's-clarion! Away grief's gasping, | joyless days, dejection.
Across my foundering deck shone

A beacon, an eternal beam. | Flesh fade, and mortal trash
Fall to the residuary worm; | world's wildfire, leave but ash:
In a flash, at a trumpet crash,

I am all at once what Christ is, | since he was what I am, and
This Jack, joke, poor potsherd, | patch, matchwood, immortal diamond,
Is immortal diamond.[21]

In an important way, the fact that there has been a Darwinian Revolution gives added meaning and understanding to Hopkins's Christianity.

Conclusion

We have entered a Darwinian world. By about 1870, there were few who did not accept evolution. In the professional scientific world, natural selection was less

---

[21] "Potsherd." This at once brings to mind the Book of Job: "So went Satan forth from the presence of the LORD, and smote Job with sore boils from the sole of his foot unto his crown. And he took him a potsherd to scrape himself withal; and he sat down among the ashes" (Job 2:7–8). The poet is identifying himself with the scrap of broken pottery that Job in his agony used to relieve his pains, and then cast away. Christ raises us up from this, the filthiest piece of trash, to "immortal diamond." Hopkins was deeply moved and influenced by Job and it is nigh a leitmotif for his great poem "The Wreck of the Deutschland" (Cotter 1995). With the pressures on traditional natural theology, he was not alone in turning to Job for insights into the nature and existence of evil in the face of a good God. Carlyle had written: "A noble Book. All men's Book! It is our first, noblest statement of the never-ending Problem,—man's destiny and God's ways with him here in this earth" (Carlyle 1993, 43).

of a success. But people knew about Darwin's ideas and in the public realm they were discussed, embraced, sometimes modified, sometimes disliked, but never ignored. The biggest critics and revisers were working in Darwin's world. Overall Darwinian science—evolution through selection, its supporters, its detractors, its modifiers—was, taken as a whole, the very paradigm of a popular science. But was it more? This is our next question.

In the same vein, Tennyson wrote of Job as "The greatest poem of ancient and modern times" (Singer 1963, 119). We will see more of Job as people wrestle with the implications of living in a post-*Origin* world.

5

God

The time has come to notch up the belt a hole or two, or less metaphorically to make a stronger case than hitherto. Thus far I have argued that, after the *Origin*, evolutionary thinking was raised from the status of a pseudoscience to that of a popular science. Now, in this and the succeeding chapters I want to argue that evolutionary thinking became something more. It became a secular religion, in opposition to Christianity. In the second half of the nineteenth century and into the first part of the twentieth century Darwinian evolutionary thinking, as characterized in the last chapter, became a belief system countering and substituting for the Christian religion: a new paradigm. Although there were ethical societies and the like, I am not making claims about organization or hierarchies or whatever. But I am saying that if you look at the belief claims of Christianity, Darwinian evolutionism offered an alternative. We do not have two world pictures talking past each other but right at each other. We have seen this already at times in the pre-Darwinian periods, but now it will intensify. Now we really do have a system that can be elaborated and developed and accepted and believed in.[1]

---

[1] The attempt to define "religion" is notoriously difficult. One can focus on one or two salient features. This is what I did in an earlier work, *The Evolution-Creation Struggle* (Ruse 2005), arguing that Christianity (particularly the more literalist form) and Darwinism are joined by a shared obsession with end times, so-called millennialism, and separated because whereas the Christians were (and are) Providentialists in thinking that we can do nothing but prepare for the return of the Lamb ("premillennialism") the Darwinians were and are Progressionists, thinking that we can and must ourselves prepare for a heaven here on Earth ("postmillennialism"). Now I want to consider religion more broadly and (as is usual) adopt a "polythetic" definition—working from a list of features none of which is individually considered necessary but a number of which are considered sufficient. I argue that Darwinism can be considered a religion because like Christianity it speaks to such issues as deity, origins, human status, morality, suffering, and more. This approach lends itself readily to a thematic treatment rather than chronological. This is appropriate because, while there is certainly change— for instance, the move to a darker perspective as the century draws to a close—there are no fixed temporal guidelines, like the formation of a hierarchy or a convention to decide dogma—although, as is shown by the treatment of Mivart and Butler, the Darwinians were pretty good at making life difficult for heretics.

Thomas Henry Huxley

This did not happen by chance. Two factors are important. First, the Darwinians—Thomas Henry Huxley in particular—set out to make a counter case to Christianity. You might say that Darwin did not entirely approve. I don't think that is true. Darwin was always more cautious—and it suited everyone that he be more cautious—but his heart was in the change. However, he was aging and sick and not inclined for battle. His supporters were and they did sally forth. Huxley, as just about everyone who writes on him agrees, was a complex character. He was the inventor of the term "agnostic" and at one level one can read his whole life negatively, as an attack on the established church (the Anglicans) and its power in Victorian Britain. There is lots of evidence in the letters and essays pointing to this kind of reading. For instance, referring to some lectures before the *Origin* was published, writing (on January 30, 1859) to one of his close friends (W. Dyster), we have: "My screed was meant as a protest against Theology and Parsondom in general—both of which are in my mind the natural and irreconcilable enemies of Science. Few see it but I believe we are on the eve of a new Reformation and if I have a wish to live thirty years, it is that I may see the foot of Science on the necks of her Enemies" (quoted by Desmond 1997, 253). He had the thirty years and a bit more and the foot did spend a lot of time on religious necks. Thanks in no small part to Huxley. "Extinguished theologians lie about the cradle of every science as the strangled snakes beside that of Hercules; and history records that whenever science and orthodoxy have been fairly opposed, the latter has been forced to retire from the lists, bleeding and crushed, if not annihilated; scotched, if not slain" (Huxley [1860] 1893, 52).

And yet, as readers soon see, there was a very positive side to what Huxley was about. He didn't want just to get rid of religion—or more precisely to get rid of theology—but to replace it with an alternative. He ended his letter to Dyster just quoted by saying: "But the new religion will not be a worship of the intellect alone." Remember the preface to this book. There was always the Calvinist about Huxley and he wanted to replace the old Christian theology with the new scientific theology of Darwinism.

> In certain passages of his writings he rises to a pitch of prophetic denunciation, and he tells his opponents that they are doomed to speedy extinction by the nature of things, and will soon be swept away from the universe. This extreme tone is probably due in part to the fact that Professor Huxley has accepted the principle of evolution more absolutely than any other man of science except Mr. Darwin himself, and that consequently he represents what might be called its religious spirit

in the most concentrated form, and partly also to the fact that his nature is essentially Puritanic, if not Calvinistic.

Continuing

> The hypothesis of evolution thus met a real and vital want in his nature, and he espoused it with a crusading zeal and insistence surprising enough to less ardent minds. In perfect harmony with this feature of his character, Professor Huxley has been known to express an ardent desire for a scientific hell to which the finally impenitent, those who persist in rejecting the new physical gospel, might be condemned. (Baynes 1873, 261)

Robert Elsmere

The second factor to be considered is the status of Christianity itself. It cannot be repeated too often that these things are comparative. The rise of evolutionism was in major way a function of the decline of Christianity. We know that, science aside, Christianity was under threat from within thanks to higher criticism and from without thanks to the rise of the industrial state and the consequent inability of the religion to speak to people's needs. Matthew Arnold's great poem "Dover Beach" was probably written in 1851, but it was published in 1867. Its central verses spoke directly to many a troubled heart, whose owner realized that he (and in many cases she) was not alone in doubting his (or her) childhood faith, nor was his loss of innocence a sign that he was an evil or immoral person.

> The Sea of Faith
> Was once, too, at the full, and round earth's shore
> Lay like the folds of a bright girdle furled.
> But now I only hear
> Its melancholy, long, withdrawing roar,
> Retreating, to the breath
> Of the night-wind, down the vast edges drear
> And naked shingles of the world.

The pressures continued. *Essays and Reviews*, a collection published four months after the *Origin* appeared (Anon. 1860), authored by Anglican divines, embraced higher criticism and in one case—that of the Reverend Baden Powell (professor at Oxford and father of the scoutmaster)—went all of the way to evolution (a view he had promoted in earlier writings). The collection caused a huge controversy—Bishop Wilberforce took time out from criticizing the *Origin* to write against this vile volume—and naturally it sold extremely well. There were prosecutions for heresy that eventually came to naught—"hell was dismissed with costs." Controversial though it may have been, the writing was on the wall. One of the contributors went on to be Archbishop of Canterbury and another Master of Balliol. Right at the heart of the establishment was recognition that Christianity was not functioning well.

Even so, no one was quite prepared for the success of *Robert Elsmere* (1888) by Mrs. Humphry Ward (1851–1920). (Her grandfather was Thomas Arnold, her uncle was Matthew Arnold, and her sister Julia was the daughter-in-law of Thomas Henry Huxley and the mother of Julian Huxley the biologist and of Aldous Huxley the novelist.) Picking up on all of the worries nagging at Victorian Christians, the story is about a young Anglican clergyman who loses his faith and who then tries to make a living doing good in the slums of London. Early on, Darwin's big hand in the story is made very clear. Robert is talking to his friend Langham.

> "Dirt, drains, and Darwin," said Langham meditatively, taking up Darwin's "Earthworms," which lay on the study table beside him, side by side with a volume of Grant Allen's "Sketches." "I didn't know you cared for this sort of thing!"
>
> Robert did not answer for a moment, and a faint flush stole into his face.
>
> "Imagine, Langham!" he said presently, "I had never read even the 'Origin of Species' before I came here. We used to take the thing half for granted, I remember, at Oxford, in a more or less modified sense. But to drive the mind through all the details of the evidence, to force one's self to understand the whole hypothesis and the grounds for it, is a very different matter. It is a revelation."
>
> "Yes," said Langham; and could not forbear adding, "but it is a revelation, my friend, that has not always been held to square with other revelations." (Ward 1888, 170–171)

In Victorian melodramas it is usually the local squire who does the dirty work, stealing the virginity of the naïve maiden. Mrs. Ward does not disappoint. However, her squire, a nonbelieving cynic, has his filthy desires turned toward our innocent vicar, whom he overwhelms with vile Germanic-type arguments.

> "*Do I believe in God?* Surely, surely! 'Though He slay me yet will I trust in Him!' *Do I believe in Christ?* Yes,—in the teacher, the martyr, the symbol to us Westerns of all things heavenly and abiding, the image

and pledge of the invisible life of the spirit—with all my soul and all my mind!"

"*But in the Man-God*, the Word from Eternity,—in a wonder-working Christ, in a risen and ascended Jesus, in the living Intercessor and Mediator for the lives of His doomed brethren?"

He waited, conscious that it was the crisis of his history, and there rose in him, as though articulated one by one by an audible voice, words of irrevocable meaning.

"Every human soul in which the voice of God makes itself felt, enjoys, equally with Jesus of Nazareth, the divine sonship, and '*miracles do not happen!*'"

It was done. (342)

His wife is not pleased.

"I can believe no longer in an incarnation and resurrection," he said slowly, but with a resolute plainness. "Christ is risen in our hearts, in the Christian life of charity. Miracle is a natural product of human feeling and imagination and God was in Jesus — pre-eminently, as He is in all great souls, but not otherwise — not otherwise in kind than He is in me or you."

His voice dropped to a whisper. She grew paler and paler.

"So to you," she said presently in the same strange altered voice, "my father — when I saw that light on his face before he died, when I heard him cry, 'Master, I come!' was dying — deceived — deluded. Perhaps even," and she trembled, "you think it ends here — our life — our love?" (364)

Apparently, Mark 12:25—"For when they shall rise from the dead, they neither marry, nor are given in marriage; but are as the angels which are in heaven"—cut little ice here.

Elsmere gets himself involved in kinds of proto-YMCA activities, even setting up a scientific Sunday school. "This was the direct result of a paragraph in Huxley's Lay Sermons, where the hint of such a school was first thrown out" (475). Expectedly, as is customary in these sorts of novels, our hero does not make it alive to the final paragraph. He mistakes something serious for a passing attack of "clergyman's throat," and having thanked God that his wife's suffering at his illness is now over, "sinking back into her arms, he gave two or three gasping breaths, and died" (604). She, one is glad to say, spends the rest of her life covering her options—Church on Sunday morning, charity work for the rest of the week.

This novel sold over a million copies legitimately and probably as many in pirated copies. Not everyone liked it.[2] Expectedly, Mr. Gladstone found fault, although author and politician got on well together. "He said that he had never read any book on the hostile side written in such a spirit of 'generous appreciation' of the Christian side" (Peterson 1970, 453). And that in a way is what makes the novel so very effective. Not only is the novel a blow as strong as any essay from the pen of Thomas Henry Huxley—and given Mrs. Ward's connections obviously a blow from within the same camp as Huxley[3]—it is not a harsh, new-atheist polemic against a dangerous creed, but a rather sad retreat from something that simply no longer works and is no longer relevant to the modern age—of the "Sea of Faith" we now hear only "its melancholy, long, withdrawing roar." We need an alternative world picture. The question to be asked, therefore, is whether Darwinism was able to provide it.

The God Question

Before we plunge in, there is a worry to be addressed, akin to the worry we addressed when looking at the science. We are going to see a wide range of views. Does it make sense to link these all under one heading of Darwinian secular religion or some such thing, especially since some of the views are not terribly secular? You cannot play entirely fast and loose with the ideas here, but overall that there is a range of views is hardly that troublesome. Think of Christianity and of how it goes all of the way from Roman Catholicism to outer versions of Protestantism like the Jehovah's Witnesses who (among other things) loathe and detest much that the Catholics hold dear. And that is before you get to the Unitarians who probably don't believe in God at all, not to mention the Mormons who believe in rather too many gods for conventional Christians. So let us apply the same tolerance to the Darwinian side. Let us agree that the essence of the position now being talked of takes Darwinian theory seriously and (we hope to show) sees it as having significant implications for our understanding of the nature of God—his very existence even—not to mention other parts of the Christian position. And by the "Darwinian theory" we mean evolution

---

[2] Interestingly, given his grumpiness about George Eliot's writings, Henry James was very impressed (Ward 1909, xxxvi–xl).

[3] About Mrs. Ward, Gladstone wrote to his daughter: "She is much to be liked personally but is a fruit of what I think must be called Arnoldism" (Peterson 1970, 445). As a deeply committed, rather conservative Christian, Gladstone felt threatened by the Arnolds' liberal attitude toward church doctrines. He saw it as a major step on the road to the agnosticism of Huxley, with whom he debated in the periodicals. Oscar Wilde joked that *Robert Elsmere* was Matthew Arnold's book of criticism, *Literature and Dogma*, without the literature.

through natural selection. That is at the very least the default position, although it was almost always more than that.[4] Such then will be the basis of our discussion and conclusions.[5]

So let us start right at the beginning with God himself. As Christina Rossetti (1830–1894) reminds us, the Christian God is a being who created the universe and all in it—the Earth and its denizens included.

> Before the mountains were brought forth, before
>   Earth and the world were made, then God was God:
> And God will still be God, when flames shall roar
>   Round earth and heaven dissolving at His nod:
> And this God is our God, even while His rod
>   Of righteous wrath falls on us smiting sore:
> And this God is our God for evermore
>   Through life, through death, while clod returns to clod.
> For though He slay us we will trust in Him;
>   We will flock home to Him by divers ways:
> Yea, though He slay us we will vaunt His praise,
>   Serving and loving with the Cherubim,
> Watching and loving with the Seraphim,
>   Our very selves His praise through endless days.
>   (Rossetti 1904, 73, written before 1882)

God owes us nothing, and yet having created freely in some sense He stands over His creation and cares about it. This follows because God is not only all powerful He is also all loving, although precisely what that might mean has been the subject of 2,000 years of debate—longer if you take into account the Jewish antecedents.[6] For the Christian, there is also all of the stuff about Jesus and his nature and his role in the scene of things, and we can and will pick up on this as we go along. Already, having dealt with Darwin, we know that bringing up the God question is not irrelevant. Darwin held to his deism—something

---

[4] Henry Adams, in England 1867–1868, commented sardonically: "Natural Selection seemed a dogma to be put in the place of the Athanasian creed; it was a form of religious hope; a promise of ultimate perfection" (Adams 1918).

[5] A tempting analogy is that Darwinism focusing on natural selection stands to the rest of evolutionism as (in the West) Catholicism stands to the rest of Christianity. Catholics and Lutherans differ over the host, but the Lutheran doctrine of consubstantiation is clearly defined against the Catholic doctrine of transubstantiation. This seems to me a helpful way of looking at things, as long as one does not get too literal.

[6] In respects, to be honest, this poem seems to owe much to Job. It is not so much of what God gives to us, but of what we owe to God—total, unconditioned loyalty and praise.

that, if anything, eased the way to evolution, for the latter confirms the former's commitment to the working of unbroken law—right through the writing of the *Origin* and even after for a while. In a celebrated letter to Asa Gray Darwin wrote:

> With respect to the theological view of the question; this is always painful to me. — I am bewildered. — I had no intention to write atheistically. But I own that I cannot see, as plainly as others do, & as I sh^d. wish to do, evidence of design & beneficence on all sides of us. There seems to me too much misery in the world. I cannot persuade myself that a beneficent & omnipotent God would have designedly created the Ichneumonidae with the express intention of their feeding within the living bodies of caterpillars, or that a cat should play with mice. Not believing this, I see no necessity in the belief that the eye was expressly designed. (Darwin 1985–, 8, 224)

But Darwin did then go straight on to affirm that he had some belief of a kind.

> On the other hand I cannot anyhow be contented to view this wonderful universe & especially the nature of man, & to conclude that everything is the result of brute force. I am inclined to look at everything as resulting from designed laws, with the details, whether good or bad, left to the working out of what we may call chance.

Later in the decade after the *Origin*, Darwin slid into agnosticism. Notwithstanding his worries about pain and suffering, it seems pretty clear that the motivation toward nonbelief was primarily theological. He could not stand the idea of eternal damnation for nonbelievers, like his own father and brother.[7]

---

[7] It is important to realize the importance of this letter. For all of Darwin's efforts to keep out social commentary and values, the *Origin of Species*, the first edition particularly, is soused in natural theology. There are many references to the Creator, as in: "Authors of the highest eminence seem to be fully satisfied with the view that each species has been independently created. To my mind it accords better with what we know of the laws impressed on matter by the Creator, that the production and extinction of the past and present inhabitants of the world should have been due to secondary causes, like those determining the birth and death of the individual" (Darwin 1859, 488). As Darwin says here, what he (as a deist) did not want was the Creator getting involved on a day-to-day basis. He was probably influenced here by Whewell who, although a sincere Anglican, was insistent that God stay outside science. In turn, Whewell would have been influenced by Kant, who was deeply indebted to his Pietist childhood, but insisted that God cannot explain in the empirical world, writing in the *Critique of Pure Reason*: "I had to deny knowledge in order to make room for faith" (Kant [1787] 1988, 117). By the time of the *Descent*, Darwin was much more "Darwinian" and the Creator is absent.

How then did those who read Darwin react? Some seem to have accepted everything and gone on secure in their Christian faith. Charles Kingsley was one. The *Water Babies* is as Christian a story as is John Bunyan's *Pilgrim's Progress*, written two centuries earlier.[8] We all know the beginning about Tom, the chimney sweep who is maltreated by his master, Grimes, and how—after being sent up a chimney and, on coming down, getting in the wrong room where he meets the beautiful daughter of the house, Ellie—he runs away and is drowned and turned into a water baby. But that is only the beginning for the full story is one of Christian redemption, as Tom slowly matures morally, learning to do things he does not like because they are the right thing to do. At the end, he helps Grimes see the error of his ways, and for this Tom earns the reward that he again becomes human.

> "You may take him home with you now on Sundays, Ellie. He has won his spurs in the great battle, and become fit to go with you and be a man; because he has done the thing he did not like."
>
> So Tom went home with Ellie on Sundays, and sometimes on weekdays, too; and he is now a great man of science, and can plan railroads, and steam-engines, and electric telegraphs, and rifled guns, and so forth; and knows everything about everything, except why a hen's egg don't turn into a crocodile, and two or three other little things which no one will know till the coming of the Cocqcigrues [fantastic animals unlike those ever seen]. And all this from what he learnt when he was a water-baby, underneath the sea.

No sex though.

> "And of course Tom married Ellie?"
>
> My dear child, what a silly notion! Don't you know that no one ever marries in a fairy tale, under the rank of a prince or a princess?

Those, like Tennyson, who were grappling with the implications of evolution saw that God as intervener in the Creation was being pushed out. As a great historian of the Scientific Revolution said about this process, God having made the magnificent machine that is the universe, was now becoming a "retired engineer" (Dijksterhuis 1961, 491). In other words, to some extent one had to go in the direction of the young Darwin toward deism. In the "Higher Pantheism,"

---

[8] Straley (2007) notes perceptively that *The Water Babies* is truly a confused gallimaufry of Lamarckian evolutionism (most probably garnered from Herbert Spencer) and undiluted Anglican Christianity. As we saw, there are threads of selection.

a poem read in 1869 at the first meeting of the Metaphysical Society (a group of believers and skeptics who met to discuss issues of mutual interest), Tennyson rather makes a virtue out of necessity, seeing God in all of the actions of unbroken law.

> Earth, these solid stars, this weight of body and limb,
> Are they not sign and symbol of thy division from Him?
> Dark is the world to thee: thyself art the reason why;
> For is He not all but thou, that hast power to feel 'I am I'?
> Glory about thee, without thee; and thou fulfillest thy doom,
> Making Him broken gleams, and a stifled splendour and gloom.
> Speak to Him thou for He hears, and Spirit with Spirit can meet —
> Closer is He than breathing, and nearer than hands and feet.
> God is law, say the wise; O Soul, and let us rejoice,
> For if He thunder by law the thunder is yet His voice.
> Law is God, say some: no God at all, says the fool;
> For all we have power to see is a straight staff bent in a pool;
> And the ear of man cannot hear, and the eye of man cannot see;
> But if we could see and hear, this Vision — were it not He?
>
> (Tennyson 1870, 202–203)

Confident, but not quite as confident as before Darwin. "The fool hath said in his heart, There is no god" (Psalm 14:1). Why then do we need to keep reassuring ourselves that this is not true?

God in Nature—and What Does That Mean?

Across the Atlantic, epitomizing New England transcendentalism, writing in a Carlyle-like fashion in his influential essay "The Over-Soul" ([1841] 2010), Emerson also played the pantheism theme, seeing a God who somehow is in nature but also part of us—not a separate distant being, but one who is at one with his creation. "Ineffable is the union of man and God in every act of the soul. The simplest person, who in his integrity worships God, becomes God; yet for ever and ever the influx of this better and universal self is new and unsearchable" (66). Likewise in the pre-*Origin* religion of Walt Whitman, for despite having given up on Christian notions like original sin, he nevertheless had a kind of spirituality focused on himself. Note, however, that although he himself is immortal, so is everyone else! Note, moreover, echoing Carlyle's natural supernaturalism, that everything is wonderful—the miraculous (immortality) and the ordinary (seeing, conceiving, learning to walk) are bound together in a deeper sense.

I do not think seventy years is the time of a man or woman,
Nor that seventy millions of years is the time of a man or woman,
Nor that years will ever stop the existence of me, or any one else.

Is it wonderful that I should be immortal? as every one is immortal,
I know it is wonderful—but my eye-sight is equally wonderful, and how
   I was conceived in my mother's womb is equally wonderful; . . .

And passed from a babe, in the creeping trance of three summers and three
   winters, to articulate and walk—All this is equally wonderful.
             (Whitman 2004, 414–415, first published 1855)

Emily Dickinson (1830–1886) picked up on these sorts of ideas, writing to a friend (around 1862): "I was thinking to-day, as I noticed, that the "Supernatural" was only the Natural disclosed" (Higginson 1891, 449).[9] Her poetry reflects this transcendentalism—the brain, thought, covers the whole of existence and in some sense includes it.

> The Brain—is wider than the Sky—
> For—put them side by side—
> The one the other will contain
> With ease—and You—beside—
>
> The Brain is deeper than the sea—
> For—hold them—Blue to Blue—
> The one the other will absorb—
> As Sponges—Buckets—do—
>
> The Brain is just the weight of God—
> For—Heft them—Pound for Pound—
> And they will differ—if they do—
> As Syllable from Sound—
>   (Dickinson 1960, 312–313—about 1863)

Of course, you might say that none of this is very Darwinian, and that is true. But it is a world picture against which Darwinian themes can be played out.[10] And in

[9] References in this book are to the one-volume reading text, edited by Thomas H. Johnson, published in 1960. This is based on the variorum edition, *The Poems of Emily Dickinson*, edited by Thomas H. Johnson, Cambridge, Mass.: The Belknap Press of Harvard University Press. Copyright © 1951, 1955 by the President and Fellows of Harvard College. Copyright © renewed 1979, 1983 by the President and Fellows of Harvard College. Copyright © 1914, 1918, 1919, 1924, 1929, 1930, 1932, 1935, 1937, 1942, by Martha Dickinson Bianchi. Copyright © 1952, 1957, 1958, 1963, 1965, by Mary L. Hampson.

[10] "Emily Dickinson herself was imbricated in a unique web of affiliation with Darwin and darwinian ideas; the key New England figures in this debate were all known to Dickinson either through

the darker world of natural selection—Carlyle, Emerson, and Whitman cut their teeth before the *Origin*—we have to start asking about the nature of this God who is so all-pervasive.[11] Do we have much more than what Aristotle would have called an "entelechy," a kind of animating power that is not necessarily all that conscious? With talk of "syllable from sound," it does seem as though God is basically the life force of nature and it is we humans, with our brains, who make sense of things. We go, for instance, from the primitive sound "um" to a range of syllables to which we humans (incorporating them in words) give different meanings—"lumbar," "dumber," "gummy," "become," and more. Thus, as Madam Natural Selection pointed out, don't look for Nature/God to give meaning to events.

> The most triumphant Bird I ever knew or met
> Embarked upon a twig today
> And till Dominion set
> I famish to behold so eminent a sight
> And sang for nothing scrutable
> But intimate Delight.
> Retired, and resumed his transitive Estate —
> To what delicious Accident
> Does finest Glory fit!
> (Dickinson 1960, 554, written about 1873)[12]

her family, her schooling, her library or the libraries at Amherst Academy and Mount Holyoke, or through the pages of the New England periodicals to which the Dickinsons subscribed" (Kirkby 2010, 7). McIntosh (2000) suggests that she would have known of Darwin's ideas as early as 1860 through Asa Gray's discussions in the *Atlantic*. "Darwin did not create Dickinson's instability of belief concerning Christianity, but he certainly helped to stimulate it" (174, n.16).

[11] Peel (2010) shows the importance of science for Dickinson, especially in her imagery. More incisively, Baym (2002) argues that overall Dickinson uses science against theology rather than as a support. Keane (2008) makes much of Darwin's influence on Dickinson's thinking about pain and suffering; Lundin (2004) stresses how Dickinson's great poems come after the *Origin* was published. Compare the earlier, almost complacency of Henry Wadsworth Longfellow on the death of his daughter (in 1848).

> She is not dead,—the child of our affection,—
> But gone unto that school
> Where she no longer needs our poor protection,
> And Christ himself doth rule.

"There was little of the speculative philosopher about Longfellow" (Conner [1949] 1973, 177).

[12] In a more theological mode, Dickinson seems to blame God for making us as we are and then punishing us straight off rather than giving us a decent chance to make good.

> "Heavenly Father" — take to thee
> The supreme iniquity

Spiders

It is this lack of meaning that struck home so forcibly, and not just for Dickinson. Either God is indifferent or God is cruel. Compare three great New England poets (including Dickinson) writing on the shared theme of spiders. First, the Puritan poet Edward Taylor (1642–1729), who uses the metaphor of the spider catching the fly for Satan catching us and needing Christ to bring about our salvation. We may be pretty pathetic, but everything makes sense in the Christian scheme of things.

> Thou sorrow, venom Elfe:
> Is this thy play,
> To spin a web out of thyselfe
> To Catch a Fly?
> For Why?

A fly is caught and allowed to escape.

> Whereas the silly Fly,
> Caught by its leg
> Thou by the throate tookst hastily
> And 'hinde the head
> Bite Dead.

And now the interpretation.

> This Frey seems thus to us.
> Hells Spider gets

> Fashioned by thy candid Hand
> In a moment contraband —
> Though to trust us — seems to us
> More respectful — "We are Dust"
> We apologize to thee
> For thine own Duplicity —
>   (Dickinson 1960, 619, written about 1879)

The sarcasm at the end suggests someone who might be ready to drop the whole Judeo-Christian conception of God and try some alternative (Zapedowska 2006). Eberwein (2013) stresses how Dickinson simultaneously wrestled with the twin challenges of Darwin and higher criticism.

His intrails spun to whip Cords thus
And wove to nets
And sets.

To tangle Adams race
In's stratigems
To their Destructions, spoil'd, made base
By venom things,
Damn'd Sins.

Fortunately, not all is lost.

But mighty, Gracious Lord
Communicate
Thy Grace to breake the Cord, afford
Us Glorys Gate
And State.

We'l Nightingaile sing like
When pearcht on high
In Glories Cage, thy glory, bright,
And thankfully,
For joy.

(Taylor 1989, 340–341)

Next, Emily Dickinson, about 1869, who is rather frightening.

A Spider sewed at Night
Without a Light
Upon an Arc of White.

If Ruff it was of Dame
Or Shroud of Gnome
Himself himself inform.

Of Immortality
His Strategy
Was Physiognomy.

(Dickinson 1960, 1138)

Is the spider making a fancy piece of finery for a woman or the death cloak for one of nature's unfortunates? And this is how he hopes to achieve immortality?

Not through an act of will but simply through physical consequences? Does God not care about intentions?[13]

Finally, look at Robert Frost (1874–1963), writing around 1912.

> I found a dimpled spider, fat and white,
> On a white heal-all, holding up a moth
> Like a white piece of rigid satin cloth —
> Assorted characters of death and blight
> Mixed ready to begin the morning right,
> Like the ingredients of a witches' broth —
> A snow-drop spider, a flower like a froth,
> And dead wings carried like a paper kite.
>
> What had that flower to do with being white,
> The wayside blue and innocent heal-all?
> What brought the kindred spider to that height,
> Then steered the white moth thither in the night?
> What but design of darkness to appall?—
> If design govern in a thing so small.
>
> (Frost 1969, 302)

The sonnet is ironically called "design," but that poses the very question. Three things, all white, come together to cause the death of the moth. Was it chance? The flower, the heal-all, should by rights be blue, in which case the spider would have stood out. The spider is white and thus camouflaged. The moth, perhaps contingently white—although had there been no spider

---

[13] As is shown by this poem from about 1862, Dickinson could write in a lighter way about spiders; although even here there is the theme of effort leading to beauty and then waste.

> The Spider holds a Silver Ball
> In unperceived Hands—
> And dancing softly to Himself
> His Yarn of Pearl — unwinds—
>
> He plies from nought to nought —
> In unsubstantial Trade —
> Supplants our Tapestries with His—
> In half the period —
>
> An Hour to rear supreme
> His Continents of Light —
> Then dangle from the Housewife's Broom—
> His Boundaries — forgot—
>
> (Dickinson 1960, 605)

it too would have been nicely camouflaged—is attracted to the white (as it is to lights and flames). Is this really design, in which case what kind of God, and if not, then how pointless it all seems. One is not surprised to learn that Frost wrote this poem while he was teaching William James in high school (Poirier 1990). He was reading James's account of how Darwin blew the argument from design into smithereens: "Darwin opened our minds to the power of chance-happenings to bring forth 'fit' results if only they have time to add themselves together. He showed the enormous waste of nature in producing results that get destroyed because of their unfitness. He also emphasized the number of adaptations which, if designed, would argue an evil rather than a good designer" (James 1907).

Suffering

In this poem of Frost, there is worry about suffering itself. As Darwin realized, a God of natural selection rather highlights this and makes it an essential part of the creation. In a later chapter, we will look at this issue theologically. For now, recognize that it occurs and that some seized on this in no uncertain terms. Winwood Reade, the explorer and anthropologist mentioned in the *Descent* and author of *The Martyrdom of Man*, a kind of secular history-cum-manifesto that was another work that upset Mr. Gladstone, has a hero (if that is the right term) in his novel *The Outcast* who is deeply affected by the Darwinian message.

> One day he came to me in trouble. He had been reading the great work of Malthus — the "Essay on Population" — and said that it made him doubt the goodness of God. I replied with the usual common-place remarks; he listened to me attentively, then sighed, shook his head, and went away. A little while afterwards he read "The Origin of Species," which had just come out, and which proves that the Law of Population is the chief agent by which Evolution has been produced. From that time he began to show symptoms of insanity — which disease, it is thought, he inherited from one of his progenitors. He dressed always in black, and said that he was in mourning for mankind. The works of Malthus and Darwin, bound in somber covers, were placed on a table in his room; the first was lettered outside "The Book of Doubt," and the second "The Book of Despair." (Reade [1875] 2012, 5)

Fortunately he meets a nice girl, but she dies and he ends as a suicide in a mad house. He leaves a manuscript describing his despair, and the cruelty of the

Darwinian process figures high. "At first, every step in the human progress was won by conflict, and every invention resulted from calamity. The most odious vices and crimes were at one time useful to humanity, while war, tyranny, and superstition assisted the development of man" (18).

Not everyone was quite so blunt about the issues as this, but the cruelty of the natural processes is an ongoing theme in prose and poetry. Here is Emily Dickinson on the subject. It is about a plant and the coming of cold weather, but note the ominous word "assassin." The poet may be reacting to the recent death (1883) at the age of seven of a favorite nephew.

> Apparently with no surprise
> To any happy Flower
> The Frost beheads it at its play—
> In accidental power—
> The blonde Assassin passes on—
> The Sun proceeds unmoved
> To measure off another Day
> For an Approving God.
>   (Dickinson 1960, 667–668, written about 1885)[14]

Almost everyone picks up on this theme. Even Yeats of all people—the man who never met a nutty view (like theosophy) that he didn't like—is sensitive to the hurts of the Darwinian struggle (McDonald 2012). A seeker of wisdom has gone to hear the echoes of a sacred spot.

> O Rocky Voice,
> Shall we in that great night rejoice?
> What do we know but that we face
> One another in this place?
> But hush, for I have lost the theme,
> Its joy or night seem but a dream;
> Up there some hawk or owl has struck,
> Dropping out of sky or rock,
> A stricken rabbit is crying out,
> And its cry distracts my thought.
>   (Yeats 1996, 346. From *Last Poems, 1938–1939*)

---

[14] "He cometh forth like a flower, and is cut down" (Job 14:2); "By the breath of God, frost is given" (Job 37:10).

The Lack of Meaning

A rabbit must be torn apart to feed a predator. What kind of God is this? But, with respect, although Darwin highlights pain and suffering, we knew about this before the *Origin*. What is new for so many is the lack of meaning. Again and again, as Emily Dickinson sensed, it is the very blindness of law rather than its consequences as such that are crushing. Robert Browning's poem "Caliban on Setebos," appearing five years after the *Origin*, has Caliban—the subhuman son of the witch Sycorax, in Shakespeare's *Tempest*—reflecting in a drunken way on his god Setebos. After the Darwinian theory, in a grotesque parody of Paley, God for Browning/Caliban is cruel even in—precisely because of—his indifference (Beer 1985; Loesberg 2008).

> Thinketh, such shows nor right nor wrong in Him,
> Nor kind, nor cruel: He is strong and Lord.
> Am strong myself compared to yonder crabs
> That march now from the mountain to the sea,
> Let twenty pass, and stone the twenty-first,
> Loving not, hating not, just choosing so.
> Say, the first straggler that boasts purple spots
> Shall join the file, one pincer twisted off;
> Say, this bruised fellow shall receive a worm,
> And two worms he whose nippers end in red;
> As it likes me each time, I do: so He.
>
> (Browning 1981, 807)[15]

And then, above all others, there is Thomas Hardy, a man for whom Darwin was his most significant guide from the very first to the very last (Hardy 1987, 259).[16] The newly Darwin-infused Hardy rages against the absent God, wanting rather one who does care enough to make life miserable (Stevenson 1932, 261)! Thus his well-known poem "Hap" (1866).

> IF but some vengeful god would call to me
>   From up the sky, and laugh: "Thou suffering thing,
>   Know that thy sorrow is my ecstasy,
>   That thy love's loss is my hate's profiting!"

[15] Holmes (2009) is particularly strong on the lack of meaning after the *Origin*, giving an extended analysis of Browning's poem and related works.

[16] Hardy's overall philosophical position is complex, or perhaps better diffuse, and changing over time (Bailey 1963). He started life as a Christian and the influence showed in his works throughout his life. Then in the early 1860s, Hardy read Darwin and became a nonbelieving pessimist, thinking all just

Then would I bear, and clench myself, and die,
  Steeled by the sense of ire unmerited;
Half-eased, too, that a Powerfuller than I
  Had willed and meted me the tears I shed.

But not so. How arrives it joy lies slain,
  And why unblooms the best hope ever sown?
—Crass Casualty obstructs the sun and rain,
  And dicing Time for gladness casts a moan. . . .
  These purblind Doomsters had as readily strown
Blisses about my pilgrimage as pain.

(Hardy 1994, 5)

Atheism

Does this mean then that there is no God? That it is not that God is indifferent or cruel but rather that he is nonexistent? This is the conclusion of the Scottish poet James Thompson (also known as Bysshe Vanolis) in his "City of the Dreadful Night," about London—a London stripped of meaning or purpose.

We bow down to the universal laws,
Which never had for man a special clause
  Of cruelty or kindness, love or hate:
If toads and vultures are obscene to sight,
If tigers burn with beauty and with might,
  Is it by favour or by wrath of Fate?

All substance lives and struggles evermore
Through countless shapes continually at war,
  By countless interactions interknit:
If one is born a certain day on earth,
All times and forces tended to that birth,
  Not all the world could change or hinder it.

blind chance. In the early 1880s he read Arthur Schopenhauer and came to believe in a kind of blind world force, the "Immanent Will." Hardy then combined this with Eduard von Hartmann's theory of the unconscious, thinking perhaps through human effort the Will becomes conscious. This was the theory of the epic drama (complete with Greek-like choruses) of the first decade of the twentieth century, *The Dynasts*. Finally, around 1910 Hardy became what he himself called an "evolutionary meliorist," seeing change moving upward through human effort. Be warned, however, that he himself said candidly in a preface at the end of his life that "no harmonious philosophy is attempted in these pages—or in any bygone pages of mine, for that matter." We shall see many counterexamples to the neat fourfold division.

I find no hint throughout the Universe
Of good or ill, of blessing or of curse;
 I find alone Necessity Supreme;
With infinite Mystery, abysmal, dark,
Unlighted ever by the faintest spark
 For us the flitting shadows of a dream.

There is nothing beyond what we sense and feel.

And now at last authentic word I bring,
 Witnessed by every dead and living thing;
 Good tidings of great joy for you, for all:
There is no God; no Fiend with names divine
Made us and tortures us; if we must pine,
 It is to satiate no Being's gall.

(Thompson [1874] 2003, 36–37; 34)

We have gone all the way from Kingsley's untouched Anglican faith to Thompson's despairing atheism. But with the possible exception of Kingsley, there is something linking all these writers. Natural selection—and note we are talking about natural selection and not some warm, fuzzy notion like Lamarckism or dynamic equilibrium—has changed their world. Or, perhaps more accurately, quoting more lines of Matthew Arnold's poem—even before Darwin we were facing a world that "Hath really neither joy, nor love, nor light,/Nor certitude, nor peace, nor help for pain"—we should say that natural selection makes this bleak vision a reality. God is at arm's length, say what you will. And that raises questions of meaning. Does he care? Is he indifferent? Is he cruel? Is he a sadist? Does he even exist? And, what is this going to mean for us? How are we to move forward? Let us see.

6

Origins

The Christian Story

Thanks to its Jewish roots, Christianity is a story of origins. Even without an absolutely literal reading of Genesis, no one (on the Christian side) doubted that God was creator, that this had happened in the conceivable past, that humankind is central, and that we have a story that is dynamic in that it leads from the past to the present and onward toward the future. The poet Christina Rossetti, who in the last chapter captured for us the notion of God, now in this sonnet captures for us the Genesis-based origins of the world and our beginnings. She stresses also the climax of the Christian story when God suffered for our sins.

> Thou Who didst make and knowest whereof we are made,
>   Oh bear in mind our dust and nothingness,
>   Our wordless tearless dumbness of distress:
> Bear Thou in mind the burden Thou hast laid
> Upon us, and our feebleness unstayed
>   Except Thou stay us: for the long long race
>   Which stretches far and far before our face
> Thou knowest,—remember Thou whereof we are made.
> If making makes us Thine, then Thine we are;
>   And if redemption, we are twice Thine own:
> If once Thou didst come down from heaven afar
>   To seek us and to find us, how not save?
> Comfort us, save us, leave us not alone,
>   Thou Who didst die our death and fill our grave.
>   (Rossetti 1904, 74)

In respects—and one truly means no real slur—evolution is a bastard off-spring of this story.[1] It too is a story of origins with events in the distant past—on neither side do we have eyewitness testimony of folk around today—and humans are central, if only as a vehicle for people to spend a lot of time showing that they are not! By and large, not too much time is spent worrying about the centrality of warthogs. So in this chapter, let us see what the creative writers had to say about origins from an evolutionary perspective. And the place to start is with the presupposition to the story, time.

Deep Time

Stress again that the immensity of time—often known as "deep time"—was no new discovery of Darwin. In the years before the *Origin*, Whitman in "Leaves of Grass" was insisting on the nigh inconceivability of history.

> It is no small matter, this round and delicious globe,
> moving so exactly in its orbit forever and ever,
> without one jolt, or the untruth of a single
> second,
> I do not think it was made in six days, nor in ten
> thousand years, nor ten billions of years,
> Nor planned and built one thing after another, as an
> architect plans and builds a house.

This said, Darwin certainly concentrated people's thinking on the age of the universe, so much so in fact that, in their ignorance of the warming effects of radioactive decay, the physicists—led by that good Presbyterian William Thompson (Lord Kelvin)—did their utmost to bring down the age to a span that would make evolution through natural selection impossible. Thompson had the figure at about 100 million years, although he thought it might be less (Burchfield 1975). One feels, however, that the novelists and poets had a better grip on things, especially that now we think the Earth over 4 billion years, the universe nearly 14 billion years, and life down here at least 3.5 billion years old.[2]

---

[1] Because of this connection, I feel free to ignore non-Western religions like Buddhism. I see Darwinism as a rival to Christianity. I do say something about non-Western religions in Ruse (2015a) and a lot more in Larson and Ruse (2016).

[2] Trying to speed evolution up a little may have been a reason why the later editions of the *Origin* have more Lamarckism than the earlier editions.

As always, that dedicated Darwinian Thomas Hardy comes to the fore. There is no more forceful or subtle treatment of time than that to be found in his novel *The Return of the Native* (1878). The story itself is a bit of a soap opera. Damon Wildeve, somewhat of a lightweight, cannot make up his mind between Thomasin Yeobright, whom he eventually marries but then rather regrets his actions, and Eustacia Vye, whom he does not marry but then rather regrets his actions. Eustacia has stars in her eyes about Clym Yeobright—cousin to Thomasin—who has just returned from Paris and wants to start a school. They do marry, but then Clym starts to lose his eyesight and becomes a furze-cutter. This is all a bit lower class, but what really upsets Eustacia is that he enjoys his new job. In the end, Eustacia and Damon run off, but they fall in a pool and drown. Clym is overwhelmed with guilt and becomes a preacher. Thomasin marries Diggery Venn, who has always had a bit of a thing for her. This atypically happy ending for a Hardy novel was not the author's original intent but was pushed on him by his publisher to suit the readers.

In a way, though, all this is froth on the top—on the top of Egdon Heath (in Hardy's imaginary county of Wessex) which is where the action takes place. It is the Heath that dominates the story and moves the characters forward or backward, even drowning a couple of them at the end. Throughout, Hardy stresses the timelessness of the Heath—always was there, is there now, will be there in the future when we are all long gone. The Heath is both hero and villain, although, as in Hardy's novels, the two notions are usually confused.

> The untameable, Ishmaelitish thing that Egdon now was it always had been. Civilization was its enemy; and ever since the beginning of vegetation its soil had worn the same antique brown dress, the natural and invariable garment of the particular formation. In its venerable one coat lay a certain vein of satire on human vanity in clothes. A person on a heath in raiment of modern cut and colours has more or less an anomalous look. We seem to want the oldest and simplest human clothing where the clothing of the earth is so primitive.
>
> To recline on a stump of thorn in the central valley of Egdon, between afternoon and night, as now, where the eye could reach nothing of the world outside the summits and shoulders of heathland which filled the whole circumference of its glance, and to know that everything around and underneath had been from prehistoric times as unaltered as the stars overhead, gave ballast to the mind adrift on change, and harassed by the irrepressible New. The great inviolate place had an ancient permanence which the sea cannot claim. Who can say of a particular sea that it is old? Distilled by the sun, kneaded by the moon, it is renewed in a year, in a day, or in an hour. The sea changed, the fields

changed, the rivers, the villages, and the people changed, yet Egdon remained. (Hardy [1878] 1999, 11–12)

There is an underlying pagan theme to Hardy's novel. The Heath is a thing unto itself—in today's terms, a Gaia-like phenomenon with an existence, a life, of its own—never born, never to die. Hardy makes much of the symbolism of the bonfire with its evocation of druids and like priests of the aged past. Although the bonfires framing the story are the successive years of Guy Fawkes Night (November the fifth), Hardy makes more of them. "The ashes of the original British pyre which blazed from that summit lay fresh and undisturbed in the barrow beneath their tread. The flames from funeral piles long ago kindled there had shone down upon the lowlands as these were shining now. Festival fires to Thor and Woden had followed on the same ground and duly had their day" (20). Even Eustacia—the beautiful Eustacia—is part of the scene, with her primitive sexuality that kills one would-be lover and drives her husband to a life of gloomy guilt. "She had pagan eyes, full of nocturnal mysteries, and their light, as it came and went, and came again, was partially hampered by their oppressive lids and lashes; and of these the under lid was much fuller than it usually is with English women" (68).

I don't think Hardy is a pagan—certainly not at this time thinking of the Earth as a living being worthy of worship—but he is using pagan ideas and sentiments to try to express something in a world without the Christian message of hope.[3] And time is an essential part of this. We are of the Earth. We came from it. We go back to it. That is all there is. Time goes on. There is no meaning, at least not in any conscious, Christian sort of way. Hardy repeats this message in his verse. Take the sad, sad poem about the lad killed in the Boer War (1899–1902), far from home, in a land he does not understand, buried without ceremony. A pointless, worthless life. He is not even a fighting man. He's just a kid who makes a lot of noise banging a piece of wood against an animal skin.

> They throw in Drummer Hodge, to rest
> Uncoffined — just as found:
> His landmark is a kopje-crest
> That breaks the veldt around:
> And foreign constellations west
> Each night above his mound.

---

[3] The manuscript of the novel is more explicitly anti-Christian than the version that was published (Paterson 1959). Because of its content, Hardy had a horrendous job getting the novel published and bowdlerized the text to achieve that end (Dalziel 2000).

> Young Hodge the drummer never knew —
> Fresh from his Wessex home —
> The meaning of the broad Karoo,
> The Bush, the dusty loam,
> And why uprose to nightly view
> Strange stars amid the gloam.
>
> Yet portion of that unknown plain
> Will Hodge for ever be;
> His homely Northern breast and brain
> Grow to some Southern tree,
> And strange-eyed constellations reign
> His stars eternally.
>
> (Hardy 1994, 80)

Young Hodge is now part of all eternity—back to the Earth, ready to be recycled again and again. He is nothing and yet, as much as any one of us, he is something. We are, always were, always will be, part of existence. And that—take it as bleak, take it as comforting—is something.[4]

Modern Science

In a way, to use an uncomfortably apt phrase, all of this is looking backward. The writers are exploring the notion of time—of deep time—and to do this they are reverting to pre-Christian notions of ages ever-lasting or perhaps eternal. It is no surprise to find that Whitman was responding at least in part to Buddhist thinking—something incidentally that was significant for Emerson. Obviously if you are going to discuss evolution, looking into the past, this is the prime way to go—and as obviously this is going to challenge the Christian. But one should not forget that, at the end of the nineteenth century, physicists—one thinks first and foremost of Albert Einstein—were going to pull apart the whole notion of time and put it back into science in ways unimaginable to earlier scientists. The deepness of time then will be just one part of the overall picture.

With reason, one might say that this is not really the geologist's or the evolutionist's concern, any more than, say, the work of Keynes on the economy is my

---

[4] This, I take it, is Hardy more at the third stage, inclined to think of some blind life force underlying everything. Schopenhauer goes back to the Romantics as does von Hartmann and a debt to Schelling. Although there are common roots and obvious overlaps, the life force of the transcendentalists seems more optimistic, more aware than the dark world of Schopenhauer particularly.

concern as I try to balance my family's finances—the mortgage, the car payment, the college fees. But of course, this is true only to a point, of both time and our finances. There is surely going to be interest in whether the future extends indefinitely as the past apparently extends indefinitely—and one might say that, just as time impinges on the Creation story, so also it impinges on the Second Coming. We will deal more with this and related topics in a later chapter. What we can say here is that, thinking in an evolutionary context, our writers were not indifferent to these sorts of issues. Notably H. G. Wells (1886–1946), in the *Time Machine* (writing a decade before Einstein), takes up the question of time and its meaning. He is not original—he cites one Professor Simon Newcomb speaking in New York—but he is forward looking.

> "Clearly," the Time Traveller proceeded, "any real body must have extension in *four* directions: it must have Length, Breadth, Thickness, and—Duration. But through a natural infirmity of the flesh, which I will explain to you in a moment, we incline to overlook this fact. There are really four dimensions, three which we call the three planes of Space, and a fourth, Time. There is, however, a tendency to draw an unreal distinction between the former three dimensions and the latter, because it happens that our consciousness moves intermittently in one direction along the latter from the beginning to the end of our lives."
> (Wells [1895] 2005, 4)

He continues: "Really this is what is meant by the Fourth Dimension, though some people who talk about the Fourth Dimension do not know they mean it. It is only another way of looking at Time. *There is no difference between Time and any of the three dimensions of Space except that our consciousness moves along it.*" This obviously opens up the possibility of time always existing in some sense, and from the viewpoint of the novel the possibility of time travel just as much as space travel. Wells is not the first to think of this in a fictional context. To take one example of many, we get something like it in Dickens's *Christmas Carol*, with the three ghosts of Christmas Past, Christmas Present, and Christmas Future. But in some way, given that space seems—or at least, seemed then—to have no bounds, it all suggests that time could be boundless likewise.

Dinosaurs

We have time. Now, we turn to filling it up with life and seeing if it all makes a coherent story. Again, let it be stressed, the *Origin* entered a world that had already done much to uncover the once-living past. Above all, those dinosaurs—down at the Crystal Palace park—thrilled and puzzled the Victorians, and they only became more pressing as the century grew on and truly fantabulous new forms were uncovered out in the American West—the most famous, *Diplodocus carnegie* ("Dippy"), being reproduced in plaster and given to museums, starting with London, all over the world. They frame our time period. Lewis Carroll wrote his famous nonsense poem about the Jabberwocky in the 1850s.

"Beware the Jabberwock, my son!
The jaws that bite, the claws that catch!
Beware the Jubjub bird, and shun
The frumious Bandersnatch!"

He took his vorpal sword in hand:
Long time the manxome foe he sought—
So rested he by the Tumtum tree,
And stood awhile in thought.

And as in uffish thought he stood,
The Jabberwock, with eyes of flame,
Came whiffling through the tulgey wood,
And burbled as it came!

One, two! One, two! and through and through
The vorpal blade went snicker-snack!
He left it dead, and with its head
He went galumphing back.

(Carroll 1871, 9)

When the poem appeared in *Alice through the Looking Glass* in 1871, the illustration was by John Tenniel, and the beast was a combination of Pterodactyl wings and the long scaly neck of a sauropod (a form of dinosaur which includes the then yet-to-be-discovered Dippy). People knew what this was all about and why it was a joke. They continued to know. In 1912 Arthur Conan Doyle (1859–1930) took a break from writing Sherlock Holmes stories to pen *The Lost World*, about Professor Challenger and his trip to South America where on a high plateau, isolated by cliffs, he finds a niche still occupied by brutes from the past, notably including dinosaurs—*Iguanodon, Stegosaurus, Allosaurus, Megalosaurus*. There are also Pterodactyls! All fantasy of course, but fantasy about the familiar.

There were, as I say, five of them, two being adults and three young ones.
In size they were enormous. Even the babies were as big as elephants,

while the two large ones were far beyond all creatures I have ever seen. They had slate-colored skin, which was scaled like a lizard's and shimmered where the sun shone upon it. All five were sitting up, balancing themselves upon their broad, powerful tails and their huge three-toed hind-feet, while with their small five-fingered front-feet they pulled down the branches upon which they browsed. I do not know that I can bring their appearance home to you better than by saying that they looked like monstrous kangaroos, twenty feet in length, and with skins like black crocodiles. (Conan Doyle [1912] 1995, 100–101)

And this almost matter-of-fact description of Iguanodons at supper is in a way the whole point. Neither Carroll nor Conan Doyle was in the religion-debunking business. Carroll was an Anglican minister and, although after a Catholic childhood he became an agnostic, notoriously Conan Doyle was an enthusiast for spiritualism and speaking with the departed. But they like everyone else were going on about brutes that clearly were major items in life's history and yet find no mention in the Old Testament. We do not read of the troubles of Noah and his family in finding room on the Ark for Diplodocus and friends. Did God really make them all and then just wipe them out in the Flood? Why should they go extinct because of the sins of humankind?

Origins of Life

Let us get more specific about the actual course of life's history and its meaning and causes. Turn first to the creative force that starts all of life. Erasmus Darwin happily supposed some form of spontaneous generation. Charles Darwin believed in something of that sort, although certainly not something continuous (which was built into Lamarck's theory). To his great friend the botanist Joseph Hooker, on February 1, 1871, he wrote that "it is often said that all the conditions for the first production of a living being are now present, which could ever have been present. But if (and oh what a big if) we could conceive in some warm little pond with all sort of ammonia and phosphoric salts,—light, heat, electricity present, that a protein compound was chemically formed, ready to undergo still more complex changes, at the present such matter would be instantly devoured, or absorbed, which would not have been the case before living creatures were formed . . ." (Darwin 1985–, 19, 53–54). In print cautiously Darwin remained silent because it was just as the *Origin* appeared that in France Louis Pasteur was putting the final nail in the coffin of naïve views of life's origination. But really, he was only speculating in a way that seemed pretty obvious to those before him and those after him. Chambers speculated about electric sparks and

Thomas Henry Huxley plunged right in with claims about deep-sea, early life forms.[5]

The poets picked up on the idea. Thus Mathilde Blind, writing in 1889:

Struck out of dim fluctuant forces and shock of electrical vapour,
Repelled and attracted the atoms flashed mingling; in union primeval,
And over the face of the waters far heaving in limitless twilight
Auroral pulsations thrilled faintly, and, striking the blank heaving surface,
The measureless speed of their motion now leaped into light on the waters.

(Blind 1899, 7)

Most poets preferred to remain fairly vague on the subject, stressing more what one might call the metaphysical aspects of life's beginnings rather than the actual messy details. In his poem with the provocative title "Genesis," Augustus Charles Swinburne is explicit in wanting a natural origin of life as opposed to the God-driven origin of Christianity—the work "a curious combination of Romantic pantheism and Positivistic agnosticism" (Roppen 1956, 181)—two strands (German and French) of the idea of Progress. His story is put in direct contrast to the creation story of the Old Testament.

In the outer world that was before this earth,
    That was before all shape or space was born,
Before the blind first hour of time had birth,
    Before night knew the moonlight or the morn;
Yea, before any world had any light,
    Or anything called God or man drew breath,
Slowly the strong sides of the heaving night
    Moved, and brought forth the strength of life and death.
And the sad shapeless horror increate
    That was all things and one thing, without fruit,
Limit, or law; where love was none, nor hate,
    Where no leaf came to blossom from no root;
The very darkness that time knew not of,
    Nor God laid hand on, nor was man found there,
Ceased, and was cloven in several shapes; above
    Light, and night under, and fire, earth, water, and air.

---

[5] That Darwin never speculated publicly on the origin of life, and that this is true even of (unpublished) early versions of the theory of the *Origin*, whereas everyone else thought such speculations came with the territory, suggests that Darwin was being very cautious, almost certainly because he hoped to elevate evolutionary thought in one step from the pseudoscience level to the professional-science level. People like Huxley, having no such ambitions and happy to stay more at the popular-science level, felt free to hypothesize.

The physical world came into being without God's help, before God indeed. And it seems that God is equally absent when life starts up and gains ground—gains ground, that is, in a way redolent of Darwinian processes.

> Then between shadow and substance, night and light,
>   Then between birth and death, and deeds and days,
> The illimitable embrace and the amorous fight
>   That of itself begets, bears, rears, and slays,
> The immortal war of mortal things that is
>   Labour and life and growth and good and ill,
> The mild antiphonies that melt and kiss,
>   The violent symphonies that meet and kill,
> All nature of all things began to be.
>   But chiefliest in the spirit (beast or man,
> Planet of heaven or blossom of earth or sea)
>   The divine contraries of life began.

And this all leads to change and growth—in a Spencerian fashion homogeneity leading to heterogeneity—although the poet does not want to leave the impression that we are going toward a happy conclusion—as presumably in the Christian story. Life is and always will be a mixture of the happy and the sad, the sweet and the bitter.

> For if death were not, then should growth not be,
>   Change, nor the life of good nor evil things;
> Nor were there night at all nor light to see,
>   Nor water of sweet nor water of bitter springs.
>   (Swinburne 1904, 2, 117–118)

Life's History

I don't think one should necessarily look for heavy-duty meaning in everything that is written, not even everything that is written by Thomas Hardy! Sometimes one is just using Darwinism (broadly construed) as background, although of course everything adds to the overall picture. And the very fact that no meaning is put in may be indicative of the author's belief that there is no meaning. Take next the actual course of life from the earliest beginnings up to the present. For one who worked for the first decade and more of his scientific career as a geologist, Charles Darwin was always curiously uninterested in the actual paths of evolution—phylogenies. Of course, he had some ideas on the subject, particularly on the evolution of barnacles. Later he speculated, correctly, that humans came out of Africa not Asia. But the *Origin* carries no picture or table of life's history—nor does the *Descent*—even though, as shown in Richard Owen's little popular book on paleontology, people had a pretty good idea of the main outlines (Owen 1860). The only diagram in the *Origin* is a very stylized and entirely theoretical tree of life, intended more to show the principle of divergence than to show the paths of evolution. But, of course, there had to be a representative tree of life, and lots of people were eager to show it and fill it in—indeed, generally uninterested in causes, it became the primary obsession of professional scientists in the decades after the *Origin*.

Hardy was sensitive to this, using the history both as background and as a vehicle ingeniously to put a familiar conviction—surely mythological—into a modern context. He picked up on the popular belief that when one is drowning or otherwise facing imminent death the whole of one's life flashes before one, like a movie in fast motion. In one of his early novels, *A Pair of Blue Eyes* (1873), the hero on a cliff edge has slipped and is clinging on, contemplating the end. Then suddenly in the cliff he sees a fossilized trilobite and this triggers the stream of consciousness, not of the hero's life but of life in general.

> Time closed up like a fan before him. He saw himself at one extremity of the years, face to face with the beginning and all the intermediate centuries simultaneously. Fierce men, clothed in the hides of beasts, and carrying, for defence and attack, huge clubs and pointed spears, rose from the rock, like the phantoms before the doomed Macbeth. They lived in hollows, woods, and mud huts—perhaps in caves of the neighbouring rocks. Behind them stood an earlier band. No man was there. Huge elephantine forms, the mastodon, the hippopotamus, the tapir, antelopes of monstrous size, the megatherium, and the myledon—all, for the moment, in juxtaposition. Further back, and overlapped by these, were perched huge-billed birds and swinish creatures as large as horses. Still more shadowy were the sinister crocodilian outlines—alligators and other uncouth shapes, culminating in the colossal lizard, the iguanodon. Folded behind were dragon forms and clouds of flying reptiles: still underneath were fishy beings of lower development; and so on, till the lifetime scenes of the fossil confronting him were a present and modern condition of things. These images passed before Knight's inner eye in less than half a minute, and he was again considering the actual present. Was he to die? (143)[6]

---

[6] It is highly probable that Hardy got his description of life's history from the sixth edition of Gideon Mantell's *The Wonders of Geology*, published in 1848, a copy of which was given to Hardy in 1858 and that he kept all his life. There are significant overlaps of themes and language, including shared phrases like "dragon forms" (Buckland 2008). In the *Origin*, Darwin simply drew on this kind

Fortunately his enterprising girlfriend tears up her underwear and fashions a rope and he is saved. One suspects that, given today's fashions, he might have been less fortunate. The reader will be happy to learn that eventually Hardy does not disappoint, because before the end the girlfriend marries the wrong chap and she dies (apparently from a miscarriage). Which seems, albeit somewhat callously, an appropriate point to pass on to our next topic.

of knowledge, of which Mantell was giving a popular exposition, and gave it an evolutionary interpretation. Hardy's text does not make explicit reference to descent, but by the time he was writing in the early 1870s, everyone would have taken the history in an evolutionary context.

7

Humans

Two Visions

"So God created man in his *own* image, in the image of God created he him; male and female created he them" (Genesis 1:27). God didn't have to create humans. He didn't have to do anything. He didn't have to make humans special. But he did, to the extent that He was prepared to die in agony on the Cross for our salvation. Darwin didn't have to write about humans, but he did. He didn't have to give us special status, but he did to the extent that he wrote a whole book about us. Here is where the Christian-Darwin contrast is so interesting and provocative. In one sense, they could not be more different. A miraculous creation of God's favorite against a naturalistic origin of one more species. In another sense, they could not be more similar. A story about one species, humankind. Or at least, so it seems, for as always the full truth is a little more complex.

How or why did Darwin think we are special? Obviously in one way because of the role of sexual selection, but we can put this on one side for a moment. We will return to it. For the moment, focus just on the fact that selection of one sort or another was crucial in our making. The point for Darwin, however, is that we weren't just made. We won. Darwin does not believe in some natural, Lamarckian-type of necessary progression up from blobs to humans, from monad to man as everyone said. But he does think we have the biggest onboard computers, that this makes us superior, and that getting big brains was something predictable given selection. "If we look at the differentiation and specialisation of the several organs of each being when adult (and this will include the advancement of the brain for intellectual purposes) as the best standard of highness of organisation, natural selection clearly leads towards highness . . ." (Darwin 1861, 134).

How did the poets and novelists deal with humans and their status? As always, there is a range. But even for those prepared to allow that there may be a God in some sense and that he might have a plan, there is an undercurrent of fear—perhaps melancholy—that evolution shows we humans might not have the status we once thought. Mark Twain made a joke out of things.

> Man has been here 32,000 years. That it took a hundred million years to prepare the world for him is proof that that is what it was done for. I suppose it is. I dunno. If the Eiffel tower were now representing the world's age, the skin of paint on the pinnacle-knob at its summit would represent man's share of that age; and anybody would perceive that that skin was what the tower was built for. I reckon they would, I dunno. (Twain [1903] 2004, 221)

Hardy, almost inevitably, saw that so-called lower forms of life are in respects more knowledgeable than we humans. A daddy longlegs (a spider), a moth, and a dumbledore (a bumble bee) fly in at night, while the author is writing. A fly is already on the page.

> Thus meet we five, in this still place,
> At this point of time, at this point in space.
> —My guests besmear my new-penned line,
> Or bang at the lamp and fall supine.
> "God's humblest, they!" I muse. Yet why?
> They know Earth-secrets that know not I.
> (Hardy 1994, 130–131, written about 1899)

Emily Dickinson has more metaphysical take on the issue.

> It's easy to invent a Life—
> God does it—every Day—
> Creation—but the Gambol
> Of His Authority—
>
> It's easy to efface it—
> The thrifty Deity
> Could scarce afford Eternity
> To Spontaneity—
>
> The Perished Patterns murmur—
> But His Perturbless Plan
> Proceed—inserting Here—a Sun—
> There—leaving out a Man—
> (Dickinson 1960, 355, written about 1863)

We may be important, but we are not that important!

Stone Age Fighting

Let us go at the topic systematically. There are lots of tales about our past and the bloody battles our ancestors fought. Often the action counts a lot more than the scientific accuracy. Typical is *Zit and Xoe* (1886) by Henry Curwen. Taking to the extreme the suppositions of people like Huxley that evolution can go in one-step jumps ("saltations") from one kind to another, the story is about two proto-humans who leapt from ape-form to human-form in one generation.

> "Wretched little beast!" cried my mother, as she angrily twisted her tail round the stoutest branch she could find, and swung herself up into a bushy banian-tree.
>
> I stood below weeping bitterly — stood, I say, because I could do nothing else: I had never been able to walk on all-fours like the others. I could not dart from tree to tree, from branch to branch, like the very smallest of my brothers and sisters.
>
> In these few words I have described the loneliness and desolation of my childhood. I was alas! tailless and hairless! I could not even chatter!

If his mother felt this way, you can imagine the shame his father felt. Fortunately, Zit (boy) meets Xoe (girl) and nature takes its course starting a new generation of human-like beings. Not, expectedly, without fights for survival.

> The shore was lined with hideous monstrous forms right down to the water's edge. But they could not pass beyond it. We were safe now, and, under the spell of some dreadful fascination, I turned to watch the terrible drama being played out before us.
>
> The Beasts had dared to declare war against Man, and were now venting their disappointed fury on each other; I could see in the distance the hatchets and spears I had so prized wielded madly and fiercely by scores of bony hands. I could hear the cries of the great beasts, as with bleeding flanks they learned for the first time what real pain was. Unsightly forms I knew of old leapt in and out of the seething crowd with such prodigious rapidity that they seemed well-nigh innumerable. Then with maddening roars each beast turned on the monstrous creature nearest, and began a combat of life and death.

There is a message here that Zit and Xoe are able to read. We humans need to cooperate or we too will go the way of the Beasts.

A little more realistic is Wells's little tale *A Story of the Stone Age,* about such conflict within the species. Uya, the leader of the pack, has got his eyes on Ugh-lomi and his girlfriend. "There was no hunting so sweet to these ancient men as the hunting of men. Once the fierce passion of the chase was lit, the feeble beginnings of humanity in them were thrown to the winds. And Uya in the night had marked Ugh-lomi with the death word. Ugh-lomi was the day's quarry, the appointed feast" (Wells [1897] 1938, 651–652). However, things don't turn out too well for the older man.

> And the third day Ugh-lomi came back, up the river. The plumes of
> a raven were in his hair. The first axe was red-stained, and had long
> dark hairs upon it, and he carried the necklace that had marked the
> favourite of Uya in his hand. He walked in the soft places, giving
> no heed to his trail. Save a raw cut below his jaw there was not a
> wound upon him. "Uya!" cried Ugh-lomi exultant, and Eudena saw
> it was well. He put the necklace on Eudena, and they ate and drank
> together. (658)

The reader is assured that Ugh-lomi and Eudena do their Darwinian duty. "And Eudena sat red in the light of the fire, gloating on him, her face flushed and her eyes shining, and the necklace Uya had made about her neck. It was a splendid time, and the stars that look down on us looked down on her, our ancestor— who has been dead now these fifty thousand years" (658).

Conan Doyle in *The Lost World* (1912) is more into interspecific conflict. It is the native humans on the plateau (the Accala) versus the ape men (the Doda). It is true that the Europeans help out, but basically it is the Accala who prove their evolutionary worth.

> Then in a moment came the panic and the collapse. Screaming and
> howling, the great creatures rushed away in all directions through the
> brushwood, while our allies yelled in their savage delight, following
> swiftly after their flying enemies. All the feuds of countless generations,
> all the hatreds and cruelties of their narrow history, all the memories of
> ill-usage and persecution were to be purged that day. At last man was
> to be supreme and the man-beast to find forever his allotted place. Fly
> as they would the fugitives were too slow to escape from the active sav-
> ages, and from every side in the tangled woods we heard the exultant
> yells, the twanging of bows, and the crash and thud as ape-men were
> brought down from their hiding-places in the trees. (Conan Doyle
> [1912] 1995, 159)

Progress to Humans?

What about putting together the parts of the picture? Do we end up with a progressive picture up to humankind as supposed by Darwin? Obviously Hardy thinks we have something like that, although he is very careful not to read any values into the process. It happened. Whether it was a good thing that it happened or whether we humans are top are questions unanswered, or at least they are in his early novel, for as we shall see, he did later have thoughts on the subject. Winwood Reade, however, for all that he thought the process terribly cruel, seems to have assumed without question that the process was progressive, upward to humankind.

> Monstrous reptiles and ungainly quadrupeds inhabited the primeval marshes of the earth; and at night the croaking of enormous frogs rose like thunder in the air. But as time flowed on the face of the earth assumed a more gentle and benignant expression; flowers blossomed in the forest, and the voices of singing birds were heard; the quadrupeds became less gigantic in size, but more graceful and varied in their forms; and finally Men appeared upon the scene, roaming in herds through the forest, clambering the trees, jabbering semi-articulate sounds. But, as language formed upon their lips, the erect posture was assumed, the fore-foot was used as a hand, weapons were invented, fire was discovered, caverns in the rock, burrows in the ground, and platforms on the trees were exchanged for huts surrounded by gardens. (Reade [1875] 2012, 15–16)

And then the evaluation, with the mandatory dig against God and his angels: "We suppose that the moral purpose of this drama is to teach the doctrine of Improvement, and to illustrate that tendency to Progress which pervades the universe." Continuing: "The evolution of mind from matter, by means of natural law, shows the innate power of that tendency or force, and the efforts by which Man achieves his own comparative perfection are no doubt intended as a protest against that habit of quiescence and content which is perhaps the natural failing of Immortals" (16–17).

In poetry too we get the upward rise and evolution of humans and their brains. A lot less portentous than Reade is this comical poem by Constance Naden (1858–1889), "Solomon Redivivus" (1886). King Solomon is talking to the Queen of Sheba and he is going to tell her a story from Darwin.

> We were a soft Amœba
> In ages past and gone,
> Ere you were Queen Of Sheba,
> And I King Solomon.

Unorganed, undivided,
We lived in happy sloth,
And all that you did I did,
One dinner nourished both:

Till you incurred the odium
Of fission and divorce—
A severed pseudopodium
You strayed your lonely course.

Evolution kept going:

Long ages passed—our wishes
Were fetterless and free,
For we were jolly fishes,
A-swimming in the sea.

We roamed by groves of coral,
We watched the youngsters play—
The memory and the moral
Had vanished quite away.

Next, each became a reptile,
With fangs to sting and slay;
No wiser ever crept, I'll
Assert, deny who may.

But now, disdaining trammels
Of scale and limbless coil,
Through every grade of mammals
We passed with upward toil.

Finally, we get to the top of the heap:

Till, anthropoid and wary
Appeared the parent ape,
And soon we grew less hairy,
And soon began to drape.

So, from that soft Amœba,
In ages past and gone,
You've grown the Queen of Sheba,
And I King Solomon.

Not, one might add, that the life of King Solomon is quite everything it is made out to be. Supposedly he was the wisest man who ever lived, but think of all those wives he had. Jim, the runaway slave in *Huckleberry Finn*, has a few words on this subject:

> Mos' likely dey has rackety times in de nussery. En I reck'n de wives quarrels considable; en dat 'crease de racket. Yit dey say Sollermun de wises' man dat ever live'. I doan' take no stock in dat. Bekase why: would a wise man want to live in de mids' er sich a blim-blammin' all de time? No—'deed he wouldn't. (Twain [1884] 1985, 85)

Perhaps it was to be expected that seriousness predominated in the verse of the German-born poet Mathilde Blind. She wrote a whole epic on what she called "The Ascent of Man." She knows all about the struggle:

> And lo, 'mid reeking swarms of earth
> Grim struggling in the primal wood,
> A new strange creature hath its birth:
> Wild—stammering—nameless—shameless—nude;
> Spurred on by want, held in by fear,
> He hides his head in caverns drear.
>
> Most unprotected of earth's kin,
> His fight for life that seems so vain
> Sharpens his senses, till within
> The twilight mazes of his brain,
> Like embryos within the womb,
> Thought pushes feelers through the gloom.
> And slowly in the fateful race
> It grows unconscious, till at length
> The helpless savage dares to face
> The cave-bear in his grisly strength;
> For stronger than its bulky thews
> He feels a force that grows with use.
>
> From age to dumb unnumbered age,
> By dim gradations long and slow,
> He reaches on from stage to stage,
> Through fear and famine, weal and woe

> And, compassed round with danger, still
> Prolongs his life by craft and skill.
>
> (Blind 1899, 14–15)

Much given to revolutionary causes, Blind worried about the innate brutality in humankind, but at the end, as shown by some kind of veiled guide, a kind of world-spirit seems to overcome all through love.

> And beside me in the golden morning
>   I beheld my shrouded phantom-guide;
> But no longer sorrow-veiled and mourning—
>   It became transfigured by my side.
> And I knew—as one escaped from prison
>   Sees old things again with fresh surprise—
> It was Love himself, Love re-arisen
>   With the Eternal shining though his eyes.
>
> (101–102)

Of course—recognizing that in the most important sense we are all now in a Darwinian world—the trouble with so much of this is seeing how Darwinian (in the sense of utilizing Darwin's mechanisms) it truly is and if Darwinian, how firmly (biological) progress can be extracted from the tale. Constance Naden certainly knew a lot about Darwin's ideas and was an astute reader (Beer 2000). But here she seems just to be having fun. Reade certainly seems Darwinian, if not in the passages just quoted then certainly in the earlier passages quoted to show how he used the Darwinian process against a good God. But he certainly takes it for granted that we are going to win in the struggle for existence and that we humans are superior to other organisms, and not just because we won—we are on the side of the "graceful" rather than the "monstrous" and "ungainly." But as people like Huxley kept pointing out, often we won because we were nastier than our opponents, not because we were nicer. It was something that Mathilde Blind wrestled with too. And her solution seems to have involved some sort of spirit force sorting it all out. Even before she gets there, the processes seem not terribly Darwinian—"He feels a force that grows with use"—being more Lamarckian or quite possibly Spencerian (which in many respects means the same thing). Spencer is big on the struggle. It is just that for him, rather than the struggle wiping out some and the others then succeeding because of nondirected variations, the struggle brings on useful features that are then passed on by Lamarckian means, whatever they might be. Of course, none of this denies that people are using evolution to provide an alternative to the Christian story, nor that others might be truer to Darwin's mechanisms and come to other conclusions.

Moving to a Darwinian Position

You can run from Darwinism, meaning pure natural selection, but what if you start to embrace it? The poet William Canton, in "Through the Ages: A Legend of a Stone Axe" (written in 1879), starts to push us in that direction. In three parts, the first tells of a Stone Age man, threatened by a saber-toothed tiger, who has an axe to defend himself. His daughter is looking on.

> With his blue eyes agleam, and
>   His wild russet hair
> Streaming back, the man travails,
>   Unwarned, unaware
> Of the lithe shape that crouches, the green eyes
>   that glare.
>
> And now, hark ! as he drives with
>   A last mighty swing
> The stone blade of the axe through
>   The oak's central ring.
> From the blanched lips what screams of wild agony
>   spring ! —
>
> There's a rush through the fern-fronds —
>   A yell of affright —
> And the savage and sabre-tooth
>   Close in fierce fight: —
> And the red sunset smoulders and blackens to night.
>
> On the swamp in the forest
>   One clear star is shown.
> And the reeds fill the night with
>   A long troubled moan —
> And the girl sits and sobs in the darkness, alone!

(Canton 1927, 51–52)

She is sad but safe. What has happened to father? Surely with the axe, a product of a thinking intelligence, he has outfought the tiger. We have to wait to learn his fate. The second part tells of the draining of the fens, under which the axe was long deposited. Then the third part introduces us to a professor and a class of girls, and in one of the display cases of the classroom lies the axe. One of the girls dreams of long ago:

> But for Phemie, through the trees in
> Her dream forest, fact and reason
> Blend with fancy, and her vision grows complete and clear
> and dread:
>
> By the swamp in the forest
>   The sylvan girl sings,
>   As his flint-headed hatchet
>   The wild woodman swings:
> But the hatchet cleaves fast in the trunk he has
>   riven, —
> The man stands unarmed as the sabre-tooth
>   springs !
>
>   (57–58)

It seems that our Stone Age man met his end. His intelligence, his tool-making skills, came to naught. Not much thought of progress here. As a race, we did survive, but the implication is that it was as much by chance as by design. We should not confuse being on the top of the evolutionary tree, because that is where today's organisms are found, with being on the top of the tree, because the tree was striving to get to that point.

Tess of the D'Urbervilles

Expectedly it is Thomas Hardy who pushes this insight to the extreme. We are just animals like the rest; part of the earth from which we came; part of the earth to which we will return. In a very non-Christian sort of way, the world was not made for us. Indeed, Hardy (writing in a notebook in 1889) worried that evolution might have made humans misfits in some sense.

> A woeful fact, that the human race is too extremely developed for its corporeal conditions, the nerves being evolved to an activity abnormal in such an environment. Even the higher animals are in excess in this

respect. It may be questioned if Nature, or what we call Nature, so far back as when she crossed the line from invertebrates to vertebrates, did not exceed her mission. This planet does not supply the material for happiness to higher existences — other planets may, although one can hardly see how. (Stevenson 1932, 266)

All these sentiments about the status of humans and the indifference of nature get expressed most powerfully in Hardy's novels, above all *Tess of the D'Urbervilles*.[1] The story is well-known. The Durbeyfields, a large and rather poor family headed by an inadequate father, learn that they are the descendants of a once-powerful family, the D'Urbervilles. Their daughter Tess is packed off to sidle up to what is (mistakenly) thought to be a remnant of the family. She gets seduced, probably raped, by the son Alec. Returning home she has a baby who dies and then she goes off to work at a dairy farm. There she meets Angel Clare—she had seen him briefly at the beginning before she went to the D'Urbervilles. Training to be a farmer, he is an idealistic young man of higher social class than she. He falls in love with her and, despite her guilt about her past, Tess finally marries him. She had thought she had confessed in a note written to him before the ceremony, but it turns out that he had not seen it and when on the wedding night she tells all he turns from her. She goes home and then to another farm, while Angel goes off to Brazil. Alec comes back into the story and finally Tess goes with him to be his mistress. Angel returns, Tess stabs and kills Alec, Angel and Tess run off for a night or two of passion before she is captured at Stonehenge. She is condemned and hanged and Angel goes off with her younger sister.[2]

There are different aspects to this story and I shall return to some later. Here I want to stress two things. First, Tess is a remarkable human being. She is stunningly beautiful in a voluptuous sort of way—she is Sophia Loren rather than Audrey Hepburn. "She had an attribute which amounted to a disadvantage just now; and it was this that caused Alec d'Urberville's eyes to rivet themselves upon her. It was a luxuriance of aspect, a fulness of growth, which made her appear more of a woman than she really was" (Hardy [1892] 2010, 45). She is the kind of woman whose loveliness comes through most strongly not when she made up

---

[1] In *The Great Tradition*, F. R. Leavis dismissed Hardy's claims to be included, quoting Henry James's patronizing assessment in a letter to Robert Louis Stevenson: "The good little Thomas Hardy has scored a great success with *Tess of the D'Urbervilles*, which is chock-full of faults and falsity, and yet has a singular charm." James may have been right about Eliot and Darwin but "singular charm" is just about the last predicate one would apply to *Tess*. Better, the "greatest work" of "the greatest artist of the Darwinian crisis" (Robinson 1980, 149).

[2] Hardy forbears to mention what his readers would have known. The law would have forbidden marriage between Angel and the sister of a dead wife.

and prepared but when she is caught unawares unexpectedly. "Her great natural beauty was, if not heightened, rendered more obvious by her attire. She was loosely wrapped in a cashmere dressing-gown of gray-white, embroidered in half-mourning tints, and she wore slippers of the same hue. Her neck rose out of a frill of down, and her well-remembered cable of dark-brown hair was partially coiled up in a mass at the back of her head and partly hanging on her shoulder— the evident result of haste" (447–448). There is something deeply earthy, pagan about her—a point made with perhaps somewhat heavy-handed symbolism by the name of her Norman ancestor, Sir Pagan d'Urberville.

Second, there is a moral purity about Tess, as is stressed by the subtitle to the work, *A Pure Woman*. When Angel has rejected her because of her past, the narrator says:

> With all his attempted independence of judgement this advanced and well-meaning young man, a sample product of the last five-and-twenty years, was yet the slave to custom and conventionality when surprised back into his early teachings. No prophet had told him, and he was not prophet enough to tell himself, that essentially this young wife of his was as deserving of the praise of King Lemuel as any other woman endowed with the same dislike of evil, her moral value having to be reckoned not by achievement but by tendency. (316)

For all her earthiness, at times there is something ethereal about Tess. "Whilst all the landscape was in neutral shade his companion's face, which was the focus of his eyes, rising above the mist stratum, seemed to have a sort of phosphorescence upon it. She looked ghostly, as if she were merely a soul at large . . . . It was then, as has been said, that she impressed him most deeply. She was no longer the milkmaid, but a visionary essence of woman—a whole sex condensed into one typical form" (155).

Yet how can there be a God, how can humans be his favored, if such an innocent—such a sinless innocent—is plunged into such torment? Part of it is nature, pure chance. Why did Tess meet Alec before she met Angel, or rather— since there was the brief encounter at the beginning—why did Tess and Angel not talk and get to know each other before Alec arrived on the scene? She goes rather to the D'Urbervilles and there the trouble starts.

> In the ill-judged execution of the well-judged plan of things the call seldom produces the comer, the man to love rarely coincides with the hour for loving. Nature does not often say "See!" to her poor creature at a time when seeing can lead to happy doing; or reply "Here!" to a body's cry of "Where?" till the hide-and-seek has become an irksome, outworn game. We may wonder whether at the acme and summit of

the human progress these anachronisms will be corrected by a finer intuition, a closer interaction of the social machinery than that which now jolts us round and along; but such completeness is not to be prophesied, or even conceived as possible. Enough that in the present case, as in millions, it was not the two halves of a perfect whole that confronted each other at the perfect moment; a missing counterpart wandered independently about the earth waiting in crass obtuseness till the late time came. Out of which maladroit delay sprang anxieties, disappointments, shocks, catastrophes, and passing-strange destinies. (46)

And then, why does she meet men—both Alec and Angel—who treat her so badly? "Why it was that upon this beautiful feminine tissue, sensitive as gossamer, and practically blank as snow as yet, there should have been traced such a coarse pattern as it was doomed to receive; why so often the coarse appropriates the finer thus, the wrong man the woman, the wrong woman the man, many thousand years of analytical philosophy have failed to explain to our sense of order" (86). Is she being punished for the sins of the fathers? Are Tess's misfortunes retribution for the appalling behavior of past D'Urbervilles?[3] Notice the jab at Christianity—ecumenical when it comes to handing out punishment, whether merited or not—which is reinforced when Tess—newly violated—meets a preacher. He is working for "the glory of God," writing on walls: "THY, DAMNATION, SLUMBERETH, NOT. 2 PET. II. 3."

> "Do you believe what you paint?" she asked in low tones.
> "Believe that text? Do I believe in my own existence!"
> "But," said she tremulously, "suppose your sin was not of your own seeking?"
> He shook his head.
> "I cannot split hairs on that burning query," he said. (96–97)

This is just a world of blind fate, without meaning, and we humans have no special status (Morton 1984). Toward the end, alone in the woods, Tess hears pheasants crying in pain, having been shot the previous day and now sinking from loss of blood. She kills them from kindness. "With the impulse of a soul who could feel for kindred sufferers as much as for herself, Tess's first thought was to put the still living birds out of their torture, and to this end with her own hands she broke the necks of as many as she could find, leaving them to lie where she had found them till the game-keepers should come—as they probably would

---

[3] As we shall see later, the attack on Tess's purity comes from within, a function of her heritage, as well as from without, the misfortunes she encounters.

come—to look for them a second time" (332). Her own end is too similar to be chance. She is caught at that shrine to paganism, Stonehenge. "It is as it should be," she murmured. "Angel, I am almost glad—yes, glad! This happiness could not have lasted. It was too much. I have had enough; and now I shall not live for you to despise me!" (469). The hangman's rope is a kindness.

> Upon the cornice of the tower a tall staff was fixed. Their eyes were riveted on it. A few minutes after the hour had struck something moved slowly up the staff, and extended itself upon the breeze. It was a black flag.
> "Justice" was done, and the President of the Immortals, in Aeschylean phrase, had ended his sport with Tess. (471–472)

There is more to be said later about this remarkable novel. We are in a world of chance, of fate, where humans—no matter their stunning beauty, their moral purity—count for naught. They came from the earth, they return to the earth. It is a world opened to us by Darwin although whether he realized fully what he had done is another question.[4]

---

[4] The reference to the President of the Immortals suggests that Hardy is moving to thoughts about an underlying—blind, indifferent, possibly malignant—life force or will.

8

Race and Class

Christianity

There are differences between human beings. Sex will get a chapter to itself. The focus here is on race and class. Christianity has significant things to say about both of these topics. So does Darwinism. Christianity—as based on both the Old Testament and the New—endorses concepts of race and of class and suggests that the differences can be significant. Whether or not you think that Adam and Eve were the unique first pair—there were pre-Adamite hypotheses around from at least the seventeenth century (Livingstone 2008)—the Old Testament particularly assumes that there are different groupings and that they are sufficiently different (whether biological or not) that some people would be specially favored by God and others not. The Israelites are the chosen people; the Egyptians, the Amalekites, the Edomites, the Canaanites, the Syrians (Arameans), the Moabites, the Ammonites, the Midianites, the Philistines, the Assyrians, the Greeks, and the Romans were not. These assumptions of difference were obviously important when in the Christian era biblical help was sought in making sense of the diverse nature of humankind. There was the mark on Cain, there was the story of Noah after the Flood—the curse on Ham (actually on his son Canaan) and his descendants was thought very helpful because it not only explained the darker-skinned races but also why they are inferior—and the Tower of Babel with the consequent different languages was also brought into play. Almost paradoxically when you think of it, the bible was also used to paint the Jews themselves as inferior. The Gospel of John came to the fore here, with the condemnation of the Jews for ignoring the Messiah and being the cause of his death. Thus: "After this Jesus went about in Galilee. He would not go about in Judea, because the Jews were seeking to kill him" (John 7:1).

Of course these things were never quite that straightforward. The Story of Ruth, one of most beautiful and moving tales in scripture, tells of a Moabite woman who shows great devotion to her mother-in-law, Naomi. She ends up married to Boaz and the great-grandmother of David as well as (according to

Matthew) an ancestor of Jesus. In the New Testament, one of the most important of the parables is that of the Good Samaritan, who is portrayed as a far better person than the Jews who passed by the suffering man. Jesus himself is willing to cure the child of a Roman, and most important, Paul explicitly reaches out to the Gentiles with the good news of the messiah. In short there is lots of grist for the mill and the same is true or even truer of class, particularly as it extends to servitude and to slavery. That people are of different classes is taken as a given—as indeed is slavery—and often these are phenomena that are at least accepted if not endorsed. Abraham's covenant with God does not mean freeing up all of the servants and slaves.

> Now Sarai, Abram's wife, bore him no children. She had an Egyptian slave-girl whose name was Hagar, and Sarai said to Abram, "You see that the Lord has prevented me from bearing children; go in to my slave-girl; it may be that I shall obtain children by her." And Abram listened to the voice of Sarai. So, after Abram had lived ten years in the land of Canaan, Sarai, Abram's wife, took Hagar the Egyptian, her slave-girl, and gave her to her husband Abram as a wife. (Genesis 16:1–3)

This all sounds like a Southern plantation before the Civil War, a fact that did not go unnoted or unappreciated. The New Testament is not a lot better. The story of the runaway slave, who goes to St. Paul, as well as the apostle's general thinking on the subject, was likewise cherished by those seeking biblical evidence for their beliefs. "Slaves, obey your earthly masters in everything; and do it, not only when their eye is on you and to curry their favor, but with sincerity of heart and reverence for the Lord" (Colossians 3:22). Again, though, these things are never completely clean cut. Certainly, the abolitionists had little trouble finding support for their position—remember, the evangelicals who take the word of the bible as foundational were those leading the charge against slavery. The Sermon on the Mount is tilted toward those disadvantaged, and the whole of Jesus's own life was spent among the humble and oppressed. He was not a big friend of the rich and powerful. Part of the problem facing someone like Paul was that his message did appeal to slaves and he had to tread carefully not to upset the social order because of this.

Darwinism

It is important to stress these ambiguities in the Christian position, because they are echoed in Darwinism and in the literary responses and interpretations. Although in Britain we were now at the time when the Empire was hitting

its peak and in America when the battle against slavery was over but the fight
for racial equality had hardly begun, many of the tools of understanding were
formed long before. With Darwin himself, two things before all else. He came
from a family absolutely and completely dedicated to the abolition of slavery.
This above all was the moral and social cause binding and driving the Darwin-
Wedgwood family (Desmond and Moore 2009). The older generation felt that
way and so did Charles and his contemporaries—something grounded particularly in the influence of his older sisters. Second, the experience of the Tierra del
Fuegians shocked and upset him perhaps more than anything in his whole life.
He had never dreamed of "savages" like these.

> At a subsequent period the Beagle anchored for a couple of days under
> Wollaston Island, which is a short way to the northward. While going
> on shore we pulled alongside a canoe with six Fuegians. These were the
> most abject and miserable creatures I any where beheld. . . . [T]hese
> Fuegians in the canoe were quite naked, and even one full-grown
> woman was absolutely so. It was raining heavily, and the fresh water,
> together with the spray, trickled down her body. In another harbour
> not far distant, a woman, who was suckling a recently-born child, came
> one day alongside the vessel, and remained there whilst the sleet fell
> and thawed on her naked bosom, and on the skin of her naked child.
> These poor wretches were stunted in their growth, their hideous faces
> bedaubed with white paint, their skins filthy and greasy, their hair en-
> tangled, their voices discordant, their gestures violent and without
> dignity. Viewing such men, one can hardly make oneself believe they
> are fellow-creatures, and inhabitants of the same world. (Darwin 1839,
> 234–235)

These twin influences—together no doubt with the views of people like Cuvier
who were convinced of the reality of the divisions—stand behind Darwin's
discussions of race, especially in the *Descent*. All humans are one stock, and yet
there are massive differences within the species. And obviously, we Europeans
have come out on top.

> There is, however, no doubt that the various races, when carefully com-
> pared and measured, differ much from each other,—as in the texture of
> the hair, the relative proportions of all parts of the body, the capacity of
> the lungs, the form and capacity of the skull, and even in the convolu-
> tions of the brain. But it would be an endless task to specify the nu-
> merous points of structural difference. The races differ also in constitu-
> tion, in acclimatisation, and in liability to certain diseases. Their mental

characteristics are likewise very distinct; chiefly as it would appear in their emotional, but partly in their intellectual, faculties. (Darwin 1871, 1, 16)

This is not to say that they are different species. "The inferior vitality of mulattoes is spoken of in a trustworthy work as a well-known phenomenon; but this is a different consideration from their lessened fertility; and can hardly be advanced as a proof of the specific distinctness of the parent races" (1, 221).

Of course, the civilized peoples are going to triumph over those less so—"The grade of civilisation seems a most important element in the success of nations which come in competition" (1, 239)—although interestingly Darwin seems to have thought that disease would do a lot rather than sheer brute force. He obviously had in mind the ways in which so many native peoples succumbed to Western illnesses. All this said, however, Darwin was not convinced that either Lamarckian factors or natural selective factors could account for all of the differences between races. While he clearly thought that intelligence and those sorts of things mattered—"The belief that there exists in man some close relation between the size of the brain and the development of the intellectual faculties is supported by the comparison of the skulls of savage and civilised races, of ancient and modern people, and by the analogy of the whole vertebrate series" (1, 145–146)—Darwin just didn't see the sorts of physical factors separating races as having had much to do with natural selection or the inheritance of acquired characteristics (a mechanism that he always accepted). Something like skin color doesn't seem explicable this way. Black, white, in between, something else, it just doesn't matter. Here as we know is where he brought in sexual selection to do the job—something we shall discuss in detail in a later chapter.

What about class? Charles Darwin was very solidly upper middle class. He appreciated servants and was respected, even loved, by them. He was more than willing to give a helping hand to someone less fortunate than himself. Remember how, in gratitude for the supportive work that he had done on mimicry, Darwin arranged that the lower-middle-class Henry Walter Bates should get a good job as secretary to the Royal Geographical Society. But he had no inherent troubles with the class system and tied it into his biology.

In all civilised countries man accumulates property and bequeaths it to his children. So that the children in the same country do not by any means start fair in the race for success. But this is far from an unmixed evil; for without the accumulation of capital the arts could not progress; and it is chiefly through their power that the civilised races have extended, and are now everywhere extending, their range, so as to take the place of the lower races. (1, 169)

It is remarkable the extent to which people were able simultaneously to argue for the abolition of slavery and for unfettered *laissez faire* in their own factories. The Darwin-Wedgwood family had little time for unions. Writing to a German correspondent in 1872, Darwin said: "I much wish that you would sometimes take occasion to discuss an allied point, if it holds good on the continent,— namely the rule insisted on by all our Trades-Unions, that all workmen,—the good and bad, the strong and weak,—sh[oul]d all work for the same number of hours and receive the same wages." Adding: "I fear that Cooperative Societies, which many look at as the main hope for the future, likewise exclude competition. This seems to me a great evil for the future progress of mankind" (Darwin 1985–, 20, 324). To the end, Darwin was a Whig, more sympathetic to the manufacturing class of which he was a beneficiary than to other segments of society. He was as much John Thornton as Roger Hamley.

Novelists on Race

H. Rider Haggard (1856–1925), author of some of the most stirring adventure stories ever penned, was sufficiently well informed about science that in his stories he could make informed jokes about sexual and natural selection, and use the name of Darwin as he did so—"Women hated the sight of me. Only a week before I had heard one call me a 'monster' when she thought I was out of hearing, and say that I had converted her to Darwin's theory" (Haggard [1886] 1991, 17).[1] As a young man Haggard spent time in Africa and his work reflects both the location and the racial attitudes. In *King Solomon's Mines*, one of the white characters gets emotionally entangled with a native girl, and the narrator expresses solid satisfaction when she gets crushed to death and hence is no longer a threat to the established order. And yet, albeit in language that today makes us squirm a little, we are told in no uncertain terms that condescension is not in order. "What is a gentleman? I don't quite know, and yet I have had to do with niggers—no, I will scratch out that word 'niggers,' for I do not like it. I've known natives who *are*, and so you will say, Harry, my boy, before you have done with this tale, and I have known mean whites with lots of money and fresh out from home, too, who *are not*" (Haggard [1885] 2006, 10).[2]

---

[1] In the version of the novel that he published first in the *Graphic* magazine, Haggard wrote of "Darwin's" theory. In the subsequent book version of the novel, he made things a little more popular and wrote of the "monkey" theory.

[2] *Prester John*, a boy's adventure story by John Buchan, written a few years later (1910), shows the same mix of condescension toward yet huge respect for Africans. The black messiah, John Laputa, is way ahead the bravest, most noble, and best-educated character in the novel.

Again, Rudyard Kipling, so often (with reason) derided as a crude imperialist, shows the same ambivalence. Take the poem "In the Neolithic Age." He uses the past to throw light on the present. First the past—the killing, the success:

> IN THE Neolithic Age savage warfare did I wage
>   For food and fame and woolly horses' pelt
> I was singer to my clan in that dim, red Dawn of Man,
>   And I sang of all we fought and feared and felt.

And then the sage's reflection that what you have done is perhaps not quite as glorious as you think.

> Then I stripped them, scalp from skull, and my hunting-dogs fed full,
>   And their teeth I threaded neatly on a thong;
> And I wiped my mouth and said, "It is well that they are dead,
>   For I know my work is right and theirs was wrong."
>
> But my Totem saw the shame; from his ridgepole-shrine he came,
>   And he told me in a vision of the night: —
> "There are nine and sixty ways of constructing tribal lays,
>   "And every single one of them is right!"

On to the moral for today:

> Still the world is wondrous large,—seven seas from marge to marge—
>   And it holds a vast of various kinds of man;
> And the wildest dreams of Kew are the facts of Khatmandhu
>   And the crimes of Clapham chaste in Martaban.
>
> Here's my wisdom for your use, as I learned it when the moose
>   And the reindeer roamed where Paris roars to-night:—
> *"There are nine and sixty ways of constructing tribal lays,*
>   *"And—every—single—one—of—them—is—right!"*
>   (Kipling 2001, 354–345)

For all that you are a "civilized" person, don't think you have an absolute lien on what is right and proper.

As it happens, we know that Kipling was not very keen on the *Descent*—which is not to say that he did not take it seriously—but he was not beyond poking fun at Herbert Spencer and suggesting that his thoughts of progress might not be quite as straightforward as he supposed. In that greatest of all novels written by an Englishman about the Raj, *Kim*, the grotesque Hurree Babu—a fat, greasy,

Bengali clerk, whose main claim to fame is a series of rejected notes to the *Asiatic Quarterly Review*—is just the sort of person to spout half-baked gems of wisdom from Spencer. Of native devils: "They are, of course, dematerialized phenomena. Spencer says." And yet, who in the end is the cleverest, the bravest, when it comes to the battle for rivalry in Asia—playing the Great Game? None other than Hurree Babu, for all that he expresses great fear of the Russians.

> "By Jove, they are not black people. I can do all sorts of things with black people, of course. They are Russians, and highly unscrupulous people. I—I do not want to consort with them without a witness."
>
> "Will they kill thee?"
>
> "Oah, thatt is nothing. I am good enough Herbert Spencerian, I trust, to meet little thing like death, which is all in my fate, you know. But—but they may beat me." (Kipling [1901] 1994, 297)

Why is the Babu so scared? Because he is a Bengali! "It was process of Evolution, I think, from Primal Necessity, but the fact remains in all the cui bono. I am, oh, awfully fearful!—" Fearful he may have been, but the Babu gets the goods and the reader knows it—and thrills along with him and realizes that he is the sort of man who earns our real respect.

> Under the striped umbrella Hurree Babu was straining ear and brain to follow the quick-poured French [of the Russian agents], and keeping both eyes on a kilta full of maps and documents—an extra-large one with a double red oil-skin cover. He did not wish to steal anything. He only desired to know what to steal, and, incidentally, how to get away when he had stolen it. He thanked all the Gods of Hindustan, and Herbert Spencer, that there remained some valuables to steal.[3]

The Heart of Darkness

Note the point being made, and it is very instructive to compare this with the Christian position. It is not so much the existence of race and its reality— whether objectively out there, subjectively constructed in here, people see it and generally accept it as a given. It is not so much that one side lords it over the

---

[3] *Kim* underlines strongly Kipling's views on the equal claims of different belief systems. The one truly holy man is the former abbot from Tibet, Teshoo Lama, searching for the River of the Arrow. The Anglican padre, Arthur Bennett, is (to say the least) insensitive to the point of stupidity. As disciple, Kim, a white man—a sahib—serves faithfully the aged lama.

other and thinks that God or science backs up this judgment. They do think this. It is rather that the authority—God or Darwin—subtly undermines this confidence and makes us, particularly if we are part of the dominant group, wonder about ourselves and our beliefs and our actions. That is the mark of a powerful and sophisticated religion. All this comes tumbling out in that most wonderful of American novels, *Huckleberry Finn*, written by a man who openly acknowledged his debts to Darwin. (Twain read the early, crucial part of the *Descent* the year it appeared.) Culturally Huck feels he should tell the authorities about Jim, the runaway slave. After all, he is someone's property. But Huck has come to know and like and respect Jim, and finds he cannot do this. The letter he has written betraying Jim cannot be sent. " 'All right, then, I'll *go* to hell'—and tore it up."

Yet, although race is important in the book—tremendously, hugely important—one senses that the real theme is the moral growth of the title character—a kid who cannot tell a truth to save his soul, although perhaps in the end that does save his soul.[4] For a more direct treatment, turn to one of the most searing pieces of creative writing on the race issue—Joseph Conrad's *The Heart of Darkness*. Apparently Conrad (1857–1924) was much influenced by Huxley's late essay on evolution and ethics (Najder 2007). This shows to the extent that both Huxley's essay and Conrad's novella start with the story of Caesar and his troops coming to invade Britain some 2,000 years ago. Especially influential was Huxley's introductory preface where he speaks of nature as a jungle and of us civilized people making and trying to maintain a garden in this wilderness. Even in success, there is a tension, a sense of unease, with the threat from outsiders, including "bipedal intruders."

> That the "state of Art," thus created in the state of nature by man, is sustained by and dependent on him, would at once become apparent, if the watchful supervision of the gardener were withdrawn, and the antagonistic influences of the general cosmic process were no longer sedulously warded off, or counteracted. The walls and gates would decay; quadrupedal and bipedal intruders would devour and tread down the useful and beautiful plants; birds, insects, blight, and mildew would work their will; the seeds of the native plants, carried by winds or other agencies, would immigrate, and in virtue of their long-earned special adaptation to the local conditions, these despised native weeds would soon choke their choice exotic rivals. A century or two hence, little beyond the foundations of the wall and of the houses and frames

---

[4] Although Huck does develop morally, as does Pip in *Great Expectations*, this does not necessarily imply that we have an evolutionary novel. This said, development can be important in such a novel, as with *Middlemarch*.

would be left, in evidence of the victory of the cosmic powers at work in the state of nature, over the temporary obstacles to their supremacy, set up by the art of the horticulturist. (Huxley [1893] 2009, 9–10)

The jungle is all around us and waiting to take over. The plants and trees, the inhabitants, wait to move in and strike. "We could have fancied ourselves the first of men taking possession of an accursed inheritance, to be subdued at the cost of profound anguish and of excessive toil. But suddenly, as we struggled round a bend, there would be a glimpse of rush walls, of peaked grass-roofs, a burst of yells, a whirl of black limbs, a mass of hands clapping, of feet stamping, of bodies swaying, of eyes rolling, under the droop of heavy and motionless foliage" (Conrad [1899] 1990, 32).

The story of *The Heart of Darkness* is well known. An Englishman, Marlow, gets a job with a Belgian company (dealing in ivory) to captain a boat up the river in the Congo, to the station where there is one of their agents, Kurtz, who is very efficient but apparently completely unstable. There is the metaphor as civilization is left and the boat goes deeper into the heart of darkness, total savagery. "The steamer toiled along slowly on the edge of a black and incomprehensible frenzy. The prehistoric man was cursing us, praying to us, welcoming us—who could tell?" (32)[5] In the end, although Kurtz is found, he dies distraught—crying "the horror, the horror"—and Marlow returns to England, lying to Kurtz's fiancée about the last words, saying that it was her name on his lips as he died.

There is much to discuss here, including the existential significance of those last words—Is this the ultimate Darwinian note of despair in the face of Godless nothingness?—but focus on the racial question. I want to make a virtue out of what many find puzzling and upsetting, perhaps without answer (Brantlinger 1988). Where, ultimately, did Conrad stand on imperialism and the racial issue? At times, he describes the situation so fully and nigh lovingly one suspects that he endorses the system.[6] Look at the way we come into the Congo. First the natives.

Brought from all the recesses of the coast in all the legality of time contracts, lost in uncongenial surroundings, fed on unfamiliar food, they sickened, became inefficient, and were then allowed to crawl away

---

[5] Note the implication that we are dealing with a world at a more primitive stage of development than Europe (Schmitt 2014, 27).

[6] Notoriously, in 1975, the Nigerian novelist Chinua Achebe accused Conrad of being a "bloody racist" and added for good measure that "Conrad had a problem with niggers." He suggested even that the novelist's fondness for that word suggested a place for psychoanalysis (Tredell 1998, 81). Well, yes, but . . . As we are about to see, things are a bit more complex in the Darwinian world.

and rest. These moribund shapes were free as air—and nearly as thin. I began to distinguish the gleam of eyes under the trees. Then, glancing down, I saw a face near my hand. The black bones reclined at full length with one shoulder against the tree, and slowly the eyelids rose and the sunken eyes looked up at me, enormous and vacant, a kind of blind, white flicker in the depths of the orbs, which died out slowly. (Conrad 1899, 14)

Absolutely appalling. Not their fault, but still. Then the European who, it is made clear, is a functionary not someone important.

When near the buildings I met a white man, in such an unexpected elegance of get-up that in the first moment I took him for a sort of vision. I saw a high starched collar, white cuffs, a light alpaca jacket, snowy trousers, a clear necktie, and varnished boots. No hat. Hair parted, brushed, oiled, under a green-lined parasol held in a big white hand. He was amazing, and had a penholder behind his ear. (15)

Say and think what you like, in the hands of a brilliant writer like Conrad, the effect and the contrast sink in. And things don't get a lot better as you get to know the natives more intimately. "An athletic black belonging to some coast tribe, and educated by my poor predecessor, was the helmsman. He sported a pair of brass earrings, wore a blue cloth wrapper from the waist to the ankles, and thought all the world of himself. He was the most unstable kind of fool I had ever seen. He steered with no end of a swagger while you were by; but if he lost sight of you, he became instantly the prey of an abject funk, and would let that cripple of a steamboat get the upper hand of him in a minute" (40). But then the native is killed.

I missed my late helmsman awfully,—I missed him even while his body was still lying in the pilot-house. Perhaps you will think it passing strange this regret for a savage who was no more account than a grain of sand in a black Sahara. Well, don't you see, he had done something, he had steered; for months I had him at my back—a help—an instrument. It was a kind of partnership. He steered for me—I had to look after him, I worried about his deficiencies, and thus a subtle bond had been created, of which I only became aware when it was suddenly broken. And the intimate profundity of that look he gave me when he received his hurt remains to this day in my memory—like a claim of distant kinship affirmed in a supreme moment. (46)

It wasn't so easily obvious, so very different and apart, after all. "Distant kinship" is there and means a great deal. Conrad affirms this point unambiguously. The Darwinian component to existence—we are all part of the same tree of life—undermines a surface reading of the situation, no less than does (let us say) the Story of Ruth or the parable of the Good Samaritan—"There is neither Jew nor Gentile, neither slave nor free, nor is there male and female, for you are all one in Christ Jesus" (Gal. 3:28). There are deeper truths. Marlow tells of those terrifying natives in the jungle edging to the banks of the river.

> The earth seemed unearthly. We are accustomed to look upon the shack
> led form of a conquered monster, but there—there you could look at
> a thing monstrous and free. It was unearthly, and the men were—No,
> they were not inhuman. Well, you know, that was the worst of it—this
> suspicion of their not being inhuman. It would come slowly to one.
> They howled, and leaped, and spun, and made horrid faces; but what
> thrilled you was just the thought of their humanity—like yours—the
> thought of your remote kinship with this wild and passionate uproar.
> Ugly. Yes, it was ugly enough; but if you were man enough you would
> admit to yourself that there was in you just the faintest trace of a re
> sponse to the terrible frankness of that noise, a dim suspicion of there
> being a meaning in it which you—you so remote from the night of first
> ages—could comprehend. (32)

In a way, recognizing this fact is as human an activity as the savagery from the bank. "Let the fool gape and shudder—the man knows, and can look on without a wink. But he must at least be as much of a man as these on the shore. He must meet that truth with his own true stuff—with his own inborn strength" (32).[7]

Conrad is ambivalent and scared at what he senses, and that is what makes *Heart of Darkness* a religious novel—a Darwinian religious novel.[8]

---

[7] One could continue with the racial theme, for instance, about Conrad's thinking of the relative fitnesses of Europeans compared to natives. For all his efficiency—"an emissary of pity and science and progress"—Kurtz doesn't make it to the end of the tale alive.

[8] This ambiguity and ambivalence runs right through the fiction (and poetry) of this era, as though the writers simply cannot fathom the huge challenges and changes occurring in their hitherto safe and—secure—world. It worries the Christians as well as the nonbelievers. Consider *Greenmantle* (1916) by the good Presbyterian John Buchan written in the depths of the Great War. The villain, Colonel Ulrich von Stumm, is a grotesque caricature of a German officer: "He was a perfect mountain of a fellow, six and a half feet if he was an inch, with shoulders on him like a shorthorn bull. He was in uniform and the black-and-white ribbon of the Iron Cross showed at a buttonhole. His tunic was all wrinkled and strained as if it could scarcely contain his huge chest, and mighty hands were clasped over his stomach. That man must have had the length of reach of a gorilla. He had a great, lazy, smiling face, with a square cleft chin which stuck out beyond the rest. His brow retreated and the

Daniel Deronda

Turn now to the Jewish question, a theme running right through our period.[9] Remarks on the prejudice are truisms, although few were as explicit as the poet T. S. Eliot. He links Jews with degeneration or perhaps lack of advance—beneath even the rats looking up from "protozoic slime."[10]

> But this or such was Bleistein's way:
> A saggy bending of the knees
> And elbows, with the palms turned out,
> Chicago Semite Viennese.
>
> A lustreless protrusive eye
> Stares from the protozoic slime
> At a perspective of Canaletto.
> The smoky candle end of time
>
> Declines. On the Rialto once.
> The rats are underneath the piles.
> The jew is underneath the lot.
> Money in furs.[11]

stubby back of his head ran forward to meet it, while his neck below bulged out over his collar. His head was exactly the shape of a pear with the sharp end topmost" ([1916] 1992, 146). Interestingly, to make things even worse, in his private quarters, he has a very suspicious taste in knickknacks and dainty furniture, not to mention embroidery. Against this, thanks to a chance encounter at a railway station, is a hugely sympathetic depiction of the Kaiser: "a far bigger tragedy than any I had seen in action" (170). He is no monster, but a man crushed by his responsibilities.

[9] With regret, I will leave untouched related issues, like that of the "Yellow Peril" in the writings of Jack London. I suspect the conclusions in the end would be similar to those dealing with blacks and Jews and other peoples who have suffered prejudice.

[10] Not strictly temporal, as in "Proterozoic," the long period before the Cambrian, but with implications of "proto"—earliest or beginning—"zoic"—animals. Also note the Jew is at the lowest level, even below the rat.

[11] To be fair, the first part of this poem – "Burbank with a Baedeker: Bleistein with a Cigar" – does not portray the presumed Gentile Burbank very well.

> Burbank crossed a little bridge
> Descending at a small hotel;
> Princess Volupine arrived,
> They were together, and he fell.

Eliot was not peculiarly anti-Semitic, given that he grew up in a society where anti-Semitism was the norm and particularly virulent in his home town of St. Louis. More an explanation than an excuse. Note the ape-like connotations of bended elbows and knees and outturned palms. Apparently this can also be linked to a love of the British music hall and the mannerisms of comics (Knowles 1998).

Most writers were more sensitive than this; even when they fall they strive to rise again. Dickens was one who had already stumbled and then regained his footing. *Oliver Twist*, the story of an orphan lad who runs away to London and falls into the clutches of a Jewish fence, Fagin, is not the *Protocols of the Elders of Zion*. It is true that Fagin is vile physically and in intent—if he corrupts Oliver, he is to get money from the lad's half-brother—but he is no worse than the thuggish thief, Bill Sykes. Dickens protested with reason that there were notorious Jewish fences—best known was Ikey Solomon—and he was just being true to life. Nevertheless, it is crude and hurtful and expectedly Jews were upset. Dickens understood and responded, drawing a portrait of Mr. Riah in *Our Mutual Friend*, the protector of Jenny Wren and as good a man as Fagin is evil. An important symbol, because, in the years after the *Origin*, the Jewish question became something of immediate urgency to the Victorians. Along with Gladstone, the other great leader was Benjamin Disraeli, admittedly a convert but in respects almost playing up to the stereotype of a Jew. I don't mean this disrespectfully. This was Disraeli's style. You couldn't pretend that he was not a Jew. His novels stressed Jewish virtues (Brantlinger 2012). He forced on people their prejudices, made them bring them out, and put them on one side—or not. As many people have found today with sexual orientation, they had to confront themselves. And that is the heart of religion.

The novelists picked up on these themes. Two of Anthony Trollope's mid-1870s novels—*The Prime Minister* and *The Way We Live Now*—feature major characters of less than sterling quality who are pretty clearly intended as Jewish. This is not to mention the odious evangelical clergyman Mr. Emilius—"of whom it was said he was born a Jew in Hungary"—who (bigamously) marries Lizzie Eustace in the *Eustace Diamonds* (1871) and who commits murder, a crime that at first is pinned on the title character, in *Phineas Redux* (1873). At the end of the century, in *McTeague,* a novel we shall discuss, the American writer Frank Norris (1870–1902) gave another less than subtle depiction of a Jew. But here, George Eliot is our key person and her novel *Daniel Deronda* our key document (Himmelfarb 2009). It is a strange story—although I shall later contest this reading, it is often with reason taken to be two stories. The first tells of the bewitching Gwendolen Harleth, penniless, who choses between potential husbands, and ends by marrying Mallinger Grandcourt, heir to the estate of Sir Hugo Mallinger. The second tells of the young man (in his mid-twenties) Daniel Deronda, the former ward of Sir Hugo. Focusing here on the Deronda side to the story (in a later chapter we shall pick up on Gwendolen too), the main theme is the search for identity and Daniel's discovery both of the Jewish faith and race and at the same time of Daniel's own background, where it turns out that he was not (as many including himself thought) the illegitimate son of Sir Hugo but of a European Jewish singer and her likewise Jewish husband. In other words, of Daniel's discovery that he is not a Protestant Englishman as he thought, but that he is himself a Jew. It is important to distinguish cause and effect. It is not that Daniel discovers himself a Jew and then searches out the Jewish religion and customs. Nor is it the case that Daniel is being primarily motivated by a growing attraction to a Jewish girl, Mirah, who has made it clear that she will not marry anyone but a co-religionist. Daniel's instinctive search for Jewish identity precedes this, and that is the mystifying, almost creepy, background of this novel.

It is about race and very much about the biological as well as cultural nature of race. You cannot flip in and out of being a Jew just by choice. " 'But I could not make myself not a Jewess,' said Mirah, insistently, 'even if I changed my belief' " (Eliot [1876] 1967, 425). Another character (Hans) loves Mirah, but it is made clear that she can never be for him because he is not Jewish. Although evolution-based, you many think that the treatment of race is not particularly Darwinian at all—except perhaps as one might say that Mirah choses Daniel because she senses that there is something Jewish about him.

> "Some minds naturally rebel against whatever they were brought up in, and like the opposite; they see the faults in what is nearest to them," said Deronda apologetically.
>
> "But you are not like that," said Mirah, looking at him with unconscious fixedness.
>
> "No, I think not," said Deronda; "but you know I was not brought up as a Jew."
>
> "Ah, I am always forgetting," said Mirah, with a look of disappointed recollection, and slightly blushing. (425)

Eliot's treatment of race does not come unvarnished out of the *Descent of Man*. It seems in respects significantly more Lamarckian and less to do with the physical and more with the emotional, the spiritual. This suggests that like *Middlemarch* the key influence here might be Spencer, but my suspicion is that it may be a work that we know Eliot studied in preparation for writing her novel, Darwin's follow-up book on humans, *The Expression of the Emotions in Man and in Animals*, published a year after the *Descent* in 1872. It is about the emotional rather than the physical and as commentators have noted it has nothing about selection and yet a huge amount about the inheritance of acquired characteristics. This fits the novel.

> If there are ranks in suffering, Israel takes precedence of all the nations—if the duration of sorrows and the patience with which they are borne ennoble, the Jews are among the aristocracy of every land—if

a literature is called rich in the possession of a few classic tragedies, what shall we say to a National Tragedy lasting for fifteen hundred years, in which the poets and the actors were also the heroes? (575)

Yes, but does this get into the blood, as one might say? Eliot implies this in the follow-up passage, which suggests incidentally that she was not quite as outside the Victorian mold as one might expect. Daniel is visiting the family of Ezra Cohen, a pawnbroker, who have taken pity on Mordecai, the brother of Mirah—weak (he is dying of tuberculosis) and yet with great inner spiritual force.

> Ezra Cohen was not clad in the sublime pathos of the martyr, and his taste for money-getting seemed to be favored with that success which has been the most exasperating difference in the greed of Jews during all the ages of their dispersion. This Jeshurun of a pawnbroker was not a symbol of the great Jewish tragedy; and yet was there not something typical in the fact that a life like Mordecai's—a frail incorporation of the national consciousness, breathing with difficult breath—was nested in the self-gratulating ignorant prosperity of the Cohens? (575)

That this aura of national consciousness is not purely cultural is made clear when we learn that Daniel has it too in some respects, inherited from a pious grandfather he not only did not know but of whom he was totally unaware. He goes to visit an old Jew in Mainz (Kalonymos) who sits him down and looks piercingly at him. Daniel "seemed to himself to be touching the electric chain of his own ancestry; and he bore the scrutinizing look of Kalonymos with a delighted awe, something like what one feels in the solemn commemoration of acts done long ago but still telling markedly on the life of to-day" (787). It is this chain with the past that determines Daniel's future destiny. His grandfather wanted above all to preserve the identity of the Jews. Daniel, finally married to Mirah, sets off to the East to start a homeland for the Jews.[12]

> I will not say that I shall profess to believe exactly as my fathers have believed. Our fathers themselves changed the horizon of their belief and learned of other races. But I think I can maintain my grandfather's notion of separateness with communication. I hold that my first duty is to my own people, and if there is anything to be done toward restoring or perfecting their common life, I shall make that my vocation. (792)

---

[12] The analogy between Daniel and Moses is unmistakable. Both are raised as non-Jews, both discover and embrace their Jewish identity, and both are then directed to the making or founding of a homeland for their fellow Jews.

Of course, this notion of a throwback to a feature that skips a generation—atavism—was well-known to Darwin who often mentioned it. So perhaps Eliot was not so far from Darwin in other respects as well.

Darwinians on Class

George Eliot is not just telling a story. She never does that! She is wrestling morally, socially, culturally, religiously with issues of race, touching at points at the most sensitive in her own society What about the other side to human variation, namely, that of class? This is not something new after Darwin. It is an ongoing theme in Dickens. In *Bleak House*, realistically it is discussed and tackled when the son of Robert Rouncewell, the ironmaster, falls in love with the maid of Lady Dedlock. Even though he has raised himself and thus his family from the lower classes right into the prosperous middle classes, the father is agreeable to this match. It is realized, however, that class matters and if Rosa the maid is to marry the son, first she must be educated up to her future station.

> All this is so frequent, Lady Dedlock, where I live, and among the class to which I belong, that what would be generally called unequal marriages are not of such rare occurrence with us as elsewhere. A son will sometimes make it known to his father that he has fallen in love, say, with a young woman in the factory. The father, who once worked in a factory himself, will be a little disappointed at first very possibly. It may be that he had other views for his son. However, the chances are that having ascertained the young woman to be of unblemished character, he will say to his son, "I must be quite sure you are in earnest here. This is a serious matter for both of you. Therefore I shall have this girl educated for two years," or it may be, "I shall place this girl at the same school with your sisters for such a time, during which you will give me your word and honour to see her only so often. If at the expiration of that time, when she has so far profited by her advantages as that you may be upon a fair equality, you are both in the same mind, I will do my part to make you happy." I know of several cases such as I describe, my Lady, and I think they indicate to me my own course now. (Dickens [1853] 1948, 396)

Class matters and it is a cause of great tension in *Our Mutual Friend* when Eugene Wrayburn, a lawyer, falls for Lizzie Hexam, the daughter of a waterman. Dickens's resolution in this story is far less realistic because Lizzie agrees to marry Eugene after he has been attacked and he lies hurt in danger of death. In a way, this is backward looking, because (as often in this novel) Dickens is relying on a Christian generosity of spirit that is going to leap across all and any difficulties. In the Darwinian world, things are tougher and grimmer, although how it all plays out is open to different interpretations. In respects, much depended on how one interpreted class differences and their causes. Were they a reflection of biology, like race only perhaps a little less so? One suspects many thought that way, including people like Darwin's cousin Francis Galton, who was busily trying to measure the IQs and like factors across and within groups. The presence of large numbers of Irish in the population would have reinforced this prejudice. It is noteworthy how, from the moment the *Origin* was published, cartoonists would portray the Irish—Paddy and Biddy—as ape-like, and many were the jokes in places like *Punch* about Mr. G. O'Rilla. These sorts of views were often reinforced with supposed Lamarckian mechanisms. People lead degraded lives, and this reflects into future generations—or conversely. We have seen a version of this kind of thinking in Samuel Butler's *The Way of All Flesh*.

Obviously not all felt this way. Rouncewell, the ironmaster, came up from the lower classes—not the very lowest, his mother is a housekeeper—and thinks that others can do likewise. If they get the right education, the potential wives of his children and others of his class can rise up and take their new places in society. Thomas Hardy more than anyone felt that class differences are significant and yet artificial. Darwinism does not guarantee a good or fair society. It is all a matter of chance at what level you are born and chance as to what level you can rise to—tradition and power are the determinants, not ability or potential in any great degree.[13] In *Tess of the D'Urbervilles*, the heroine is better educated than other members of her family and clearly a much nicer person. A lot of good it does her. She goes to the faux D'Urbervilles where she is treated like a serf by the mother and seduced by the son. Then she meets up with Angel. One wonders had she been the daughter of an earl whether, after confession time on the wedding night, he would have rejected her. As it is, when he has vanished from the scene to South America, Tess goes to seek help from his family. The class barriers are so great that she makes no contact and returns with so little hope that she ends as the mistress of Alec.

In *The Return of the Native*, Clym goes near-blind, has to give up hopes of becoming a schoolteacher, drops a social class by becoming a furze-cutter, rather enjoys it, and that basically is the end of his relationship with Eustacia. In *The Woodlanders*, the story is sparked by the fact that, although the very decent Giles Winterbourne seems all set to marry his childhood sweetheart, Grace Melbury, she unfortunately has been educated out of her class. Her father thinks that she is too good for Giles and directs her toward the more socially desirable—he is

---

[13] This is the unspoken background to "Drummer Hodge." The wretched, ignorant child dies for the Empire, to the glory and riches of others (Riquelme 1999).

a doctor—Edgar Fitzpiers. This man turns out to be a cad of the first order, off with his mistress until she drops him. And then poor Giles gives shelter to the fleeing Grace, protecting her virtue by sleeping outside in appalling weather, and promptly dies—lamented only by a poor girl, Marty South, who earlier in the novel had sold her beautiful hair to the woman who becomes Edgar's mistress. Even attempts to escape your class seem dogged by disaster since Grace is re-united with Edgar, who clearly will not remain faithful for ten minutes beyond the final page.

Most crushing of all is the class system in Hardy's last completed and most pessimistic novel, *Jude the Obscure*.[14] It is the story of Jude Fawley, a young man who becomes a stonemason but who teaches himself Latin and Greek, hoping thereby to go to the university at Christminster (Oxford). He fails in his aims in part because he gets entangled with his false on-again, off-again, on-again wife Arabella, who starts their relationship by tricking him into marriage (by pre-tending she is pregnant)—an act the author makes clear is precisely the sort of thing that might happen at (and probably only at) the social level of Jude and Arabella. But his failure is not just or even primarily a function of Jude's passions and weaknesses. Jude is clearly gifted and desperately keen to better himself. The respect and approval that he gets is less than zero, from his childhood where he is berated for having his thoughts on other things, to where he goes to work in Christminster and gets a rebuff from the college authorities.

BIBLIOLL COLLEGE.

SIR,—I HAVE READ YOUR LETTER WITH INTEREST; AND, JUDGING FROM YOUR DE-SCRIPTION OF YOURSELF AS A WORKING-MAN, I VENTURE TO THINK THAT YOU WILL HAVE A MUCH BETTER CHANCE OF SUCCESS IN LIFE BY REMAINING IN YOUR OWN SPHERE AND STICKING TO YOUR TRADE THAN BY ADOPTING ANY OTHER COURSE. THAT, THEREFORE, IS WHAT I ADVISE YOU TO DO. YOURS FAITHFULLY, T. TETUPHENAY.

TO MR. J. FAWLEY, Stone-mason. (Hardy [1895] 1960, 138)

Jude is destined, as he says later, to be an "outsider" to the end of his days. Arabella clears off to Australia and Jude takes up with his already-married cousin Sue. But they too get entangled in class and convention. Although both Jude and Sue get divorces from their respective spouses, there is still the stigma, quite apart from the fact that Sue can no longer bring herself to enter another marriage with another man. At the end of the book, even as he lies dying (of pneumonia), Jude is scorned and made to remember his position. "Certain sounds from with-out revealed that the town was in festivity, though little of the festival, whatever it

---

[14] This novel is way gloomier than anything warranted by Darwin. The influence of Schopenhauer would fit the bill.

might have been, could be seen here. Bells began to ring, and the notes came into the room through the open window, and travelled round Jude's head in a hum" (486). Then there is a musical performance.

> The powerful notes of that concert rolled forth through the swinging yellow blinds of the open windows, over the housetops, and into the still air of the lanes. They reached so far as to the room in which Jude lay; and it was about this time that his cough began again and awakened him.
>
> As soon as he could speak he murmured, his eyes still closed: "A little water, please."
>
> Nothing but the deserted room received his appeal, and he coughed to exhaustion again—saying still more feebly: "Water—some water—Sue—Arabella!"
>
> The room remained still as before. Presently he gasped again: "Throat—water—Sue—darling—drop of water—please—oh please!"
>
> No water came, and the organ notes, faint as a bee's hum, rolled in as before. (487)

As always with Hardy, the bleakness of the Darwinian vision is complemented by the complicity of the Christian religion in failing entirely to ameliorate the emptiness of existence. Christminster, the institution that turns its back on Jude, who wants above all to become a minister of religion, is itself a bastion of established Christianity. And the comforts of Christianity are false and destructive. When we first meet Sue, she is nigh pagan. She buys plaster statuettes of Venus and Apollo for her room. Then later, when she is living with Jude, Little Father Time—the sadly named child of Jude and Arabella—fearing that they were a burden on the family's strained finances, kills himself and the two children of Jude and Sue: "a piece of paper was found upon the floor, on which was written, in the boy's hand, with the bit of lead pencil that he carried: *Done because we are too menny*" (405). Poor Sue has a miscarriage and a religious crisis. Are her tragedies punishment for leaving her original husband and living unwed with Jude? She leaves Jude whom she does love and returns to this husband whom she does not love and forces herself to have (very unwelcome) sex with him, because now she believes that this is the Christian thing to do.[15] To what end? In response to

---

[15] As Eagleton ([1974] 1988) notes about Sue's behavior, "there isn't, when one comes down to it, much to be said in her defence" (41). Note that, throughout the novel, Sue seems to be a free agent—as not marrying Jude—in a way that many (or all) of the characters in earlier novels are not. Everyone in *The Return of the Native* seems controlled by the heath.

an optimistic hope, Jude's official wife—speaking the truth for once in her life—makes the final sour comment:

> "Well—poor little thing, 'tis to be believed she's found forgiveness somewhere! She said she had found peace!
>
> "She may swear that on her knees to the holy cross upon her necklace till she's hoarse, but it won't be true!" said Arabella. "She's never found peace since she left his arms, and never will again till she's as he is now!" (494)[16]

As always, our Darwinian writers are doing more than just describing facts. They are offering social commentary in a way redolent of a religious world picture. A secular world picture against the spiritual world picture of Christianity.

---

[16] Explicitly, *Jude the Obscure* is Hardy's retelling of the Book of Job, except, as the critic Harold Bloom notes, this is the world of Thomas Hardy not that of the God of the Old Testament. "A spirit like Jude's is condemned to die whispering the Jobean lament: "Let the day perish wherein I was born." [Job 3:3] *Jude the Obscure* is Hardy's book of Job, and like Job is too dark for tragedy, while unlike Job it is just the reverse of theodicy, being Hardy's ultimate declaration that the ways of the Immanent Will towards man are unjustifiable" (Bloom 2005, 4). Apparently an earlier version of the novel had Jude cursing God on his deathbed.

9

Morality

The Problem of Morality

After her death, a perceptive friend wrote of a meeting with George Eliot:

> I remember how, at Cambridge, I walked with her once in the Fellows'
> Garden of Trinity, on an evening of rainy May; and she, stirred some-
> what beyond her wont, and taking as her text the three words which
> have been used so often as the inspiring trumpet-calls of men—the
> words *God, Immortality, Duty*—pronounced, with terrible earnestness,
> how inconceivable was the *first,* how unbelievable the *second,* and yet
> how peremptory and absolute the *third.* Never perhaps have sterner ac-
> cents affirmed the sovereignty of impersonal and unrecompensing Law.
> I listened, and night fell; her grave, majestic countenance turned toward
> me like a sibyl's in the gloom; it was as though she withdrew from my
> grasp, one by one, the two scrolls of promise, and left me the third scroll
> only, awful with inevitable fates. And when we stood at length and
> parted amid that columnar circuit of the forest trees, beneath the last
> twilight of starless skies, I seemed to be gazing, like Titus at Jerusalem,
> on vacant seats and empty halls—on a sanctuary with no Presence to
> hallow it, and heaven left lonely of a God.

> (Myers 1881)

This was the big problem. If God is gone or at least pushed back to a position
of irrelevance, what then of morality? This was the worry in *Nemesis of Faith.*
Without God, can there be a moral code, and even if there is one will anyone
take note of it? The one thing one can say above all else of Christianity is that
it filled a need. What should one do? How should one treat one's family, one's
neighbors, one's fellow countrymen, the inhabitants of other lands? And what
about the non-human animals and plants? Christianity had answers. Have no

God other than me. Don't murder people. Have respect for your mother and father. Treat others as you would want to be treated yourself.

> Hearing that Jesus had silenced the Sadducees, the Pharisees got to-gether. One of them, an expert in the law, tested him with this question: "Teacher, which is the greatest commandment in the Law?"
>
> Jesus replied: " 'Love the Lord your God with all your heart and with all your soul and with all your mind.' This is the first and greatest commandment. And the second is like it: 'Love your neighbor as yourself.' All the Law and the Prophets hang on these two commandments." (Matthew 22:34–40)

And there are many other commands, particularly about gender relationships and sexual behavior. So significant was the role of Christianity that Darwin worried that, without it, all would fall into moral chaos, and Thomas Henry Huxley, of all people, elected to the first London School Board, argued strongly for religious instruction in state schools.

Darwinism sets the problem. How can something based on the struggle for existence make room for morality? As she prepares to leave Jude, Sue puts the matter starkly. "Your worldly failure, if you have failed, is to your credit rather than to your blame. Remember that the best and greatest among mankind are those who do themselves no worldly good. Every successful man is more or less a selfish man. The devoted fail . . . 'Charity seeketh not her own' " (Hardy [1895] 1960, 437).[1] The evolutionists had responses. In the *Descent*, Darwin took very seriously the evolution of morality and as we saw he thought a moral group, a tribe, would have an advantage over other groups without such morality. Getting down to details, he offered ways in which natural selection might bring on belief in something like the Love Commandment. One cause might have been what is today known as "reciprocal altruism." You scratch my back and I'll scratch yours. "In the first place, as the reasoning powers and foresight of the members became improved, each man would soon learn that if he aided his fellow-men, he would commonly receive aid in return. From this low motive he might acquire the habit of aiding his fellows; and the habit of performing benevolent actions certainly strengthens the feeling of sympathy which gives the first

---

[1] Unlike others—Gaskell, London, Gissing, Wharton—one senses that Hardy's sympathies are with the losers. For some like Tess in losing they triumph—"Angel, I am almost glad—yes, glad! This happiness could not have lasted." For others it is because the losers are good people and like Jude go under because of this. Marty South's lament for the dead Giles: "If ever I forget your name, let me forget home and Heaven!—But no, no, my love, I never can forget 'ee; for you was a GOOD man, and did good things!" (Ingham 2003, 115)

impulse to benevolent actions. Habits, moreover, followed during many generations probably tend to be inherited" (Darwin 1871, 1, 163–164). Then Darwin
added: "But there is another and much more powerful stimulus to the development of the social virtues, namely, the praise and the blame of our fellow-men.
The love of approbation and the dread of infamy, as well as the bestowal of praise
of blame, are primarily due, as we have seen in the third chapter, to the instinct
of sympathy; and this instinct no doubt was originally acquired, like all the other
social instincts, through natural selection" (1, 164). He elaborated: "To do good
unto others—to do unto others as ye would they should do unto you,—is the
foundation-stone of morality. It is, therefore, hardly possible to exaggerate the
importance during rude times of the love of praise and the dread of blame"
(1, 165).

Herbert Spencer went a different way, arguing that thanks to the progressive
nature of the evolutionary process—progress in everything from biology through
language and on to culture—what we find is that morality emerges and our duties are
to ensure that this happens by removing barriers and facilitating the process. "Ethics
has for its subject-matter, that form which universal conduct assumes during the last
stages of its evolution" (Spencer 1879, 21). Continuing: "And there has followed the
corollary that conduct gains ethical sanction in proportion as the activities, becoming less and less militant and more and more industrial, are such as do not necessitate
mutual injury or hindrance, but consist with, and are furthered by, co-operation and
mutual aid." As noted earlier, Spencer's thinking is rather more subtle than many give
him credit for. Although at times he does sound totally committed to an extreme and
harsh form of *laissez faire,* the essence of his evolutionism was that with progress the
struggle will fall away and organisms will live in harmony. It was precisely because of
this that he felt that he could identify the end point of evolution with that which is
the ethically highest. What distorts our understanding is that often his followers were
given to pushing a far more stern position than he. Thus William Graham Sumner,
the American sociologist: "The glib generalities in which we sometimes hear people
talk, as if you could set moral and economic forces separate from and in antithesis to
each other, and discard the one to accept and work by the other, gravely misconstrue
the realities of the social order" (Sumner 1914).

This kind of thinking, known today as "Social Darwinism,"[2] did not go unchal-
lenged. Philosophers like Henry Sidgwick (1876) and his student G. E. Moore

---

[2] I am uncomfortable with this terminology. It was hardly used in the nineteenth century and
gained currency only after 1940 with its use by Richard Hofstadter in an admittedly seminal study of
nineteenth-century social evolutionism. Although it is now so standard that I will continue to use it,
what worries me is that there is a tendency to separate "Social Darwinism" (bad) from "Darwinism"
(good), and to suggest that it is not really a Darwinian idea but owes more to others, particularly
Spencer. As a hitherto-egregious sinner in this regard now repenting: the ideas are in Darwin—he

(1903) thought that it is fallacious philosophically to identify that which evolved with that which is good. For Moore, this was an paradigmatic example of what he called the "naturalistic fallacy." Thomas Henry Huxley, in the essay on evolution and ethics mentioned several times already, likewise took great exception to the thinking—he argued that it is far from the case that those attributes that lead to success in the struggle are necessarily those that we think good. Indeed, often it is the very opposite. "Man, the animal, in fact, has worked his way to the headship of the sentient world, and has become the superb animal which he is, in virtue of his success in the struggle for existence" (Huxley 1893, 51). Continuing:

> For his successful progress, throughout the savage state, man has been largely indebted to those qualities which he shares with the ape and the tiger; his exceptional physical organization; his cunning, his sociability, his curiosity, and his imitativeness; his ruthless and ferocious destructiveness when his anger is roused by opposition.
>
> But, in proportion as men have passed from anarchy to social organization, and in proportion as civilization has grown in worth, these deeply ingrained serviceable qualities have become defects. After the manner of successful persons, civilized man would gladly kick down the ladder by which he has climbed. He would be only too pleased to see "the ape and tiger die."[3]

The Christian Opposition

With this kind of background among the evolutionists, as you can imagine the novelists and poets were all over the map, united only in their agreement with George Eliot that this issue is really, really important and that after Darwin things cannot stand still. Expectedly, there were those who went on arguing that only with religion can one have a sound basis for moral behavior, and just as expectedly, Disraeli was one of these voices. *Lothair* (1870) tells the story of a young nobleman who has two guardians, one a Presbyterian and the other a Catholic convert, a cardinal. The hero is entangled with Theodora, a young woman with

---

endorsed capitalism fully and we saw his views on unions—and Spencer's responsibility is there but not uniquely so.

[3] Notwithstanding the comments in the last footnote, by the 1890s Darwin was dead but Spencer was not only alive but still pushing strongly his philosophy of the benefits of struggle and the end point of social Progress. In writing this essay, Huxley explicitly had Spencer in his sights. For Spencer, and for Darwin in respects too, the bloody struggle leads to moral sentiments. For Huxley, this is never so. Morality is opposed to the products of the struggle.

very radical ideas, but he knows only too well that the state of bliss that this brings on cannot last indefinitely. And then what? The scientists are of little help.

> Chance, necessity, atomic theories, nebular hypotheses, development, evolution, the origin of worlds, human ancestry—here were high topics, on none of which was there lack of argument; and, in a certain sense, of evidence; and what then? There must be design. The reasoning and the research of all philosophy could not be valid against that conviction. If there were no design, why, it would all be nonsense. . . Atheism may be consistent with fine taste, and fine taste under certain conditions may for a time regulate a polished society; but ethics with atheism are impossible; and without ethics no human order can be strong or permanent. (197)

As Disraeli said, when it came to apes or angels, he was with the heavenly choir.

At the end of the century, the Irish novelist George Moore made the same points. *Evelyn Innes* tells the story of a young woman who runs off to Paris with her lover (Sir Owen Asher) and becomes an opera singer. Give Sir Owen credit, he knows his way to a girl's heart, not to mention the lower parts of her anatomy.

> That she was at that moment preparing to receive him brought a little dizziness into his eyes, and compelled him to tear off his necktie. Then, vaguely, like one in a dream, he began to undress, very slowly, for she had told him to wait a quarter of an hour before coming to her room. He examined his thin waist as he tied himself in blue silk pyjamas, and he paused to admire his long, straight feet before slipping them into a pair of black velvet slippers. He turned to glance at his watch, and to kill the last five minutes of the prescribed time he thought of Evelyn's scruples. She would have to read certain books—Darwin and Huxley he relied upon, and he reposed considerable faith in Herbert Spencer. (Moore 1898, 146–147)[4]

Fortunately for her immortal soul—tiring of Owen she has even had sex with a man during a performance of *Tristan and Isolde*—the heroine falls in with a Monsignor.

> With a little pathetic air, Evelyn admitted that Owen had used every possible argument to destroy her faith. She had read Huxley, Darwin, and a little Herbert Spencer.

---

[4] The American reprint of 1923 neatly excises (without mention) this and the succeeding paragraphs. One assumes it was the sex that offended the American publisher and not the reference to Darwin.

"Herbert Spencer! Miserable collections of trivial facts, bearing upon nothing. Of what value, I ask, can it be to suffering humanity to know that such and such a fact has been observed and described? Then the general law! rubbish, ridiculous rubbish!" (332–333)

It is not easy for one who has fallen so low to regain the higher moral ground.

That sense of right and wrong which, like a whip, had driven her here could be nothing else but the voice of her soul; therefore there was a soul, and if there was a soul it could not die, and if it did not die it must go somewhere; therefore there was a heaven and a hell. But in spite of her desire to convince herself, remembrance of Owen's arguments whistled like a wind through her pious exhortations, and all that she had read in Huxley and Darwin and Spencer; the very words came back thick and distinct, and like one who finds progress impossible in the face of the gale, she stopped thinking. (391–392)

But thank God—thank God—the faith conquers all. "That you should think like this is part of the teaching of the man whose object was to undermine your faith; it is part of the teaching of Darwin and Huxley and Spencer. You were per-suaded that to live with a man to whom you were not married differed in no wise from living with your husband. The result has proved how false is such teaching" (397). In the end, it is not quite certain who saves her soul—God Almighty or Richard Wagner—although perhaps there is not much difference between the two. Having been led into sin through one opera, through another—though tempted, Tannhäuser never returns to the Venusberg—she finds her guide and support. [5]

The Evolutionist Response

What did the evolutionists have to say? Someone like Kingsley hardly counts, inasmuch as his position seems unchanged after Darwin from before. We ought

---

[5] Evelyn is not alone in being led astray by her dreadful influences. The heroine of Arnold Bennett's *Sacred and Profane Love* (1905) is another with a rocky sexual career, likewise finding *Tristan* somewhat of an aphrodisiac. "He held me; he clasped me, and, despite my innocence, I knew at once that those hands were as expert to caress as to make music. I was proud and glad that he was not clumsy, that he was a master. And at that point I ceased to have volition . . . ." ([1905] 1906, 61). She was primed. "I discovered *The Origin of Species* in the Free Library. It finished the work of corruption. Spencer had shown me how to think; Darwin told me what to think. The whole of my upbringing went for naught thenceforward" (23). As with Evelyn, lifelong guilt was close at

to behave in a good Christian way. Tom finds salvation in following God's rule. "He has won his spurs in the great battle, and become fit to go with you and be a man; because he has done the thing he did not like" (Kingsley [1863] 2008, 188). Among those more inclined to the view that the good is more or less defined by the outcome of evolution, one senses that—at a reasonably restrained level—Gissing endorses something along these lines. Certainly there seems a respect for Jasper Milvain over Edwin Reardon for simply having the energy and nous to make a life for himself. Edwin's girlfriend, Marian Yule, ends without man or money, and her willingness to do whatever is right and "good" does not entirely endear her to the author. We have already been told that she is a bit of a wimp, and this kind of conversation rather confirms this judgment.

> "Decide my fate for me, Marian," he pursued, magnanimously. "Let us make up our minds and do what we decide to do. Indeed, it doesn't concern me so much as yourself. Are you content to lead a simple, un-ambitious life? Or should you prefer your husband to be a man of some distinction?"
>
> "I know so well what your own wish is. But to wait for years—you will cease to love me, and will only think of me as a hindrance in your way."
>
> "Well now, when I said five years, of course I took a round number. Three—two might make all the difference to me."
>
> "Let it be just as you wish. I can bear anything rather than lose your love."
>
> "You feel, then, that it will decidedly be wise not to marry whilst we are still so poor?"
>
> "Yes; whatever you are convinced of is right."
>
> (Gissing [1891] 1976, 509–510)

It is little wonder that Jasper goes off with Amy, who is a woman who knows her mind and appreciates success and its benefits.

There is expectedly some fairly standard Social Darwinian writing. All the tales of humans winning out over apes or lower forms—as in the *Lost World*—fall into this category. The same is true of much of Jack London's work. Spitz is beaten by Buck. "Only Spitz quivered and bristled as he staggered back and forth, snarling with horrible menace, as though to frighten off impending death. Then Buck sprang in and out; but while he was in, shoulder had at last squarely met shoulder. The dark circle became a dot on the moon-flooded snow as Spitz

---

hand. That very night she was being carried away in Wagnerian ecstasies, the aunt who reared her died suddenly, having had the forethought to leave her niece "a magnificently-bound copy of *The Imitation of Christ*" (78).

disappeared from view. Buck stood and looked on, the successful champion, the dominant primordial beast who had made his kill and found it good" (London [1903] 1990, 24). But it is more than just this. Everyone now benefits from Buck's success, dogs and men. "Highly as the dog-driver had forevalued Buck, with his two devils, he found, while the day was yet young, that he had undervalued. At a bound Buck took up the duties of leadership; and where judgment was required, and quick thinking and quick acting, he showed himself the superior even of Spitz, of whom Francois had never seen an equal" (26). And slackers are pulled back into line.

> Pike, who pulled at Buck's heels, and who never put an ounce more of his weight against the breast-band than he was compelled to do, was swiftly and repeatedly shaken for loafing; and ere the first day was done he was pulling more than ever before in his life. The first night in camp, Joe, the sour one, was punished roundly—a thing that Spitz had never succeeded in doing. Buck simply smothered him by virtue of superior weight, and cut him up till he ceased snapping and began to whine for mercy. (26)[6]

There was a fair amount of poetry along Social Darwinian lines. Robert Bridges's "To a Socialist in London" (1903) is a good example. You think God has made everything nice and easy for us?

> —'Simple it is, (you say) God is good,—Nature is ample,—
> 'Earth yields plenty for all,—and all might share in abundance, . . .

Friend, you forget the Malthusian pressures.

> When goods are increas'd, mouths are increas'd to devour them:
> If the famine be reliev'd this season in India, next dearth
> Will be a worse.

How can we interpret nature but to say LIFE LIVETH ON LIFE?

> That the select creatures, who inherit earth's domination,
> Whose happy existence is Nature's intelligent smile,
> Are bloody survivors of a mortal combat, a-tweenwhiles
> Chanting a brief pæan for victory on the battlefield?

---

[6] Notice how this cooperation fits in with Spencer's organicism. "From the lowest living forms upwards, the degree of development is marked by the degree in which the several parts constitute a co-operative assemblage" (Naso 1981, 17, quoting Spencer 1862).

Since that of all their kinds most owe their prosperous estate
Unto the art, whereby they more successfully destroy'd
Their weaker brethren, more insatiably devour'd them;
And all fine qualities, their forms pictorial, admired,
Their symmetries, their grace, & beauty, the loveliness of them,
Were by Murder evolv'd, to 'scape from it or to effect it.

(Bridges 1953, 426–428)

The Critics

Others were not so sure that throwing over conventional morality and grab-
bing what you can is necessarily the way to go. Jack London was one! He knew
his Huxley as well as his Darwin and Spencer, and he was well up on the debate
over ethics, finding it very stimulating. Obviously this did not mean giving up on
Darwin-Spencer, but in some of his stories he clearly worked in pro-Huxley sentiments. In London's story *The Scarlet Plague* (1912), a new disease wipes out almost
all human beings. One of the survivors, a professor of classics, ruminates on the appalling behavior of people under such huge stresses, not to mention the often grotesque actions of those who do survive. One of the most successful was "an iniq-
uitous, moral monster, a blot on the face of nature, a cruel, relentless, bestial cheat
as well." The professor concludes in a very non-Spencerian fashion that Progress is
never permanent and that the best we can do is fight the beast within us.[7]

> "The gunpowder will come. Nothing can stop it—the same old story
> over and over. Man will increase, and men will fight. The gunpowder
> will enable men to kill millions of men, and in this way only, by fire and
> blood, will a new civilization, in some remote day, be evolved. And of
> what profit will it be? Just as the old civilization passed, so will the new.
> It may take fifty thousand years to build, but it will pass. All things pass."
> (Spencer 1912, 540)[8]

---

[7] To be fair to Spencer, he was not unaware that societies do break down and dissolve (Spencer
1867). The problem is that so often he seems to acknowledge counterinstances to his main theses
without making much effort to harmonize the whole.

[8] London died young, in 1916 at the age of forty. It is easiest to say that his inconsistent positions
are the mark of a man who did not live long enough to work out a mature philosophy. Better to say
that he is reflecting what we have just seen in Gissing (and earlier in Gaskell) and shall see later in
Edith Wharton—a sense that morality has to be more than just Malthusian struggle but yet an admiration for those with the strength to go out and compete and the drive to win. The Christian idea
of humility and acceptance of life's woes—"Blessed *are* the meek: for they shall inherit the earth"
(Matthew 5:5)—something with which Sue consoles Jude—cuts little ice here.

Others felt the same way about the limitations of simplistic moral evolution-ism. In Theodore Dreiser's *Sister Carrie*, the heroine has got herself nicely set up as a mistress. But is this what morality is about?

> For all the liberal analysis of Spencer and our modern naturalistic philosophers, we have but an infantile perception of morals. There is more in the subject than mere conformity to a law of evolution. It is yet deeper than conformity to things of earth alone. It is more involved than we, as yet, perceive. Answer, first, why the heart thrills; explain wherefore some plaintive note goes wandering about the world, un-dying; make clear the rose's subtle alchemy evolving its ruddy lamp in light and rain. In the essence of these facts lie the first principles of morals.
>
> "Oh," thought Drouet, "how delicious is my conquest."
>
> "Ah," thought Carrie, with mournful misgivings, "what is it I have lost?"
>
> Before this world-old proposition we stand, serious, interested, confused; endeavouring to evolve the true theory of morals—the true answer to what is right. (Dreiser [1900] 1991, 68–69)

Moreover, as some perceptive people realized, it is one thing to talk about tri-umph and might and so forth, but there is always the threat from the poor and the weak and the disposed. Bitterness can lead to dreadful vengeance. Thus Wilfrid Scawen Blunt, writing against the British occupation of Ireland.

> Scientists tell us the world has no direction or plan,
> Only a struggle of Nature, each beast and nation at grips,
> Still the fittest surviving and he the fittest who can.
> You are that fittest, the lion to-day in your strength. To-morrow?
> Well, who knows what other will come with a wider jaw?

Indeed:

> Granted your creed of destruction, your right of the strong to devour,
> Granted your law of Nature that he shall live who can kill,
> Find me the law of submission shall stay the weak in his hour,
> His single hour of vengeance, or set a rein on his will.

Better a Christian ethic, than that of Darwin.

> I hold the justice of Heaven
> Larger than all the science, and welled from a purer fount;

God as greater than Nature, His law than the wonders seven,
Darwin's sermon on Man redeemed by that on the Mount.
                                        (Blunt 1914, 2, 251–252)

Some critics thought that it was religion precisely that was a major negative factor in this discussion. *The Jungle*, by Upton Sinclair (1878–1968), tells
the horrific story of a Lithuanian immigrant, Jurgis Rudkus, who comes to
America and works in the stockyards in Chicago at the turn of the century.
He and his family suffer appalling hardships—his wife Ona is pushed into
prostitution before she dies in childbirth, his only surviving child drowns in
a puddle on an unkempt road, the house is lost when he is jailed for beating
up the man who misused Ona, and so the awful tale continues. The descrip-
tions of the sausage making turn the stomach—so much so that Sinclair was
a major force in the enactment of food-safety laws. A striking metaphor is of
Sinclair's human beasts being used by the system as much as the hogs led to
slaughter.

> There was a long line of hogs, with squeals and lifeblood ebbing away
> together; until at last each started again, and vanished with a splash into
> a huge vat of boiling water.
>   It was all so very businesslike that one watched it fascinated. It was
> porkmaking by machinery, porkmaking by applied mathematics. And
> yet somehow the most matter-of-fact person could not help thinking of
> the hogs; they were so innocent, they came so very trustingly; and they
> were so very human in their protests—and so perfectly within their
> rights! They had done nothing to deserve it; and it was adding insult
> to injury, as the thing was done here, swinging them up in this cold-
> blooded, impersonal way, without a pretense of apology, without the
> homage of a tear. (Sinclair [1906] 2001, 29)

Jurgis reflects: "And now was one to believe that there was nowhere a god of
hogs, to whom this hog personality was precious, to whom these hog squeals
and agonies had a meaning? Who would take this hog into his arms and comfort
him, reward him for his work well done, and show him the meaning of his sacrifice?" (30) Later he comes to see how it all applies to him and his family, and
indeed to everyone up and down the food chain: "a hog was just what he had
been—one of the packers' hogs. What they wanted from a hog was all the profits
that could be got out of him; and that was what they wanted from the working-
man, and also that was what they wanted from the public. What the hog thought
of it, and what he suffered, were not considered; and no more was it with labor,
and no more with the purchaser of meat" (264).

This is not a writer who has much truck with religion. Sinclair speaks of religion as the "Archfiend's deadliest weapon" (279) against the poor and suffering. Expectedly, therefore, notwithstanding the trials of the downcast, Sinclair is a strong believer in the possibility of Progress. In fact, one of the major criticisms of religion is that it stands against this philosophy—"Religion oppressed his mind, and poisoned the stream of progress at its source" (279). However, Progress is not going to happen in some Spencerian fashion by making people better. Most of the downtrodden in *The Jungle* end up dead or pushed into crime or prostitution, and those at the other end of the scale are certainly not the highest by any standard. There is an encounter between Jurgis and the son of one of the owners of the meatpacking business, a young man who seems taken straight from the pages of a P. G. Wodehouse farce.[9] Crucially, Sinclair does not dispute the Malthus-Darwin system of economic laws or the thinking of these men about the way they usually function in a cruel fashion. How then are things to be improved? By using the laws of nature to our own ends. Sinclair was a committed socialist and he puts this thinking into the mouth of a journalist:

> It was a process of economic evolution, he said, and he exhibited its laws and methods. Life was a struggle for existence, and the strong overcame the weak, and in turn were overcome by the strongest. Those who lost in the struggle were generally exterminated; but now and then they had been known to save themselves by combination—which was a new and higher kind of strength. It was so that the gregarious animals had overcome the predaceous; it was so, in human history, that the people had mastered the kings. The workers were simply the citizens of industry, and the Socialist movement was the expression of their will to survive. The inevitability of the revolution depended upon this fact, that they had no choice but to unite or be exterminated; this fact, grim and inexorable, depended upon no human will, it was the law of the economic process, of which the editor showed the details with the most marvelous precision. (273)

In *The Jungle* there is no explicit reference to Darwin; perhaps reflecting the Germanic origins of much American socialism, there is a reference to Friedrich Nietzsche as the "prophet of evolution"—but notice how the struggle for existence makes a key appearance. This fits the pattern. Whether or not there are explicit references—and often there are—everyone has Darwin and his work

---

[9] Sinclair is not subtle. It would have been interesting had he tackled the fact that many Chicago business owners were major philanthropists, whose legacy includes the Chicago Art Institute, one of the great collections of the world.

at the back—often at the front—of their mind. This is true whether or not they have grasped the details of Darwin's own work or have some version of it (as in the case of Sinclair) that might owe more to other thinkers, not necessarily sympathetic to Darwin. As always, this overall grappling with Darwin and evolution confirms the kind of case being made. Do not look for nor expect uniformity of belief. One does not get it with Christianity. Why should one expect it of Darwinism?

Thomas Hardy

What do our two great novelists have to say on these issues about morality and proper conduct? The heavily Darwin-influenced Hardy does not look for meaning as such in nature—that is the very point of his overall position. Nature after Darwin has no interest in us. Even when the Immanent Will appears on the scene there is not much joy for humans. Hardy would endorse Richard Dawkins's take on a passage by A. E. Housman:

> For Nature, heartless, witless Nature
> Will neither know nor care.
> DNA neither knows nor cares. DNA just is. And we dance to its music.
> (Dawkins 1995, 133)

This said, Hardy is an intensely moral man. The discussion of class showed us that. Perhaps more than any of our writers, he is the one who worries about free will. As all agree, if we are to be moral beings, then we must have some dimension of free choice. A rock falling under the laws of physics has no freedom, and hence no moral standing. If the rock by chance hits a robber thus allowing the victim to escape, it merits no praise. If the rock by chance smashes a windscreen thus causing a fatal accident, it merits no blame. Most, although not all, Christians endorse some version of what is known as "libertarianism," meaning nothing to do with political freedom and everything to do with free actions lying outside the causal nexus. For someone like Kant, it is not that causation is denied but that it is thought irrelevant (and impossible) for choice. If I do X, I could have done otherwise, and this is not an option when all is determined. Others endorse "compatibilism." Here the opposition is not between freedom and determinism but between freedom and restraint or lack of it. If I do X freely, then I am not restrained. I am not in chains, I am not hallucinating or hypnotized or whatever. Someone like Hume argues that not only is freedom possible given determinism, but it would not be possible without determinism. If I were not, for example, controlled by childhood training, I would not be acting freely. I would be the pawn of my emotions. This may not be a popular Christian option, but there are some—Calvinists particularly—who are drawn to it.

For obvious reasons, Darwinians are going to be drawn to compatibilism. The more you argue that the world is law-like, the more ready you are to include human beings in the system. This was certainly Darwin's position, from the very start. It wasn't a matter of tension. It just seemed obvious: "thinking over these things, one doubts the existence of free will, every action determined by heredetary [*sic*] constitution, example of others, or teaching of others" (Barrett et al. 1987, M. 27). It was also Hardy's. *Tess* is a fascinating example of a novelist working out these ideas in fiction. Life is pretty mean to Tess. She has a sad family background—her mum is nice but weak and limited, and her dad is a total loser; she is pushed into sex by Alec; she gets pregnant and loses the kid; and we are not yet halfway through the novel! Yet, she is a good-looking girl, she is intelligent, she has a reasonably good education, she is a nice person, and much more. Is she just a victim of circumstances, or is she responsible for her fate? In part, obviously she is a victim. I think she really was raped by Alec and had no choice on that. In part, though, she is not. When her baby dies, she is determined that it be buried in consecrated ground and it is. "So the baby was carried in a small deal box, under an ancient woman's shawl, to the churchyard that night, and buried by lantern-light, at the cost of a shilling and a pint of beer to the sexton, in that shabby corner of God's allotment where He lets the nettles grow, and where all unbaptized infants, notorious drunkards, suicides, and others of the conjecturally damned are laid" (Hardy [1892] 2010, 116). Don't we give Tess great moral credit for this?

My reading is that Hardy does allow free will and judgment. I don't see much of a moral issue about Tess stabbing Alec—perhaps I should, but he had it coming—however, I do see more of a moral issue about her having become his mistress. Not much, given the way she has been cast aside by her husband, Angel. But allow that it does sully her purity. It still fits beautifully with a Darwinian reading of freedom—"every action determined by hereditary constitution" (let us correct Darwin's spelling). As we shall see in detail shortly, a huge leitmotiv of the novel is the degenerate blood of the D'Urbervilles. They have sunk since the founder came over with Duke William in 1066. Tess is the end point of this, both victim but also perpetrator. In a way, it is all very Calvinistic. She is part of the causal network, but she is still responsible. You may think this an inadequate analysis of freedom, but it is what Darwin offers (and is not idiosyncratic) and it is what Hardy takes up and uses and illustrates.

What about the morality in Hardy? Sometimes his poetry seems almost unimaginably bleak, suggesting that there is no point to life and that morality counts for naught. No surprise that World War I brought out these feelings. Take first a sonnet—"The Pity of It"—written in the early years of the war. It stresses the way in which the killing is going on between cousins, close kin, not aliens or total strangers. Note also how nonjingoistic it is. It may be Kaiser Wilhelm who was to blame. But it equally could be people on our side. The point is that they are causing great suffering and deserve condemnation.

> I walked in loamy Wessex lanes, afar
> From rail-track and from highway, and I heard
> In field and farmstead many an ancient word
> Of local lineage like "Thu bist," "Er war,"
> "Ich woll", "Er sholl", and by-talk similar,
> Nigh as they speak who in this month's moon gird
> At England's very loins, thereunto spurred
> By gangs whose glory threats and slaughters are.
>
> Then seemed a Heart crying: "Whosoever they be
> At root and bottom of this, who flung this flame
> Between kin folk kin tongued even as are we,
> "Sinister, ugly, lurid, be their fame;
> May their familiars grow to shun their name,
> And their brood perish everlastingly."
>
> (Hardy 1994, 500)[10]

See how after the war Hardy feels no triumph, no sense that right has prevailed. In "Christmas 1924," there is bitterness at what was done—poison gas was the ultimate obscenity—and contempt at the ineffectiveness of Christianity. This poem is as brilliantly short as it is brilliantly brutal.

> "Peace upon earth!" was said. We sing it,
> And pay a million priests to bring it.
> After two thousand years of mass
> We've got as far as poison-gas.
>
> (Hardy 1994, 848)

Yet, the pagan theme that runs right through Hardy's work suggests not just a oneness with the earth—as in Drummer Hodge—but also a oneness with each other. There is no God or gods, there is no supernatural salvation, but we humans

---

[10] Christians likewise were bemused by the violent conflict between relatives and neighbors. In *Greenmantle* the hero, racked with fever, stays with the family of a woodcutter, the man away fighting. "I thought we could never end the war properly without giving the Huns some of their own medicine. But that woodcutter's cottage cured me of such nightmares" (Buchan [1916] 1992, 191). There was hatred of those who caused the war. But the sentiments are Hardy's. "What good would it do Christian folk to burn poor little huts like this and leave children's bodies by the wayside? To be able to laugh and to be merciful are the only things that make man better than the beasts."

can and must hang together. There is a kind of blind force—the Immanent Will—that infuses everything. Herein lie morality and duty. We see this in the poem "A Plaint to Man" written around 1910. God is speaking to us, saying first that for some reason as we evolved we had need of God and so created Him.

> When you slowly emerged from the den of Time,
> And gained percipience as you grew,
> And fleshed you fair out of shapeless slime,
>
> Wherefore, O Man, did there come to you
> The unhappy need of creating me —
> A form like your own for praying to?

But now that need is vanishing or gone, and we humans are on our own.

> And now that I dwindle day by day
> Beneath the deicide eyes of seers
> In a light that will not let me stay,
>
> And to-morrow the whole of me disappears,
> The truth should be told, and the fact be faced
> That had best been faced in earlier years:
>
> The fact of life with dependence placed
> On the human heart's resource alone,
> In brotherhood bonded close and graced
>
> With loving-kindness fully blown,
> And visioned help unsought, unknown.
>
> (296)

Find the resources within yourself, for they are not to be found elsewhere. One cannot but be struck by the similarity of thought to that of existentialism. In *The Brothers Karamazov* (1880), Dostoevsky has one of his characters say: "God does not exist, so all things are permitted."[11] Of course, neither Dostoevsky nor any who followed him—notably Jean Paul Sartre who popularized that

---

[11] A modern translation (with the key phrase in bold) runs: "Rakitin now—he doesn't like God, doesn't like Him at all. To people like him, God is a sore spot. But they hide it, they lie, they pretend. 'Will you,' I asked him, 'try to develop these ideas in your literary criticism?' 'They won't let me do it too openly,' he said, and laughed. 'But tell me,' I asked him, 'what will happen to men? **If there's no God** and no life beyond the grave, doesn't that mean that **men will be allowed to do whatever they want**?' 'Didn't you know that already?' he said and laughed again. 'An intelligent man can do

saying—thought that was the end of the matter. It is rather the beginning of moral inquiry. We are seeing parallel thoughts in that most English of writers, Thomas Hardy.[12]

George Eliot

And so to George Eliot. We see in her novels an attempt to work out a secular account of morality, against a background of Spencer and Darwin too, for all that she grumbled about Darwin's thinking. She and Lewes studied Darwin and thought deeply about the evolution of morality, although perhaps with respect to the *Descent* being more inclined to give the social a bigger role than the biological. But these were differences within the paradigm, as it were, and they agreed fully with the overall naturalistic approach. This comes through particularly in Eliot's novel, *Daniel Deronda*, and is the reason why I see it as more integrated than do other readers. Although clearly in living unmarried with Lewes she was not about to be constrained by the norms of society, Eliot was no radical trying to destroy them.[13] In the twin characters of Gwendolen Harleth and Daniel Deronda, Eliot is showing us the consequences of our actions and using these as justification for (good) moral behavior.[14] There is nothing very mysterious. We are told right from the beginning that Gwen is a wonderful person, beautiful in her distinctive way, intelligent, interesting, and a very attractive young

anything he likes as long as he's clever enough to get away with it. But you, you got caught after you killed, so today you have to rot in prison.' He's real swine to say that to my face; a few months ago I used to throw people like that out of the window. But now I just sit and listen to him" (Dostoevsky [1880] 1983, 788). The speaker is one brother Mitya (Dmitri), falsely accused of the murder of his father, to another brother Aloysha (Alexei). Ratikin is a journalist, repeating ideas he got from the third brother, Ivan.

[12] Inasmuch as we ever do, we are seeing a move to evolutionary meliorism. Hardy studied Henri Bergson's *Creative Evolution* with care, although expectedly far from uncritically.

[13] Although some (including Huxley) would not bring their wives to meet her, socially George Eliot was no pariah. The Darwins, not being bourgeois in the way of the Huxleys, had no reservations. Charles met her several times, explicitly asked that his daughter be allowed to visit, and a very thrilled Emma finally had the opportunity to tell the novelist to her face how much she enjoyed her fiction (Browne 2002, 405).

[14] As noted earlier, Eliot had translated David Strauss, so although Eliot is searching for a non-religious backing for morality, it is surely the case that biblical scholarship along with evolution was behind this drive. Expectedly, this is not the only place in her fiction where Eliot makes this kind of argument. Of *Middlemarch*, a very perceptive critic writes: "At its simplest level, George Eliot wants to suggest that crime does not pay. If organic social harmony is to be preserved, wrongdoing must be shown to have undesired consequences for the perpetrator" (Shuttleworth 1984, 153). Newton (1974) also picks up on this theme in *Middlemarch*, suggesting that Dorothea gains happiness thanks to her essential goodness and Lydgate does not because of his self-centered attitude to life.

woman. She is also spoiled and incredibly self-centered. If life isn't directed to Gwen's pleasures and comforts, she doesn't want to know about it. We learn that at once from the title of Book One—"The Spoiled Child." The plot of the story is sparked by the failure of a bank in which her family has parked its money. "The first effect of this letter on Gwendolen was half-stupefying. The implicit confidence that her destiny must be one of luxurious ease, where any trouble that occurred would be well clad and provided for, had been stronger in her own mind than in her mamma's, being fed there by her youthful blood and that sense of superior claims which made a large part of her consciousness" (Eliot [1876] 1967, 44). Not a thought for poor old mother or anyone else. All "poor Gwen." "There was no inward exclamation of 'Poor mamma!' Her mamma had never seemed to get much enjoyment out of life, and if Gwendolen had been at this moment disposed to feel pity [she is more angry than anything other] she would have bestowed it on herself—for was she not naturally and rightfully the chief object of her mamma's anxiety too?" (45)

This is just the beginning. Gwen is not a monster and it is made clear through the novel that she does have redeeming features—she is fun to be with: "even those ladies who did not quite like her, felt a comfort in having a new, striking girl to invite" (72)—but it is me, me, me, all the time. And this leads her into making the disastrous marriage with a rich man, Henleigh Mallinger Grandcourt, who turns out to be a thoroughly unpleasant human being, without a modicum of feeling for anyone but himself. And so Gwen ends up really unhappy. Even when Grandcourt drowns—and note that there is some ambiguity about how much she did or did not help him in distress—the misery persists. And she finally realizes what she has done. "It is because I was always wicked that I am miserable now" (825). But it is too late. Daniel, whom she really does fancy, has a different girlfriend (Mirah) and is about to get married and head off East to found a Jewish homeland.

Now take Daniel. He has been brought up as a gentleman with no clear aim of getting a profession. He doesn't know where he comes from but as Sir Hugo's ward he is in pretty good hands. He too is blessed with looks, social decency, and so forth. But, from the start, it is the well-being of others that is his concern. Even in Chapter One, before he knows anything of Gwen, he is rescuing her bracelet for her from the pawnbrokers where she has taken it after her losses at the gambling table. And this kind of behavior continues. In what is really rather heavy-handed symbolism, Daniel too has the chance to rescue someone from drowning (Mirah who is in despair). He not only succeeds but takes her to the family of his friend (Hans) and from then on is concerned about her welfare, even before he falls in love with her. When his friend has eyesight troubles, Daniel sacrifices his own time (and hence his chances at a scholarship) to help because the friend needs to succeed (and get money) more than he does. "Daniel

had the stamp of rarity in a subdued fervor of sympathy, an activity of imagination on behalf of others which did not show itself effusively, but was continually
seen in acts of considerateness that struck his companions as moral eccentric-
ity" (218). And his moral goodness continues, not just to Mirah but also to her
ailing brother, Mordecai. And in the end, he finds true contentment, not only in
his relationship with Mirah but in the real course of action and plan that he has
found for his life. In following his plan, he will serve others and find personal
happiness.

Is this Darwinian? Is this Spencerian? It doesn't matter. What matters is
Eliot's finding a solution to her own demand in the Fellows' Garden at Trinity.
A solution making no appeal to the will of the Almighty but firmly grounded
within the space opened by the evolutionists.[15] She was an exceptional thinker,
one of the truly great contributors to the English literary tradition. In our context, she was another helping shape and articulate the Darwinian alternative to
the Christian religion.[16]

[15] Note the difference in this respect between *Nemesis of Faith* and *Robert Elsmere* (Ashton 1989).
In Froude's novel, loss of faith leads the hero into a very morally ambiguous relationship with another
man's wife. In Ward's post-George Eliot novel, the hero's loss of faith leads him into even-greater
moral behavior in the slums of London. Mrs. Ward herself was nigh-Kantian in her belief in an unfal-
tering and categorical moral code, and in respects socially conservative (Peterson 1976). She always
opposed women's suffrage.

[16] It has been suggested that George Eliot's early novel *Silas Marner* (1861) could be her rework-
ing of the story of Job (Fisher 2003). It is the tale of a weaver unfairly cast out of his community
apparently by the will of God (lots are thrown and he is the loser), who then has his savings stolen,
and only slowly regains his sense of self-worth and happiness—coming back to the beginning like
Job—through his caring love for a little girl who appears at his fire hearth, her golden curls a far better
exchange for his lost sovereigns. This would fit nicely with Eliot's secular perspective, that the way to
recoup from life's undeserved misfortunes lies less in worshiping the deity and more through making
an effort yourself to buck up and get on with things. There are interesting parallels and contrasts
here with Dickens's *Bleak House*, a novel written pre-*Origin* by a Christian. Job laments: "Let the day
perish wherein I was born" (Job 3:3). The central figure of Esther is told by her stern godmother
(aunt): "It would have been far better, little Esther, that you had had no birthday, that you had never
been born!" (Dickens [1853] 1948, 17). But whereas Job resolves things through repentance and
faith, Esther—brimming with love—resolves things by confronting her own insecurities and rising
above them. The Esther searching her mother is a very different Esther from the one who left her
godmother's house. Progress is starting to edge out Providence (Larson 1985, 161–162).

Sex

Christianity

Sex can be a rotten business sometimes.

> "It was all Mrs. Bumble. She *would* do it," urged Mr. Bumble; first look-
> ing round to ascertain that his partner had left the room.
> "That is no excuse," replied Mr. Brownlow. "You were present on the
> occasion of the destruction of these trinkets, and indeed are the more
> guilty of the two, in the eye of the law; for the law supposes that your
> wife acts under your direction."
> "If the law supposes that," said Mr. Bumble, squeezing his hat em-
> phatically in both hands, "the law is a ass—a idiot. If that's the eye of
> the law, the law is a bachelor; and the worst I wish the law is, that his
> eye may be opened by experience—by experience." (Dickens [1837]
> 1948, 399)

This is humorous, but the Victorians felt the power and dread of sexuality.
Kipling expressed feelings that many felt.

> When Nag the basking cobra hears the careless foot of man,
> He will sometimes wriggle sideways and avoid it if he can.
> But his mate makes no such motion where she camps beside the trail.
> For the female of the species is more deadly than the male.

This does not hold just in the animal world.

> When the early Jesuit fathers preached to Hurons and Choctaws,
> They prayed to be delivered from the vengeance of the squaws.
> 'Twas the women, not the warriors, turned those stark enthusiasts pale.
> For the female of the species is more deadly than the male.

And note how it all gets tangled up with religion, with the poor sap of a male trying to appeal to his God to justify his superiority, with but limited effect.

> And Man knows it! Knows, moreover, that the Woman that God gave him
> Must command but may not govern—shall enthral but not enslave him.
> And *She* knows, because *She* warns him, and Her instincts never fail,
> That the Female of Her Species is more deadly than the Male.
> (Kipling 2001, 379–380)

Sex plays a big part in religions, and this is especially true of the Christian religion. It just has to, if religion is to have any grip on the human imagination. From our births, sex is just about the most important thing in our lives, starting with (at least as it was in my childhood) whether we are to be dressed in blue or in pink! Families are based on sex—that is why the controversy over gay marriage is so important for both sides—huge amounts of our daily lives, physical and emotional, are based on sex, and almost all social decisions and consequences involve sex at some level. The story of Christianity highlights sex, starting with Adam and Eve, and going through to the gospels and on to the story of Paul. It is also prescriptive—sexual requirements and prohibitions—and this has been ongoing. Christianity and sexuality did not stop with Revelation but continue down to the present. Witness, for instance, the battles over women priests and bishops in the Anglican Church.

It is virtually impossible to say briefly what the attitude of Christianity is towards sex, but surely one can say that there are two, somewhat conflicting, main themes. On the one hand, sex is a good thing. God created Adam and Eve, man and woman, for companionship but also for procreation. Having children is a good thing both personally and for society. It is right and proper to fall in love, to reproduce, to cherish one's offspring and also more generally to support one another in these activities. On the other hand, sex is a worrisome thing. Adam and Eve sinned and were kicked out of Eden where they had to work for their livings and childbirth would be difficult and painful; the Messiah was apparently celibate which seems prima facie a little bit odd if he is supposed to be fully human; and so it goes on to the various restrictions on priesthood, on sex outside marriage, and even on sex within marriage—with respect to contraception for instance. Often—usually—males are given the dominant role in Christian discussions— "Wives, submit yourselves to your husbands, as is fitting in the Lord" (Colossians 3:18)—but the power (and danger) of women is fully recognized. We are sinners because Adam sinned, but it was Eve who put him up to it. Sex is important but it isn't easy.

Darwinism and Sexuality

Darwinism is as obsessed with sex as is Christianity.[1] Darwin wrote of the struggle for existence, but he knew and at once made clear that mere existence means nothing. "I should premise that I use the term Struggle for Existence in a large and metaphorical sense, including dependence of one being on another, and including (which is more important) not only the life of the individual, but success in leaving progeny" (Darwin 1859, 62). Without sex, evolution grinds to a rapid halt. When it came to humankind, sex took on an even greater role and importance, because it was here that sexual selection kicked in in a big way. Remember that there are two kinds of sexual selection, selection through male combat and selection through female choice, although Darwin made it clear that neither variety was the exclusive lien of one sex. Of North American Indians Darwin quotes one observer: "It has ever been the custom among these people for the men to wrestle for any woman to whom they are attached; and, of course, the strongest party always carries off the prize" (Darwin 1871, 2, 324). This is as typical a case of male combat as two stags fighting. But often we get cases of males choosing their mates on beauty rather than females doing the choosing. Indeed: "In civilised life man is largely, but by no means exclusively, influenced in the choice of his wife by external appearance ..." (2, 338). Actually Darwin is a bit more nuanced and realistic than this. "Civilised men are largely attracted by the mental charms of women, by their wealth, and especially by their social position; for men rarely marry into a much lower rank of life" (2, 355–356). That, of course, is why the Eugene Wrayburn-Lizzie Hexam union was such a fraught business.

Sexual selection through female choice in humans goes the other way too.

> In Northern Africa "a man requires a period of from 'eight to ten years to perfect his coiffure.' With other nations the head is shaved, and in parts of South America and Africa even the eyebrows are eradicated. The natives of the Upper Nile knock out the four front teeth, saying that they do not wish to resemble brutes. Further south, the Batokas knock out the two upper incisors, which, as Livingstone remarks, gives the face a hideous appearance, owing to the growth of the lower jaw; but these people think the presence of the incisors most unsightly, and

---

[1] This is a major reason why there is so much material to be discussed, and not just in this chapter. Given the obsession, evolutionary themes were a means through which the somewhat socially repressed Victorians could think and write legitimately about sexuality.

on beholding some Europeans, cried out, 'Look at the great teeth!'"
(2, 340)

As always though, Darwin knew the power of social position and money. "With
respect to the opposite form of selection, namely of the more attractive men by
the women, although in civilised nations women have free or almost free choice,
which is not the case with barbarous races, yet their choice is largely influenced
by the social position and wealth of the men; and the success of the latter in life
largely depends on their intellectual powers and energy, or on the fruits of these
same powers in their forefathers" (2, 356).

Sexual Selection in Fiction

Novelists and poets loved this sort of stuff, and expectedly it runs right through
our period—at all levels. Famously, at the end of *Tarzan of the Apes*, Jane sup-
presses "the psychological appeal of the primeval man to the primeval woman in
her nature" and, on very Darwinian lines, makes the sensible decision to marry
the apparent Lord Greystoke (William Cecil Clayton) instead of the (unac-
knowledged) true Lord Greystoke (Tarzan).

> Did not her best judgment point to this young English nobleman,
> whose love she knew to be of the sort a civilized woman should crave,
> as the logical mate for such as herself?
>   Could she love Clayton? She could see no reason why she could not.
> Jane was not coldly calculating by nature, but training, environment
> and heredity had all combined to teach her to reason even in matters of
> the heart. (Burroughs [1912] 2008, 340)

Fortunately, for those whose lives would be lessened without the twenty-five
sequels, this proves not to be a lasting commitment.[2]
    Sexual selection is likewise the underlying theme of George Meredith's *The
Egoist* (1879), a novel about a young woman trying to wriggle out of an unfortunate engagement.

> A deeper student of Science than his rivals, he appreciated Nature's com-
> pliment in the fair one's choice of you. We now scientifically know that

---

[2] Edgar Rice Burroughs owned a copy of the *Descent of Man* and it was a big influence on a
Martian science-fiction trilogy, penned at just the time of *Tarzan* (Parrett 2004, xviii). He believed in
God but could not stand established religion because of its perceived opposition to science.

in this department of the universal struggle, success is awarded to the bettermost. You spread a handsomer tail than your fellows, you dress a finer top-knot, you pipe a newer note, have a longer stride; she reviews you in competition, and selects you. The superlative is magnetic to her. She may be looking elsewhere, and you will see—the superlative will simply have to beckon, away she glides. She cannot help herself; it is her nature, and her nature is the guarantee for the noblest races of men to come of her. In complimenting you, she is a promise of superior off-spring. Science thus—or it is better to say—an acquaintance with science facilitates the cultivation of aristocracy. Consequently a successful pursuit and a wresting of her from a body of competitors, tells you that you are the best man. What is more, it tells the world so. (Meredith [1879] 1968, 71–72)

As it happens, Meredith (1828–1909) is poking fun at the chap who thinks this way. The gist of the novel is that sexual selection does work, but it is a lot more subtle than many take it to be. Young women don't necessarily go for the most obvious choice—intelligence, sensitivity and a lot of other things come into play too (Smith 1995; Williams 1983). That said, it was seen that Darwin was right about the lure of power and status. For all that there is a snide remark about how ugly men who choose pretty women as mates do not guarantee beauty in the offspring, George Eliot is no less committed to sexual selection in *Daniel Deronda* (1876).[3] The Darwinian theme is unmistakable (Beer 1983).

Some readers of this history will doubtless regard it as incredible that people should construct matrimonial prospects on the mere report that a bachelor of good fortune and possibilities was coming within reach, and will reject the statement as a mere outflow of gall: they will aver that neither they nor their first cousins have minds so unbridled; and that in fact this is not human nature, which would know that such speculations might turn out to be fallacious, and would therefore not entertain them. (Eliot [1876] 1967, 123)

---

[3] About a young woman who inherited from her father her plain looks—"underhung and with receding brow resembling that of the more intelligent fishes"—Eliot wrote "considering the importance which is given to such an accident in female offspring, marriageable men, or what the new English calls "intending bridegrooms," should look at themselves dispassionately in the glass, since their natural selection of a mate prettier than themselves is not certain to bar the effect of their own ugliness" (Eliot [1876] 1967, 149). In the *Descent*, Darwin had said that the British aristocracy "from having chosen during many generations from all classes the more beautiful women as their wives, have become handsomer, according to the European standard of beauty, than the middle classes" (Darwin 1871, 2, 356).

Eliot begs to differ. A woman has beauty and youth to sell. A man has power and money and status to offer. It is a business transition pure and simple. Gwendolen escapes the dreary life of a governess through the bargain of her marriage to Grandcourt.

> All the while they were looking at each other; and Grandcourt said, slowly and languidly, as if it were of no importance, other things having been settled—
>
> "You will tell me now, I hope, that Mrs. Davilow's [Gwen's mother] loss of fortune will not trouble you further. You will trust me to prevent it from weighing upon her. You will give me the claim to provide against that."
>
> The little pauses and refined drawlings with which this speech was uttered, gave time for Gwendolen to go through the dream of a life. As the words penetrated her, they had the effect of a draught of wine, which suddenly makes all things easier, desirable things not so wrong, and people in general less disagreeable. She had a momentary phantasmal love for this man who chose his words so well, and who was a mere incarnation of delicate homage. Repugnance, dread, scruples—these were dim as remembered pains, while she was already tasting relief under the immediate pain of hopelessness. She imagined herself already springing to her mother, and being playful again. Yet when Grandcourt had ceased to speak, there was an instant in which she was conscious of being at the turning of the ways.
>
> "You are very generous," she said, not moving her eyes, and speaking with a gentle intonation.
>
> "You accept what will make such things a matter of course?" said Grandcourt, without any new eagerness. "You consent to become my wife?" (347)

And so she does. But Grandcourt is playing the same game. He wants a charming, attractive woman as his wife—one who is not "used goods" like the mistress we learn that he had. He also wants a woman of spirit whom he can control and break. It certainly doesn't sound like the usual passions.

> "I am going to marry the other girl."
> "Have you fallen in love?" This question carried a strong sneer.
> "I am going to marry her." (163)[4]

---

[4] Given that Eliot read Darwin's *Expression of the Emotions in Man and Animals* in preparation for this book, it is interesting to note that Darwin gives a very full discussion of blushing and that blushing is a major attribute of both of Eliot's central young women, as in (Gwendolen) "She knew Grandcourt's

Thomas Hardy

George Eliot is a truly great artist, but there is always something a little bit cerebral even in the most intense of her fictional relationships. Perhaps it was the pagan in him, but Hardy had the sense of raw animal passion. In the *Descent*, Darwin has an extended discussion of music and our feelings for it. It puzzles him, obviously, because he doesn't see the immediate utility. "With man song is generally admitted to be the basis or origin of instrumental music. As neither the enjoyment nor the capacity of producing musical notes are faculties of the least direct use to man in reference to his ordinary habits of life, they must be ranked amongst the most mysterious with which he is endowed" (Darwin 1871, 2, 333). However, in a very familiar pattern, going back to such things as bird songs and their sexual power, Darwin relates this to humankind: "the suspicion does not appear improbable that the progenitors of man, either the males or females, or both sexes, before they had acquired the power of expressing their mutual love in articulate language, endeavoured to charm each other with musical notes and rhythm" (2, 337). Adding: "The impassioned orator, bard, or musician, when with his varied tones and cadences he excites the strongest emotions in his hearers, little suspects that he uses the same means by which, at an extremely remote period, his half-human ancestors aroused each other's ardent passions, during their mutual courtship and rivalry" (337).

Hardy picks up on this.[5] Tess is working with three other girls as a milkmaid. Angel turns up to train as a farmer and carries all four girls across a puddle when they are on the way to church. They all fall for him and the sexual tension is high. You can smell the pheromones.

> The air of the sleeping-chamber seemed to palpitate with the hopeless passion of the girls. They writhed feverishly under the oppressiveness of an emotion thrust on them by cruel Nature's law—an emotion

indistinct handwriting, and her mother was not surprised to see her blush deeply" (336) and (Mirah) "But when she uttered the words she blushed deeply" (680). If you check (taking almost at random) a pre-*Origin* novel like *Bleak House*, you find a lot of blushing there too, so perhaps one should be careful at drawing firm lines of descent. That said, in a way that is not true of Dickens, Eliot makes blushing work for her and picks up on specific Darwinian points, for instance, about the link between blushing and confusion. "Her annoyance at what she imagined to be the obviousness of her confusion robbed her of her usual facility in carrying it off by playful speech, and turning up her face to look at the roof, she wheeled away in that attitude. If any had noticed her blush as significant, they had certainly not interpreted it by the secret windings and recesses of her feeling. A blush is no language: only a dubious flag-signal which may mean either of two contradictories" (Eliot [1876] 1967, 474).

[5] So does Sherlock Holmes in *The Study in Scarlet*, telling Watson that Darwin thinks musical ability predates speech. "Perhaps that is why we are so subtly influenced by it. There are vague memories in our souls of those misty centuries when the world was in its childhood" (Conan Doyle [1887] 2003, 33).

which they had neither expected nor desired. The incident of the day had fanned the flame that was burning the inside of their hearts out, and the torture was almost more than they could endure. The differences which distinguished them as individuals were abstracted by this passion, and each was but portion of one organism called sex. (Hardy [1892] 2010, 175)

Angel makes his choice, Tess. Now he must catch her. It is his playing on the harp that does it.

Tess had heard those notes in the attic above her head. Dim, flattened, constrained by their confinement, they had never appealed to her as now, when they wandered in the still air with a stark quality like that of nudity. To speak absolutely, both instrument and execution were poor; but the relative is all, and as she listened Tess, like a fascinated bird, could not leave the spot. Far from leaving she drew up towards the performer, keeping behind the hedge that he might not guess her presence. (146–147)

"A stark quality like that of nudity"![6] "Tess was conscious of neither time nor space. The exaltation which she had described as being producible at will by gazing at a star came now without any determination of hers; she undulated upon the thin notes of the second-hand harp, and their harmonies passed like breezes through her, bringing tears into her eyes. The floating pollen seemed to be his notes made visible, and the dampness of the garden the weeping of the garden's sensibility" (147). This animal-like girl—remember her lushness, her full-breastedness, her passionate nature—is captured—"the dampness of the garden" ready for the "floating pollen." This is of the order of—and plays the same essential but unsettling role as—David's lust for Bathsheba. Sex is good, but oh it is so animal and hence so dangerous.[7]

---

[6] Music has the same erotic undertones in the end-of-the-century novel, *The Awakening*, by Kate Chopin. "One piece which that lady played Edna had entitled 'Solitude.' It was a short, plaintive, minor strain. The name of the piece was something else, but she called it 'Solitude.' When she heard it there came before her imagination the figure of a man standing beside a desolate rock on the seashore. He was naked" (Chopin [1899] 1994, 25).

[7] There are many other places in Hardy's writings where one can look profitably for themes of sexual selection (Ebbatson 1982). Two recent writers have drawn attention to Darwin's discussion of blushing in the *Expression* and the major role that blushing plays in *A Pair of Blue Eyes*—as in "'Forgive me,' she said, laughing a little, a little frightened, and blushing very deeply" (Mallet 2009; Richardson 1998). Perhaps so, although given that Darwin's work did not appear until late in 1872 by which time Hardy was already serializing his novel, it might be safest to say simply that Hardy was writing in a Darwinian mode.

Women on Darwinism on Sex

Darwin (and Huxley) had some pretty Victorian ideas about the sexes. Neither of them thought that women could compete with men. Their brains are not big enough. They just don't have the intelligence needed; nor do they have the drive. Expectedly, this was fodder for that enterprising duo, Gilbert and Sullivan. Their 1884 operetta *Princess Ida*, based on Tennyson's poem "The Princess," tells the story of a school for young women, isolated from men. Poking fun at the great evolutionists, one of the mistresses expresses a Darwin-inspired perspective on things with a very different conclusion.

> A Lady fair, of lineage high,
> Was loved by an Ape, in the days gone by
> The Maid was radiant as the sun,
> The Ape was a most unsightly one.
> So it would not do;

The ardent primate does his best.

> With a view to rise in the social scale,
> He shaved his bristles, and he docked his tail,
> He grew moustachios, and he took his tub,
> And he paid a guinea to a toilet club

Still no luck. He continued as "the apiest Ape that ever was seen!" So desperate measures are taken.

> He bought white ties, and he bought dress suits,
> He crammed his feet into bright tight boots
> And to start in life on a bran new plan,
> He christened himself Darwinian Man!

Again, however, he was out of luck.

> For the Maiden fair, whom the Monkey craved,
> Was a radiant Being,
> With a brain far-seeing
> While a Man, however well-behaved,
> At best is only a monkey shaved!
>
> (Bradley 1988, 261–263)

Ultimately, though, the women jump back into line and do their Darwinian duty, getting married.

This is parody. More than one female author was made of sterner stuff, willing to accept the overall Darwinian picture but taking a serious view of the alternatives. In "The Ballad of the Ichthyosaurus," a poem published in *Punch* in 1885, May Kendall wrote semihumorously about the struggle.

> Ere Man was developed, our brother,
> We swam and we ducked and we dived,
> And we dined, as a rule, on each other —
> What matter, the toughest survived.
>
> (Kendall 1887, 14)

She recognized women's lowly role, but (in "Woman's Future") expected evolution (perhaps in a Spencerian fashion) to put things right.

> Complacent they tell us, hard hearts and derisive,
> In vain is our ardour; in vain are our sighs:
> Our intellects, bound by a limit decisive,
> To the level of Homer's may never arise.
> We heed not the falsehood, the base innuendo,
> The laws of the universe, these are our friends,
> Our talents shall rise in a mighty crescendo,
> We trust Evolution to make us amends.

It is in part our own faults because we spend our time drinking tea and knitting. More effort is needed.

> Oh, rouse to a lifework — do something worth doing!
> Invent a new planet, a flying-machine.
> Mere charms superficial, mere feminine graces,
> That fade or that flourish, no more you may prize;
> But the knowledge of Newton will beam from your faces,
> The soul of a Spencer will shine in your eyes.
>
> (Kendall 1887, 38–39)

One suspects that someone's leg is being pulled a little here.

Certainly, if you want leg pulling to a serious purpose, look no further than the poetry of Constance Naden. She knew all about sexual selection and she knew that it did not work always as well as an aged, upper-middle-class male like Charles Darwin might suppose. Her delightful poem "Natural Selection" (actually more about sexual selection), written around 1885, hits the nail right on the head. Ultimately, none of us are really that clever. We are driven by forces over which we don't have much control. Reason and common sense don't have much say in these things.

> I HAD found out a gift for my fair,
>   I had found where the cave men were laid:
> Skulls, femur and pelvis were there,
>   And spears that of silex they made.
>
> But he ne'er could be true, she averred,
>   Who would dig up an ancestor's grave—
> And I loved her the more when I heard
>   Such foolish regard for the cave.
>
> My shelves they are furnished with stones,
>   All sorted and labelled with care;
> And a splendid collection of bones,
>   Each one of them ancient and rare;
>
> One would think she might like to retire
>   To my study—she calls it a "hole"!
> Not a fossil I heard her admire
>   But I begged it, or borrowed, or stole.
>
> But there comes an idealess lad,
>   With a strut and a stare and a smirk;
> And I watch, scientific, though sad,
>   The Law of Selection at work.
>
> Of Science he had not a trace,
>   He seeks not the How and the Why,
> But he sings with an amateur's grace,
>   And he dances much better than I.
>
> And we know the more dandified males
>   By dance and by song win their wives—
> 'Tis a law that with *avis* prevails,
>   And ever in *Homo* survives.

> Shall I rage as they whirl in the valse?
>   Shall I sneer as they carol and coo?
> Ah no! for since Chloe is false
>   I'm certain that Darwin is true.[8]
>
> (Naden 1999, 207–208)

There was always something a little bit pompous about Herbert Spencer. He was the sort of man who, if you commented favorably on his genius in his presence, would accept your judgment gravely with thanks and agreement. Constance Naden too cannot help teasing him, at the same time respecting his work and Darwin's. Another of her poems, "The New Orthodoxy," like "Natural Selection" from a collection called "Evolutionary Erotics," has a young woman joshing her boyfriend for his stick-in-the-mud ways.

> Things with fin, and claw, and hoof
> Join to give us perfect proof
> That our being's warp and woof
>   We from near and far win;
> Yet your flippant doubts you vaunt,
> And—to please a maiden aunt—
> You've been heard to say you can't
>   Pin your faith to Darwin!
>
> Then you jest, because Laplace
> Said this Earth was nought but gas
> Till the vast rotating mass
>   Denser grew and denser:
> Something worse they whisper too,
> But I'm sure it *can't* be true—
> For they tell me, Fred, that you
>   Scoff at Herbert Spencer!
>
> (205)

We learn in this poem that although Fred went to Oxford, she (Amy) went to the women's college at Cambridge, Girton. Both May Kendall and Constance

---

[8] I do not see Naden putting down women in this poem, suggesting that the girl alone is flighty and shallow (Murphy 2002). Here and elsewhere I see her astutely poking fun at young people of both sexes, suggesting that often they are dominated by their (Darwinian) emotions and that reason doesn't come into things very much. This all fits in with a philosophical theory she elaborated and embraced, "Hylo-Idealism," a kind of evolutionary monism that sees everything as part of a world force or spirit, that in some sense she identified with the feminine (Thain 2003).

Naden were educated women, with strong social consciousness. One senses the self-respect in the poems. Like those formidable mother superiors in the middle ages who were not about to let males run over them, so these women represented a new age of female awareness. To his credit, Spencer was not unappreciative, writing on Naden's far-too-early death: "I can think of no woman, save 'George Eliot,' in whom there has been this union of high philosophical capacity with extensive acquisition. Unquestionably her subtle intelligence would have done much in furtherance of rational thought; and her death has entailed a serious loss" (Hughes 1890, 89–90). He felt the need to qualify his judgment by adding: "While I say this, however, I cannot let pass the occasion for remarking that in her case, as in other cases, the mental powers so highly developed in a woman are in some measure abnormal, and involve a physiological cost which the feminine organization will not bear without injury more or less profound." Naden died after an operation to remove ovarian cysts. Female readers take note.

Darwinian Sex: The American Dark Side

Henry James's first truly great novel, *Portrait of a Lady* (1881), has a heroine who owes much to Dorothea Brooke and Gwendolen Harleth (Levine 1963). Isabel Archer is a young American who comes to England and is unexpectedly left a fortune by a somewhat distant relative. She has already refused two suitors, the English nobleman Lord Warburton and the American businessman Caspar Goodwood, but then is enchanted into marriage by an older, penniless American living in Italy, Gilbert Osmond. The story is of Isabel's growing distaste for Osmond, and her realization that he married her only for her fortune, needing it to launch his own daughter, Pansy—who it turns out at the end of the novel was the result of an adulterous relationship with a woman, Madame Merle, who was the force behind the trapping of Isabel.

Isabel is faced with options like Gwendolen but much resembles Dorothea and her choice of Casaubon, taking as husband a man with few visible virtues but whom romantically she has vested with desirability.

> She had had a more wondrous vision of him, fed through charmed senses and oh such a stirred fancy!—she had not read him right. A certain combination of features had touched her, and in them she had seen the most striking of figures. That he was poor and lonely and yet that somehow he was noble—that was what had interested her and seemed to give her her opportunity. There had been an indefinable beauty about him—in his situation, in his mind, in his face. She had felt at the same time that he was helpless and ineffectual, but the feeling had taken

the form of a tenderness which was the very flower of respect. He was like a sceptical voyager strolling on the beach while he waited for the tide, looking seaward yet not putting to sea. It was in all this she had found her occasion. She would launch his boat for him; she would be his providence; it would be a good thing to love him. (James [1881] 2011, 449)

Henry James (1843–1916) had met Darwin ten years before he started on the novel, and later got to know both George Eliot and George Lewes as well as Herbert Spencer. He also had a brother, William James, who, especially in the realm of psychology, was rapidly moving into being the most sensitive thinker of his age about the implications of Darwin's theorizing (James 1880a, b).[9] There is little surprise that it is Darwinian sexual selection that sets much of the background of the novel, combined with dashes of Spencerian thinking about the ways in which women have adapted to please men (Bender 1996, 136).[10] First Spencer: "the men of the conquering races which gave origin to the civilized races, were men in whom the brutal characteristics were dominant; and necessarily the women of such races, having to deal with brutal men, prospered in proportion as they possessed, or acquired, fit adjustments of nature" (Spencer [1873] 1889, 375). Then James: "It was astonishing what happiness she could still find in the idea of procuring a pleasure for her husband" (437). This said, James is obviously using Darwinian theory as a foil to see what combinations are permissible. Some of the thinking is fairly straightforward.[11] Osmond wants Isabel's money, especially to launch his own child. Isabel's friends cannot believe that she will not choose either Warburton or Goodwood, conventional choices—Warburton and Goodwood are a bit taken aback too. But as with Eliot and Dorothea, James sees that the sexual dance is not always straightforward and that some people are able to deceive (as with Osmond) or open to deception (as with Isabel). *Portrait of a Lady* is anything but anti-Darwinian. *The Descent of Man* sets the background. But it does set out to show—as did Constance Naden—that the foreground can be a great deal more complex than Darwin suggests.

---

[9] The rapidity and enthusiasm with which the American Pragmatists—very professional philosophers and psychologists—took up not just evolution but Darwinian evolution through natural selection is another good reason for regarding very cautiously claims about non-Darwinian Revolutions, and so forth (Ruse 2009).

[10] We saw earlier how in a rather condescending way, James saw Darwinism seeping right through *Middlemarch* (James 1873). Sauce for the English goose was sauce for the American gander.

[11] One is hardly being unduly dirty-minded in noting that there are times when James lays it on with a trowel, as when writing of Goodwood's "disagreeably strong push, a kind of hardness of presence in his way of rising before her," or of his parting kiss to Isabel "as if he were pressing something that hurt her." He was out of luck: "I can't understand, I can't penetrate you!"

Many of the same things apply to Edith Wharton, another novelist so influenced by Darwinian thinking that in her autobiography she wrote of Darwin as an "Awakener" and acknowledged the "wonder-world of nineteenth century science" that included the *Origin* and such writers as Huxley, Spencer, and Haeckel (Singley 1998).[12] Again, it is sexual selection that sets the background of her story, *The House of Mirth*, although in a cruder and more overt fashion than any of our other writers (Saunders 2009). Lily Bart, age twenty-nine and unmarried, belongs to the highest level of the New York social scene. Time is moving on and her options are stark—get married or face poverty and exclusion. Fortunately she is stunningly beautiful, so she has an asset to sell. The story chronicles her failure to catch a husband—a rich young socialite, Percy Gryce; a clever lawyer, Lawrence Selden; a master of finance, Simon Rosedale; another woman's husband, George Dorset. Ever more in need of money—she loses through bridge playing, her clothing expenses are high, Lily's aunt cuts Lily almost entirely out of her will—Lily sinks lower and lower in the social circle, until she is forced to work in a hat factory. In the end, she overdoses on chloral [hydrate], probably accidentally, but by then she does not much care.

Why is Lily so unsuccessful? In each case, there is a good answer. Gryce is totally boring. Selden doesn't make much money. Rosedale is a Jew. Dorset? Well, he is someone else's husband. But before the book is over, you start to get a sense that there is a pattern here, particularly when you learn that years earlier she had had these issues with an Italian count. Prima facie it is because Lily is a woman of intelligence and morality. She couldn't marry Gryce. She would go mad within minutes. She couldn't go after Dorset. He is already married. When she is almost down and out, Rosedale is still prepared to take her on, as long as she gets on side with Dorset's wife, who (for reasons to do with her own behavior) has taken after Lily. All she needs to do is blackmail this woman, which Lily is able to do since she has come into possession of some incriminating letters. But Lily cannot. And so the story goes.

And yet, one senses that our author shares somewhat of the sentiment toward Lily that George Gissing has toward his losers. This is a tough hard world, and if you are not prepared to play the game, you have only yourself to blame. It is made very clear that Lily is no angel. She likes material possessions and she doesn't want to work for them. She knows she would look "hideous in dowdy clothes" (Wharton [1905] 2002, 59). She has an "incurable dread of discomfort and poverty" and fears "that mounting tide of dinginess against which her mother had so passionately warned her" (204). She is not unaware of her nature

---

[12] A full analysis of the work of Edith Wharton, and of others like Frank Norris, would bring in the influence of the French naturalist writer, Émile Zola. This complements, not contradicts, what is being said about these Anglophone writers (Lehan 2005).

but she is powerless to change. Nor indeed is her creator about to condemn her for that. The Darwinian world in which we all live had made her one way and not another, adapted for one lifestyle and not another.

> She had learned by experience that she had neither the aptitude nor the moral constancy to remake her life on new lines; to become a worker among workers, and let the world of luxury and pleasure sweep by her unregarded. She could not hold herself much to blame for this ineffec-tiveness, and she was perhaps less to blame than she believed. Inherited tendencies had combined with early training to make her the highly specialized product she was: an organism as helpless out of its narrow range as the sea-anemone torn from the rock. She had been fashioned to adorn and delight; to what other end does nature round the rose-leaf and paint the humming-bird's breast? And was it her fault that the purely decorative mission is less easily and harmoniously fulfilled among social beings than in the world of nature? That it is apt to be hampered by material necessities or complicated by moral scruples? (244–245)

Lily's trouble is not so much that she is too moral, although it is true that she does invoke morality (genuinely) to justify some of her actions, but that when push comes to shove she simply will not buckle down and do the necessary—pretend to a boring rich young man, marry a Jew, be willing to give up posses-sions to go with a man she really likes. Take the woman who is destroying Lily socially. Comparing her to Lily, a good friend says: "Every one knows you're a thousand times handsomer and cleverer than Bertha; but then you're not nasty. And for always getting what she wants in the long run, commend me to a nasty woman" (34–35). And then when the chance comes Lily's way, she can do noth-ing. The husband George Dorset comes to Lily and begs her to use information against his wife.

> Here was a man who turned to her in the extremity of his loneliness and his humiliation: if she came to him at such a moment he would be hers with all the force of his deluded faith. And the power to make him so lay in her hand—lay there in a completeness he could not even remotely conjecture. Revenge and rehabilitation might be hers at a stroke—there was something dazzling in the completeness of the opportunity.
> She stood silent, gazing away from him down the autumnal stretch of the deserted lane. And suddenly fear possessed her—fear of herself, and of the terrible force of the temptation. All her past weaknesses were like so many eager accomplices drawing her toward the path their feet

had already smoothed. She turned quickly, and held out her hand to Dorset.

"Goodbye—I'm sorry; there's nothing in the world that I can do." (198)

Thomas Henry Huxley would have said that this is the mark of a civilized person. I doubt that is fully Wharton's view. Morality is one ingredient in the stew, but not the only one.[13] She does not agree with Spencer that what has evolved is by definition right, but she does think that success is what counts and that ultimately that is all that there is to be said.[14] Lily would have agreed fully with the prescription of Marion in *New Grub Street* for the desirable mate:

He was so human, and a youth of all but monastic seclusion had prepared her to love the man who aimed with frank energy at the joys of life. A taint of pedantry would have repelled her. She did not ask for high intellect or great attainments; but vivacity, courage, determination to succeed, were delightful to her senses. Her ideal would not have been a literary man at all; certainly not a man likely to be prominent in journalism; rather a man of action, one who had no restraints of commerce or official routine. But in Jasper she saw the qualities that attracted her apart from the accidents of his position. (Gissing [1891] 1976, 219–220)

Like Marion, unfortunately, Lily doesn't have the guts to go out and grab what she wants. In Gissing's novel it was Amy who seized her chances and won the prize. Next time around Marion and Lily should take note of Amy's philosophical guides: "though she could not undertake the volumes of Herbert Spencer, she was intelligently acquainted with the tenor of their contents; and though she had never opened one of Darwin's books, her knowledge of his main theories and illustrations was respectable" (397). Enough said.[15]

---

[13] No one learning of Edith Wharton's heroic work in World War I for the suffering in France and Belgium can have any doubts about her moral backbone; but her indefatigable efforts for those in need make the very point I am arguing.

[14] Not quite all. What makes the *House of Mirth* deeply tragic is that at some level Lily's lack of vigor stems from a realization that the society in which she mixes is shallow and trivial. Its prizes are not worth having (Singley 1995, 69). The title is taken from Ecclesiastes (7:4). The first part refers to Lily; the second to the society she rejects. "The heart of the wise is in the house of mourning; but the heart of fools is in the house of mirth." In a sense, Lily is more free than Lydgate – she is not just a victim of fate – but less so than Fred – she is not able to take up the reins of life and move forward.

[15] Theodore Dreiser in *Sister Carrie* has a negative attitude to evolutionary success. His main character succeeds. She drags herself up from nowhere to success and riches. But to what end? "In

H. Rider Haggard

Women get crushed by the Darwinian world. But Kipling flags us that things are more complex. Men suffer too. *She* (1886), by H. Rider Haggard, hints at the beginning that this is going to be a Darwinian story. It tells the tale of a Cambridge don, Horace Holly, and his ward, Leo Vincey. Leo at the start of the adventure is just twenty-five and handsome to the point of being beautiful, with curly fair hair. Holly is tremendously intelligent, speaks many languages, is very strong physically, and is incredibly ugly. Remember how he was so simian in appearance he had converted a woman to Darwin's theory!

They set off for Africa with their servant Job and end up with a group of natives, the Amahaggers, who worship a mysterious woman, Ayesha, "*She-who-must-be-obeyed.*" Leo starts a relationship with one of the women of the tribe, Ustane, but this is a preliminary to meeting Ayesha. She is 2,000 years old and has been waiting for the incarnation of her lover Kallikrates, whom she killed in a rage. At the very sight of her face, both Holly and Leo fall desperately in love with her, but Leo is the chosen one, apparently being Kallikrates reborn. Ayesha intends that she and Leo will unite and rule the world—shades of Cecil Rhodes—but first he must stand in the sacred fire. She shows him how, but unfortunately it has the reverse effect on her. She ages before their horrified eyes and ends a mere withered mummy.[16] Job dies of fright, but Leo is comforted by her assurance that she will return.[17]

This is a Darwinian nightmare with sexual selection gone completely out of control. Apart from poor Holly's problems, when the adventurers meet the Amahaggers it turns out that men are virtually powerless when it comes to sexual encounters and liaisons. "When a woman took a fancy to a man she signified her preference by advancing and embracing him publicly, in the same way that this handsome and exceedingly prompt young lady, who was called Ustane, had embraced Leo. If he kissed her back it was a token that he accepted her, and the arrangement continued until one of them wearied of it" (Haggard [1886] 1991, 79). But that is a mere preliminary to the shenanigans of Ayesha. She is the Platonic form of *femme fatale*. A man has no choice but to fall in love with her

---

your rocking-chair, by your window dreaming, shall you long, alone. In your rocking-chair, by your window, shall you dream such happiness as you may never feel" (Dreiser [1900] 1991, 369).

[16] Actually, more interesting and revealing than a mummy. "There, too, lay the hideous little monkey frame, covered with crinkled yellow parchment, that once had been the glorious *She.*" Ayesha has reverted to an earlier form of being—recapitulation in reverse (Ruddick 2007).

[17] Hunter (1983) argues convincingly that Conrad's *Heart of Darkness* is in an important sense a riff on *She.* This is supported not only by the similarity of plot—Europeans going into darkest Africa to find the horrifying being at its center—but also by the almost plagiaristic use by Conrad of Haggard's language, starting with the light that pierced through "the heart of the darkness" (240).

once he sees her face. Holly insists on seeing her and is trapped for the rest of his life. And yet, it is a sick attraction, for with the great beauty comes an aura of evil, of something entirely wrong.

> About the waist her white kirtle was fastened by a double-headed snake of solid gold, above which her gracious form swelled up in lines as pure as they were lovely, till the kirtle ended on the snowy argent of her breast, whereon her arms were folded. I gazed above them at her face, and—I do not exaggerate—shrank back blinded and amazed. I have heard of the beauty of celestial beings, now I saw it; only this beauty, with all its awful loveliness and purity, was *evil*—at least, at the time, it struck me as evil. How am I to describe it? I cannot—simply I cannot! The man does not live whose pen could convey a sense of what I saw. (143)

One starts to sense why this novel, published in 1886, was a best-seller from the moment it appeared, having sold almost 100 million copies in the years since. (The *Da Vinci Code* has sold rather less than half of that number.) In a way found only in the bible—think Delilah, think Jezebel, think Salome—it mixes fabulous beauty with evil intent or consequences. Sex is overwhelming, but it comes at great cost—and it is generally women who are the cause of all the problems. And take note that Ayesha is not yet finished. Ustane makes the mistake of refusing to relinquish Leo. Ayesha says nothing; she merely looks at the poor woman. "Ustane put her hands to her head, uttered one piercing scream, turned round twice, and then fell backwards with a thud—prone upon the floor. Both Leo and myself rushed to her—she was stone dead—blasted into death by some mysterious electric agency or overwhelming will-force whereof the dread *She* had command" (202–203). This really is a perverted form of male combat. And Leo, who is understandably very upset at the loss of what Holly assures the reader is the legitimate African equivalent of a wife, is next. "I saw him struggle—I saw him even turn to fly; but her eyes drew him more strongly than iron bonds, and the magic of her beauty and concentrated will and passion entered into him and overpowered him—ay, even there, in the presence of the body of the woman who had loved him well enough to die for him" (204–205). Apparently no blame should be attached, although Leo is not pleased with himself. To no avail. "I do not understand what I do. For what I want to do I do not do, but what I hate I do" (Romans 7:15).

She is a fairy story so Haggard is able to put things right in the end. We learn that the Amahaggers' women's power is tolerated only up to a point. Finally men get mad. "'Then,' he answered, with a faint smile, 'we rise, and kill the old ones as an example to the young ones, and to show them that we are the strongest. My poor wife was killed in that way three years ago. It was very sad, but to tell thee the truth, my son, life has been happier since, for my age protects me from the young ones'" (107). And of course *She-who-must-be-obeyed* also gets her comeuppance as she withers away in a kind of reverse evolution back to the monkey stage and beyond. But the "damage," if that is the right term, has been done. Sexual selection has been turned on its head, to reveal the awful powers of sexuality and what can happen when it gets out of hand. And even in death, it holds its power. Holly and Leo are broken men. "For we felt—yes, both of us— that having once looked Ayesha in the eyes, we could not forget her for ever and ever while memory and identity remained. We both loved her now and for all time, she was stamped and carven on our hearts, and no other woman or interest could ever raze that splendid die" (262).[18]

D. H. Lawrence

> My candle burns at both ends;
> It will not last the night;
> But ah, my foes, and oh, my friends--
> It gives a lovely light.
>
> (Millay 1922, 9)

The American poet Edna St. Vincent Millay (1892–1950) made no bones about her not-very-private life. This little squib probably refers not only to her bisexuality but also to her huge bedroom appetite. But none of it seems very deep or long-lasting.

> What lips my lips have kissed, and where, and why,
> I have forgotten, and what arms have lain
> Under my head till morning; . . .
>
> (Millay 1956)

She saw the biological side to things, but thought it really went no further.

> I cannot say what loves have come and gone,
> I only know that summer sang in me
> A little while, that in me sings no more.

---

[18] Confirming these deep-seated fears of the female, Adams (1989) notes perceptively that Nature in both Tennyson's *In Memoriam*—"red in tooth and claw"—and Darwin's *Origin*—"constantly destroying life"—is female. She is our mother, but she is not about to spoil the child. Remember that Dixon's Natural Selection was "Madame" not "Monsieur." As with Haggard, Tennyson shows a rather shaky confidence that men will prevail when in *The Princess* (echoed by Gilbert and Sullivan) he has Ida eventually realize her proper role as a wife and mother.

As we enter fully into the twentieth century, is there not another option, one that breaks with the constraints of the Victorian era but does not at once embrace the *Playboy* philosophy, seeing sexuality as little more than sophisticated farmyard activity? Agree that sex can be repressive and soul-destroying, especially if it goes unchanneled. Is it not possible that sex is liberating—not just a good thing but *the* good thing and the source of all things creative? The ultimate font of life? This is something one associates more with pagan customs and religions with their various fertility rites and sacred sexual orgies and the like. But, if only at a folk level, this kind of thinking is important in many places where Christianity is the dominant religion. One would expect aspects of this kind of thinking to find their way into Darwinism—or perhaps someone influenced by Darwinism would seize upon it precisely to show how Darwinism (or evolutionary thinking generally) takes one away from the sterile and repressive thinking of Christianity and opens up a new, freer, more authentic form of life and expression.

D. H. Lawrence (1885–1930) is promising, fertile territory, although one realizes at once that this will not be an easy task. After all, this is the man who wrote: "Myself, I don't believe in evolution, like a string hooked onto a first cause . . . I prefer to believe in what the Aztecs call Suns: that is, worlds successively created and destroyed" (Lawrence [1927] 1974, 12). However we do know that as a young man he had read Darwin, Huxley, Haeckel, and Spencer and at least for a while fallen under their spell (Granofsky 2003, 13). One can find these influences if one looks carefully, especially if one is willing to blend in some of the popular ideas—the philosophy of the Frenchman Henri Bergson, who (in *L'Évolution créatrice,* 1907) supposed a vital force (*élan vital*) infusing and guiding evolution—when Lawrence was writing. The novels that spring to mind are *The Rainbow* (1915) and its sequel *Women in Love* (1921).[19] To take the novels together, it is the story of the Brangwen family. We start with Tom, who marries a Polish widow, Lydia, with a child, Anna. Tom and Anna forge a bond and, after Anna marries Tom's nephew Will, Tom eventually comes to give them support. Neither Tom and Lydia nor Anna and Will seem terribly well suited, but they do connect strongly sexually. Anna and Will have eight children, the oldest of

---

[19] One cannot overemphasize the influence that Bergson (translated as *Creative Evolution,* 1911) had on intellectual society in the second decade of the twentieth century (Canales 2015). Julian Huxley's first book, *The Individual in the Animal Kingdom* (1912), was typical in its slavish devotion to the Frenchman's philosophy (Ruse 1996). Lawrence read Bergson in 1913 and was a little contemptuous: "the Bergson book was very dull. Bergson bores me. He feels a bit thin" (Lawrence 1979, 544). This would not have been the first (or last) time he encountered Bergson's ideas. He wrote for places where Bergsonian themes were discussed, especially the *English Review,* and he mixed with fellow contributors and Bergsonian enthusiasts like the Huxley brothers, Julian and Aldous (Meyers 1990; Vogeler 2008). So one should take Lawrence's snide remark with a pinch of salt. At times, particularly in *Women in Love,* he is virtually quoting *Creative Evolution.*

whom is Ursula, and it is her story that occupies the rest of the first novel, *The Rainbow*. She hitches up with Anton Skrebensky, the son of a family friend, and after a lesbian fling with one of her teachers, has a continued affair with Anton until he goes off to India. She finds herself pregnant (but then miscarries) and having tried unsuccessfully to contact Anton faces life on her own. Except now, in the second novel, her younger sister Gudrun comes on the scene. Ursula gets involved with a school inspector, Rupert Birkin (Lawrence himself lightly disguised) and Gudrun with Gerald Crich, the son of a local mine owner. Gerald takes over the family business and his relationship with Gudrun deteriorates. Ursula and Rupert, however, realize that they can and do love each other, while keeping their own independence. At the climax, the two couples go off for a skiing holiday in the Swiss Alps. Gerald and Gudrun quarrel and he walks out into the snow and freezes to death. Rupert and Ursula stay content together after Ursula persuades Rupert that although he rather wanted a second (parallel) relationship with Gerald, one marriage at a time is enough.

This is a story through time and it is a story of change, of Progress. Rupert and Ursula are way advanced beyond Tom and Lydia. Lawrence flags us from the beginning that we are dealing with something biological. Anna is in childbirth. "The rent was not in his body, but it was of his body. On her the blows fell, but the quiver ran through to him, to his last fibre. She must be torn asunder for life to come forth, yet still they were one flesh, and still, from further back, the life came out of him to her, and still he was the unbroken that has the broken rock in its arms, their flesh was one rock from which the life gushed, out of her who was smitten and rent, from him who quivered and yielded" (Lawrence [1915] 1949, 74). But what is the meaning of these people's existence? What is it that drives them forward, making for advance and purpose? It has to be something mystical, ethereal almost. Lydia, reared a Catholic, finds it in her religion. "She shone and gleamed to the Mystery, Whom she knew through all her senses, she glanced with strange, mystic superstitions that never found expression in the English language, never mounted to thought in English" (103). But this can never do for the next generations. Ursula loses her religious beliefs. Religion "became a tale, a myth, an illusion, which, however much one might assert it to be true as historical fact, one knew was not true—at least, for this present-day life of ours" (283).

All is not lost. Lawrence in some primeval, pagan way reaches out to sexual activity as the alternative, authentic option. It is the ultimate source of creativity and freedom. Will and Anna may not altogether care for each other, but bedtime is another matter.

> But now he had given way, and with infinite sensual violence gave himself to the realization of this supreme, immoral, Absolute Beauty, in the body of woman. It seemed to him, that it came to being in the body of

woman, under his touch. Under his touch, even under his sight, it was there. But when he neither saw nor touched the perfect place, it was not perfect, it was not there. And he must make it exist.

But still the thing terrified him. Awful and threatening it was, dangerous to a degree, even whilst he gave himself to it. It was pure darkness, also. All the shameful things of the body revealed themselves to him now with a sort of sinister, tropical beauty. All the shameful, natural and unnatural acts of sensual voluptuousness which he and the woman partook of together, created together, they had their heavy beauty and their delight. Shame, what was it? It was part of extreme delight. It was that part of delight of which man is usually afraid. Why afraid? The secret, shameful things are most terribly beautiful.

They accepted shame, and were one with it in their most unlicensed pleasures. It was incorporated. It was a bud that blossomed into beauty and heavy, fundamental gratification. (237–238)

It doesn't take much insight to see that it is anal sex that they are practicing here and that that is the very point—one is breaking through convention, going beyond shame, to the ultimate point of creativity. Lawrence stresses immediately that Will has now a new dimension of freedom that expresses itself in creative activity. "And gradually, Brangwen began to find himself free to attend to the outside life as well. His intimate life was so violently active, that it set another man in him free. And this new man turned with interest to public life, to see what part he could take in it" (238).

One senses a vital force, an *élan vital*, at work here—the metaphor that Lawrence uses repeatedly is that of "blood"—"he transferred to her the hot, fecund darkness that possessed his own blood" (446); "she had the potent dark stream of her own blood" (449); "the rainbow was arched in their blood and would quiver to life in their spirit" (496). The key is a dimension of freedom that explicitly Bergson finds wanting in conventional Darwinism. For all that he sees humans as the outcome, not only does the French philosopher stress the increased freedom potential as evolution takes us upward—the nervous system becomes a *"reservoir of indetermination"*—he makes absolutely central the possibility of different routes of change ("divergent directions") and stresses that this too points to creative possibilities. Lawrence's debt to this thinking continues through to the end of the novels. Ursula is taking a biology course and discussing the nature of life with her teacher. "May it not be that life consists in a complexity of physical and chemical activities, of the same order as the activities we already know in science? I don't see, really, why we should imagine there is a special order of life, and life alone—" (440). Can this be enough? Can one thus explain life's purpose? "For what purpose were the incalculable physical and chemical activities nodalized in this shadowy, moving speck under her microscope? What was the will which nodalized them and created the one thing she saw? What was its intention? To be itself? Was its purpose just mechanical and limited to itself?" (441) There has to be more—however much we know physically and chemically, "it does not follow that chemistry and physics will ever give us the key to life"—and this is the continuing theme of *Women in Love*. Ursula and Rupert explore the dimensions of their existence through their sexual relationship. They too are into anal sex as a prerequisite to freedom.[20]

> They might do as they liked—this she realised as she went to sleep. How could anything that gave one satisfaction be excluded? What was degrading? Who cared? Degrading things were real, with a different reality. And he was so unabashed and unrestrained. Wasn't it rather horrible, a man who could be so soulful and spiritual, now to be so—she balked at her own thoughts and memories: then she added—so bestial? So bestial, they two!—so degraded! She winced. But after all, why not? She exulted as well. Why not be bestial, and go the whole round of experience? She exulted in it. She was bestial. How good it was to be really shameful! There would be no shameful thing she had not experienced. Yet she was unabashed, she was herself. Why not? She was free, when she knew everything, and no dark shameful things were denied her. (Lawrence [1921] 1960, 464)

But true freedom demands more. It comes in the sexual union but one that preserves the individual. Rupert fears that we (white people) are finished as a race. "Was there left now nothing but to break off from the happy creative being, was the time up? Is our day of creative life finished?" Then he sees the way forward. "There was the paradisal entry into pure, single being, the individual soul taking precedence over love and desire for union, stronger than any pangs of emotion, a lovely state of free proud singleness, which accepted the obligation of the permanent connection with others, and with the other, submits to the yoke and leash

---

[20] Is this obsession with heterosexual anal sex—it occurs also in *Lady Chatterley's Lover*—a metaphor for homosexual activity? It could be, especially if we read the activity not as Rupert penetrating Ursula's anus with his penis but as Ursula shoving her finger up his behind (prostate massage). "She had thought there was no source deeper than the phallic source. And now, behold, from the smitten rock of the man's body, from the strange marvellous flanks and thighs, deeper, further in mystery than the phallic source, came the floods of ineffable darkness and ineffable riches" (354). For all that in this novel Lawrence's attitude to homosexuality is accepting and positive, outside his fiction, Lawrence was aggressively homophobic. In parallel, Lawrence's ambivalence here is another good reason for not taking as definitive his stated, negative attitude to Bergson.

of love, but never forfeits its own proud individual singleness, even while it loves and yields" (287).

Gerald's relationship with Gudrun fails because (in a Bergsonian fashion) she sees that people like him are machines and thus never free. "The essence of mechanical explanation, in fact, is to regard the future and the past as calculable functions of the present, and thus to claim that *all is given*" (Bergson 1911, 40). Such people are automata. "Let them become instruments, pure machines, pure wills, that work like clock-work, in perpetual repetition. Let them be this, let them be taken up entirely in their work, let them be perfect parts of a great machine, having a slumber of constant repetition. Let Gerald manage his firm" (Lawrence [1921] 1960, 524). And this, in the end, revealing that Lawrence is telling a tale about evolution, is where it is at. In the sexual act, properly understood and performed, lies true freedom and creativity and the way forward to the future.

> God can do without man. God could do without the ichthyosauri and the mastodon. These monsters failed creatively to develop, so God, the creative mystery, dispensed with them. In the same way the mystery could dispense with man, should he too fail creatively to change and develop. The eternal creative mystery could dispose of man, and replace him with a finer created being. Just as the horse has taken the place of the mastodon.
>
> It was very consoling to Birkin, to think this. If humanity ran into a CUL DE SAC and expended itself, the timeless creative mystery would bring forth some other being, finer, more wonderful, some new, more lovely race, to carry on the embodiment of creation. The game was never up. The mystery of creation was fathomless, infallible, inexhaustible, forever. Races came and went, species passed away, but ever new species arose, more lovely, or equally lovely, always surpassing wonder. The fountainhead was incorruptible and unsearchable. It had no limits. (538)

My very strong suspicion is that Charles Darwin would not have enjoyed *The Rainbow* or *Women in Love*. One doubts that, however pretty the girl and however happy the ending, people doing such rude things to their bodies could ever fit his formula for a good novel. But Lawrence is playing his part in our story. Sex—the ecstasy and the guilt—are right up there as fundamental to the human experience. As Christianity makes sex a central part of its story, so Lawrence made sex a central part of his evolutionary story. It has a very different role from that played in Christianity—and yet, and this reinforces the Darwinism-as-religion theme, sex is still not the happy coupling of healthy young animals. It is as fraught with meaning and cosmic responsibility as for a young Catholic pair who, after an elaborate ceremony, have just been given the go-ahead by their priest.

11

Sin and Redemption

The Problem of Evil

Take up now the oft-mentioned problem of evil, the biggest challenge to Christianity. If God is both all good and all powerful, why is there so much suffering in the world? Why is there natural or physical evil, such as the Lisbon earthquake, and why is there moral evil, such as the carnage in the French Revolution? There are standard responses. In the case of natural evil, the reply is a version of an argument made popular by Leibniz and parodied by Voltaire. God can only do the possible. God cannot make 2 + 2 = 5 and God cannot make us safe from fire without making it very painful if we get burned. Natural evil is the cost of a functioning universe. In the case of moral evil, it is argued that it happens as a function of human free will. The Christian agrees with Lawrence that it is better that we have such will than that we be automata, machines. But why, even given free will, should we cause such pain and harm? Because we are tainted with original sin. There are different traditions on this, but the standard response is that God made us good but we fell into sin—Adam and Eve disobeyed the Lord—and the rest of us are thereby tainted.

Unlike Christians, Darwinians do not see that natural evil is a problem. Obviously they do not like it and may feel one has a moral obligation to reduce it, but it is just something that happens. No one causes it, no one is to blame.[1] Moral evil is something fairly readily explicable given Darwinism. We have

---

[1] In handling both natural and moral evil, post-Darwinians (believers and nonbelievers) felt free to invoke and as appropriate modify traditional, theistic responses. This is why the argument from Job seemed increasingly attractive. "I'm God; I created the world; I make the rules; don't whine." Hopkins responded by using the Resurrection as the second part of the story, the secular novelists Hardy and Eliot had their takes on things. Expectedly, we find a poet like Robert Frost, wrestling with pain and suffering, using Job (Faggen 1997, 222). In "Home Burial" (Frost 1969, 54, written 1914), a husband's frustration at not getting through to his grieving wife—"I shall laugh the worst laugh I ever laughed./I'm cursed. God, if I don't believe I'm cursed."—reflects the biblical language and thoughts—"Curse God and die" (Job 2:9).

a natural inclination to selfishness. That is to be expected given that selection works for the individual. In many cases this inclination is countered or masked by the biological virtues of cooperation. But not always, and so we are going to expect humans to be a mix of (what we would call) the good and the bad. Given natural variations and circumstances, we would expect some people to be better than others. Clearly things like technology are also going to be involved. A homicidal maniac armed with an iron axe is going to be a lot more dangerous than such a maniac with but his fists. Huxley, as we have seen, was pretty good on these sorts of issues, and he was opposed to Spencer who would have been more likely to endorse any product of evolution as in some sense good and would have thought it wrong to oppose the workings of evolution. For that reason, a Spencerian might be more likely to argue that we should let nature's inadequates decline and die. Darwin himself was more nuanced, although note that in respects he does seem to think morality was "incidental." "The aid which we feel impelled to give to the helpless is mainly an incidental result of the instinct of sympathy, which was originally acquired as part of the social instincts, but subsequently rendered, in the manner previously indicated, more tender and more widely diffused. Nor could we check our sympathy, if so urged by hard reason, without deterioration in the noblest part of our nature" (Darwin 1871, 1, 168–169).

All this said, there is no doubt that, as the century moved along, unsullied thoughts of social Progress began to decline. Prosperity brought its own problems—appalling inner-city slums where the unfortunate and unwanted tended to gather. Also, there were increasing tensions and conflicts between nations, especially among Europeans over the race to control Africa. Britain and Germany exemplified the unease with both sides starting a massive naval buildup. This unease was reflected in evolutionary thinking and many was the article or treatise devoted to the ubiquity of biological degeneration. E. Ray Lankester, one of the most prominent evolutionists toward the end of the century—a student of Huxley, professor at Oxford, and then director of the British Museum (Natural History)—harped incessantly on this theme. Following then-general practice, he tied it in with the biogenetic law of Haeckel, that ontogeny recapitulates phylogeny, seeing organisms reverting to earlier less advanced stages of their evolutionary history. The ascidian or sea squirt starts life as a tadpole-like creature but ends as a sponge-like invertebrate stuck to the sea bottom. Apparently it is all a matter of ease of getting food and other necessities of life. "Any new set of conditions occurring to an animal which render its food and safety very easily attained, seems to lead as a rule to Degeneration" (Lankester 1880, 33). Lankester's own life was fraught with psychosexual problems—he could only relate sexually to prostitutes and not to women of his own social class—and he thought them a function of his earlier easy life—as a student at all-male institutions, first at

school and then at Oxford (Ruse 1996). It was natural therefore to read this into
the history and present state of humankind. "The traditional history of mankind
furnishes us with notable examples of degeneration. High states of civilisation
have decayed and given place to low and degenerate states" (58). He added ominously, in case people thought he was writing in the abstract, "Possibly we are all
drifting, tending to the condition of intellectual Barnacles or Ascidians" (60). It
hardly needs adding that one mark of degenerate people is that they are going to
be a lot less moral than advanced people.

Robert Louis Stevenson

How do our writers respond to these kinds of issues? Start with the ever-
fascinating novella by Robert Louis Stevenson (1850–1894), *The Strange Case
of Dr. Jekyll and Mr. Hyde* (1886). This is the well-known story of a respectable
medical doctor, Dr. Henry Jekyll, who invents a potion that turns him into a
monster, Mr. Edward Hyde. The latter starts off by trampling all over a young
girl, for which transgression he is forced to pay £100, most of it in the form of a
check drawn to the account of the respectable Dr. Jekyll. Then, with a cane, Hyde
beats to death a man—Sir Danvers Carew M.P.—an incident that again can be
connected to Dr. Jekyll. Finally, after another man has died of shock from some
unknown incident involving Jekyll, very worried friends burst in on Dr. Jekyll, to
find the body of Hyde in Jekyll's clothing. A suicide note tells them that Jekyll,
given to dreadful private vices, had discovered a way to turn himself into Hyde
to avoid detection, but that unfortunately increasingly he (Jekyll) was unable to
control the transformations and was becoming Hyde all of the time. So Jekyll
killed himself to avoid the inevitable capture and execution.[2]

What makes this story particularly pertinent to our study is that it can be read
two ways—underlining that Christianity and Darwinism are rivals, different reflections of the same reality. First, it can be seen as a Christian story about original sin. Even the best of us have this dark side with which we are besmirched. We
cannot escape it. There is reason to think that Stevenson—a Scot, so he would
have known all about original sin from living in that dour Presbyterian land

[2] "Such irregularities as I was guilty of"? Could these involve homosexuality? Reference is made
to the "very pretty manner of politeness" of "beautiful" Sir Danvers when he "accosted" Mr. Hyde.
Why was he in a lonely street at night in the first place? Perhaps pertinently, the novella was composed just at a time when homosexuality was much discussed and a law making such practices illegal
was passed in Parliament (Showalter 1990). Interestingly, adaptations, like the excellent 1931 movie
starring Frederick March, give Jekyll a girlfriend, not to mention a future father-in-law who is trying
to put off the marriage. Add a girl of easy virtue to whom Jekyll is attracted and whom Hyde finally
kills, and the Freudian stew is complete.

of the North—was inspired by the history of Deacon Brodie, an eighteenth-century Edinburgh worthy, a respectable cabinet maker and city counselor by day and a burglar by night, whose life ended on the gallows. Second, the story can be read as an evolutionary parable, about the animal always within and the risk of degeneration to an earlier lower form. There are many hints in the text for both readings. On the one hand, Hyde is identified as Satanic, the ultimate personification of good turned to evil.

> Mr. Hyde was pale and dwarfish, he gave an impression of deformity without any nameable malformation, he had a displeasing smile, he had borne himself to the lawyer with a sort of murderous mixture of timidity and boldness, and he spoke with a husky, whispering and somewhat broken voice; all these were points against him, but not all of these together could explain the hitherto unknown disgust, loathing, and fear with which Mr. Utterson [a lawyer friend of Jekyll] regarded him. "There must be something else," said the perplexed gentleman. "There is something more, if I could find a name for it. God bless me, the man seems hardly human! Something troglodytic, shall we say? or can it be the old story of Dr. Fell? or is it the mere radiance of a foul soul that thus transpires through, and transfigures, its clay continent? The last, I think; for, O my poor old Harry Jekyll, if ever I read Satan's signature upon a face, it is on that of your new friend." (Stevenson [1886] 2003, 17)

Then the other side. Dr. Jekyll's terrified servant tells of what he has seen. "Well, when that masked thing like a monkey jumped from among the chemicals and whipped into the cabinet, it went down my spine like ice. Oh, I know it's not evidence, Mr. Utterson. I'm book-learned enough for that; but a man has his feelings, and I give you my Bible-word it was Mr. Hyde!" (37) And in the suicide note there is more reference to the simian nature of Hyde. "Hence the ape-like tricks that he would play me, scrawling in my own hand blasphemies on the pages of my books, burning the letters and destroying the portrait of my father; and indeed, had it not been for his fear of death, he would long ago have ruined himself in order to involve me in the ruin" (61). We have here a being who has regressed to an earlier stage of development and with this comes evil.[3]

---

[3] Freud did not look upon homosexuality as evil. In his "letter to an American mother" he is remarkably tolerant and understanding (Ruse 1988b). However, regression does play a significant role in his thinking about the etiology of homosexuality, and we do know how very important were evolutionary themes (especially those of recapitulation) in his theorizing (Sulloway 1979). Influenced by the same biology, savvy readers would have known the score. Darwin was certainly empathetic to notions of recapitulation, although how much is a matter of some controversy (Richards and Ruse 2016). His study of barnacles underlined the belief that same-sex activity is primitive: "my species

Bram Stoker

Some of these same themes are to be found in another famous work of fiction from that era, *Dracula* (1897) by Bram Stoker (1847–1912). The story of a Transylvanian vampire who decides to set up shop in England, it (deservedly) continues to spark countless spinoffs particularly in the world of the movies.[4] Dracula invites a London lawyer, Jonathan Harker, to his castle to do the legal paperwork on real estate purchases in England, intending after his own departure to leave the poor man to the mercies of his three undead females. Fortunately, Harker escapes and, although he falls sick, his girlfriend Mina is able to join him and they at once get married. Meanwhile Dracula, who (in the form of a dog) jumps ashore at Whitby in Yorkshire, has started to prey on Mina's friend, Lucy. Her neck punctured by his teeth, he is drinking her blood and she is getting weaker daily. Unfortunately, even though the knowledgeable Dr. Van Helsing is summoned from Holland, nothing can save her and she dies. Except she doesn't, she becomes one of the undead, the "bloofer lady" preying on small children in the Hampstead region. Finally, she finds peace after a stake is driven through her heart, her head cut off, and her mouth filled with garlic. Van Helsing and friends chase Dracula back to Transylvania where finally he is killed—just as well, since he had started to do to Mina what he had done to Lucy.

As with *Jekyll and Hyde*, the combination—the entwining—of Christian and evolutionary symbolism is remarkable. Dracula is the apotheosis of the corrupt and vile. He is the one beyond Christian salvation, who draws back before the crucifix and whose undead female partners dread the communion wafer—poor, polluted Mina gets a scar on her forehead from the touch of one. At the same time, he is the ultimate symbol of evolutionary degeneration. He has—a fact that Mina states explicitly—just the signs that criminologists like Cesare Lombroso were assuring people is the mark of atavism, of regression to a more primitive state.[5]

---

theory convinced me, that an hermaphrodite species must pass into a bisexual species [meaning a species with separate sexes] by insensibly small stages, & here we have it, for the male organs in the hermaphrodite are beginning to fail, & independent males ready formed" (Darwin 1985–, 4: 140. Letter to Joseph Hooker, May 10, 1848). Note how Lankester picks on barnacles as the epitome of the degenerate.

   [4] Why England? It could be part of a general concern about Britain's increasingly fragile hold on world supremacy, threatened by the growth of Germany and America (Arata 1990). In *She*, Ayesha has plans for going off to London and usurping Queen Victoria.

   [5] Is Dracula a Jew with all the implications that this might be taken to have about degeneracy? There is a lot of stuff about blood and contamination, about gold and hoarding, and even a comment about the Count's "ook nose." Add to this the fact that the book was published just at a time when England was worrying about an influx of poor Eastern European Jews, that Stoker was the theater manager for Sir Henry Irving, who played Shylock 250 times, and that so much of the story

His face was a strong—a very strong—aquiline, with high bridge of the thin nose and peculiarly arched nostrils; with lofty domed forehead, and hair growing scantily round the temples but profusely elsewhere. His eyebrows were very massive, almost meeting over the nose, and with bushy hair that seemed to curl in its own profusion. The mouth, so far as I could see it under the heavy moustache, was fixed and rather cruel-looking, with peculiarly sharp white teeth; these protruded over the lips, whose remarkable ruddiness showed astonishing vitality in a man of his years. For the rest, his ears were pale, and at the tops extremely pointed; the chin was broad and strong, and the cheeks firm though thin. The general effect was one of extraordinary pallor. (Stoker [1897] 1993, 24–25)

In case we have any doubt, we are told explicitly that Dracula used to be a great man, but now he has regressed to the state of being childlike. "Soldier, statesman, and alchemist—which latter was the highest development of the science-knowledge of his time. He had a mighty brain, a learning beyond compare, and a heart that knew no fear and no remorse. He dared even to attend the Scholomance, and there was no branch of knowledge of his time that he did not essay. Well, in him the brain powers survived the physical death; though it would seem that memory was not all complete. In some faculties of mind he has been, and is, only a child . . ." (321–322).[6]

Note also how his powers come to him through a perverted parody of Christianity. As we are reminded many times in the novel, central to the Christian faith—to the Roman Catholic faith—is the miracle of transubstantiation, where the bread and the wine are turned into the body and blood of Christ. It is the physical presence of the Savior that is so important. Closing up the tomb of Lucy, for example, van Helsing uses putty filled with something that crumbles. What is it? " 'The Host. I brought it from Amsterdam. I have an Indulgence.' It was an answer that appalled the most sceptical of us, and we felt individually that in the presence of such earnest purpose as the Professor's, a purpose which could thus use the to him most sacred of things, it was impossible to distrust" (224). For Dracula and his minions, it is equally the life force within the body of a human, his or her blood, that gives power and, if not eternal life, renewing

is consciously putting Christianity up front in the fight against Dracula, and the idea is at least plausible (Halberstam 1993). Although Stoker's full first name was Abraham, he was not himself a Jew, although he was probably homosexual, which strikes me as rather less relevant than others seem to think.

[6] The Scholomance was a school of black magic, run by the Devil, reputedly located in Transylvania.

life. Opening up his coffin, there "lay the Count, but looking as if his youth had been half renewed, for the white hair and moustache were changed to dark iron-grey; the cheeks were fuller, and the white skin seemed ruby-red underneath; the mouth was redder than ever, for on the lips were gouts of fresh blood, which trickled from the corners of the mouth and ran over the chin and neck" (59).[7]

Readers of *Dracula* note that gender roles in the novel are remarkably complex. Lucy seems the apotheosis of the fragile Victorian maiden. She has no less than three suitors for her hand, all of whom prove eager to have blood transfused when she is in dire need.[8] She finds lasting peace only when she is symbolically penetrated with the stake through her heart. Mina, however, comes across as significantly more enterprising and intelligent than her new husband, Jonathan Harker. There are references to her status as one of the "New Women"—the kind of young female who went biking in bloomers and who made her own decisions about careers and marriage. "Some of the 'New Women' writers will someday start an idea that men and women should be allowed to see each other asleep before proposing or accepting. But I suppose the New Woman won't condescend in future to accept; she will do the proposing herself. And a nice job she will make of it, too!" (99). It will come as no surprise to learn van Helsing's opinion. "She has man's brain—a brain that a man should have were he much gifted—and a woman's heart." He does cover his tracks by adding: "The good God fashioned her for a purpose, believe me, when He made that so good combination" (250).

Frank Norris

Cross the Atlantic for a third instance of evolutionary degeneration, to be found in Frank Norris's *McTeague*, published in 1899 two years after *Dracula*. In respects the American novel could not be farther from Robert Louis Stevenson's British fantasy. In grim, realistic terms it tells the story of an inadequate, untrained man practicing dentistry in San Francisco. He falls in love with one of his patients, Trina Sieppe, and they marry. Trina has won $5,000 in a lottery, but she refuses to use her capital, insisting that they live on his earnings plus a little that she can earn. Unfortunately, a rival for Trina's hand, Marcus Schouler, tells the authorities that McTeague is unlicensed, he loses his job, and the pair descend into poverty. They split, she becomes a total miser reveling in her wealth, he

---

[7] The crucial role of blood reminds one of Lawrence, and in both cases blood does seem to be a life force. But whereas for Lawrence it is creative, for Stoker it is degenerate.

[8] In good Darwinian fashion she opts for the lord, leaving the asylum doctor and the Texan with dashed hopes.

returns and kills her, and then with a little avian pet makes for the desert where, having killed his rival, he faces certain death from lack of water.

> As McTeague rose to his feet, he felt a pull at his right wrist; something held it fast. Looking down, he saw that Marcus in that last struggle had found strength to handcuff their wrists together. Marcus was dead now; McTeague was locked to the body. All about him, vast interminable, stretched the measureless leagues of Death Valley.
>
> McTeague remained stupidly looking around him, now at the distant horizon, now at the ground, now at the half-dead canary chittering feebly in its little gilt prison. (Norris 1899, 442)

Yet it was the Scotsman's reading of evolutionary degeneration that lay deep in the heart of Norris's tale (McElrath and Crisler 2010). McTeague is a brute, and when he has Trina under the chloroform he cannot help himself. "Suddenly the animal in the man stirred and woke; the evil instincts that in him were so close to the surface leaped to life, shouting and clamoring" (30). Let us say that the brute within wins out, although to his credit McTeague does propose when she comes around. Not that Trina turns out to be a great deal better. We learn that Jews have the lust for gold in their blood. "It was impossible to look at Zerkow [a local junk man] and not know instantly that greed—inordinate, insatiable greed—was the dominant passion of the man. He was the Man with the Rake, groping hourly in the muck-heap of the city for gold, for gold, for gold. It was his dream, his passion; at every instant he seemed to feel the generous solid weight of the crude fat metal in his palms" (43).[9] Trina has the same affliction, to a really quite perverted degree.

> She had her money, that was the main thing. Her passion for it excluded every other sentiment. There it was in the bottom of her trunk, in the canvas sack, the chamois-skin bag, and the little brass match-safe. Not a day passed that Trina did not have it out where she could see and touch it. One evening she had even spread all the gold pieces between the sheets, and had then gone to bed, stripping herself, and had slept

---

[9] As a student at Berkeley, the future novelist had fallen under the spell of the geologist Joseph Le Conte. A native of Georgia, a one-time slave owner, and violent racist, Le Conte (1891) argued strongly against the degenerate evolutionary effects of mixing different peoples, and this is reflected strongly in *McTeague* (Bender 2004, 35). Zerkow marries Maria, a Mexican. Their child is doomed, dead within ten days. No wonder really, "combining in its puny little body the blood of the Hebrew, the Pole, and the Spaniard" (Norris 1899, 240). Remember Darwin's worries about the effects of mixed breeding on vitality.

all night upon the money, taking a strange and ecstatic pleasure in the touch of the smooth flat pieces the length of her entire body. (360–361)

Shades of Zeus and Daneä. It is a wonder she did not end up pregnant.

Is anyone a free agent? That is an open question. What is clear is that good and evil in *McTeague* are set in an evolutionary context as much as, say, good and evil in *Pilgrim's Progress* are set in a Christian context. "Do not store up for yourselves treasures on earth, where moths and vermin destroy, and where thieves break in and steal" (Matthew 6:19).[10]

Thomas Hardy

Degeneration. Can one say more about this in a broader context, perhaps edging on causal questions? Against the indifference of nature, it is a running theme through *Tess of the D'Urbervilles*. We start right off at the beginning of *Tess* with establishing the previously high status of the D'Urbervilles:

> Your ancestor was one of the twelve knights who assisted the Lord of Estremavilla in Normandy in his conquest of Glamorganshire. Branches of your family held manors over all this part of England; their names appear in the Pipe Rolls in the time of King Stephen. In the reign of King John one of them was rich enough to give a manor to the Knights Hospitallers; and in Edward the Second's time your forefather Brian was summoned to Westminster to attend the great Council there. You declined a little in Oliver Cromwell's time, but to no serious extent, and in Charles the Second's reign you were made Knights of the Royal Oak for your loyalty. (Hardy [1892] 2010, 4)

Already though we are being primed for the worst. We learn of Tess's father: "Yes, that's the d'Urberville nose and chin—a little debased" (4). And don't get your hopes up: "chasten yourself with the thought of 'how are the mighty fallen.'" That is the constant message through the book. After Tess marries Angel, they are about to leave the church in their carriage and for some unknown

---

[10] Le Conte stressed that the human "is possessed of two natures—a lower, in common with animals, and a higher, peculiar to himself. The whole mission and life-work of man is the progressive and finally the complete dominance, both in the individual and in the race, of the higher over the lower. The whole meaning of sin is the humiliating bondage of the higher to the lower" (Le Conte 1891, 330). McTeague clearly therefore has some dimension of freedom and subsequent responsibility; unfortunately, his reason fails to control his animal inheritance (Pizer 1961).

reason Tess shudders at its sight. Angel enlightens her. "A certain d'Urberville of the sixteenth or seventeenth century committed a dreadful crime in his family coach; and since that time members of the family see or hear the old coach whenever—But I'll tell you another day—it is rather gloomy" (256). Apparently that crime stayed in Angel's memory for when he has abandoned Tess he blames himself for having been false to his own standards. "He was embittered by the conviction that all this desolation had been brought about by the accident of her being a d'Urberville. When he found that Tess came of that exhausted ancient line, and was not of the new tribes from below, as he had fondly dreamed, why had he not stoically abandoned her in fidelity to his principles?" (311) Angel really should have checked first. The place he rented for their wedding night once belonged to the D'Urbervilles. Two portraits are still in place. "The long pointed features, narrow eye, and smirk of the one, so suggestive of merciless treachery; the bill-hook nose, large teeth, and bold eye of the other suggesting arrogance to the point of ferocity, haunt the beholder afterwards in his dreams" (260). If that isn't enough warning, the pictures don't only upset Tess: "her fine features were unquestionably traceable in these exaggerated forms."[11] As I said earlier, for all of her purity, it is little wonder that she ends as Alec's mistress before she kills him.[12]

H. G. Wells

Darwinian though Hardy may have been, he is not very informative about how the degeneration gets into the blood. It all seems very Lamarckian. H. G. Wells

---

[11]

> I am the family face;
> Flesh perishes, I live on,
> Projecting trait and trace
> Through time to times anon,
> And leaping from place to place
> Over oblivion.

(Hardy 1994, 395, written around 1890)

[12] Was the killing of Alec simply a matter of biological determinism, or did Tess have choice? Hardy himself suggested the former: "The murder that Tess commits is the heredity quality, to which I more than once allude, working out in this impoverished descendent of a once noble family" (quoted in Greenslade 1994, 162). Perhaps—although because Angel rejected her as used goods, there is the suggestion that she acted deliberately. "How can we live together while that man lives?— he being your husband in nature, and not I. If he were dead it might be different" (290). In killing Alec, Tess puts things right. "It came to me as a shining light that I should get you back that way" (457). Although a compatibilist would allow both determinism and freedom at this point, I doubt that the implied sense of fate sits well with freedom.

in the *Time Machine* makes much more of a scientific effort to explain things. The traveler has gone forward in time and meets the Eloi, friendly rather naïve folk. It is noteworthy how the differences between the sexes seem less pronounced than they are for us humans today.

> Seeing the ease and security in which these people were living, I felt that this close resemblance of the sexes was after all what one would expect; for the strength of a man and the softness of a woman, the institution of the family, and the differentiation of occupations are mere militant necessities of an age of physical force; where population is balanced and abundant, much childbearing becomes an evil rather than a blessing to the State; where violence comes but rarely and off-spring are secure, there is less necessity—indeed there is no necessity—for an efficient family, and the specialization of the sexes with reference to their children's needs disappears. (Wells [1895] 2005, 29–30)

As Darwin could have told you, with his views about women being child-men, this is not necessarily a good thing. "What, unless biological science is a mass of errors, is the cause of human intelligence and vigour? Hardship and freedom: conditions under which the active, strong, and subtle survive and the weaker go to the wall; conditions that put a premium upon the loyal alliance of capable men, upon self-restraint, patience, and decision" (32). We need struggle for advance and without it degeneration sets in. The traveler adds that he fears that this is already starting to become true of our own society. I am not sure that Wells's traveler entirely approved of the New Woman with her aspirations to take the roles of males.

However, the traveler realizes that this cannot be all of the true story. If the Eloi are doing so little, if they have given up using machines, how is it that they have great palaces to sleep in, and nice clothes and sandals with complex metal ware? There has to be a second species, doing all of the hard work. And, of course, there is, the subterranean Morlocks. These are in their way as degenerate as the Eloi. But it wasn't simply that the Eloi had gone one way and the Morlocks another, the latter living underground and degenerating in their own way separate from the Eloi. "So, in the end, above ground you must have the Haves, pursuing pleasure and comfort and beauty, and below ground the Have-nots, the Workers getting continually adapted to the conditions of their labour" (48). In an almost Hegelian fashion, the master-slave relationship means that as the master exploits the slave, so the slave exploits the master. The Morlocks start using the Eloi for their own ends. "The Upper-world people might once have been the favoured aristocracy, and the Morlocks their mechanical servants: but that had long since passed away. The two species that had resulted from the evolution of man were

sliding down towards, or had already arrived at, an altogether new relationship"
(57). The Eloi were living courtesy of the Morlocks, who provided them with
food and lodging and clothing, but as wanted took them for food! The Eloi were
like cattle or sheep.

> So, as I see it, the Upper-world man had drifted towards his feeble pret-
> tiness, and the Under-world to mere mechanical industry. But that
> perfect state had lacked one thing even for mechanical perfection—
> absolute permanency. Apparently as time went on, the feeding of the
> Under-world, however it was effected, had become disjointed. Mother
> Necessity, who had been staved off for a few thousand years, came back
> again, and she began below. The Under-world being in contact with ma-
> chinery, which, however perfect, still needs some little thought outside
> habit, had probably retained perforce rather more initiative, if less of
> every other human character, than the Upper. And when other meat
> failed them, they turned to what old habit had hitherto forbidden. (79)

Wells gives an account both of speciation and of degeneration. There is not too
much in the way of details, but it seems that this comes through selective processes. As always in these accounts, we are getting more than just a story. The
author is giving us a moral message. If we let things slide as they are going today,
with the rich getting ever softer and idler, and the poor ever more exploited and
degraded, we are making for no future paradise. "For you know very well that
the day of the Lord will come like a thief in the night. While people are saying,
"Peace and safety," destruction will come on them suddenly, as labor pains on a
pregnant woman, and they will not escape" (1 Thessalonians, 5:2–3)

Salvation

Is there no way forward? In the Christian story we may be tainted by sin, but we
can hope for salvation through the Blood of the Lamb. And there is the command laid on us to help others, although there is some debate as to whether
helping others is at all to gain credit or whether to mark our gratitude for having
ourselves been saved. There were those who wrote in evolutionary terms who
simply kept the old Christian solutions. Charles Kingsley was a prime example.[13]

---

[13] So unchanged was Kingsley that in the 1870s, after the *Descent of Man*, he broke with what he
took to be Darwin's materialism, even endorsing the critical but spiritually infused *Genesis of Species*
(1871) by St. George Mivart (Hale 2013). This despite the fact that Mivart was a Roman Catholic
and Kingsley was the arch-Protestant whose attack on the integrity of John Henry Newman had
spurred the latter to write his *Apologia Pro Vita Sua* (1864).

Grimes the chimney sweep, the master of Tom, is a pretty dreadful person. He broke his poor old mother's heart. "I ran away from her and took up with the sweeps, and never let her know where I was, nor sent her a penny to help her" (Kingsley [1863] 2008, 182). He is sorry. "I've made my bed, and I must lie on it. Foul I would be, and foul I am, as an Irishwoman said to me once; and little I heeded it. It's all my own fault: but it's too late" (183). It is never too late, he learns. He is forgiven, although he is sent off to sweep the crater of Mount Etna. "And for aught I know, or do not know, he is sweeping the crater of Etna to this very day" (184). Better, one supposes, than being stuck up a chimney with a fire warming your backside, which was his earlier punishment for having inflicted such a dreadful thing upon Tom.

In the end Evelyn Innes was saved by confession of her sins and a return to faith. Although how permanent the change would be is left somewhat up in the air. "She strove to distinguish her soul; it seemed flying before her like a bird, making straight for some goal which she could not distinguish. She could distinguish its wings in the blue air, and then she lost sight of them; then she caught sight of them again, and they were then no more than a tremulous sparkle in the air. Suddenly the vision vanished, and she found herself face to face with herself—her prosaic self which she had known always, and would know until she ceased to know everything" (Moore 1898, 477). Was that really going to make it all of the way? She was pretty certain that she would never again lead a life of nonstop sin. But the casual sin? For all that there will be remorse, it could happen. "He who repents, he who had once felt the ache of sin, may fall into sin again." Best not to worry perhaps: "his sinning is of no long duration!"[14]

Hardy, we know, was not very keen on any of this. You might repent and return (or go) to faith. Whether it will make you really better and truly happy is another matter. You could be just stuck in some sterile miserable mode of existence that gives comfort to neither you nor anybody else. This is the fate of poor Sue in *Jude the Obscure*. She has gone back to her husband and remarried him. Now comes the penalty.

> He gloomily considered her thin and fragile form a moment longer as she crouched before him in her night-clothes. "Well, I thought it might

---

[14] Moore wrote a sequel, *Sister Teresa*, and could not make up his mind quite what was going to happen to his heroine—join a monastery (first edition, 1901) or set up a home for handicapped children (second edition, 1909). Either way, Sir Owen is out of luck. "The gates of love open, and we pass into the garden and out of it by another gate, which never opens for us again" (Moore [1909] 1929, 279–280).

end like this," he said presently. "I owe you nothing, after these signs; but I'll take you in at your word, and forgive you."

He put his arm round her to lift her up. Sue started back.

"What's the matter?" he asked, speaking for the first time sternly. "You shrink from me again?—just as formerly!"

"No, Richard—I—I—was not thinking—"

"You wish to come in here?"

"Yes."

"You still bear in mind what it means?"

"Yes. It is my duty!"

Placing the candlestick on the chest of drawers he led her through the doorway, and lifting her bodily, kissed her. A quick look of aversion passed over her face, but clenching her teeth she uttered no cry. (Hardy [1895] 1960, 480)

As the landlady says: "Ah! Poor soul! Weddings be funerals 'a b'lieve nowadays. Fifty-five years ago, come Fall, since my man and I married! Times have changed since then!" (408)

George Eliot

Is there then no hope of redemption for the person caught in an evolutionary novel? In *The Way of All Flesh*, Samuel Butler suggests that the shock of prison changes Ernest Pontifex, although whether he was truly a sinner when he went to prison (rather than rather naïve and stupid) is a moot point. George Eliot as always is more balanced and thought-provoking than most. Given the challenge that she has set herself, it would be unthinkable were she not to see some way forward. She does not think everyone is a saint or could be converted to even a moderately good form of life. Lapidoth, the father of Mirah and Mordecai in *Daniel Deronda*, is a truly dreadful man. He enters the novel wanting to make his daughter the mistress of a middle-aged count, in order it seems to get the count to pay off his gambling debts. When he appears again later in the novel, it is but to sponge off his children. And it gets no better. He is thinking of cadging from Daniel but then sees that foolishly Daniel has taken off his ring and has no hesitation in stealing it. As he reasons, "any property of Deronda's (available without his formal consent) was all one with his children's property, since their father would never be prosecuted for taking it." No great matter. Daniel loses his ring but gets the daughter. "Mirah, let me think that he is my father as well as yours—that we can have no sorrow, no disgrace, no joy apart. I will rather

take your grief to be mine than I would take the brightest joy of another woman"
(Eliot [1876] 1967, 863).

I am not sure—I doubt that George Eliot is sure—whether Gwendolen
reforms, although undoubtedly her own suffering and the influence and example of Daniel do lead to a much greater self-awareness. But Fred Vincy in
Middlemarch certainly does change his ways for the better. He is never an evil
person like Lapidoth—I think Eliot would not believe herself if she reformed
that sort of person—but Fred is careless and selfish and causes others—
especially including those he has greatest reason to thank—great distress. He
has had Mary Garth's father, Caleb, cosign a loan for him and instead of repay-
ing when he has some money he goes off and buys a horse that turns out to
be absolutely worthless. There is at least a suggestion that Fred is rather casual
about the money he owes because his family is of a higher social class than the
Garths. Then he changes. He doesn't get a legacy that he expected. Mary whom
he loves makes it very clear that she thinks his behavior leaves much to be desired. He realizes that a better man than he, the local vicar, also loves Mary but
is magnanimous in standing aside. Caleb offers Fred a job—"The lad is good at
bottom, and clever enough to do, if he's put in the right way; and he loves and
honors my daughter beyond anything, and she has given him a sort of promise
according to what he turns out. I say, that young man's soul is in my hand; and
I'll do the best I can for him, so help me God!" (Eliot [1874] 2011, 647)—and
Fred knuckles down to work. He doesn't always find it easy and temptations lie
along the way.

> As to money just now, Fred had in his mind the heroic project of
> saving almost all of the eighty pounds that Mr. Garth offered him, and
> returning it, which he could easily do by giving up all futile money-
> spending, since he had a superfluous stock of clothes, and no expense
> in his board. In that way he could, in one year, go a good way towards
> repaying the ninety pounds of which he had deprived Mrs. Garth, un-
> happily at a time when she needed that sum more than she did now.
> Nevertheless, it must be acknowledged that on this evening, which
> was the fifth of his recent visits to the billiard-room, Fred had, not
> in his pocket, but in his mind, the ten pounds which he meant to re-
> serve for himself from his half-year's salary (having before him the
> pleasure of carrying thirty to Mrs. Garth when Mary was likely to be
> come home again)—he had those ten pounds in his mind as a fund
> from which he might risk something, if there were a chance of a good
> bet. Why? Well, when sovereigns were flying about, why shouldn't he
> catch a few? (771)

But he does succeed. "Fred remained unswervingly steady" (953). He ends up writing books on agriculture, happy with a good wife and three little boys. Eliot shows how on her secular approach to morality, as with Christianity, there are failures but there can be successes too. People after Darwin continued to recognize sin but knew that it must and could be dealt with.

12

The Future

Promises, Promises

This is surely the most optimistic—or naïve—chapter of them all. Christianity makes big promises. Heaven, eternal life, bliss with the Creator. There is some considerable debate about the exact form this afterlife is going to resemble. I like to think of it as a new Mozart opera every night, fish and chips in the intermission, and no student papers to mark when I get home. I suspect most people if pushed have something like this in mind—existence down here only better. Rupert Brooke pokes gentle fun at this.

> Fish (fly-replete, in depth of June,
> Dawdling away their wat'ry noon)
> Ponder deep wisdom, dark or clear,
> Each secret fishy hope or fear.
> Fish say, they have their Stream and Pond;
> But is there anything Beyond?

The fish rather think there is.

> We darkly know, by Faith we cry,
> The future is not Wholly Dry.
> Mud unto mud! — Death eddies near —
> Not here the appointed End, not here!
> But somewhere, beyond Space and Time.
> Is wetter water, slimier slime!
> And there (they trust) there swimmeth One
> Who swam ere rivers were begun,
> Immense, of fishy form and mind,
> Squamous, omnipotent, and kind;
> And under that Almighty Fin,

The littlest fish may enter in.
Oh! never fly conceals a hook,
Fish say, in the Eternal Brook, . . .

Paradise!

And in that Heaven of all their wish,
There shall be no more land, say fish.

Gentle fun, but one that does actually conceal a hook. Does heaven make sense, is it plausible, or is it nothing but a projected wish fulfillment? If God exists, one presumes that at least heaven is in some sense an option. But what if God does not exist? Is there hope of some kind of heaven here on Earth? And if so, what would it be like? There is a range of answers.[1] Let us begin at the bottom, as it were, with those who are doubtful about any kind of heaven, up there or down here.

Thomas Hardy

Thomas Hardy begs us to take him first. In the end, where does he stand on the God question and the implications for immortality? For the early Hardy (1860s): Nothing. No meaning. Nothing. Thus "Nature's Questioning."

"Has some Vast Imbecility,
    Mighty to build and blend,
    But impotent to tend,
Framed us in jest, and left us now to hazardry?

"Or come we of an Automaton
    Unconscious of our pains?. . .
    Or are we live remains
Of Godhead dying downwards, brain and eye now gone?

"Or is it that some high Plan betides,
    As yet not understood,
    Of Evil stormed by Good,
We the Forlorn Hope over which Achievement strides?"

Thus things around. No answerer I. . . .
    Meanwhile the winds, and rains,

---

[1] While there is hardly going to be exact overlap, I much doubt that there is any less of a range among Christian answers.

> And Earth's old glooms and pains
> Are still the same, and gladdest Life Death neighbors nigh.
>   (Hardy 1994, 58)

Is life the end result of some crazy divinity, a machine, a dying God, or just nothing? Who knows? Who cares? The laws of nature just keep grinding on and death awaits us all.

Things seem not to get much better. In "God's Funeral," written around 1910, Hardy sees a procession of people following the body of the Almighty.

> I saw a slowly-stepping train —
> Lined on the brows, scoop-eyed and bent and hoar —
> Following in files across a twilit plain
> A strange and mystic form the foremost bore.

He reflects how we invented God and worked on Him through the ages.[2]

> O man-projected Figure, of late
> Imaged as we, thy knell who shall survive?
> Whence came it we were tempted to create
> One whom we can no longer keep alive?
>
> Framing him jealous, fierce, at first,
> We gave him justice as the ages rolled,
> Will to bless those by circumstance accurst,
> And longsuffering, and mercies manifold.
>
> And, tricked by our own early dream
> And need of solace, we grew self-deceived,
> Our making soon our maker did we deem,
> And what we had imagined we believed,

But now the God idea has run out of steam and usefulness. It had to go.

> Till, in Time's stayless stealthy swing,
> Uncompromising rude reality
> Mangled the Monarch of our fashioning,
> Who quavered, sank; and now has ceased to be.
>   (Hardy 1994, 297–299)

---

[2] Almost certainly this reflects Feuerbach's belief (in *The Essence of Christianity* translated into English by George Eliot) that God is a human invention (Schweik 1999).

Hardy does not speak for everyone. In fact, one is not sure he speaks for himself all of the time. Much of the time he is pagan-like—whether there be an Immanent Will or not—seeing things just having existence and going on indefinitely. Neither good nor bad, just there. This is certainly the theme of a novel like *The Return of the Native*. Egdon Heath always was, is now, and always will be. We are just puppets who dance on its surface for a while. Sometimes, he is quite negative. This comes across, understandably, in late poems after the Great War. Yet, at the end of "God's Funeral" he is less absolutely negative than one might expect. He is still ruminating on the death of God.

> Still, how to bear such loss I deemed
> The insistent question for each animate mind,
> And gazing, to my growing sight there seemed
> A pale yet positive gleam low down behind,
>
> Whereof, to lift the general night,
> A certain few who stood aloof had said,
> 'See you upon the horizon that small light --
> Swelling somewhat?' Each mourner shook his head.
>
> And they composed a crowd of whom
> Some were right good, and many nigh the best. . ..
> Thus dazed and puzzled 'twixt the gleam and gloom
> Mechanically I followed with the rest.

The last stanza is slightly ambiguous about whom the crowd might be. I take it that it is the "certain few" of the previous stanza and not everyone. So although the speaker doesn't at once pick up positively, at least he or she is "dazed and puzzled." In an entirely secular way this would mesh with the thoughts we have seen by him of the possibility of humans going it alone and improving things. It also ties in with the optimism he expresses (around 1908) at the end of the *Dynasts* (Bailey 1956). We start (back around 1903) with the Immanent Will, an unconscious force driving things along.

> SHADE OF THE EARTH
> What of the Immanent Will and Its designs?
>
> SPIRIT OF THE YEARS
> It works unconsciously, as heretofore,
> Eternal artistries in Circumstance,
> Whose patterns, wrought by rapt aesthetic rote,

Seem in themselves Its single listless aim,
And not their consequence.

CHORUS OF THE PITIES [aerial music]
Still thus? Still thus?
Ever unconscious!
An automatic sense
Unweeting why or whence?
Be, then, the inevitable, as of old,
Although that SO it be we dare not hold!

SPIRIT OF THE YEARS
Hold what ye list, fond believing Sprites,
You cannot swerve the pulsion of the Byss,
Which thinking on, yet weighing not Its thought,
Unchecks Its clock-like laws.
                    (Hardy [1903-1906-1908] 2013, 11)

Echoing *Tess of the D'Urbervilles,* it is possible for the Spirit Sinister (one of the emanations of the Immanent Will) to play havoc with human life. In direct descent from Job, Hardy used the Spirit Sinister to bring on the Napoleonic Wars by getting George III to reject Napoleon's peaceful overtures (Bailey 1946). Yet at the end, through the Will achieving consciousness thanks to human effort, things ahead look brighter. Perhaps we are on the way to evolutionary meliorism.

CHORUS
But—a stirring thrills the air
    Like to sounds of joyance there
      That the rages
      Of the ages
  Shall be cancelled, and deliverance offered from the darts
      that were,
  Consciousness the Will informing, till It fashion all things fair!
(423)

Pulling back however, in the second decade of the new century, Hardy writes about the sinking of the *Titanic,* explicitly linking the building of the ship with the formation of the iceberg, things that through blind destiny were fated to collide.

VI

Well: while was fashioning
This creature of cleaving wing,
The Immanent Will that stirs and urges everything

VII

Prepared a sinister mate
For her — so gaily great —
A Shape of Ice, for the time far and dissociate.

VIII

And as the smart ship grew
In stature, grace, and hue,
In shadowy silent distance grew the Iceberg too.

IX

Alien they seemed to be;
No mortal eye could see
The intimate welding of their later history,

X

Or sign that they were bent
By paths coincident
On being anon twin halves of one august event,

XI

Till the Spinner of the Years
Said "Now!" And each one hears,
And consummation comes, and jars two hemispheres.
(Hardy 1994, 279)

Not much evolutionary meliorism there or much help from the Immanent Will. And this was before the Great War, when the poison gas ruined everything.[3]

---

[3] Hardy told his wife that he would not have ended *The Dynasts* as he did had he known the Great War was coming (Dean 1977, 34).

H. G. Wells

After Darwin, Hardy saw no meaning in life or the world. At times he tried
to break from this through a faith in humankind possibly informing and di-
recting an Immanent Will or possibly humans acting alone—and perhaps he
did—but then (whatever he said) despair and pessimism crushed much human
hope.[4] Others were negative for a slightly different reason. Like Spencer—like
Darwin himself—they were quite prepared in principle to see an upward rise in
both society and evolution. It was just that they thought that this was no longer
true. With E. Ray Lankester they thought that evolutionary progress had run
its course and now they were in a time of decay and loss. For some perhaps this
was a cyclical thing. Now you get rise. Then decay and degeneration. Then rise
again. Others were not so sure. It was not only the social factors that influenced
them. The science did also. In particular, the second law of thermodynamics
stated definitively that although, for a while, you may stop things running down
in certain parts of the universe, in the end all is futile. The future is heat decay
with everything grinding to a halt.[5] H. G. Wells was sensitive to this belief. (He
makes explicit mention, in the 1931 edition of the *Time Machine*, of the influence of the second law on his thinking in the 1890s.) The final stops of the
time traveler (i.e., before he takes off again and vanishes for evermore) are ever-
closer to the end of time. He has pushed way into the future and what he finds
does not please.

> The sky was no longer blue. North-eastward it was inky black, and
> out of the blackness shone brightly and steadily the pale white stars.
> Overhead it was a deep Indian red and starless, and south-eastward it
> grew brighter to a glowing scarlet where, cut by the horizon, lay the
> huge hull of the sun, red and motionless. The rocks about me were of

---

[4] To be fair, for all that Hardy denied that he was trying overly hard to be fully consistent, he was
aware of the tensions in his thinking, and toward the end (in 1922) we find him saying that seeing the
downside to things is a necessary stage to seeing the upside: "If way to the Better there be, it exacts
a full look at the Worst: that is to say, by the exploration of reality, and its frank recognition stage by
stage along the survey, with an eye to the best consummation possible: briefly, evolutionary meliorism" (quoted by Bailey 1963, 585).

[5] Darwin worried about this one. To Hooker, he wrote: "I quite agree how humiliating the slow
progress of man is; but everyone has his own pet horror, & this slow progress, or even personal an-
nihilation sinks in my mind into insignificance compared with the idea, or rather I presume certainty,
of the sun some day cooling & we all freezing. To think of the progress of millions of years, with every
continent swarming with good & enlightened men all ending in this; & with probably no fresh start
until this our own planetary system has been again converted into red-hot gas.—*Sic* transit gloria
mundi, with a vengeance" (Darwin 1985–, 13, 56, written February 9, 1865).

a harsh reddish colour, and all the trace of life that I could see at first was the intensely green vegetation that covered every projecting point on their south-eastern face. It was the same rich green that one sees on forest moss or on the lichen in caves: plants which like these grow in a perpetual twilight. (Wells [1895] 2005, 82)

There is worse to come. He sees a monstrous creature and then many more. "Can you imagine a crab as large as yonder table, with its many legs moving slowly and uncertainly, its big claws swaying, its long antennae, like carters' whips, waving and feeling, and its stalked eyes gleaming at you on either side of its metallic front? Its back was corrugated and ornamented with ungainly bosses, and a greenish incrustation blotched it here and there. I could see the many palps of its complicated mouth flickering and feeling as it moved" (83).

He moves on through time. "At last, more than thirty million years hence, the huge red-hot dome of the sun had come to obscure nearly a tenth part of the darkling heavens" (84). The crabs are gone. "I saw nothing moving, in earth or sky or sea. The green slime on the rocks alone testified that life was not extinct." All was quiet in a dreadful manner. "'The darkness grew apace; a cold wind began to blow in freshening gusts from the east, and the showering white flakes in the air increased in number. From the edge of the sea came a ripple and whisper. Beyond these lifeless sounds the world was silent" (85). There was no light. "The sky was absolutely black." But then. Was it just a rock? Was it an illusion? "As I stood sick and confused I saw again the moving thing upon the shoal—there was no mistake now that it was a moving thing—against the red water of the sea. It was a round thing, the size of a football perhaps, or, it may be, bigger, and tentacles trailed down from it; it seemed black against the weltering blood-red water, and it was hopping fitfully about." The traveler had had enough. "So I came back" (86).

Transcendentalism

Turn now to those who did see some glimmers of hope. The American transcendentalists might be fertile territory. Walt Whitman modifies a strand of Lamarckism—probably taken from Chambers—to suggest that something might persist after death.

> How can the real body ever die and be buried?
>> Of your real body and any man's or woman's real body,
>> Item for item it will elude the hands of the corpse-cleaners and
>>> pass to fitting spheres,

Carrying what has accrued to it from the moment of birth to the
    moment of death.

(Whitman 2004, 58)

Emily Dickinson is not exactly positive, but then again she is not exactly negative either. Did she believe, or not? There is certainly an empathy for belief and
perhaps a yearning for the hereafter. Somewhat poignantly she remarked in a
letter of 1872 to Elizabeth Holland, drawing the connection between joy and
sadness: "Why the Thief ingredient accompanies all Sweetness Darwin does not
tell us." The sentiment is echoed in this poem.

> That it will never come again
> Is what makes life so sweet.
> Believing what we don't believe
> Does not exhilarate.
>
> That if it be, it be at best
> An ablative estate —
> This instigates an appetite
> Precisely opposite.

(Dickinson 1960, 706, date unknown)

Somewhat amusingly, the first two lines were posted on the London Underground
in 2009 as part of the British Humanist's Association "Atheist Bus" campaign.
Perhaps so. "Ablative" means distant or separation. I sense more regret and sense
of loss in some way, reflecting into our emotions here and almost a need to be
happy and enjoy life. Other poems strike me as more positive about the hereafter, even if hardly as confident as Billy Graham at one of his revivalist meetings.
Take that most famous poem, "Because I could not stop for Death."

> Because I could not stop for Death —
> He kindly stopped for me —
> The Carriage held but just Ourselves —
> And Immortality.
>
> We slowly drove — He knew no haste
> And I had put away
> My labor and my leisure too,
> For His Civility —
>
> We passed the School, where Children strove
> At Recess — in the Ring —

We passed the Fields of Gazing Grain —
We passed the Setting Sun —

Or rather — He passed Us —
The Dews drew quivering and Chill –
For only Gossamer, my Gown –
My Tippet — only Tulle —

We paused before a House that seemed
A Swelling of the Ground —
The Roof was scarcely visible —
The Cornice — in the Ground —

Since then — 'tis Centuries — and yet
Feels shorter than the Day
I first surmised the Horses' Heads
Were toward Eternity —
        (Dickinson 1960, 350, written about 1863)

There is initial promise here of immortality and moreover of something essentially good. Death "kindly" stopped for me and took me, apparently without
regret or longing, past children and the cornfields and the beauty of the sun going
down. Then at the end of the poem, we learn that the speaker died long ago. Not
much seems to have happened since then, but at the same time one senses that
that "not much" was not a stress or a bad thing. It is more a gentle peace in a quiet
grave—"a swelling of the ground." This fits with the kind of transcendentalism
so crucial in understanding this poet—a metaphysics which might or might not
involve a personal God but which also somewhat paradoxically makes a personal
God rather less important. Although note that there is a shade of worry (Vendler
2010, 225–230). This is not necessarily the revivalist's happy hereafter. There is a
chill in the air and we might not be adequately clothed. And the final promise is
of eternity not immortality. This meshes with the understated natural theology
that pervades Dickinson's poetry—there is a point to everything, but don't push
to get the immediate understanding thrust on you by Paley's eye, and be prepared for a kind of indifference that is alien to Christianity. A worm is eaten by a
bird. At first, the worm's existence had seemed senseless. Now it all fits together.

Our little Kinsmen — after Rain
In plenty may be seen,
A Pink and Pulpy multitude
The tepid Ground upon.
A needless life, it seemed to me

Until a little Bird
As to a Hospitality
Advanced and breakfasted —
As I of He, so God of Me
I pondered, may have judged,
And left the little Angle Worm
With Modesties enlarged.

(Dickinson 1960, 420, written about 1864)

Note that we are kinsmen to the worm, not to the bird (who seems more God-like). It all makes sense, but the sense is not necessarily focused on our well-being. Cold comfort for us—and Upton Sinclair's pigs![6]

Optimism

And so we come to those more positive. For all of his doubts and his worries in the post-*Origin* era, ultimately Tennyson continued to believe. Moreover, he believed not just in a god or gods but in a personal God. One who cares for us and who in some sense is guaranteeing that this life is not all. This comes through in a short poem—"God and the Universe"—written late in his life, about worries stemming from the vastness of the universe. The world we live in is huge, it is scary, but "fear not." There still exists the "Power which alone is great."

Will my tiny spark of being wholly vanish in your deeps and heights?
Must my day be dark by reason, O ye Heavens, of your boundless nights,
Rush of Suns, and roll of systems, and your fiery clash of meteorites?

"Spirit, nearing yon dark portal at the limit of thy human state,
Fear not thou the hidden purpose of that Power which alone is great,
Nor the myriad world, His shadow, nor the silent Opener of the Gate."

(Tennyson 1892, 110–111)

The old man never lost faith in evolution or, ultimately, in the conviction of "In Memoriam" that we have evolved upward and yet God has plans for further

---

[6] There are obvious parallels here with Hardy's Immanent Will, hardly surprising since ultimately they both stem from German Romanticism and the idea of the deity as a kind of unthinking world force – as in Carlyle also – rather than the super-rational, creator being of Christianity. As with the turn to Job, we are seeing people looking for meaning and explanation in a world that is not the one of their childhood.

upward movement. Even to the end, as in "The Making of Man" (1892), with "the crowning Age of ages," we get the whiff of Chambers![7]

One did not have to be a believer to be positive, although obviously a non-believer is going to restrict his positive outlook to this world and not to the next. George Eliot, writing before the themes of degeneration became practically the norm, and obviously in respects in the glow of Spencer, was positive about the prospects of social Progress. This was the sentiment expressed at the end of *Middlemarch*, and in the case of Daniel Deronda (although probably not Gwendolen) there is a bright future anticipated. Daniel tells Gwen of his plans.

> "What are you going to do?" she asked, at last, very mildly. "Can I understand the ideas, or am I too ignorant?"
>
> "I am going to the East to become better acquainted with the condition of my race in various countries there," said Deronda, gently—anxious to be as explanatory as he could on what was the impersonal part of their separateness from each other. "The idea that I am possessed with is that of restoring a political existence to my people, making them a nation again, giving them a national center, such as the English have, though they too are scattered over the face of the globe. That is a task which presents itself to me as a duty; I am resolved to begin it, however feebly. I am resolved to devote my life to it. At the least, I may awaken a movement in other minds, such as has been awakened in my own." (Eliot [1876] 1967, 875)

As for the Jews, so also for women. Remember May Kendall and her hopes for the rise of women. Stop knitting and crocheting and start using your minds.

> Alas, is it woolwork you take for your mission,
> Or Art that your fingers so gaily attack?
> Can patchwork atone for the mind's inanition?
> Can the soul, oh my sisters, be fed on a plaque?
> Is this your vocation? My goal is another,
> And empty and vain is the end you pursue.
> In antimacassars the world you may smother;
> But intellect marches o'er them and o'er you.
>
> (Kendall 1887, 38–39)

---

[7] Should Tennyson really be included on the Darwinian side? Surely yes, if you think of him as compared to Disraeli and Christina Rossetti. But he does show that the divisions between the rival positions is not a clear-cut black-and-white affair, as one expects in a Kuhn-style revolution. Stress again that, without considering Darwinism, Christianity itself shows huge variation with some asserting things that others think heretical and some denying things that others think crucial. You can hardly fault Darwinism for having a similar range or that there is overlap.

One suspects strongly that Mina Harker, from *Dracula*, would have loved this poem.

The same might not have been entirely true for D. H. Lawrence, although his Bergsonian enthusiasms certainly inclined him to an optimistic view of the future.

> The fountain-head was incorruptible and unsearchable. It had no limits. It could bring forth miracles, create utter new races and new species, in its own hour, new forms of consciousness, new forms of body, new units of being. To be man was as nothing compared to the possibilities of the creative mystery. To have one's pulse beating direct from the mystery, this was perfection, unutterable satisfaction. Human or inhuman mattered nothing. The perfect pulse throbbed with indescribable being, miraculous unborn species. (Lawrence [1921] 1960, 538–539)

One wonders whether these unborn species will show quite the same obsession with male power and the phallus as does Lawrence. Is this the heaven on Earth we should hope for? Reading *Women in Love* one gets the impression that while Ursula's various orifices serve the end of Progress, the same can hardly be said of her clitoris. It seems curiously idle—at least unmentioned—in the energetic activities, shameful or not, between her and Rupert.

George Meredith

End our survey of reactions to Darwinism with George Meredith. Overall, unlike his friend Thomas Hardy, he was an optimist. He saw the problems posed by Darwinism, but in the end thought that life moves up and that this is good. He was, however, remarkably clear-headed about how we ought to behave toward the future.

> The lover of life holds life in his hand,
> Like a ring for the bride.
> The lover of life is free of dread:
> The lover of life holds life in his hand,
> As the hills hold the day.
>
> But lust after life waves life like a brand,
> For an ensign of pride.
> The lust after life is life half-dead:
> Yea, lust after life hugs life like a brand,
> Dreading air and the ray.

For the sake of life,
For that life is dear,
The lust after life
Clings to it fast.
For the sake of life,
For that life is fair,
The lover of life
Flings it broadcast.

The lover of life knows his labour divine,
And therein is at peace.
The lust after life craves a touch and a sign
That the life shall increase.

The lust after life in the chills of its lust
Claims a passport of death.
The lover of life sees the flame in our dust
And a gift in our breath.

(Meredith 1870, 182–183)

What is the poet saying? He is dealing with the theme that we have seen in the poetry of Emily Dickinson. He says that life is good. Enjoy it for what it is and focus on the present not the future. Above all, don't let your life here and now be ruined by the fear of death and the thought that life will end. That is the way to making up fables about the future and how we will endure—thinking we have a "passport of death." Take up the gift that we have and don't spoil it because it is not all that you want. It is a good in itself and needs no encore to have great value. Heaven is now.

That is not a bad note on which to end this survey.

13

Darwinism as Background

Professional Evolution

In the early part of the twentieth century, biologists developed a theory of heredity based on the insights of the nineteenth-century Moravian monk Gregor Mendel. Around 1930, a number of mathematically gifted biologists used this theory to create a new theoretical discipline, "population genetics," a picture of the nature and change of genetic ratios in populations, as impacted upon by mutation and above all natural (and sexual) selection (Provine 1971). With the theory in place, empirical scientists moved in and by mid-century there was an active field of neo-Darwinian studies, one that saw Darwinian selection as central and effective because of the underlying genetic foundations—genetic foundations that with the discovery of the double helix by James Watson and Francis Crick in 1953 were soon to be put in molecular terms. Evolutionary biology as science finally had a basis from which people could study the many areas noted by Darwin—behavior (especially social behavior), paleontology, biogeography, classification (taxonomy), anatomy, and embryology, to name the major items (Ruse 2006). Some of the most exciting work focused on our species. At the time of Darwin, although Neanderthals were known, there were no "missing links." Then at the end of the century, the first genuine fossil of a pre-human form—Java Man (now known to be *Homo erectus*)—was uncovered. In 1924, the first Australopithecine (the genus before *Homo*, our genus) was found in South Africa, and by the 1950s the science was going flat out (Ruse 2012).[1]

---

[1] In the second decade of the century, things were thrown off course by what was probably the greatest scientific fraud of all time: Piltdown Man, discovered in Britain, a being with a human-sized brain and an ape-like jaw. It was revealed as a fraud in the 1950s. In *Anglo-Saxon Attitudes* (1956), the novelist Angus Wilson wrote a wonderful fantasy based on the Piltdown incident, conceiving of the fraud in terms of a Lawrencian figurine (i.e., a pagan model with a massively erect penis) put in the grave of the saintly bishop who converted the British heathen.

With the rise of neo-Darwinism—more commonly in the United States known as the "synthetic" theory of evolution—came full-blooded professionalism (Ruse 1996). Evolutionists moved from the museums into university departments, training was formalized with new crops of doctoral students—influential here were E. B. Ford in England and the Russian-born Theodosius Dobzhansky in the United States—grants were applied for and obtained, and new journals like *Heredity* and *Evolution* were founded and flourished. Darwin's dream had finally been recognized. From pseudoscience to popular science, and now from popular science to professional science. So what does all this mean for our story? You might think that it brings it to an end. One of the most distinctive marks of professional science as opposed to pseudoscience and even to popular science is that although it is ruled by "epistemic values"—norms for doing good science like predictive fertility and internal consistency—it expels social and cultural values. In a museum you might say or at least hint that Earth is better than Mars because it can support life, but as a geologist or astronomer this is forbidden. So when we look at all of the things that might lead one to speak of evolutionism/ Darwinism as a religion or as working from a religious perspective, you might think that these would all be expelled from professional science—and since that is what we have from around 1930, that is the end of our story.

And yet, things are never quite this simple. Professional evolutionary biology may have arrived, but that did not spell the demise of popular evolutionary biology. People were still going to be interested in issues like religion, about morality, about class, about so many of the things that had obsessed earlier evolutionists. It is just that one might now expect somewhat of a change of emphasis. Given that evolution is now so integral a part of culture, perhaps people pretty much accepted some form of Darwinism and moved on. Christianity is certainly not gone, especially not in America, where the Scopes Monkey Trial of 1925, when a young man was prosecuted for teaching evolution in the classrooms of Tennessee, was still a very public and raw memory. But overall the science-religion conflict was not the major burning topic (Larson 1997).[2] One would expect writers to be more concerned with the big issues of the day—social conditions like racism (particularly for those living in the South of the United States), the Depression, World War II, the subsequent Cold War—that sort of thing. Evolution will be there—but more as background.[3] Let us illustrate this point by turning to three

[2] Keep this point in mind. My story is not "evolution/Darwinism in popular culture" or some such thing, but "Darwinism as religion." If by 1930 that battle had been fought, the interesting question is why—to contrast with something comparable like female suffrage—this was not the end of the story. Given this change of emphasis, against the background of my large survey, I now feel able to be more focused and representative, with less need to be comprehensive.

[3] Paradoxically, just as Darwin's theorizing was achieving professional status, the rise of interest in Freud and Marx, rival bases for secular world pictures, pushed Darwinism in the public domain

major novelists, two American and one British, two prewar and one postwar, all of whom won the Nobel Prize for Literature.

Absalom, Absalom!

William Faulkner (1897–1962) who won the Prize in 1949 lived in Mississippi, and Yoknapatawpha County, the fictional setting of many of his novels, is set in that state. His novel *Absalom, Absalom!* (1936) is not easy to read, using multiple flashbacks, different narrators not all of whom are (or are intended to be) reliable, and with stream-of-consciousness sentences so gargantuan that the reader nigh expires for want of a full stop. Rather spoiling the fun, my brief synopsis will follow the author's own helpful chronology that he gives at the end of the book. The central figure, one hesitates to call him a hero, is Thomas Sutpen, born in what is now West Virginia of poor white stock around 1807. While he was still a child, the family moved South, where he not only encountered Negro slaves for the first time but realized that his family was very low on the social scale.[4] At about the age of fourteen he ran away and ended up in Haiti, where some years later he married his first wife, had a son, deserted them (when he discovered that she was one-eighth Negro), and moved back to the United States and to the state of Mississippi. There, with a gang of slaves, he built a large house on a hundred square miles of land he had acquired somewhat shadily, had a daughter (Clytie) with one of his female slaves, married a local white woman (Ellen), and had two more children, Henry and Judith. At college, Henry became friends with one Charles Bon who turned out to be Thomas's son from Haiti (suspicion was that his mother engineered the meeting) and Charles (with Henry's knowledge of the relationship) became the fiancé of his half-sister Judith.

The Civil War now intervened, with Thomas, Henry and Charles serving the South. Rosa, Ellen's sister, moved in after their father starved himself in the attic lest he be coopted into the war. At the end, Thomas and Henry returned to the family homestead, where Henry shot Charles when he learnt of his black blood – "So it's the miscegenation, not the incest, which you cant bear" (Faulkner [1936] 1986, 285). Henry vanished, Thomas returned, and tried to marry Rosa, but was rejected when he said the condition is that she have a son. So instead

---

to one side a bit. Remember the Freud-like revisions in the (1931) movie version of the Dr. Jekyll and Mr. Hyde story. Likewise in 1931—the year it was written—Aldous Huxley's *Brave New World* owes as much to Freud as it does to Darwin. Mark Greif (2015), discussing American novels of the mid-twentieth century, suggests that—thanks to the influx of European scholars fleeing Hitler—existentialism became a major influence. Freud and Marx make appearances but Darwin is virtually invisible.

[4] I use Faulkner's language for African-Americans.

Thomas impregnated the granddaughter of a poor white man working on the property, but when she had a daughter he repudiated her, at which point grand-father killed her and daughter, having first murdered Thomas. Meanwhile appearing on the scene was Charles Etienne St. Valery Bon, Charles's son, whose mother was an octoroon (one-eighth Negro) from New Orleans. Before he died (as does Judith) of yellow fever, he married a Negro woman and had a son, Jim Bond. At the end, Henry turned up and Clytie burnt down the house with both of them in it, lest he get arrested for the murder of Charles. Jim Bond was the sole survivor, and the forecast was that his type "are going to conquer the western hemisphere" (302).

Like a Verdi opera, *Absalom, Absalom!* is a lot more rewarding that than one might guess from the program notes. Focusing here on possible Darwinian elements, and avoiding fascinating side issues like the Freudian nature of the relationship between Henry and Charles, let alone Charles and Judith, one can be sure that, thanks to the Scopes Trial of 1925, Faulkner like every other educated Southerner would have been up on the evolution question. More specifically, we know that he was sufficiently interested in (and presumably sympathetic to) Darwin's ideas that a year after the novel appeared he prompted his step-son Mac to begin study of anthropology and biology and gave him a copy of the *Origin of Species* for Christmas. The internal evidence of the novel also bears out the interest in evolution. Two things in particular stand out.

First, the whole scope of the story. It reminds one of nothing so much as that ultra-Darwinian novel, *Tess of the D'Urbervilles*. We learn (and I work chronologically now) right from the beginning that heredity counts. Sutpen like Tess comes from a really inadequate family, describable in animal terms– "as cattle, as cattle, creatures heavy and without grace, brutely evacuated into a world without hope or purpose for them, who would in turn spawn with brutish and vicious prolixity, populate, double treble and compound" (190). Like Tess, Sutpen seems to have a slightly better education than the rest and this is put down to his biological heritage – some of his blood had been "bred in mountains" and "did permit him to listen when the teacher read aloud" (195). Crushed when (on moving South) a Negro servant tells him not to use the front door but to go around the back, he gets the grand "design" to make money and have social power himself. Hence the move to the West Indies and then, when he has some capital, to Mississippi with his band of slaves.

But, as with Tess, there is degenerate blood there and its effects cannot be blocked. We learn (admittedly from a not-entirely-reliable reporter) that Thomas "looked about upon the scene which was still within his scope and compass and saw son gone, vanished, more insuperable to him now than if the son were dead since now (if the son still lived) his name would be different and those to call him by it strangers and whatever dragon's outcropping of Sutpen blood the son might sow on the body of whatever strange woman would therefore carry on the tradition, accomplish the hereditary evil and harm under another name and upon and among people who will never have heard the right one" (148). Thanks to Thomas's own actions, thanks to chance happenings outside his control (the war particularly), the grand house that he has built ends a degenerate ruin, his land is gone, and the only surviving successor is Jim Bond, an "idiot negro" (301). As in Hardy's post-Darwinian world, there is no God, there is no false hope, there is only chance from the luck of the genes and the fortunes of nature. Tess's hopes collapse and so do Sutpen's designs. The novels are not identical. Tess is a much nicer person than Sutpen. But the metaphysics is similar.

Then second, there is the whole race and (to a lesser extent) class thing. Obviously Faulkner's thinking is not straight out of the *Descent of Man*. There was quite enough home-grown material to fill the novel and fifty more. But it is all very much in the pattern given credence by the evolutionists and especially the hierarchy of races one finds in Darwin and subsequent writers. Let there be no mistake about it. Negroes are seen as much ape-like as is Stevenson's Mr. Hyde. The language is non-stop. When Sutpen turns up with his twenty slaves in tow, they are described as "his band of wild niggers like beasts half tamed to walk upright like men" (4). This is nothing to the description of Charles Etienne's wife. She is a "coal black and ape-like Woman" (166). He flaunts the "ape-like body of his charcoal companion" (167). She is a "black gargoyle" (170) and she resembles "something in a zoo" (169). The very violence of the language, however, cautions one to take care. No matter the shock for Darwin from the Tierra del Fuegians, Faulkner's is not the language or the sentiment of the *Descent*. Apart from anything else, Darwin had seen Fuegians who had gone to England and had taken on Western ways. He knew that much of the difference between us and natives in their habitats was cultural. More than this. Darwin is the man who abhors slavery—"this odious deadly subject" (Darwin 1985–, 3, 242, letter to Charles Lyell, August 25, 1845). The absolute moral stand oozes out of every pore of his body. It is his King Charles's head. From the *Journal of Researches* talking of the land of "Brava Gente"—"I bear them no good will—a land also of slavery, and therefore of moral debasement" (Darwin 1839, 592)—to the *Descent of Man*—"The great sin of Slavery has been almost universal, and slaves have often been treated in an infamous manner" (Darwin 1871, 1, 94). During the civil war, Asa Gray the botanist promoter of Darwinism in America, an ardent abolitionist, told his English friend: "You are the only Britisher I ever write to on this subject, and, in fact, for whose opinions about our country I care at all" (Darwin 1985–, 11, 302, letter from Gray to Darwin, April 11, 1863).

In *Absalom, Absalom!* slavery is taken as a fact and the emancipation that takes place in the middle of the time-line is something that makes absolutely no difference to the way that the white people treat the black people. This is not a novel that celebrates Negro freedom. It is certainly not *Huckleberry Finn*. I do not in any sense imply that this indifference, or the characterizations above, convey the sentiments of Faulkner. He is a novelist, putting words into the mouths of his characters. And this flags us to the fact that however much of a Darwinian background there may be in this novel, and there is and it is genuine, this is not really a Darwinian novel in the way true of *Tess of the D'Urbervilles*. Hardy's theme is the cruelty of fate in a Darwinian universe. Faulkner's theme is the complex relationships between whites and blacks in the American South. There is nothing in Darwin to say that someone who is one-sixteenth Negro is therefore Negro. In fact, one suspects the very opposite. It is like saying that because we now know that all white people have some Neanderthal DNA, all white people are Neanderthals (as opposed to black people who have none). Darwin's ultimate story is that we are all brothers and sisters under the skin.

Faulkner is examining how and why people can take such stands as they do. They all live in such symbiotic relationship with those very people they disparage. Sutpen lives with and works with and eats with and wrestles with his Negroes. He has no qualms about sex with his female slaves or bringing up the offspring in his own house. And yet he turns from a son who is virtually white because of those few drops of blood that was "tainted and corrupt" (263). And then he couples with the granddaughter of the lowest menial on the estate because she is pure white and might give him the all-desired son, Henry having now vanished. This son is no better. He has no objection to a half-brother marrying their sister but then balks because the man is one-sixteenth Negro. A woman (Rosa) is the daughter of a man who kills himself rather than fight for the South, and yet she is horrified when a half-black woman (Clytie) addresses her by her first name and dares to touch her and to stop her from dashing upstairs to the room with the body of Charles—"that black arresting and untimorous hand on my white woman's flesh" (111). I am not saying that Faulkner solves any of these issues, or even sets out to solve them. I am not sure as a novelist he had to. What he is doing is pushing these sorts of facts up before us, telling us that if we are to understand human nature—if we are to understand the American South—then we had better start right here. How can people all of one species get themselves into such an appalling cultural mess? This is an important theme handled quite brilliantly, but it is not primarily a Darwinian theme and it is certainly not something taking on the role of religion in all of this. These are not Faulkner's issues.

The Grapes of Wrath

John Steinbeck (1902–1968), who won the Nobel Prize in 1962, was from California. *The Grapes of Wrath*, his novel set in the Depression about the

migrants to California and their horrendous challenges and trials, has been controversial since it was published in 1939. Some see it as a searing, profound in-
dictment in fiction of America and its culture. Others a sentimental tale, way
overexaggerated. It is perhaps something of both, but its narrative power endures
and no one can read it without being deeply disturbed and if not inspired then
with a huge sense of admiration for people who simply refuse to be crushed by
life's adversities. The story is a simple one of a family, ruined by the dust storms
and leaving their native Oklahoma for the West and the hope of work and a new
life. The Joads are Granma and Granpa; Ma and Pa; various children, including
Tom, just out of jail where he has spent four years for killing a chap in a fight;
Noah, the oldest and a bit odd; Rose of Sharon (the name of a local flower),
pregnant, and her husband, Connie; sixteen-year-old Al, who is good at cars and
who has the hormones of a randy billy goat; other assorted small children; Uncle
John Joad, ever sad because he did not save his wife from peritonitis; and, tag-
ging along with them, the Reverend Jim Casy who used to be a preacher but is no
longer. It is the story of their journey along Route 66 to the Promised Land and
of the grave disappointments—no work, no money, gross prejudice, appalling
weather, and more—when they arrive in California. It is the story of violence, of
killings, and of sad failures to survive, ending with the stillborn child of Rose of
Sharon. It is also the story of human endurance and of the will to persist despite
all misfortunes. It is the story of those who grow stronger as the days go by—Ma
Joad, the matriarch of the family, and Tom Joad, her favorite son—and those
who fade away—Granma and Granpa who die on the road, Noah Joad who just
walks away from the family, and Connie, the son-in-law who deserts his wife. It is
despite all a story of hope in some sense, although ominously the narrator warns
of social explosions that might occur if the valve of inequality and injustice is not
released.

We know that Steinbeck was deeply influenced by evolutionary ideas, both
at college—he spent some undergraduate years at Stanford—and then in the
1930s, when he became a close friend of Ed Ricketts, a professional biologist
(who had studied at the University of Chicago) and owner of a biological supply
house (Astro 1973). Through both sources, Steinbeck absorbed the truth and
importance of evolution, but (especially through Ricketts) an evolution of a distinctive kind (that was the trademark of Chicago), a form of holism that saw
the key features of the process as promoting unity and integration (Ruse 2013).
There was Bergson in the background with his creative notions of evolutionary
change, there was Clyde Warder Allee at Chicago arguing for animal aggrega-
tions and seeing phenomena like the ants' nest as the paradigm for future progress, and above all there was the holistic thinking of the South African statesman
Jan Smuts. "Evolution is not merely a process of change, of regrouping of the
old into new forms; it is creative, its new forms are not merely fashioned out

of the old materials; it creates both new materials and new forms from the synthesis of the new with the old materials" (Smuts 1926, 89). Evolution tends to create wholes, to bring parts together, but transforming into new higher entities that could not simply be deduced from the components. "We must have time to think and to look and to consider. And the modern process—that of looking quickly at the whole field and then diving down to a particular—was reversed by Darwin. Out of long long consideration of the parts he emerged with a sense of the whole" (Steinbeck [1942] 1962, 60). See how Steinbeck weaves this philosophy into a condemnation of the way in which the big banks, which had, through their mortgages, driven people like the Joads off their land and now, using mega-tractors, were plowing it all up to grow (the soil-depleting) cotton.

> And in the tractor man there grows the contempt that comes only to a stranger who has little understanding and no relation. For nitrates are not the land, nor phosphates; and the length of fiber in the cotton is not the land. Carbon is not a man, nor salt nor water nor calcium. He is all these, but he is much more, much more; and the land is so much more than its analysis. The man who is more than his chemistry, walking on the earth, turning his plow point for a stone, dropping his handles to slide over an outcropping, kneeling in the earth to eat his lunch; that man who is more than his elements knows the land that is more than its analysis. But the machine man, driving a dead tractor on land he does not know and love, understands only chemistry; and he is contemptuous of the land and of himself. (Steinbeck [1939] 2006, 115–116)

Infusing this kind of thinking with a good dose of Emersonian transcendentalism about universal world souls, and the mix was complete.[5] Steinbeck had a philosophy that structures the *Grapes of Wrath* from beginning to end. For all the trials and tribulations, the picture is one of Progress, of things improving or about to improve, no matter what the setbacks.

> To build a wall, to build a house, a dam, and in the wall and house and dam to put something of Manself, and to Manself take back something of the wall, the house, the dam; to take hard muscles from the lifting, to take the clear lines and form from conceiving. For man, unlike any

---

[5] Apparently Steinbeck thought the Emersonian flavor was more a matter of parallel thinking than direct influence (Railsback 1995, 48). Perhaps so, but there was a huge amount of this kind of thought among the Chicago biologists. "Ricketts' world-view . . . finds an understanding response in Goethe, Wordsworth, and Whitman" (28). The point is that not only did Steinbeck's book reflect evolutionary thinking, it reflected evolutionary thinking 1930s-style.

other thing organic or inorganic in the universe, grows beyond his
work, walks up the stairs of his concepts, emerges ahead of his ac-
complishments. This you may say of man—when theories change and
crash, when schools, philosophies, when narrow dark alleys of thought,
national, religious, economic, grow and disintegrate, man reaches,
stumbles forward, painfully, mistakenly sometimes. Having stepped
forward, he may slip back, but only half a step, never the full step back.
This you may say and know it and know it. (150)

I am not sure how Darwinian any of this is, but it is certainly evolutionary and
progressive. We know he read Bergson with ideas of P/progress coming through
our facing suffering and stress (Railsback 1995). In addition, for Steinbeck, as
he makes clear repeatedly, some form of organicism, holism, is a key feature of
the picture. Again and again, the point is made about the importance of family.
"The eyes of the whole family shifted back to Ma. She was the power. She had
taken control. 'The money we'd make wouldn't do no good,' she said. 'All we got
is the family unbroke. Like a bunch a cows, when the lobos are ranging, stick all
together. I ain't scared while we're all here, all that's alive, but I ain't gonna see us
bust up'" (169–170).[6] On the road, come the evenings, we see the formation of a
group, even just a temporary one, as migrant families camp together and make a
mini-society, with its own rules and ways of living together. "Every night a world
created, complete with furniture—friends made and enemies established; a
world complete with braggarts and with cowards, with quiet men, with humble
men, with kindly men. Every night relationships that make a world, established;
and every morning the world torn down like a circus" (194).

And through it all is the transcendentalists' world soul. When Tom kills a
man and has to leave the family he promises that he will be there whenever there
is injustice or unkindness or people suffering.

Tom laughed uneasily, "Well, maybe like Casy says, a fella ain't got a
soul of his own, but on'y a piece of a big one—an' then—"
"Then what, Tom?"
"Then it don' matter. Then I'll be all aroun' in the dark. I'll be
ever'where—wherever you look. Wherever they's a fight so hungry
people can eat, I'll be there. Wherever they's a cop beatin' up a guy, I'll
be there. If Casy knowed, why, I'll be in the way guys yell when they're
mad an'—I'll be in the way kids laugh when they're hungry an' they

---

[6] According to Steinbeck's first wife, Carol, Steinbeck made Ma the key figure because he was
influenced by the claims of the social anthropologist Robert Briffault that the female is the dominant
figure in the family or clan (Astro 1973, 133).

know supper's ready. An' when our folks eat the stuff they raise an' live in the houses they build—why, I'll be there." (419)

Does Steinbeck take up the question of religion and does he see it as anti-thetical to the holistic evolutionary thinking that underlies his story? At one level, this is surely the case. Christians are portrayed in a hostile way as oppos-ing the creative forces driving humans forward. For a while the Joads end up in a government-run camp—portrayed very favorably as an example of what can be done when people of good will band together for the common weal. There are hot showers, flush lavatories, Saturday evening get-togethers and dances, and overall a general sense of cooperation and goodwill. The naysayers are the Christians. "The string band took a reel tune up and played loudly, for they were not practicing any more. In front of their tents the Jesus-lovers sat and watched, their faces hard and contemptuous. They did not speak to one another, they watched for sin, and their faces condemned the whole proceeding" (335). Likewise, preachers are not given much praise—it is implied that they are only in it for money—and a crazy old woman scares the wits out of the pregnant Joad daughter, Rose of Sharon, telling her that she is going to have a stillborn child because she danced and that sort of thing.

And yet, there is the central character of the Reverend Jim Casy, a former preacher and nonstop seducer, and now a repentant sinner. He wrestles with his guilt and with his faith. But when the time comes, he proves himself a Christ-like figure—in case the reader does not quite get it, the two share initials. Tom cannot afford to get in trouble in California, else he will be shipped back to Oklahoma for breaking parole. It is Casy who steps up to the plate, getting ar-rested in Tom's place. Then later, it is Casy who leads the strike for higher wages and gets murdered for his troubles. "We come to work there. They says it's gonna be fi' cents. They was a hell of a lot of us. We got there an' they says they're payin' two an' a half cents. A fella can't even eat on that, an' if he got kids—So we says we won't take it. So they druv us off. An' all the cops in the worl' come down on us" (382–383). It is the man who killed Casy who gets retribution from Tom: "Tom leaped silently. He wrenched the club free. The first time he knew he had missed and struck a shoulder, but the second time his crushing blow found the head, and as the heavy man sank down, three more blows found his head" (386).

Evolution is in *The Grapes of Wrath* and so is Christianity in various ways. The two interact—in some forms Steinbeck finds it stultifying and opposed to true creativity; in other forms, Steinbeck finds it a key element in the push forward. Casy did important things and left a legacy, most important, he left Tom deter-mined now to carry on and use and spread the Emersonian message. Casy may not have redeemed all of mankind, but he provided a moral light, to go with Ma's fundamental stability and determinism to move forward as family, and Tom's new role as ever-present force and conscience. At the end, Rose of Sharon, her baby stillborn but with a new force herself, opens her full breast to give suck to a starving man. Perhaps more Freudian than Darwinian, but part of the picture. "'There!' she said. 'There.' Her hand moved behind his head and supported it. Her fingers moved gently in his hair. She looked up and across the barn, and her lips came together and smiled mysteriously" (455). If not Christian, then at least in some sense deeply spiritual.[7]

Yet, to leave things here would be misleading. The background is evolutionary and religion plays a key role, but the story is not about the science-religion relationship. It is about the Depression, its nature, how it affected people, how they responded. It is about human need and human greed. It is about hope and the crushed spirit. It's an important novel because the Depression was important and demanded a response from the nation's novelists and other creative artists— *The Grapes of Wrath* was made into a truly great movie, a work in its own right, directed by John Ford whose excesses for once became virtues, and with painfully moving performances by Henry Fonda as Tom Joad and Jane Darwell as Ma. (The movie is more optimistic and focuses more exclusively on the family.) None of this is criticism, far from it. Rather, it is to place the novel in its time and to point to the factors that did (as one would expect) influence the author.

The Inheritors

William Golding (1911–1993), an Englishman who won the Nobel Prize for Literature in 1983, will always be famous for his first novel, *The Lord of the Flies* (1954), the story of original sin emerging in a group of schoolboys stranded on a South Sea island. However, it was his second novel, *The Inheritors* (1955), about human origins, that was his personal favorite. This has as its background the science of paleoanthropology, the study of human evolution. Somewhat naturally, by the 1950s, with the discrediting of Piltdown and the findings from Africa, this field of science attracted the attention of novelists and has indeed given rise to a whole genre labeled "prehistorical fiction." The structure of *The Inheritors*, one of the earliest and certainly most distinguished examples, is simple. To their utter

---

[7] Does one also see the Book of Job? "Then said his wife unto him, 'Dost thou still retain thine integrity? Curse God, and die'. But he said unto her, 'Thou speakest as one of the foolish women speaketh. What! Shall we receive good at the hand of God, and shall we not receive evil?'" (Job 2:10). There is a spirit in Ma and Tom that is very Job-ean. Don't curse God. Don't die. Fight and triumph over hardship. This is the spirit of Gaskell, of Gissing, of Wharton, of London. In the Darwinian world, having guts is a moral virtue. The contrast with Matthew 5:5—"Blessed are the meek: for they shall inherit the earth"—could not be greater.

disaster, a small band of Neanderthals comes into contact with modern humans, *Homo sapiens*. The Neanderthals die—often killed—one by one. The humans survive and go off at the end, carrying their somewhat ambiguous trophy, the last surviving Neanderthal, a baby.

On this story Golding erects a very sophisticated metaphorical framework. Almost everything is told from the viewpoint of one of the Neanderthals, Lok, and Golding presents his thought processes as very different from those of humans. Although one of the Neanderthals (Fa, a female) shows rudiments of being able to think things through, the assumption is that overall the group does not have much in the way of reasoning power. All experiences and interactions are presented as immediate, mainly through the senses, which are (especially the nose) conceived as very much more powerful than those of humans. Thus when one of the humans shoots an arrow at the Neanderthals, we get a phenomeno-logical description of the stick that comes close by Lok's head and of the point at one end and the feathers at the other. Sexual intercourse between the humans, observed by uncomprehending Neanderthals, gets a similar treatment.

> The two people beneath the tree were making the noises fiercely as though they were quarrelling. In particular the fat woman had begun to hoot like an owl and Lok could hear Tuami gasping like man who fights with an animal and does not think he will win. He looked down at them and saw that Tuami was not only lying with the fat woman, but eating her as well, for there was black blood running from the lobe of her ear. (Golding [1955] 1962, 175)

The humans come across as—well, as humans. They can reason, they have technology—they can make canoes that can be paddled upstream against the current—they have complicated and rather violent religious practices centered on stags (which they hunt and kill), and very obviously they are violent, trying to kill the other, the strangers. At the end of the novel we find that they regard the Neanderthals as dangerous, referring to them as "devils." They are also ap-parently caste or class conscious because the youthful male is planning on killing the older, still-dominant male, and to take his place as leader.

The Neanderthals are peaceful by nature. They feel themselves as at one with their surroundings, and their god, Oa, seems to be somewhat of an Earth mother. They eat meat but only that which is from animals killed by others. Most important, a lot of their insights come from picture making or conceiving. These seem to be not just internal but to give information about external events. When Ha (a Neanderthal male) disappears, the old male Mal gets pictures of what has happened. Ha runs toward a cliff. "There is another smell of a nobody. Going up the cliff and coming back. But the smell of Ha stops. There is Ha going up the cliff over the weed-tails when the sun has gone down; and then nothing" (66). This the end of Ha who presumably got pushed over the edge by a human. "There is the scent of others." Not only do the Neanderthals have this telepathic or clairvoyant capacity, but it is something that is shared in the group.

> Quite without warning, all the people shared a picture inside their heads. This was a picture of Mal, seeming a little removed from them, illuminated, sharply defined in all his gaunt misery. They saw not only Mal's body, but the slow pictures that were waxing and waning in his head. One above all was displacing the others, dawning through the cloudy arguments and doubts and conjectures until they knew what it was he was thinking with such dull conviction.
> "Tomorrow or the day after, I shall die." (39)

Critics of prehistorical fiction complain that the authors do not take enough care to ensure that their claims about earlier hominins are in line with contemporary scientific research. Certainly this charge can be leveled against Golding's picture of the Neanderthals. There was little evidence for his supposition of their nigh-saintly and in respects extremely naïve natures, making them so different from humans. Even when he was writing, the assumptions were that Neanderthal life internal and external was not so very different from ours. But this really is to miss the point and confirms the wisdom of Golding's publisher who refused to send the manuscript to experts on human evolution (Carey 2009). This is a work of imaginative fiction, not a scientific treatise. This said, *The Inheritors* is obviously a work that is based on an evolutionary understanding of human prehistory. First there were the gentle folk like the Neanderthals. Then there were the violent folk like the humans. You can even put it in Darwinian terms, because the humans pretty much stamp out the Neanderthals and they do so because of their superior technology and so forth, not to mention their desire to eliminate possible threats from the Neanderthals. Yet there are very non-Darwinian elements, notably the peaceful nature of the Neanderthals, their picture imaginations, and especially their clairvoyant powers. This is much more like Alfred Russel Wallace than Darwin. Golding's recent biographer (John Carey) suggests that the picturing comes from Wells, who had speculated that "Primitive man probably thought very much as a child thinks, that is to say, in a series of imaginative pictures" (Carey 2009, 180). This could well be true, although overall there is an older and deeper source. As a young man, Golding had fallen under the spell of Rudolf Steiner, the Austrian esoteric thinker, the founder of the system known as "anthroposophy," as well as of the Waldorf School system, based on his principles. By the time he was writing his novels, Golding had rejected the basic claims of Steiner—which are an imaginative fusion of theosophy and German

Naturphilosophie—but he always had a sympathy for the overall organicist view of Steiner and used various ideas in his fiction. For instance, Golding's next book after *The Inheritors, Pincher Martin* (1956), is based on Steiner's thinking about the Doppelgänger (Ruse 2013).

If you look at Steiner's major work, *Occult Science: An Outline*, you find that (among all sorts of weird claims about beings on other planets, not to mention the sun and moon) Golding cherry-picked a number of ideas, including picture thinking—in earlier times humans had "a predominating picture consciousness" (Steiner [1914] 2005, 164)—that tells about real events—"he experiences inwardly in pictures what is going on outside him" (174)—and group thinking—"the soul felt a kind of Group Ego reaching back to distant ancestors, and the individual man felt himself a member of the group" (186). Unfortunately, during evolution—Steiner was deeply influenced by the idealistic morphological thinking of the late nineteenth-century German evolutionist Ernst Haeckel—"this common consciousness, uniting individuals with their forefathers, was gradually lost" (196). One suspects that the idea of group thinking, to be found both in Golding's novel and through the notion of "group soul" in Steinbeck's novel, have different sources. Golding from Steiner, although similar ideas in Olaf Stapeldon's science fiction novel from 1930, *Last and First Men*, may have been important. Steinbeck from Emerson (or other transcendentalist thinkers). This is no big matter because both Steiner and Emerson go back to shared elements of German thought, particularly that of Friedrich Schelling.

Steiner also gives us a clue to the overall intent of Golding's novel. It is clearly not about evolution as such, and even less is it about the conflict between science and religion. Like *The Lord of the Flies* before it, the novel is about human nature—in particular about original sin, the natural depravity in us all. We are tainted, a view that Golding got from his experiences in World War II, and that infuses not only the first two novels but the third, *Pincher Martin*, as well. The novel is certainly about P/progress of a kind. The humans are far more advanced than the Neanderthals when it comes to rational thought and technology. But it has been at a cost, namely, the loss of innocence and of our more spiritual side that binds us together in a peaceful group and makes us one with our fellows and the world as a whole. This explicitly is Steiner's message. In what is (or should be) as much an embarrassment to today's devotees as Noah's Flood is to Christians, Steiner embraced the idea of Atlantis, a long-disappeared land in the middle of the Atlantic Ocean. Humans were there and then left. And (without in any sense implying that Golding accepted Atlantis) while there was a rise up in some sense of the word, there was a falling off in another sense. Apparently "the post-Atlantean evolution of mankind had meant for the physical world an ascent—but at the same time a decline for the spiritual world" (Steiner [1914] 2005, 217). I spoke of a metaphorical framework. For Golding, the

Neanderthals are our innocent ancestors or cousins (who may or may not have actually existed); the humans—the "inheritors"—are *Homo sapiens* today (who certainly do exist). "God saw every thing that he had made, and, behold, it was very good" (Genesis 1: 31). That was no longer a given in the Darwin-produced, mid-twentieth-century world of William Golding.

14

Darwinian Theory Comes of Age

This would seem to be the end of our story. By the mid-twentieth century, evolutionary ideas—owing more or less to Darwin's actual science—were commonplace and natural groundings for serious writers of fiction. But the battle, whether won or lost, had moved on. It was no longer the science-religion debate that was people's immediate focus. Minds had been made up on that. Novelists were now—as one might very much expect—turning to the pressing themes of their day—the Depression and social inequality, the wars of the century and what they tell about human nature, and more. Yet to cry "finis" now would be premature. In part—a part we shall explore in this chapter—the reason is internal to evolutionary studies. In part—a part we shall explore in Chapters 15 and 16, the final chapters of this book—the reason is external to evolutionary studies. Let us move briskly to the first part.

The year 1959 was the hundredth anniversary of the publication of the *Origin of Species*. In the world of professional science, evolutionary biology was now a well-established branch of science and about to take off with stunning conceptual advances as well as the gathering of huge amounts of pertinent empirical information. In the area of social behavior, the then-graduate student William Hamilton (1964) was formulating his model of (what came to be known as) "kin selection," where one sees natural selection benefiting the individual inasmuch as it benefits close relatives. Following this explanatory breakthrough came other models, and these and related discoveries were brought together in one massive volume in 1975, *Sociobiology: The New Synthesis*, by Harvard biologist Edward O. Wilson. Other areas of evolutionary biology likewise were moving forward rapidly, often because of the application of molecular techniques to old and hitherto-insoluble problems (Lewontin 1974). Computers were important too—paleontology (or as it came to be known, "paleobiology") was totally revamped. The father did the science (Sepkoski 1994) and the son wrote the history (Sepkoski 2012). These new and very successful expansions and extensions of evolutionary theory—firmly Darwinian in that natural selection was seen increasingly to be the key to full understanding—led to new confidence in professional evolutionary biologists.

This confidence reflected an optimism about the worth and correctness of the approach they were taking, together with a willingness to proselytize, to share their enthusiasm with others. There were always popularizers of evolution—but now the numbers increased by an order of magnitude—and naturally, since this was popular science, value issues and the like, including religious issues, came to the fore. Picking out just one example—the best of them all—the late Stephen Jay Gould, Harvard professor, paleontologist, baseball fanatic, choral singer, wrote a monthly column—"This View of Life"—for thirty years (from around 1970 to around 2000) in the popular magazine, *Natural History*. He covered just about everything—racism, war, family, America, sports (naturally!), and religion. He spun off best-selling collections of his essays, as well as independent books on evolution, and included here was one work devoted exclusively to the science-religion relationship: *Rocks of Ages* (1999).

Expectedly, this kind of activity—and Gould was the best of many—attracted the attention of creative writers, novelists, and poets, and we find that they turned increasingly to evolution, not as with writers like Steinbeck and Golding as a foundation for tackling other issues but as a source of problems and topics to be written about in their own right.[1] The focus was less a matter of evolution's conflict with religion and more a matter of picking up on problems raised by nineteenth-century thinkers, problems that today's writers felt merited more attention—both in light of new knowledge about evolution's processes and in light of new thinking at what one might call the theological or philosophical level. Let us look at three representative examples.[2]

The French Lieutenant's Woman

Set back in the 1860s, the third novel of John Fowles (1926–2005), published in 1969, is an early exemplar of so-called neo-Victorian fiction (Glendening 2013). It is also, and here one needs to know the jargon, a notable instance of that kind of postmodern writing known (perhaps a little pretentiously) as "metafiction,"

---

[1] Of course, people like Faulkner and Steinbeck and Golding went beyond the professional science finally being produced. Writers are interested in values, just the sorts of things that professional science excludes. The point is that now there was a flood of popular science, often raising precisely the sorts of things of interest to writers.

[2] Refreshed interest in Darwinism might also have been a function of the fact that, as the second half of the twentieth century got under way, enthusiasm for the rival pictures of Freud and Marx was ebbing. Not completely so. Think *Portnoy's Complaint* by Philip Roth: "Who does Mommy love more than anything in the whole wide world? I am absolutely punchy with delight, and meanwhile follow in their tight, slow, agonizingly delicious journey up her legs the transparent stockings that give her flesh a hue of stirring dimensions" (Roth [1969] 1994, 45). But even here, we have as much debunking parody as acceptance.

meaning that the author plays games with both the characters and the readers, manipulating the former rather like a puppeteer and sometimes making them do one thing and sometimes another, whether they want to or not, and stepping out of authorial role and commenting to the latter on aspects of what is happening or not happening or could happen. It is "metafiction" because, as metamathematics is not mathematics but about mathematics, so metafiction is not just the story but comments on the story. Most famously, going one up on *Caleb Williams* and *Great Expectations*, Fowles offers three endings to his novel—rearranging the lives of his characters—and discusses these endings—inviting the reader to share in the authorial process.

The main story is fairly simple. A well-connected young man, Charles Smithson—he has a private income of his own and he is the presumptive heir of an unmarried uncle who has both estates and a baronetcy—is engaged to a young woman, Ernestina Freeman—the only daughter of a very rich store owner. (The model is clearly Selfridges in England or Macy's in the United States.) They are in love if not entirely passionately so, and spending time before the marriage with relatives, in the town of Lyme Regis, on the South Coast of England. They see a strange-looking young woman on the quay looking out to sea. It turns out that she is one Sarah Woodruff, a former governess, who fell in love with a young French naval officer who was rescued from the sea and spent time recovering at her place of employ. He left for home and she quit her job and now spends all her time apparently mourning his departure and waiting for his return. There was some question about their actual relationship and she has become known as the "French Lieutenant's Woman."

The story takes a predictable course. Charles is fascinated by Sarah, who has managed to get another job as companion to a demanding old woman. Charles meets with Sarah on her afternoon walks and his feeling grows. Sarah gets the sack for walking in places that the old woman has forbidden and goes off to stay in a hotel in Exeter. Meanwhile Charles's uncle declares his intention of marrying and starting a family. Although he is no longer so good a catch, Ernestina declares her fidelity and her father in London, whom Charles goes up to see, backs his daughter, although he does suggest that now Charles has no prospects as a landed squire he might think about joining the family business—trade, an unappealing prospect to the upper-class Charles. On the way home, the train passes through Exeter. Charles stays onboard and returns home to Ernestina. They marry, have lots of kids, Sarah is forgotten, and Charles ends by going into the business and rather liking it.

But this is only the first ending. The second version of the story has Charles leaving the train in Exeter, going to Sarah's hotel, where they have sex, Charles then realizing that Sarah was a virgin—even though on their last meeting she had told him that she and the Frenchman had consummated their relationship.

Charles is understandably upset and confused but writes to Sarah that he means to break off with Ernestina and join up with her. Unfortunately his servant does not deliver the letter, and though poor Charles breaks with Ernestina and earns the enmity of her father, Sarah has vanished. Charles goes off to America and finally discovers the whereabouts of Sarah in London. He returns, declares his love, discovers that their brief bout led to a daughter, and happiness for the three seems assured.

Then there is the third ending. Charles comes back to Sarah, she basically says she was leading him along all of the time and doesn't give a fig for him, but she will marry him still if that is what he wants. It turns out that that is not what Charles wants and he is left out in the cold—and although a sadder man nevertheless a wiser man.

> He walks towards an imminent, self-given death? I think not; for he has at last found an atom of faith in himself, a true uniqueness, on which to build; has already begun, though he would still bitterly deny it, though there are tears in his eyes to support his denial, to realize that life, however advantageously Sarah may in some ways seem to fit the role of Sphinx, is not a symbol, is not one riddle and one failure to guess it, is not to inhabit one face alone or to be given up after losing one throw of the dice; but is to be, however inadequately, emptily, hopelessly into the city's iron heart, endured. And out again, upon the unplumb'd, salt, estranging sea. (Fowles [1969] 1998, 467)

Why is this sometimes enjoyable, sometimes irritating, story relevant to our tale?[3] Charles has a hobby—fossil hunting and the paleontology behind it. (Lyme Regis was noted for its important fossil beds.) This—the story opens in 1868—leads easily into discussions of Darwin and the *Origin of Species*. As in the novels of Hardy, it is less the science as such that is fundamental and more the metaphysical implications. In particular—and although Fowles locates his discussion in the Victorian era, one suspects he must have had more recent writings also in mind—the implications for humans and their freedom. "Darwinism, as its shrewder opponents realized, let open the floodgates to something far more serious than the undermining of the Biblical accounts of the origins of man; its deepest implications lay in the direction of determinism and behaviorism, that is, towards philosophies that reduce morality to a hypocrisy and duty to a straw hut in a hurricane" (120).

A lot of the novel is concerned with showing how the characters are driven by forces over which they have no control. Sarah obsesses about the French

---

[3] I am sure I am not alone in wishing Sarah would be a bit more positive about Charles.

lieutenant. Charles obsesses about Sarah. The local doctor gives Charles a book about a Frenchman in a situation similar to his who ended up accused and tried. "The day that other French lieutenant was condemned was the very same day that Charles had come into the world. For a moment, in that silent Dorset night, reason and science dissolved; life was a dark machine, a sinister astrology, a verdict at birth and without appeal, a zero over all." Adding: "He had never felt less free" (235).

Or when Sarah and Charles fall for each other.

> "My dear Miss Woodruff, pray control yourself. I –"
> "I cannot."
> The words were barely audible, but they silenced Charles. He tried to tell himself that she meant she could not control the gratitude for his charity . . . he tried, he tried. But there came on him a fleeting memory of Catullus: "Whenever I see you, sound fails, my tongue falters, thin fire steals through my limbs, an inner roar, and darkness shrouds my ears and eyes." (249)

But we have been primed for more than this. The author is going to complexify things. Is Charles really so bound? Yes, in version one of the story. Not so obviously in versions two and three of the story. Charles had a choice: "and while one part of him hated having to choose, we come near the secret of his state on that journey west when we know that another part of him felt intolerably excited by the proximity of the moment of choice. He had not the benefit of existentialist terminology; but what he felt was really a very clear case of the anxiety of freedom—that is, the realization that one is free and the realization that being free is a situation of terror" (340–341).

Charles had been caught in the conventions of the day—marrying a pretty heiress whom he did not really love. He breaks from this to engage with a woman who was by any standards half mad. "You know your choice. You stay in prison, what your time calls duty, honor, self-respect, and you are comfortably safe. Or you are free and crucified. Your only companions, the stones, the thorns, the turning backs; the silence of cities, and their hate" (362). Hitherto he had been caught in the mechanistic grind of modern life. "That was what had deceived him; and it was totally without love or freedom . . . but also without thought, without intention, without malice, because the deception was in its very nature; and it was not human, but a machine" (363). It is an in joke that the family name of Ernestina and her father is "Freeman."

Surely if you are crucified on the Cross you are hardly free? Somehow, however, this leads to "uncrucifixion." "What he saw now was like a glimpse of another world: a new reality, a new causality, a new creation. A cascade of concrete visions—if you like, another chapter from his hypothetical autobiography—poured through his mind" (365). And this is freedom. Thinking of taking Sarah to Italy, "did stand, however banally, for the pure essence of cruel but necessary (if we are to survive—and yes, still today) freedom" (366). Freedom, despite Darwinism's implication of determinism. Does this work? There are still grave problems. Fowles himself throws water on his own claims. Consider when Charles enters Sarah's room in the hotel in Exeter.

> Again his eyes were fixed on her. The nightgown buttoned high at the neck and at her wrists. Its whiteness shimmered rose in the firelight, for the lamp on the table beside him was not turned up very high. And her hair, already enhanced by the green shawl, was ravishingly alive where the firelight touched it; as if all her mystery, this most intimate self, was exposed before him: proud and submissive, bound and unbound, his slave and his equal. He knew why he had come; it was to see her again. Seeing her was the need; like an intolerable thirst that had to be assuaged. (346)

No prizes for guessing what is about to happen. "Her legs parted. With a frantic brutality, as he felt his ejaculation about to burst, he found the place and thrust" (349–350). This, to be honest, does not sound much like a man in control of himself.

Three possibilities suggest themselves. Remember the two schools of (philosophical) thought about free will. "Compatibilism" argues that you can have both free will and determinism, suggesting the true dichotomy is between freedom and constraint. A man walking down the road is free. A man dragged down the road in chains is not. We could argue—our first possibility—that in some sense Charles is significantly freer in the second and (especially) the third endings, because he is not constrained by the norms of a repressive society but makes up his own mind about what he values and wants to do. As in the hotel room, he does not always seem that free, but overall his actions are those of a man who is as they say "doing his own thing."

Rivaling compatibilism there is "libertarianism" (not to be confused with social philosophies like those of Ayn Rand), arguing that freedom exists outside the causal chain. This was the position of Immanuel Kant, and it is often put in terms of reasons versus causes. Freedom belongs to the realm of reason and can exist no matter what the underlying causal structure. I live and breathe and so forth, but I reason whether to stay onside with the comfortable option (first ending) or to go for something more desirable if fraught with problems (second and third endings). In the novel—our second possibility—there is some warrant for this approach. The final chapter has as a second epigraph a line from one of Matthew Arnold's notebooks: "True piety is *acting what one knows.*" The author comments that in pursuing our ends: "The fundamental principle that should guide these actions, that I believe myself always guided Sarah's, I have set as the second epigraph. A modern existentialist would no doubt substitute "humanity" or "authenticity" for "piety," but he would recognize Arnold's intent" (466–467). This certainly suggests that the Charles of the second and perhaps even more the third ending has greater freedom than the Charles of the first ending.

The third possibility is to go to the metalevel and think about the fact that we do have three endings. Is the author trying to bring in freedom here, if not for the characters directly more in the cosmic scheme of things? Fowles suggests that this might be so, for at one point he enters the story himself, sitting looking at Charles in a railway carriage (on the way to London to find Sarah). He likens himself to God and asks what is he to do with his characters now? Charles he knows wants to find Sarah. Sarah is ambiguous. Does she want to be found or not? Normally the author fixes the fight and we get the solution the author wants. Fowles does not want to do this. He does not want to fix the fight. "That leaves me with two alternatives. I let the fight proceed and take no more than a recording part in it; or I take both sides in it. I stare at that vaguely effete, but not completely futile face. And as we near London, I think I see a solution; that is, I see the dilemma is false. The only way I can take no part in the fight is to show two versions of it" (406).

Does this solve the problem of freedom? I am not sure that it does. It seems almost that chance is deciding the fate of the characters. At most, the characters will realize that there might have been other possibilities—of the first ending, the author writes "the last few pages you have read are not what happened, but what he spent the hours between London and Exeter imagining might happen" (339). Fate—or the stern laws of nature—decreed otherwise. This is a faint notion of freedom. The happy note for us is that we here do not have to decide among these options nor do we have to judge whether any of them work. It is enough for us to recognize here that we have a novelist grasping—as did Hardy a century before him—that Darwinism challenges complacent notions of human freedom. Hardy wrestled with the problem and had stimulating insights but hardly solved the problem—did Tess freely murder Alec or not? Fowles legitimately picks up the challenge and tries to move the discussion forward. That in itself makes his novel worth discussing.[4]

---

[4] Another notable neo-Victorian addition to the literature, likewise dealing with the problem of free will, is A. S. Byatt's novella *Morpho Eugenia* (1992).

The Honorary Consul

Fowles deals with one problem still festering from Victorian times, but one that blows up in our time, the possibility of freedom in a Darwinian world. Although the notion of "uncrucifixion" is central, he stresses that after early enthusiasms Charles no longer has religious convictions and that the recognition of the importance of Christ was not a "St. Paul on the road to Damascus" experience (Fowles [1969] 1998, 365). Now we turn to a writer who was a committed Christian. Sensitive to the ways in which religion is always under secular attack, where science particularly is a favorite battering ram against the gates of faith, he deals with another problem, at least if not more important, that of evil—not so much specifically the pain and suffering raised by the Darwinian process—that is for the next chapter—but the problem of evil more generally, for from the start of his early conversion to Catholicism, the English novelist Graham Greene (1904–1991) labored, through the often-tortured world of his fictional characters, to make sense of God, of humans, of their relationships. How do we reconcile the evil that lies in people's hearts and the terrible things that they do with the existence of a loving Creator God?[5] In later life, by his own admission, Greene was much attracted to the theology of the French Jesuit paleontologist, Teilhard de Chardin (1955). The priest, who was deeply influenced by the creative evolutionism of Henri Bergson, was one of a number—as we shall see his thinking bears resemblances to process theology reaching back to the Anglo-American philosopher Alfred North Whitehead (1929)—who strove to move from the immovable, unchanging deity of classical theology—much influenced by Platonic thought, Augustine thought of God as being akin to the Form of the Good, in a sense being like a mathematical concept outside time and space—to a God who is here with us now, who works alongside us and who co-creates and has human-like features including suffering with us. For Teilhard de Chardin therefore evil was not so much a consequence of a world thanks to Darwin bereft of a God—as it is in *Tess of the D'Urbervilles*—but something to be conquered and transcended in an evolutionary fashion by humans working with God. Evolution is not the problem; it is the solution.

This world picture infuses Greene's late novel, *The Honorary Consul*. A character—almost a parody of a Greene figure, a priest who has married

---

[5] Expectedly we find elements of Job in Greene's thinking, perhaps most fervently in *Brighton Rock* (1938) where an old priest in the confessional speaks about God to Rose, the girl who has married the central figure, the young criminal Pinky. She wishes she had committed suicide as had he, so they could be damned together: "You can't conceive, my child, nor can I or anybody the . . . appalling . . . strangeness of the mercy of God" (Greene [1938] 1991, 246). It is all a bit Hardy-like though, because Rose thinks that Pinky's love for her will redeem the situation whereas we know his final (recorded) message to her is one of hate—"the worst horror of all" (267).

and now joined a revolutionary group who wanted to seize the Argentinian American Ambassador and force the Paraguayan dictatorship to hand over captured rebels (and who even more typically has seized the wrong person)— explains the Teilhard-influenced theology that drives him forward.[6] "He made us in His image—so our evil is His evil too. How could I love God if He were not like me? Divided like me. Tempted like me" (Greene [1973] 1974, 260). Continuing: "The God I believe in must be responsible for all the evil as well as all the saints. He has to be a God made in our image with a night side as well as a day side . . . It is a long struggle and a long suffering, evolution, and I believe God is suffering the same evolution that we are, but perhaps with more pain" (261). Then: "God when he is evil demands evil things. He can create monsters like Hitler. He destroys children and cities. But one day with our help he will be able to tear his evil mask off forever. How often the saints have worn an evil mask for a time, even Paul. God is joined to us in a sort of blood transfusion. His blood is in our veins and our tainted blood runs through his" (262–263).

This last passage is remarkably parallel to a powerful but negative poem written around the same time by the English poet Ted Hughes, about a dark Doppelgänger of God called "Crow":

> When God, disgusted with man,
> Turned towards heaven.
> And man, disgusted with God,
> Turned towards Eve,
> Things looked like falling apart.
>
> But Crow. . Crow
> Crow nailed them together,
> Nailing Heaven and earth together —
>
> So man cried, but with God's voice.
> And God bled, but with man's blood.

The poet continues, reading this as the beginning of true evil.

> Then heaven and earth creaked at the joint
> Which became gangrenous and stank -
> A horror beyond redemption.
>
> The agony did not diminish.

---

[6] In the 1940s, the English weekly *The New Statesman and Nation* ran a competition asking for parodies of Greene's style. Entering under a pseudonym, the author—alas—came only second.

Man could not be man nor God God.

The agony

Grew.

Crow

Grinned

Crying: "This is my Creation,"

Flying the black flag of himself.[7]

(Hughes 1971, 57)[8]

Hughes, like Greene/Teilhard de Chardin, sees God in human terms. He sees also that humans and God are forever joined together. For the poet, this points to dark, dark evil—"a horror beyond redemption." For Greene, however, the priest's theology points to the triumph of God. Teilhard de Chardin believed that evolution proceeds upward and at some point it reaches what he called the noösphere, where we find the Omega Point that he identified with Jesus Christ, the Redeemer (Teilhard de Chardin 1955). The struggle for man and God ends in success. "I believe in the Cross and the Redemption. The Redemption of God as well as of Man. I believe that the day side of God, in one moment of happy creation, produced perfect goodness, as a man might paint one perfect picture. God's intention for once was completely fulfilled so that the night side can never win more than a little victory here and there." He continues: "With our help. Because the evolution of God depends on our evolution. Every evil act of ours strengthens his night side, and every good one helps his day side. We belong to him and he belongs to us. But now at least we can be sure where evolution will end one day—it will end in a goodness like Christ's. It is a terrible process all the same, and the God I believe in suffers as we suffer while he struggles against himself—against his evil side" (Greene [1973] 1974, 262).

---

[7] "Crow Blacker Than Ever" from COLLECTED POEMS by Ted Hughes. Copyright © 2003 by The Estate of Ted Hughes. Reprinted by permission of Faber and Faber and Farrar, Straus and Giroux, LLC.

[8] In *Dracula*, Arthur (Lord Godalming), having given blood to Lucy, felt "since then as if they two had been really married and that she was his wife in the sight of God." The fact that Lucy's two other suitors had also given blood, not to mention Dr. Van Helsing, and so on Arthur's reading we have a bit of a group thing going here, is passed over in dignified silence. "None of us said a word of the other operations, and none of us ever shall." Later in the novel, Dracula and Mina actually drink each other's blood, and remember that the now-polluted Mina is scarred by a holy wafer that touches her forehead. Fortunately, the death of Dracula restores her purity although the blood of Dracula does live on in her son.

Note that although Greene, as always, is wrestling with evil, and although he brings evolution to bear on the issue, and although he sees that the evolutionary process involves pain and struggle, he is obviously not thinking at a directly biological level. Nevertheless, he is relying on a particular interpretation of the biological world. A novelist, a poet, is entitled to a certain artistic elasticity. It is no real criticism of Golding to say that his Neanderthals were not like those that we now know, or even as they were known back in the 1950s. But if you go with ideas that are completely repudiated by scientists, then the extent to which you can be said to be working with the authority of science becomes questionable. This is particularly pertinent in the case of Teilhard de Chardin, for (as we shall see in the next chapter) his thinking was savaged by a very distinguished member of the scientific community, and there are reasons why—starting with the fact that selection was never his main force of change, but rather a form of Lamarckian striving.

This said, although the details of his science were questioned, not all evolutionists rejected his vision (Ruse 1996). Theodosius Dobzhansky in America and Julian Huxley in England, two of the leading evolutionists in the mid-century, were enthusiastic Teilhardians—even though paradoxically Dobzhansky was a (Russian) Orthodox Christian and Huxley an atheist (although ever with a liking for Bergsonian vitalism).[9] One should not therefore think that Greene was totally out of the scientific loop. Somewhat humorously, while no one had too much time for the Lamarckian elements in Teilhard's thought, although Gould spoke strongly against the evolutionary progressivism that is so crucial to the Teilhardian picture—in an attempt to destroy his reputation as a scientist, Gould (1980) even went so far as to pin the Piltdown hoax on Teilhard de Chardin (a suggestion treated with the contempt it merited)—many other prominent professional scientists are ardent evolutionary progressionists. They may not have too much time for the Omega Point, but the science (interpreted in a Darwinian fashion) they accept. Also, paradoxically one suspects that Teilhard de Chardin's

---

[9] As an undergraduate at Oxford, Julian Huxley won the Newdigate Prize for poetry. Later in life, he broke into verse about the virtues of progress.

> The Ant herself cannot philosophize–
> While Man does that, and sees, and keeps a wife,
> And flies, and talks, and is extremely wise...
> Yet our Philosophy to later Life
> Will seem but crudeness of the planet's youth,
> Our Wisdom but a parasite of Truth.

This is from a sonnet entitled "Man the Philosophizer" (Huxley 1932, 53). That it should come from the same family that two generations before had produced "Dover Beach" surely proves that, notwithstanding my enthusiasm for the power of the Internet, not all change is Progress.

theology, firmly repudiated by his Church when he wrote—he was forbidden to publish and his masterwork, *The Phenomenon of Man*, appeared only after his death—now finds more favor. Again, however, none of this is really our worry. As with Fowles, we are seeing an attempt to move things forward in a post-Darwinian world.

Galapagos

The novelist Kurt Vonnegut (1922–2007) was a force—a moral, uncompromising, uncomfortable force—unto himself. Thrown into the Battle of the Bulge in 1944 as a lowly private, he was captured, shipped to Dresden, and survived the allied firebombing only because he was incarcerated in an underground slaughterhouse. This led to his celebrated novel, *Slaughterhouse Five*, combining as did other of his novels hair-raising and deeply moving factual episodes with science-fiction fantasy about ghosts and other worlds. His fiction and his life was one of protest against the evils of society—especially his own American society—and typically at the end of his life he was to be found raging against the invasion of Iraq. In a memorable line that will take some topping, on comparing President George W. Bush with Adolf Hitler, Vonnegut's judgment was that at least Hitler had been elected. Expectedly he was a fervent nonbeliever, and although for a while he worshipped with the Unitarian-Universalists, he was essentially an agnostic at the least and at his death was president of the American Humanist Association.

Stylistically and in content *Galapagos* is a novel that could have been written only by Vonnegut. Mixing magic with realism, it tells the story about events in 1986 (a year to the future of the date of the novel's appearance), from the supposed present a million years hence, using as narrator (Leon Trout) a ghost. The action takes place around a cruise ship, the *Bahía de Darwin*, about to depart from Ecuador for the Galapagos Archipelago, on what has been billed as the "nature cruise of the century." All had looked pretty good and the celebrity list signed up for the journey was highly impressive—Jackie Kennedy Onassis was one of the intended participants. However, a world financial crisis brought all of the wonderful dreams crashing down (Vonnegut was using a South American financial crisis as material) and after war breaks out between neighboring South American states only a motley group manage a getaway. These include the captain, Adolf von Kleist, who it turns out has not the slightest idea about steering the ship; Mary Hepburn, a widow of good intentions; James Wait, a confidence man who preys on unsuspecting females, who dies moments after marrying Hepburn (on board ship); Hisako Hiroguchi, a pregnant Japanese woman who will give birth to Akiko Hiroguchi, who thanks to a mutation passed on from the effects of Hiroshima will have a furry covering over her whole body; and six young native women who don't seem to speak anyone's language very much. "These were orphans from the Ecuadorian rainforest across the mountains to the east—from far, far away. Their parents had all been killed by insecticides sprayed from the air, and a bush pilot had brought them to Guayaquil, where they had become children of the streets" (Vonnegut [1985] 1999, 164).

The boat ends up beached on one of the Galapagos Islands, Santa Rosalia (not a real one). It turns out that there is lots to eat—boobies, finches, iguanas, crabs, penguins—so they can survive. Reproduction is a little bit of a problem, because with Wait gone the only people really ready for sex are the captain and Mary Hepburn, and she is past her reproductive stage. But over time, Akiko and the native girls come on reproductive-ready board, and with some imaginative action by Mary—after intercourse with the captain, she dips her finger into her sperm-full vagina and then shoves it appropriately (as one might say) into the girls—they all get pregnant and the human race continues. Which is just as well, because on the mainland, and indeed all around the world, starting at the annual Frankfurt Book Fair—one supposes that one place was as good as any—a new parasite appeared that eats up all of the eggs in the human ovary.

What is going on here, or rather what has gone wrong here? And what is going to happen? What has gone wrong is hammered into the reader's consciousness again and again. It is the Thomas Hardy problem. Humans have overevolved. We have massive great brains and they only lead us into trouble. At the beginning, talking about the confidence trickster, James Wait:

> It is hard to believe nowadays that people could ever have been as brilliantly duplicitous as James Wait—until I remind myself that just about every human being back then had a brain weighing about three kilograms! There was no end to the evil schemes that thought machines that oversized couldn't imagine and execute.
>
> So I raise this question, although there is nobody around to answer it: Can it be doubted that three-kilogram brains were once nearly fatal defects in the evolution of the human race?
>
> A second query: What source was there back then, save for our overly elaborate nervous circuitry, for the evils we were seeing or hearing about simply everywhere?
>
> My answer: There was no other source. This was a very innocent planet, except for those great big brains. (8–9)

They led to monstrous machines of war, to famine, to misery and destruction. They are nothing but a source of evil and suffering.

What happens? Vonnegut makes it clear that improvement does not come from our planning or execution. Pure luck saves the human race. The captain certainly did not steer the ship to the island intentionally. He had no idea how he was doing. The islands were not provided for our necessities by design. It just so happened that they did. "Nature chose to be generous, so there was enough to eat" (297). And what happened in the future—now past from the viewpoint of the narrator—was not intended. Over the years, thanks particularly to the boost given by the furry Japanese girl, humans evolved through natural selection into seal-like beings. And with this went a diminution of brain size and in turn a lack of interest in doing the things that led to destruction, quite apart from a physical inability to get up to mischief.

> As for human beings making a comeback, of starting to use tools and build houses and play musical instruments and so on again: They would have to do it with their beaks this time. Their arms have become flippers in which the hand bones are almost entirely imprisoned and immobilized. Each flipper is studded with five purely ornamental nubbins, attractive to members of the opposite sex at mating time. These are in fact the tips of four suppressed fingers and a thumb. Those parts of people's brains, which used to control their hands, moreover, simply don't exist anymore, and human skulls are now much more streamlined on that account. The more streamlined the skull, the more successful the fisher person. (201–202)

Vonnegut is what you might call a blunt-instrument thinker. Nothing very subtle here. He is against what conventionally is called Progress at the technological level but also at the social level, and he is obviously dubious about medical Progress also given the apparent inability to control the egg-eating parasite. He is clearly also much more relativistic about the course of biological history. He doesn't see much progress to humans and basically looks upon the future seal-people as just as good as us, if not better. You might wonder if Vonnegut is flailing at windmills because he is attacking nineteenth-century notions of biological progress, but as noted earlier this is not so. Whatever they may say professionally, it is rarely so for evolutionists. Most of them tend to have a sneaking feeling that humans overall are better and we have won the evolutionary battle. A popular argument for such progress, going back through Julian Huxley's first little book—*The Individual in the Animal Kingdom* (1912)—and reaching back to Darwin himself, invokes what are known today as biological "arms races"— lines respond to each other with better adaptations, prey get faster and so predators get faster. Enthusiasts argue that, as in real arms races, where electronics have become more and more important, so in biological arms races on-board computers (a.k.a. brains) have become increasingly important. Ideas like this were increasingly being pushed just at the time that Vonnegut was writing (early 1980s) so I am not sure that there is cause and effect, but the novelist was certainly writing against real targets.

One might also add, as a kind of ironic footnote, that in the 1950s with atomic testing in the air, many were worried about the knock-on effects of mutations. People like Dobzhansky, who argued for (what molecular biology revealed) the normal existence of much variation in natural populations, were not that concerned. Bomb radiation might even be a good thing, adding to the pot. Again there is no reason to think that Vonnegut was writing in the light of this, but his fantasy about the furry Japanese girl—different because of the bomb—fits nicely with this. I am not sure Vonnegut thought of this as a good thing, but he would have appreciated the irony. One stupid thing leads by chance to another thing, something that can be used for good. In a way, we have Thomas Hardy's message updated. People are kidding themselves if they think that evolution is going to give them slick and comfortable answers. But perhaps there is hope despite this. The epigraph to his book, a quotation from the diary of Anne Frank, leads us full circle to suggest that Vonnegut is not such a cynical curmudgeon after all. "In spite of everything, I still believe people are really good at heart." If she of all people could say that, who are the rest of us to naysay?

Conclusion

What we have seen in this and the previous chapter makes good sense. Evolution (usually meaning Darwinism) is generally accepted. Some writers pick up on this and use it as background against (what are for them) more pressing social issues. Then as the professional science itself developed and flourished, there was in tandem an increase in evolution at the popular science level, and this stimulated writers to pick up on some of the issues that had so concerned the Victorians. They hoped to bring some clarity and new insights to the divisions between modern evolutionists and those many (like social scientists and philosophers) who take a keen interest in these sorts of things. A conclusion that might seem to be the end to our story. As we shall see, however, ours is a tale that ends with a bang not a whimper.

15

The Divide Continues

Although people are still interested in evolution and religion, apparently the focus had moved away from direct interest in the science-religion relationship— particularly the relationship as something meaning warfare between competing belief systems—to broader, more pressing issues. Sputnik, launched in 1957, brought earlier concerns right back into the limelight. Terrified that they were losing the Cold War to the Russians, Americans poured money into science promotion including education, and evolutionary theory, now building on thirty years of professional activity, was made a central component of this new and vigorous drive.[1] This in turn sparked a reaction by concerned Christians who, already frightened (and elated) that the Cold War spelled the end of time and the promised return of Christ, were increasingly sensitive to what they saw as the materialistic and antireligious odor of modern science. Even those who were not out and out biblical literalists feared that evolution posed a considerable threat to their faith commitments. Expectedly, scientists in turn reacted to the religious responses and so there was and continues to be increased tension on the science-religion front, with Darwinian evolution right at the heart of things.

Starting on the side of science, even in 1961, in Britain we find the Nobel Prize–Winning biologist Peter Medawar reviewing Teilhard de Chardin's masterwork, *The Phenomenon of Man*, writing of "a feeling of suffocation, a gasping and flailing around for sense"; "a feeble argument, abominably expressed"; "the illusion of content"; and "alarming apocalyptic seizures" (1961, 99–100). And that was just the first paragraph. In the next decade, in America, Edward O. Wilson followed his big work on sociobiology with a Pulitzer Prize–winning sequel about our own species, *On Human Nature* (1978). In a book that he directed to the general public he argued for the relevance of evolution—of the genes as naturally selected—to the widest range of issues, including morality, individual variation (like sexual orientation), and religion. He was blunt in his

---

[1] Although most prominent and immediate, expectedly, Sputnik was not the only factor sparking concern about the Russians outstripping the Americans (Rudolph 2015).

thinking. The "epic" of evolution means only one thing: "Theology is not likely to survive as an independent intellectual discipline" (192).

And then above all, back in Britain, there was and is Richard Dawkins—perhaps not so much the Charles Darwin of his day but the Herbert Spencer, inasmuch as he clearly aimed both to speak to and to stimulate and provoke his fellow professional biologists, and also—thanks to his felicitous style and genius with metaphor—to address the general public (Dawkins 1976, 1986). He has shown no hesitation in assuming that a fluidity in writing about science qualifies him to talk (very critically) on matters philosophical and theological. Cheetahs seem wonderfully designed to kill antelopes. "The teeth, claws, eyes, nose, leg muscles, backbone and brain of a cheetah are all precisely what we should expect if God's purpose in designing cheetahs was to maximize deaths among antelopes" (Dawkins 1995, 105). Conversely, "we find equally impressive evidence of design for precisely the opposite end: the survival of antelopes and starvation among cheetahs." One could almost imagine that we have two gods, making the different animals, and then competing. If there is indeed but one god who made both animals, then what is going on? What sort of god makes this sort of encounter? "Is He a sadist who enjoys spectator blood sports? Is He trying to avoid overpopulation in the mammals of Africa? Is He maneuvering to maximize David Attenborough's television ratings?" (105) The answer is inevitable.

> In a universe of blind physical forces and genetic replication, some people are going to get hurt, other people are going to get lucky, and you won't find any rhyme or reason in it, nor any justice. The universe we observe has precisely the properties we should expect if there is, at bottom, no design, no purpose, no evil and no good, nothing but blind, pitiless indifference. (133)

There is thank God—or perhaps thank Darwin—an alternative. "The feeling of awed wonder that science can give us is one of the highest experiences of which the human psyche is capable. It is a deep aesthetic passion to rank with the finest that music and poetry can deliver" (1998, x).

Expectedly, the creative writers started to weigh in.

Philip Appleman

A long-time professor at Indiana University, Philip Appleman (b. 1926) is a poet whose credentials include the editing (through three versions) of *Darwin: Norton Critical Edition*, which means he has probably had a greater influence than any other human on the average American undergraduate's grasp of Darwinism. One of his deservedly best-known poems is an evolutionary-themed ode to the automobile. The Indianapolis 500, the famous race, is held in the capital of the state every year and Appleman gives a kind of ironic and yet at times almost melancholic reflection on his state's obsession with that mode of transport. First there is reference to the race and (here is the irony) that at the end the cars are back where they started. Then a very Darwinian reflection on the evolution of the automobile as—in the pursuit of ever-more efficient performance and greater speed—one kind of part gives way to a superior part. And how the losers—the fêted of yesteryear—are simply cast aside, unwanted and unloved.

> In Indianapolis they drive
> five hundred miles and end up
> where they started: survival
> of the fittest. In the swamps
> of Auburn and Elkhart,
> in the jungles of South Bend,
> one-cylinder chain-driven runabouts fall
> to air-cooled V-4's, a-speed gearboxes,
> 16-horse flat-twin midships engines—
> carcasses left behind
> by monobloc motors, electric starters,
> 3-speed gears, six cylinders, 2-chain drive,
> overhead cams, supercharged
> to 88 miles an hour in second gear, the age
> of Leviathan . . .

Then an interlude and an italicized passage from the end of the *Origin* itself, and a genuine appreciation of the tremendous new racing machines that keep appearing—powerful and stunning to look at, truly awesome.

> *There is grandeur in this view of life,*
> *as endless forms*
> *most beautiful and wonderful*
> *are being evolved.*

Finally, and here is the melancholy, a likening of the glorious automobiles of the past to the dinosaurs and other fabulous beasts of the past, once the masters of all that they could see, and now dead and buried, as if they had never existed. A nice echoing of the race itself—huge effort, great innovations, tremendously exciting, but at the end—going nowhere!

And then
the drying up, the panic,
the monsters dying: Elcar, Cord,
Auburn, Duesenberg, Stutz—somewhere
out there, the chassis of Studebakers,
Marmons, Lafayettes, Bendixes, all
rusting in high-octane smog,
ashes to ashes, they
end up where they started.

(Appleman [1984] 2009, 65)

For Appleman, Darwinian evolutionary theory is the greatest discovery of all time and it behooves us as humans to accept this and explore the full implications of what it means to be evolved beings—no more, but certainly no less. Knowledge, morality, good behavior, and everything else can only be based on our human nature as fashioned by natural selection. "If we come to maturity by recognizing what is outside us, we come to wisdom by knowing what is inside" (Appleman 2014, 37). Those automobiles. In one sense, such a triumph of science and engineering. We are nigh God-like in what we can achieve. And yet, at another level, in the end without ultimate meaning. But seeing that is in itself important. Things are born, they grow, they live, they decline, they die, they rot. That's it. And that in its way is wonderful. That's enough. We don't and shouldn't look for spiritual or divine purpose and all the dangerous nonsense that goes with such a search. Above all, we must recognize that religion, a natural belief development of ignorant and frightened ancestors, something that claims to give those ultimate answers, has long outlived its usefulness and now is positively harmful. "Religion stalks across the face of human history, knee-deep in the blood of innocents, clasping its red hands in hymns of praise to an approving God" (27).

Appleman pulls no punches in his poetry. Noah is told to build a boat and the materials and dimensions are specified carefully.

And then
the Voice tells him why.

His sons, Shem, Ham, and Japheth, just cannot handle this news.

"He's going to drown them all?" Japheth whispers,
"Every last woman and child? What for?"
Noah's mind is not what it used to be; lately
it strays like a lost lamb, his ancient voice
A bleat: "Ahh —

wickedness, I think that's
what He said — yes, wickedness."

The sons are outraged.

"He's going to murder
the lot of them, just
for making a few mistakes? For being — human?"

But being dutiful sons they do it.

"Ours not to reason why," says Shem, the firstborn
and something of a prig. "Ours but to build the ark."

Not easy, as you might expect, keeping the lambs away from the lions, and getting in a year's supply of bananas for the monkeys. But they do it and the rains come and the ark floats clear. Of course the boys look out of the windows and see the fate of one particularly beautiful friend.

Japheth caught
one final glimpse, and of course it had to be Zillah,
holding her baby over her head
till water rolled over her
and she sank, and the baby
splashed a little, and then
there was silence upon the waters,
and God was well pleased.

And so the story draws to its end. The waters subside and humans and animals disembark.

And Noah knows, in his tired bones,
that now he will have to be fruitful, once more,
and multiply, and replenish the earth
with a pure new race of people who
would never, *never* sin again,
for if they did,
all that killing would be for nothing,
a terrible embarrassment
to God.

(Appleman 1996, 178–186)

Not much more you can say after that, except to turn to today's holy men for poetic inspiration.

> The first time?
> So long ago — that brown-eyed boy . . .
> How can I say this, Your Reverences,
> so you'll understand? Maybe
> it was the tilt of his pretty neck
> when he pondered the mysteries – Grace,
> the Trinity — the way his lower lip
> curled like a petal, the way . . .
> But you know what I mean — down
> from your pulpits and into the dirty streets —
> you *know*, there are some provocations
> the good Lord made no sinew
> strong enough to resist.

In any case, we have the love of David for Jonathan to guide us in our conduct. After all, was it really so very wrong?

> What? I? "Ruined their lives"?
> Wait a minute, let's get this straight —
> my passion *gave* them a life, gave them
> something rich and ripe in their green youth,
> something to measure all intimate flesh against,
> forever. After that,
> they ruined their own lives, maybe.
> But with me they were full of a love
> firmer than anything their meager years
> had ever tasted . . .

And let's not be hypocrites. We all know how this is going to be resolved.

> Oh, I know where I'm headed —
> to "therapy" as we always say,
> a little paid vacation
> with others who loved not wisely
> but too young — and also, of course,
> with the usual slew of dehydrating
> whiskey priests. But don't forget
> that when they say I'm "recovered" again,

they'll send me off to another parish,
with more of those little lambs — a priest,
after all, is a priest forever.[2]

(251–255)

Religion is evil and its offerings are corrupt. True happiness, true joy, "does not depend upon mysticism or dogma or priestly admonition. It is the joy of human life, here and now, unblemished by the dark shadow of whimsical forces in the sky. Charles Darwin's example, both in his work and in his life, helps us to understand that that is the only 'heaven' we will ever know. And it is the only one we need" (Appleman 2014, 69). It isn't just that Appleman thinks that God doesn't exist. He loathes and detests all that is done and said in the name of God. Morality has been a constant theme of my story. No one engages in the science-religion issue just as a matter of epistemology, as a matter of true or false. It is always a moral issue. Can you believe in God? Should you believe in God? Where does science take you? Is evolution the route to license and immorality? Appleman's rage is something we should understand and respect, even if we do not necessarily share it.

The Christian Opposition

To be strictly accurate, Christians had not all waited until Sputnik before they were awoken from their slumber. Already in the 1930s and 1940s, the Christian apologist and fantasy novelist C. S. Lewis and his fellow writers (most famous of whom was J. R. R. Tolkien of hobbit fame)—the so-called Inklings—were showing that they did not much care for science, and that they cared for the scientists (notable representative Julian Huxley) even less (Bud 2013). Lewis's *Space Trilogy*—especially the final volume, *That Hideous Strength* (published in 1945)—shows all the marks of the mind-set. There are masses of stuff about the ways in which scientific thought leads to materialism and a downgrading of human nature, something truly revealed only through the Christian religion. The main action takes place in and around a place known as the National Institute for Co-ordinated Experiments. There is some question as to who runs this place, and about its purpose, but you can be sure that it is up to no good.

The physical sciences, good and innocent in themselves, had already, even in Ransom's own time, begun to be warped, and had been subtly

---

[2] Appleman (1996). Copyright 1996 by The University of Arkansas Press. Reproduced with the permission of the University of Arkansas Press, www.uapress.com.

maneuvered in a certain direction. Despair of objective truth had been increasingly insinuated into the scientists; indifference to it, and a concentration upon mere power, had been the result. Babble about the *élan vital* and flirtations with panpsychism were bidding fair to restore the *Anima Mundi* of the magicians. Dreams of the far future destiny of man were dragging up from its shallow and unquiet grave the old dream of Man as God. The very experiences of the dissecting room and the pathological laboratory were breeding a conviction that the stifling of all deep-set repugnances was the first essential for progress. (Lewis [1945] 1996, 203)[3]

And so on and so forth, at great length.

Lewis's writings have had a curiously switchback existence (McGrath 2013). Popular in the 1940s and 1950s—I was brought up on the *Screwtape Letters*—they fell out of favor. Then suddenly, perhaps because of the filming of his *Narnia* series of children's books, he was taken up and now is the darling of the evangelicals, something that he as a rather conservative Anglican would have found ironic to say the least. He is not alone. I do not want to imply that the contemporary science-religion debate (especially coming from the side of religion) is exclusively American, but in the Christian West it very much tends to be, and elsewhere is often—like Coca-Cola—an American import. The debate or clash occurs most obviously and vehemently where extreme evangelicals—literalists or Creationists—are involved (Ruse 1988a). So also for the fiction.

> He approached the bed, knowing what he would find. The indented pillow, the wrinkled covers. He could smell her, though he knew the bed would be cold. He carefully peeled back the blankets and sheet to reveal her locket, which carried a picture of him. Her flannel nightgown, the one he always kidded her about and which she wore only when he was not home, evidenced her now departed form.
>
> His throat tight, his eyes full, he noticed her wedding ring near the pillow, where she always supported her cheek with her hand. It was too much to bear, and he broke down. He gathered the ring into his palm and sat on the edge of the bed, his body racked with fatigue and grief. He put the ring in his jacket pocket and noticed the package she had mailed. Tearing it open, he found two of his favorite homemade cookies with hearts drawn on the top in chocolate.

---

[3] Actually, with the Bergsonian references, the problem is not materialism but its opposite, vitalism. Lewis and his somewhat precious drinking pals would have thought this the road to heresy.

What a sweet, sweet woman! he thought. *I never deserved her, never loved her enough!* He set the cookies on the bedside table, their essence filling the air. With wooden fingers he removed his clothes and let them fall to the floor. He climbed into the bed and lay facedown, gathering Irene's nightgown in his arms so he could smell her and imagine her close to him.

And Rayford cried himself to sleep. (LaHaye and Jenkins 1995, 75–76)

It is not often that one feels a huge sympathy for airline pilots, especially when apparently they spend most of their time in the air trying to get into the panties of the prettiest flight attendant, but it is hard not to shed a tear for Rayford Steele (Captain, Pan-Continental Airlines). He has come home to find his wife missing. She has not, as one might presume, run off with the milkman. Rather, the End of Time is on its way, and she and other true believers have been raptured up to heaven to join Jesus.

This is an extract from the *Left Behind* series, by Tim LaHay and Jerry B. Jenkins, dealing with life after the Rapture.[4] It is one of a very successful series—sixteen volumes so far and with over 65 million sales starting to assume Rider Haggard proportions—that is backed by video games and toys and children's versions and much more. And this is but the tip of an iceberg. Yet, with some regret, in the spirit of my earlier discussions—literalism is not traditional Christianity but an idiosyncratic American invention of the first part of the nineteenth century to speak to social and other needs facing a new nation in a hostile land (Noll 2002; Numbers 2006)—I am going to stay with mainstream Christians who accept evolution—Darwinism even—but who think that this is the beginning rather than the end of the discussion. So let us look as a counter to Philip Appleman at a woman who is one of America's leading Christian poets.

Pattiann Rogers

Deeply religious in a nonpreachy sort of way—she was raised first Presbyterian and then in a fundamentalist group but has moved on—Pattiann Rogers (b.

---

[4] According to Dispensationalist theology, the history of Earth is divided into periods at the end of which major upheavals occur. Noah's Flood, for instance, is the end of one such dispensation. The final end is on its way. First true believers will be lifted up to heaven ("raptured") to join Jesus in fully resurrected bodies. Next will be the Great Tribulation, when at least 75% of the remaining humans will be destroyed. After this, Jesus will come back to Earth, defeat Satan in the battle of Armageddon, and then rule for 1,000 years (the millennium) before the Day of Judgment.

1940) expresses a profound love of nature and appreciation of the science behind it. One thinks obviously again of Hopkins and she admits the influence and also (as one would expect) of Dickinson, but her main source of inspiration is Whitman.

> I swear I think now that everything without exception has an eternal Soul!
> The trees have, rooted in the ground! the weeds of the sea have! the animals!
> (Whitman 2004, 455)

One looks therefore for transcendentalism—"Matter is not dead but alive, not dumb but aware" (Conner [1949] 1973, 100–101)—and it is there. In particular, there is the value placed on the very fact of life itself—the mystery, the insistence, the worth. The world throbs with life and that is good. Take "Opus from Space." In a way, it almost comes across as pagan—but not really. There is a "raging to be born" and that this is a "singular honor."

> Almost everything I know is glad
> to be born — not only the desert orangetip,
> on the twist flower or tansy, shaking
> birth moisture from its wings, but also the naked
> warbler nesting, head wavering toward sky,
> and the honey possum, the pygmy possum,
> blind, hairless thimbles of forward,
> press and part.

All of nature pushes and shoves, trying to be born and to savor existence.

> Almost everything I know rages to be born,
> the obsession founding itself explicitly
> in the coming bone harps and ladders,
> the heart-thrusts, vessels and voices
> of all those speeding with clear and total
> fury toward this singular honor.
> (Rogers 2001, 426–428)

Note, however, that although within this poem there is force and pushing and so forth, it is not the struggle for existence and there is no blind force leading to tragedy as easily as to comedy or to happiness. There is just an urge to being. One does not really have to bring God into the story, although He may well be there. Life itself is of value. We are right back with Emerson. "In the morning I awake, and find the old world, wife, babes, and mother, Concord and Boston, the dear old spiritual world, and even the dear old devil not far off. If we will take the good we find, asking no questions, we shall have heaping measures. The great gifts are not got by analysis" (Emerson [1844] 1920, 197).

This said, Rogers wrestles with the problem of pain and suffering brought on by the evolutionary process and of how we might reconcile this with a caring God. She explores several possible ways of doing this, including two which have both found favor recently by those traveling in the same direction as she. Again one finds a turning to the Book of Job and an exploration of the theology given there.[5] God's creation comes tumbling out. Forget pain and suffering. Things are alive.

First God:

> 39 Knowest thou the time when the wild goats of the rock bring forth? or canst thou mark when the hinds do calve?
>
> ² Canst thou number the months that they fulfil? or knowest thou the time when they bring forth?
>
> ³ They bow themselves, they bring forth their young ones, they cast out their sorrows.
>
> ⁴ Their young ones are in good liking, they grow up with corn; they go forth, and return not unto them.
>
> ⁵ Who hath sent out the wild ass free? or who hath loosed the bands of the wild ass?

Don't argue with me. Don't question me. I am God. I give life.
Now Rogers.

> This is the only rite of holiness
> I know: fierce barb of bacteria, that hot,
> hot, coal, that smoldering challenge
> clearing, for twelve millennia at least,
> in all directions from its dark, subzero
> cellar of frozen glacial rock.
>
> This is the noise of heavenly
> hosts: trumpet-blaring chaparrals
> and shinneries, cymbal-banking greasewood
> and jojodba deserts, bubble of hellbinders, slips

---

[5] Holmes (2009) notes the importance of Job for contemporary poets. I have tried to show that this is a tradition with roots back through the nineteenth century—as one might have expected. Deliberately I quote from the King James Version to bring out the poetic parallels.

of heliotropes, tweakings of brush mice
and big-eared bats, wheezings of rusty wheels,
grasshopper sparrows, autumn leaves ticking
across gravel on their paper pricks.

Continuing and concluding:

This is the only stinging, magenta-cruel,
fire-green huffing, bellowing mayhemic
spirituality I will ever recognize:
the one shuddering with veined lightning,
cackling with seeded consolations, howling
with winter pities, posturing with speared
and fisted indignities, surly as rock, ruder
as weeds, riotous as billbugs, tumultuous
as grapevine beetles, as large black, burying
beetles, bare, uncovered to every perception
of god, and never, never once forgiving
death.

(440–441)

A world created, take it for what it is, and ask not about good or bad. "If God or a Creator or a spiritual presence is all-good and all-powerful, as we often posit in the Judeo-Christian tradition, how can suffering of the innocent occur? It's an old, old question. Archibald MacLeish put it like this in his play *J.B.*, based on the story of Job: If God is God, he is not good. If God is good, he is not God" (Perry and Zade 2012, 92, interviewing Rogers).

Contrasting, we find another approach in Rogers's poetry, one that in a sense makes a virtue of pain and suffering. We have seen hints of this kind of approach in Steinbeck's thinking—strife and hardship lead to Progress. In Rogers's case, the way forward is found in the already-mentioned, related "process philosophy/theology" of Alfred North Whitehead (1929). As in the case of Bergson and Teilhard de Chardin, one stresses the constant motion, of becoming, of everything, and in particular one sees evolution as the greatest proof and manifestation of this. Converting this thinking into theological terms, one argues—in a way that traditional thinkers like Augustine, not to mention Aquinas and Calvin, would think deeply heretical—that God and his creation too are in a state of becoming, and that in some sense the world in which we find ourselves is as yet incomplete (Ruse 2015a). God under this conception is co-creator, having voluntarily relinquished his absolute powers—this is known as "kenosis"—and thus in a sense although God suffers when pain occurs he cannot prevent it. In fact, he suffers precisely because he cannot prevent it. All this is expressed in her poem, "The Possible Suffering of a God during Creation." We set right out with a God who feels that most human of emotions, despair. Trying to get it right and not succeeding.

> It might be continuous — the despair he experiences
> Over the imperfections of the unfinished, the weaving
> Body of the imprisoned moonfish, for instance,
> Whose invisible arms in the mid-waters of the deep sea
> Are not yet free, or the velvet-blue vervain
> Whose grainy tongue will not move to speak, or the ear
> Of the spitting spider still oblivious to sound.

Then there is the pain from the act and method of creation—that awful Darwinian process.

> And maybe he suffers from the suffering
> Inherent to the transitory, feeling grief himself
> For the grief of shattered beaches, disembodied bones
> And claws, twisted squid, piles of ripped and tangled,
> Uprooted turtles and crowd rock crabs and Jonah crabs,
> Sand bugs, seaweed and kelp.

And in the end, he doesn't know if he has succeeded or will succeed. A feeling that it was or will be all worthwhile.

> Maybe he wakes periodically at night,
> Wiping away the tears he doesn't know
> He has cried in his sleep, not having had time yet to tell
> Himself precisely how it is he must mourn, not having had time yet
> To elicit from his creation its invention
> Of his own solace.[6]

(182–183)

See here how there is nothing but unremitting labor and strife and hardship. God cannot even take pleasure from the hoped-for end point. He is too bound up with what he is doing to pull back and admire or to take hope from what he

---

[6] "Opus from Space," "Against the Ethereal," and "The Possible Suffering of a God during Creation" from Rogers (2001). Copyright © 2001 by Pattiann Rogers. Reprinted with permission from Milkweed Editions. www.milkweed.org.

has done and what lies ahead and the joys of completion. Unlike Teilhard de Chardin, who likewise sees a continuous process of creation, there is no upward progress, nor is there the promise of Christ at the end. This could be read as a message of despair, but process theologians draw the opposite conclusion. Our lives are made meaningful because we are not alone. The knowledge that we are sufficiently responsible to share with God the trials of creation is in itself a great good and source of joy. This hardly comes through in Rogers's poem, but it is there in the background.

Rogers is not very consistent. On the one hand, she suggests that God is so powerful that anything He does or says goes. On the other hand, God is so weak that He is down in the world of evil like the rest of us. In a sense, so what? Thomas Hardy would have empathized. A poet has the license to try out different approaches. In another sense, why is this a fault? Surely it is open to anyone who takes seriously the problem of evil to explore different approaches finding value in each and all and leaving matters at that. It is the same problem. Rogers (before her Graham Greene, and before him John Steinbeck and others) is trying to see evil less as a problem to be explained away in the face of a good God and more something as itself part of the positive creative process. She like the others, therefore, turns to evolution and finds not yet further challenges to her faith—"I cannot persuade myself that a beneficent & omnipotent God would have designedly created the Ichneumonidæ with the express intention of their feeding within the living bodies of caterpillars, or that a cat should play with mice"—but a way forward because of evolution. At the end of the nineteenth century, the High-Church Anglican theologian Aubrey Moore wrote: "Science had pushed the deist's God farther and farther away, and at the moment when it seemed as if He would be thrust out altogether, Darwinism appeared, and, under the guise of a foe, did the work of a friend." Continuing: "In nature everything must be His work or nothing. We must frankly return to the Christian view of direct Divine agency, the immanence of Divine power from end to end, the belief in a God in Whom not only we, but all things have their being, or we must banish him altogether" (Moore 1890, 99–100). Christian authors like Rogers would agree wholeheartedly with this sentiment.[7] Appleman has it all wrong. Darwinism does not vanquish Christianity. Christianity absorbs Darwinism and thereby grows.

---

[7] With the turn to evolution, should Rogers be considered outside or opposed to the paradigm? As with Tennyson, in part it is all a matter of self-identification. Rogers is clearly on the other side from Appleman. But over the 150 years or so since the *Origin*, there has surely been somewhat of a shift of the dividing line (for conventional Christians) with a move toward greater acceptance of evolutionary ideas. As with Copernicus so with Darwin—what it means to be a Christian has changed.

16

Conflicting Visions

Twin Towers

One could continue looking at other poets also trying to make the case for Christianity in a Darwinian world. Amy Clampitt (1920–1994), born of Quaker parents and raised in the Midwest (Iowa), did not start seriously to write poetry until midlife and published only in later life. A perceptive friend wrote of Clampitt having "periods of religious experience in adulthood that ranged from doubt to intense Episcopalianism to disillusionment, and then to some sort of private peace with her enduring inconsistencies," and it comes out in Clampitt's poetry (Salter 1997, xiv). Influenced by Frost and before him Hardy, she dwells on life's pains and miseries. Charles Darwin and the death in childhood of his beloved daughter Annie.

> Think of Charles Darwin mulling over
> whether to take out his patent on
> the way the shape of things can alter,
> hearing the whir, in his own household,
> of the winnowing fan no system
> (it appears) can put a stop to,
> winnowing out another little girl,
> for no good reason other than
> the docile accident of the unfit,
> before she quite turned seven.[1]

(68)

---

[1] Actually, Annie Darwin was ten when she died.

And yet this is from a poem with the title "Good Friday," that sacred day when the blameless Christian God met his death on the cross to save us from our sins. How literally Clampitt believes any of this—she writes of Good Friday as a "therapeutic outlet"—one feels the mystical Quakerism that senses but does not comprehend. One has another intimation of the theology of Job, of a God who allows and perhaps even commits what we judge evil. A Creator God whose power is absolute and who is above good and evil. "Who has a claim against me that I must pay? Everything under heaven belongs to me" (Job 41:11). This is not the Leibnizian God, constrained by the law of noncontradiction. This is a God of whom we are aware and in whom we are in awe, but a God who ultimately is hidden from us.

> [4] Where wast thou when I laid the foundations of the earth? declare, if thou hast understanding.
> [5] Who hath laid the measures thereof, if thou knowest? or who hath stretched the line upon it?
> [6] Whereupon are the foundations thereof fastened? or who laid the corner stone thereof;
> [7] When the morning stars sang together, and all the sons of God shouted for joy?

For Clampitt, all of this is close to what is known as "apophatic" theology, where one can only say of God what He is not—we cannot speak of God yet to say that in some sense He is beyond our ken and understanding. Clampitt wrestles with evil generally and with evil as a function of nature's creative processes. The language may be that of earlier poets, but she should be read almost in a post-modern way as she tries to move on beyond the nihilism of the Darwinian world of Thomas Hardy.

Of course, this does not end the debate and it probably never will be over. Expectedly, Appleman had a few choice things to say about Job.

> God horns in with that scandalous
> non sequitur. "No," he says,
> "You don't suffer because you sin.
> You suffer because I say so."
>
> (Appleman 1996, 206)

In the end, all turns out nicely for Job, because God rewards him for his fidelity. "As I always say, toadying is good for business." Let's just hope that God is busy now with other things.

> It's hard enough to bring up a family
> in these troubled times, without admitting
> that almighty God has morals
> of a Babylonian butcher. (207)

An ongoing debate that may wax and wane but that will probably outlast us all. Climax more than enough for now are reactions to the terrible events of 9/11. It was Muslims who flew the airliners into the World Trade Center, but this made little difference. The nonbelievers exploded with rage. Finally, will people see the damage that religion does? Will they recognize the evil that lurks at the heart of every faith system? "The God of the Old Testament is arguably the most unpleasant character in all fiction: jealous and proud of it; a petty, unjust, unforgiving control-freak; a vindictive, bloodthirsty ethnic cleanser; a misogynistic, homophobic, racist, infanticidal, genocidal, filicidal, pestilential, megalomaniacal, sadomasochistic, capriciously malevolent bully" (Dawkins 2006, 31). The works poured forth, especially from a central four, the New Atheists. *The God Delusion* (2006), by Richard Dawkins; *The End of Faith* (2004), by then-student Sam Harris; *God Is Not Great* (2007), by journalist Christopher Hitchens; and *Breaking the Spell* (2006), by philosopher Daniel Dennett. And to counter them, works by Christians showing that things are not as simple as the nonbelievers suggest. *The Dawkins Delusion* (2007), by Protestant theologian Alister McGrath and his wife Joanna; *God and the New Atheism* (2008), by Catholic theologian John Haught; *God's Undertaker* (2009), by Oxford mathematician John Lennox; and so the story goes on in large numbers. Expectedly Darwinism is in the thick of it. If only you would accept Darwinism fully—meaning something along the lines of Thomas Hardy's views cubed—you would see that Christianity is false and pernicious. If only you would accept Darwinism at its true worth—an epistemological pimple on the unwashed nether regions of life—you would see how our *sensus divinitatis*—a kind of theological equivalent of Skype with God at the other end—makes all else irrelevant. Expectedly, just as there are atheist novelists, so there are Christian novelists. Let us conclude our story by turning to two of today's most-praised writers of fiction, both of whom hold very strong views on the significance of Darwinism, both of whom write in the light of these views, and both of whom write in the knowledge of the renewed tensions between evolution and Christianity. Two of today's most-praised writers of fiction who hold completely diametric views on these subjects.

Ian McEwan (b. 1948)

Not always approvingly, critics have noted how Ian McEwan's plots are often melodramatic, perhaps owing more to pulp fiction than they should, but for once this tendency plays well.[2] The story *Enduring Love* (1997) opens with a picnic shared by a couple, Joe Rose, a science writer, and his long-term partner, Clarissa Mellon, an academic. They see a hot-air balloon in trouble—a young child is aboard and it threatens to take off without an adult—and Joe (along with five other men) rushes to help. Unfortunately, five of the six let go and the balloon soars carrying aloft the sixth, a physician, John Logan, who finally lets go and falls to his death. It turns out that one of the other would-be helpers is a young man, Jed Parry, who has a psychological affliction known as erotomania or de Clérambault's syndrome, so named after the French psychiatrist who first described it. On the basis of their balloon encounter, Jed falls obsessively in love with Joe, convinced that the feeling is reciprocated. The rest of the story is about how this works out. For a long time, Joe's girlfriend—and police included—thinks that Joe is exaggerating. Even when Jed's obsession turns to resentment and he pays to have Joe assassinated—something that fails to come off—no one takes Joe seriously. This all leads to so much tension that Clarissa walks out on Joe. (Up to this point they had been very much in love but one senses underlying issues because Clarissa is infertile.) Finally, Joe gets a gun (illicitly) and when Jed threatens Clarissa, Joe shoots Jed (nonfatally), the police now believe him, and Jed gets locked up in an asylum, where he spends his days writing declarations of love to Joe. A subplot about Logan's presence is resolved when we learn (to his wife's relief) that he was not there with a girlfriend but because he had given a pair of private lovers (a fifty-year-old professor and his twenty-year-old student) a lift, and in an almost offhand manner we learn that Joe and Clarissa get back together and adopt a child. One presumes that this last fact is true, although readers of another of McEwan's novels, *Atonement*, will know that he is not above playing John Fowles's trick of multiple endings, not all of which give the reader the happy ending he or she is hoping for.

Ian McEwan has always had a keen interest in science and this comes through strongly in this novel—most particularly by making Joe a science writer. One of McEwan's great strengths is in showing how people's professional lives can be interesting, and we get a real sense of Joe as a man who uncannily gets into the feelings of scientists and their work. Although as a writer it is evolutionary biology that really interests him—Joe made his breakthrough into the field with a book on dinosaurs and now we learn that it is neo-Darwinism, particularly evolutionary psychology and genetics, that are the hot fields—a basic underlying theme of the book is that of science generally versus irrationality, especially irrationality

---

[2] Bradley (2009), having noted how the New Atheists speak of the world of evolution in nigh-biblical terms of awe and wonderment, stressing its beauty, suggests that perhaps we can think of novelists like Ian McEwan as akin to the authors of the Judeo-Christian fables, attempting to use metaphor and myth to convey deep truths.

as found in religious mania.[3] Joe stands for a world run by unbroken law and the attempt of humans to ferret out its nature. We learn that he is an atheist without religious belief. Jed to the contrary is a man of emotions and deep religious conviction. From the beginning he is trying to convert (a very unwilling) Joe. On their first meeting:

> 'Look, we don't know each other and there's no reason why you should trust me. Except that God has brought us together in this tragedy and we have to, you know, make whatever sense of it we can?' Then, seeing me make no move, he added, 'I think you have a special need for prayer?'
>
> I shrugged and said, 'Sorry. But you go right on ahead.' I Americanised my tone to suggest a lightheartedness I did not feel.

It continues:

> 'I don't think you understand. You shouldn't, you know, think of this as some kind of duty. It's like, your own needs of being answered? It's got nothing to do with me, really, I'm just the messenger. It's a gift.'
>
> As he pressed harder, so the last traces of my embarrassment disappeared. 'Thanks, but no.' (McEwan 1997, 25)

More specifically, expectedly, it is evolutionary biology that counts. Joe puts the balloon incident in the language of the sociobiologists or (in human terms) evolutionary psychologists. Surely letting go was the reasonable thing to do?

> No failure. So can we accept that it was right, every man for himself? Were we all happy afterwards that this was a reasonable course? We never had that comfort, for there was a deeper covenant, ancient and automatic, written in our nature. Co-operation—the basis of our earliest hunting successes, the force behind our evolving capacity for language, the glue of our social cohesion. Our misery in the aftermath was proof that we knew we had failed ourselves. But letting go is in our nature too. Selfishness is also written on our hearts. This is our mammalian conflict—what to give to the others, and what to keep for yourself. Treading that line, keeping the others in check, and being kept in check by them, is what we call morality. (14)

---

[3] The English writer on things evolutionary, Adrian Desmond, wrote a best-seller published in 1976: *The Hot-Blooded Dinosaurs: A Revolution in Palaeontology.*

A major theme of the book is the wrestling match with this dilemma. Why did
Logan do what he did when it led to his death and the others did what they did
and survived—yet felt awful? Clearly in one sense it was selfishness and expectedly biology promotes just that. His actions were explicable, as long as one
could assume (as did his wife) that Logan was out there with an illicit girlfriend
and by hanging on he was trying to impress a much younger woman. When he
did it because it was right, that took more explaining. But one can explain it—as
Joe at the end explains it to the wife—in terms of some people simply being
better than others. Evolutionary psychology can accommodate this, if only to
inspire others. "The kind of courage the rest of us can only dream about." And
note it seems to have been this kind of healing scenario that opened the path
for Joe and Clarissa to reconnect. How could one let something like this go
unanswered?

The case of Jed is somewhat more complex and ambiguous. It is made
clear in an appendix that his condition was probably triggered by incidental
social factors, which could range from a missing father through inheritance
of wealth that made possible a psychologically isolating situation to the very
excitement of the balloon incident. How far biology in the form of genetics
was responsible is left unanswered. The main thing is that we are not dealing
with a rational person and in this case religion was intimately involved. It
is interesting to note that it is admitted that religion does not normally get
so involved, suggesting that the author did this deliberately to contrast with
Joe's atheistic rationality. Be this as it may, the overall theme is that we are
what we are because of our evolved past as much as because of individual
happenstance.

> We do not arrive in this world as blank sheets, or as all-purpose learning
> devices. Nor are we the 'products' of our environment. If we want to
> know what we are, we have to know where we came from. We evolved,
> like every other creature on earth. We come into this world with limi-
> tations and capacities, all of them genetically prescribed. Many of our
> features, our foot shape, eye color, are fixed, and others, like our social
> and sexual behavior, and our language learning, await the life we live
> to take their course. But the course is not infinitely variable. We have a
> nature. (69–70)

Much is made of Darwin's claim that human expressions are the same from culture to culture. At Heathrow airport: "I saw the same joy, the same uncontrol-
lable smile, in the faces of a Nigerian earth mama, a thin-lipped Scottish granny
and a pale, correct Japanese businessman as they wheeled their trolleys in and
recognized a figure in the expectant crowd" (4). One is not surprised that at

the end of the book McEwan acknowledges his debt to Edward O. Wilson's *On Human Nature*. It shows.

The dreadful events of 9/11 hardened McEwan's stance:

> Few of us, I think, in the mid-1970s, when The Selfish Gene was pub-
> lished, would have thought we would be dedicating so much mental
> space to discussing religious faith in this new century. We thought that
> since it has nothing useful at all to say about cosmology, the age of the
> earth, the origin of species, the curing of disease or any other aspect of
> the physical world, it had retreated finally to where it belongs, to the
> privacy of individual conscience. We were wrong. A variety of sky-god
> worshippers with their numerous, mutually exclusive certainties (all of
> which we must "respect") appears to be occupying more and more of
> the space of public discourse. (McEwan 2006)

Saturday, a novel that appeared four years after the Twin Towers inferno—
"Now we breathe a different air" (McEwan [2005] 2006, 37)—shows a yet-
deeper commitment to science, to Darwinian-type thinking, and a like distrust
of faith and emotion-based systems. In respects, this and the earlier novel share
plot elements. Both involve a decent human—this time, the neurosurgeon
Henry Perowne—in contact with a crazed human being—this time Baxter, a
thug who suffers from Huntington's chorea. Taking place in London all within
one day, the story is of Perowne going out to play squash, diverted down a
street because of a major rally against the proposed invasion of Iraq, where he
bashes his car against that of Baxter. Able to talk his way out of a potentially
violent situation (by noting and remarking on Baxter's illness which has not
yet taken over his body), Perowne and his family are later (at home) terrorized
by Baxter who has discovered his address. In the end, Perowne knocks Baxter
down the stairs, and then spends the rest of the evening operating on Baxter
who has sustained a bad head injury. It is left hanging whether Perowne does
this out of altruism, simply because that is what he does for a living, or because
he knows that he is simply guaranteeing Baxter a year or two of dreadful existence as the chorea takes over.

Again, it is the life of science (or its technological implications as in neuro-
surgery) that is the underlying theme of the novel, combined with a view that
religion and all kinds of irrationality are what science combats and conquers—
although there is an edge to things missing earlier. The operation on Baxter is a
success. None of this is Darwinian as such, but to make sure the reader knows that
it is the Darwinian metaphysics that underlies this attitude, not only is Perowne
given a Darwinian biography to read—given the date, one speculates: Was it

the first volume of Janet Browne's (1995) magisterial biography that had just appeared?—but the implications are spelled out. Like a tune that one cannot get out of one's head, Perowne thinks again and again of that most famous line toward the end of the *Origin*: "There is a grandeur in this view of life."

> Kindly, driven, infirm Charles in all his humility, bringing on the earth-worms and planetary cycles to assist him with a farewell bow. To soften the message, he also summoned up a creator in later editions, but his heart was never really in it. Those five hundred pages deserved only one conclusion: endless and beautiful forms of life, such as you see in a common hedgerow, including exalted beings like ourselves, arose from physical laws, from war of nature, famine and death. This is the grandeur. And a bracing kind of consolation in the brief privilege of consciousness. (56)[4]

Unlike the earlier novel, the crazy one is not a religious maniac, but there is enough to make one wary of religion, and indeed of the whole Arab/Islamic way of life. Perowne is strongly in favor of Progress. "Life in it [London] has steadily improved over the centuries. For most people, despite the junkies and beggars now. The air is better, and salmon leaping in the Thames, and otters are return-ing. At every level, material, medical, intellectual, sensual, for most people it has improved." Continuing: "He remembers some lines by Medawar, a man he ad-mires: 'to deride the hopes of progress is the ultimate fatuity, a last word in poverty of spirit and meanness of mind'" (77). Think of Islam—"Waiting at red lights he watches three figures in black burkhas emerge from a taxi on Devonshire Place" (123–124)—where the males alone are allowed to enter the twentieth century— "But the men, the husbands—Perowne has had dealings with various Saudis in his office—wear suits, or trainers and track suits, or baggy shorts and Rolexes, and are entirely charming and worldly and thoroughly educated in both traditions. Would they care to carry the folkloric torch, and stumble about in the dark at midday?" (124).[5]

Perowne sees a plane in flames. As it happens, it turns out not to be that tragic, but at the time of viewing he did not know this. Why was it happening? "A man of sound faith with a bomb in the heel of his shoe. Among the terrified pas-sengers many might be praying—another problem of reference—to their own God for intercession. And if there are to be deaths, the very God who ordained them will soon be funereally petitioned for comfort" (17–18). You cannot

---

[4] As you know, this is not my take on the *Origin*, although I think it is closer to the *Descent*.

[5] Obviously now evolution is being opposed not just to Christianity but to all religions.

win an argument against something so irrational. "Even the denial of God, he was once amazed and indignant to hear a priest argue, is a spiritual exercise, a form of prayer: it's not easy to escape from the clutches of the believers" (18). Interestingly, although Perowne's adult daughter is portrayed as much against the prospect of the Iraq war, Perowne himself—having met one of Saddam's victims—is a lot more ambivalent. (Among the New Atheists, Hitchens notoriously was for the war.) The only real change from *Enduring Love* is that McEwan is now self-consciously aware that it is one thing to write against religion and irrationality, but it would be another to include all nonscientific activity in this category.[6] Poetry is given a favorable treatment—both Perowne's daughter and father-in-law are poets, and at a crucial moment Baxter is distracted by the beauty of Matthew Arnold's "Dover Beach." Dare one suggest that the choice of this particular poem—which is printed at the end of the novel—is not random, but chosen precisely because it tells of the loss of faith? It is not very psychologically convincing that the poem would have had the supposed calming effect on Baxter, but it is a crucial support of McEwan's metaphysical world picture that with the death of God we are on our own and our only hope comes from humankind.

> Ah, love, let us be true
> To one another! for the world, which seems
> To lie before us like a land of dreams,
> So various, so beautiful, so new,
> Hath really neither joy, nor love, nor light,
> Nor certitude, nor peace, nor help for pain;
> And we are here as on a darkling plain
> Swept with confused alarms of struggle and flight,
> Where ignorant armies clash by night.

Marilynne Robinson (b. 1943)

Cross the Atlantic and turn to the novels of a woman, a Christian, who garners the same praise as McEwan. Somewhat ironically, given themes in her fiction, one of her greatest admirers is Barack Obama, the first black president of the United States (Obama and Robinson 2015). Although I do not take her to

---

[6] To be fair, it is not so much "change" as "development," for as Clark and Gordon (2003) point out McEwan does wrestle somewhat in *Enduring Love* with the limits of science and the need of a broader humanistic perspective. McEwan speaks of "continuing a conversation" on this topic and Clark and Gordon remark perceptively that "it's a conversation that has clearly not come to an end" (81).

be a crude Creationist—the first chapter of Genesis "is startlingly compatible with the idea of evolution"—Marilynne Robinson is as wary of Darwinism as McEwan is enthusiastic. Her essay on the topic (that dates from 1997) contains just about all of the standard criticisms. It promotes and cherishes selfishness. It is anti-Christian. "Darwinism was the appropriation of certain canards about animal breeding for the purpose of social criticism, together with a weariness in European civilization with Christianity, which did cavil, if anything did, at the extraordinary cruelty of industrial and colonial civilization" (Robinson [1998] 2005, 32–33). It is materialistic (35). It is (or at least taken to be) antimorality. "Whether Darwin himself intended to debunk religion is not a matter of importance, since he was perceived to have done so by those who embraced his views. His theory, a science, is irrelevant to the question of truth of religion. It is only as an inversion of Christian ethicalism that he truly engages religion" (36–37). It is anti-religion generally (38). It is itself a religion. "Faith is called faith for a reason. Darwinism is another faith—a loyalty to a vision of the nature of things, despite its inaccessibility to demonstration" (39). It is so back to back with Creationism, they are peas in a pod. It claims not to be progressivist, but it is. "I am aware that many Darwinists do not argue that the complexity of organisms is a mark of progress in evolution, yet the idea is implicit in their model of adaptation" (45). After all this, the reader will not be surprised to learn that natural selection is a tautology and that Darwinism led to both Freud and Hitler.

Turn now to Robinson's trilogy, *Gilead* (2004), *Home* (2008), and *Lila* (2014) for the alternative picture. The central figure is an aged Congregationalist minister, the Reverend John Ames, in a small town, Gilead, in Iowa. When we meet him in the first novel—the time is the mid-1950s, Eisenhower is running again for president—Ames is married to a much younger woman, Lila, and has a near-seven-year-old son. Ames's grandfather was also a minister and an abolitionist, not afraid to take up weapons for the cause. His father, a minister, had been a pacifist. Ames himself has had a long and sad life. His first wife, a childhood friend, died in childbirth and the child (a girl) did not survive either. For forty years, Ames remained a lonely widower. Then, about eight years earlier than the telling of the story, Lila had appeared from nowhere, poor and friendless—a passion sprang up between them, they married, and the son (Robert) was conceived and born. Connecting with *Home* (taking place at the same time) is one of the adult sons of Ames's best friend, the Presbyterian minister, the Reverend Robert Boughton. John Ames (Jack) Boughton is a ne'er-do-well, an alcoholic, who impregnated a young girl (very much from the wrong side of the tracks) and ignored both mother and child, the latter (a girl) dying at a very young age. With more than echoes of the Prodigal Son, Jack is loved above all others by his father, but Ames cannot stand him—he thinks with reason that this son is downright mean.

Inasmuch as these are stories with a plot—and it is no criticism to say that in many respects they are more philosophical/theological reflections exploring the psychology of human beings—*Gilead* and *Home* center on the discovery (made clear in *Gilead* but not introduced into *Home* until the end) that Jack has for ten years been living in a common-law relationship with a black woman and that they have a child (a boy also called Robert). This discovery brings Ames to a love of Jack. Speaking in his mind to his friend Boughton: "I blessed that boy of yours for you. I still feel the weight of his brow on my hand. I said, I love him as much as you meant me to. So certain of your prayers are finally answered, old fellow. And mine too, mine too. We had to wait a long time, didn't we?" (Robinson [2004] 2005, 279).

Lila takes us back about eight years to the appearance of Ames's future wife in Gilead. Abused by her family as a very small child, she was stolen away by a woman called Doll. A life of trial follows, living vagabond-like on the road— this was the time of the Depression—and then when Doll gets arrested (and subsequently escapes and vanishes) for killing the man who was probably Lila's father, Lila spends time first in a brothel in St. Louis and then cleaning hotel rooms, until she runs off to Iowa and ends (without design) in Gilead. Living in a shack on the edge of town she starts coming to church, suddenly she proposes to Ames—"You ought to marry me"—and marriage and parenthood follow.

We are in the world of John Calvin—it is stressed that both Presbyterians and Congregationalists are in the tradition of Calvin—with a strong flavor of New England transcendentalism. "The moon looks wonderful in this warm evening light, just as a candle flame looks beautiful in the light of morning. Light within light. It seems like a metaphor for something. So much does. Ralph Waldo Emerson is excellent on this point" (Robinson [2004] 2005, 136). Let me isolate three themes, one from each book.[7] First let us look at the Calvinist notion of predestination. This is in complete contrast to the blind randomness Thomas Hardy extracted from Darwinism. For Calvin, God's sovereignty is everything, meaning that ultimately He knows all things and He decides all things. In *Gilead* particularly, this is the underlying foundation. Ames's first wife and child die, unexpectedly, when basically they should not have done. This was part of God's plan. Ames could have remarried but did not—whether as part of his God-given nature or part of his reaction to the deaths, from which he never recovered. Lila appearing on the scene and their subsequent marriage and the birth of a healthy child are again part of God's plan. And the subsequent reconciliation with Jack—a man born with a flawed nature—also falls into place. None of this is chance. All of it is the will and scheme of the Almighty. And if you are in any doubt about this, in both *Gilead* and *Home* there are explicit discussions of predestination. Jack challenges Ames about this doctrine. It is accepted totally, although—in a passage identical in both novels—Ames admits its full meaning is beyond his ken. "I tell

---

[7] Although from any perspective, these are major themes, I stress that I am not doing a general analysis of the trilogy but focusing on aspects pertinent to our story.

them there are certain attributes our faith assigns to God: omniscience, omnipotence, justice, and grace. We human beings have such a slight acquaintance with power and knowledge, so little conception of justice, and so slight a capacity to grace, that the workings of these great attributes together is a mystery we cannot hope to penetrate" (Robinson [2004] 2005, 171, 2008, 220).

The problematic issue with all systems that make God so all-powerful is how then one makes room for the equally important matter of human freedom. A major intent of Robinson is to show precisely that her characters are free and merit judgment. Ames had psychological as well as (in his mind) contractual reasons not to remarry—he had made a commitment to the first wife—but nevertheless it was in some sense his choice to lead an adult life of such loneliness. Then when Lila appears, they too have a choice about marriage. Jack clearly merits forgiveness given the concern he has for his black wife and child. It may be that God gave him his original nature and that God was involved in the change. But there is more. Although it is stressed that Lila has great native intelligence, she is presented as a bit of a holy innocent or fool. Yet it is she who makes clear that there is change and humans deserve merit for their efforts. "A person can change. Everything can change" (Robinson 2008, 227). And Jack thanks her for bringing comfort to his troubled soul.

Finally, think about Ames and Jack. The older man hates Jack for personal reasons. He himself lost wife and child. Then Jack has a girlfriend and ignores her and his child, even to the point where the latter dies and it is his own family who take her and bury her. Finally, Ames is given the comfort of his own wife and child. And it turns out that Jack has wife and son, and cares deeply about them. Obviously there are all sorts of psychological causal factors at work here, but overall and in the end it is Jack who changes and Ames who responds and forgives and loves. No more than with the discussions of freedom in the earlier chapters am I saying that this is all entirely satisfactory. What I am saying is that Robinson is acknowledging the challenges and taking them on and offering an alternative to a position that many think has been dictated by Darwinism.

Home in respects is a darker work. Although the true nature of Jack's wife and child—that they are black—is not revealed until the end, it hangs over everything and we the readers know from the earlier novel what is at stake. Jack essentially is looking to see if Gilead is a place that he can bring his family and settle into. Remember, this is the town where Ames's grandfather was a minister—that grandfather so deep in the movement to free the slaves that he even went to war and lost an eye—and who was much involved in the passage of slaves up to free territories. Now 100 years later, blacks cannot comfortably live in Gilead. There were once black families but they have all left and the black church was set afire—or an attempt was made to do so. Moreover, the ministers—the men of God—are doing little about this and showing complacency. This is the time of civil rights demonstrations in the South, events that are being shown on the newly acquired televisions. "'The colored people,' his father said, 'appear to me to be creating problems and obstacles for themselves with all this—commotion. There's no reason for all this trouble. They bring it on themselves.'" Jack protests and the conversation continues.

> "So you know some colored people, there in St. Louis."
> "Yes. They've been kind to me."
> His father regarded him. "Your mother and I brought you children up to be at ease in any company. Any respectable company. So you could have the benefit of good friends. Because people judge you by your associations. I know that sounds harsh, but it's the truth."
> Jack smiled. "Yes, sir, believe me, I know what it is to be judged by my associations."
> "You could help yourself by finding a better class of friends." (Robinson 2008, 156–157)

Even the best of us are tainted. We are all marked by original sin. No better demonstration could be given of the futility of hopes or claims of Progress. Without the grace of God we are as nothing.

Lila brings up this matter of grace precisely. A major theme is that of trying to make sense of suffering and pain. In some respects, the solution offered is that of the poet Keats, that this world is a vale of soul making. It is through suffering that things are made better. The authority of Calvin is invoked—"people have to suffer to really know grace" (Robinson 2014, 131). Lila has a taste for the more difficult books of the Old Testament and her husband responds. "I guess I've had my time of suffering. Not so much by Ezekiel's standards. And there might be more to come. At my age, I'm sure there is. But at least I've had enough of it by now to know that this is grace" (132). As with our other Christian writers, Job is also invoked. Ames worries that he is so happy now. Could it possibly have been part of God's plan that his first wife and child had to die to make possible his joy now? And what of his own old age? He is soon going to leave a rather defenseless wife and young child. He has no real savings or anything else. The story of Hagar and Ishmael is raised, another mother and son without help or hope whom the Lord comforted and succored. But ultimately it is all a mystery. Effects of the thoughts and actions of a sovereign God.

> Sorrow is very real, and loss feels very final to us. Life on earth is difficult and grave, and marvelous. Our experience is fragmentary. Its parts don't add up. They don't even belong in the same calculation. Sometimes it is hard to believe they are all parts of one thing. Nothing makes sense

until we understand that experience does not accumulate like money, or memory, or light years and frailties. Instead, it is presented to us by a God who is not under any obligation to the past, except in his eternal, freely given constancy. (223)

Robinson does not bring Darwin or Dawkins or sociobiology into her novels. But they are there in the shadows. She is writing from within the other paradigm, the other world picture, the other religion. "I am content to place humankind at the center of Creation" (Robinson 2015, 9). You may or may not accept it. But you should see that she is very self-conscious about what she is doing. Presenting the case that makes Darwinism not just false in important respects but deeply irrelevant to the human condition and to our understanding of it. "If there is a scientific mode of thought that is crowding out and demoralizing the humanities, it is not research in the biology of the cell or the quest for life on other planets. It is this neo-Darwinism, which claims to cut through the dense miasmas of delusion to what is mere, simple, and real" (12). For her, Joe's disquisition on selfishness and altruism—inspired by the rising balloon and that only one hung on—is so beside the point as to be farcical. They all had a choice, and Logan alone showed himself a moral giant. The others were pigmies. No amount of Darwinian theorizing is going to take credit from Logan or excuse Joe and the others. No amount of Darwinian theorizing is needed to give meaning to the life of John Ames, his little family, and his friends and others in his community. For Ian McEwan, Progress is everything. Providence is a dated superstition, one that retards the forward course of modern life. For Marilynne Robinson, Progress is a false hope. People were no better in the middle of the twentieth century than they had been in the middle of the nineteenth. Worse perhaps. Without Providence, without God's grace, we have nothing. No hope, no joy, no genuine relationships with our Maker and with ourselves. We have come a full circle and are back where we started.

EPILOGUE

At the end of *A Portrait of a Lady* the reader is left hanging.[1] Isabel has returned to her vile husband, Gilbert Osmond. Is this going to be permanent or will she leave once and for all, perhaps to divorce and marry Caspar Goodwood? The last line has Henrietta, Isabel's friend, saying to Caspar: "Just you wait." Wait for what? Wait for Isabel to turn up on his doorstep? Or wait until he has grown up and forgotten her? Real life is a bit like that. Rarely do we get a happy ending. Rarely do we get an ending. And that is our story. In the past 300 years, something really important has happened. People have come to see that there were no miracles, no Creator God pleased with the job He had done, no promise or guarantee that we humans are special. Like all other organisms, we have been produced by a long, slow, natural process of change, of blind evolution and that is it. Charles Darwin was not the only figure in this story, but he was way and afar the most important. Whether one accepted it in whole, in part, or little at all, natural selection brought on by the struggle for existence struck a chill in people's hearts. We miss the import of what happened if we think of the "revolution"— and it is fully appropriate to use this term and to credit it to Darwin—simply as a matter of fact, of disinterested science. Making the crucial distinctions between pseudoscience and popular science, and popular science and professional science, it was at the popular science level that Darwinism struck hardest and had the greatest effect. And seen in this light, there was something we can properly speak of not just as a revolution in science but as a religious revolution, whether you want to speak without qualification of Darwinism as a religion or more cautiously of Darwinism as offering a new, secular religious perspective.

---

[1] I refer now to the original 1881 edition. In the revised 1908 edition, I read James as saying (what he had always intended) that the return to Osmond is final. Bender (1996, 138) suggests that James is reflecting a Spencerian observation that women are attracted to men who treat them badly.

It has clearly not vanquished all existing religions, Christianity in particular, the religion against which Darwinism was formed and fought and grew and matured. Even for believers, however, the world has changed and is less obvious. It isn't really true that for Marilynne Robinson we are back where we started. The great Congregationalist hymn-writer Isaac Watts wrote not only of the sacrifice on the Cross but also in a natural theological vein of the way in which the world testifies to the Creator.

> Joy to the world, the Lord is come!
> Let earth receive her King;
> Let every heart prepare Him room
> And heaven and nature sing.
>
> Joy to the earth, the Savior reigns!
> Let men their songs employ,
> While fields and floods, rocks, hills, and plains
> Repeat the sounding joy.[2]

In the post-Darwinian world, not only does nature not sing, it is hard to hear the tunes of Heaven either. Witness the way in which John Ames turned to Job for solace. He is part of a movement that reaches back into the nineteenth century for both believers and nonbelievers as they tried to make sense of a world without Archdeacon Paley's friendly God. Confidence in Divine Providence has been replaced by fear of those Purblind Doomsters. After Darwin, meaning has been drained from the world and all is laid on faith. "Where wast thou when I laid the foundations of the earth? declare, if thou hast understanding."

This is no obviously happy ending. Is it an ending at all? For some, there is nothing. For others, there is still hope, whether from outside or from within. Perhaps we can find value still in the world or perhaps we can find value in our hearts. Appropriately, let us give the last word to Thomas Hardy in his 1899 poem "The Darkling Thrush," a melancholic reflection on the existentially barren nature of our world, acknowledging that even now for some there is something true and beautiful to be seen and grasped. But not all of us can readily share in the optimism. It is all so ambiguous in the Darwinian world.

> I leant upon a coppice gate
>   When Frost was spectre-grey,
>   And Winter's dregs made desolate

---

[2] Emily Dickinson's style owes a huge amount to Isaac Watts, whose hymns were a major part of her Christian childhood. Obviously she turns his message the other way (Wolosky 1988).

The weakening eye of day.
The tangled bine-stems scored the sky
   Like strings of broken lyres,
And all mankind that haunted nigh
   Had sought their household fires.

The land's sharp features seemed to be
   The Century's corpse outleant,
His crypt the cloudy canopy,
   The wind his death-lament.
The ancient pulse of germ and birth
   Was shrunken hard and dry,
And every spirit upon earth
   Seemed fervourless as I.

At once a voice arose among
   The bleak twigs overhead
In a full-hearted evensong
   Of joy illimited;
An aged thrush, frail, gaunt, and small,
   In blast-beruffled plume,
Had chosen thus to fling his soul
   Upon the growing gloom.

So little cause for carolings
   Of such ecstatic sound
Was written on terrestrial things
   Afar or nigh around,
That I could think there trembled through
   His happy good-night air
Some blessed Hope, whereof he knew
   And I was unaware.

(Hardy 1994, 134)

BIBLIOGRAPHY

Adams, H. 1918. *The Education of Henry Adams*. Boston: Houghton Mifflin.

Adams, J. E. 1989. Woman red in tooth and claw: Nature and the feminine in Tennyson and Darwin. *Victorian Studies* 33: 7–27.

Allen, L., B. Beckwith, J. Beckwith, S. Chorover, D. Culver, N. Daniels, et al. 1976. Sociobiology: another new biological determinism. *BioScience* 26: 182–186.

Anon. [D. T. Ansted] 1860a. Species. *All the Year Round* 3 (58): 174–178.

———. [D. T. Ansted] 1860b. Natural Selection. *All the Year Round* 3 (63): 293–299.

———. [D. T. Ansted] 1861. Transmutation of Species. *All the Year Round* 4 (98): 519–521.

Anon. [J. W. Parker] 1860. *Essays and Reviews*. London: Longman, Green, Longman, and Roberts.

Ansted, D. T. 1860. *Geological Gossip: Or, Stray Chapters on Earth and Ocean*. London: Routledge, Warne, and Routledge.

Appleman, P. 1996. *New and Selected Poems, 1956–1996*. Fayetteville: University of Arkansas Press.

———. 2000. *Darwin: Norton Critical Edition*. New York: Norton.

———. [1984] 2009. *Darwin's Ark*. Bloomington, IN: Indiana University Press.

———. 2014. *The Labyrinth: God, Darwin, and the Meaning of Life*. New York: Quantuck Lane Press.

Arata, S. D. 1990. The Occidental tourist: "Dracula" and the anxiety of reverse colonization. *Victorian Studies* 33: 621–645.

Ashton, R. 1989. Doubting clerics: From James Anthony Froude to *Robert Elsmere* via George Eliot. *The Critical Spirit and the Will to Believe*. Edited by D. Jasper and T. R. Wright, 69–87. London: Macmillan.

Astro, R. 1973. *John Steinbeck and Edward F. Ricketts: The Shaping of a Novelist*. Minneapolis: University of Minnesota Press.

Bailey, J. O. 1946. Hardy's "Mephistophelian Visitants." *PMLA* 61: 1146–1184.

———. 1956. *Thomas Hardy and the Cosmic Mind: A New Reading of the Dynasts*. Chapel Hill: University of North Carolina Press.

———. 1963. Evolutionary meliorism in the poetry of Thomas Hardy. *Studies in Philology* 60: 569–587.

Barrett, P. H., P. J. Gautrey, S. Herbert, D. Kohn, and S. Smith, eds. 1987. *Charles Darwin's Notebooks, 1836–1844*. Ithaca, NY: Cornell University Press.

Bates, H. W. 1862. Contributions to an insect fauna of the Amazon Valley. *Transactions of the Linnean Society of London* 23: 495–515.

———. 1863. *The Naturalist on the River Amazon*. London: John Murray.

Bateson, W. 1909. Heredity and variation in modern lights. In *Darwin and Modern Science*. Edited by A. C. Seward, 85–101. Cambridge: Cambridge University Press.

———. 1922. Evolutionary faith and modern doubts. *Science* 55: 1412.

Baym, N. 2002. *American Women of Letters and the Nineteenth-Century Sciences*. New Brunswick, NJ: Rutgers University Press.

Baynes, T. S. 1873. Darwin on expression. *Edinburgh Review* 137: 492–508.

Beach, J. W. [1936] 1966. *The Concept of Nature in Nineteenth-Century English Poetry*. New York: Russell and Russell.

Beer, G. 1983. *Darwin's Plots: Evolutionary Narrative in Darwin, George Eliot, and Nineteenth Century Fiction*. London: Routledge and Kegan Paul.

———. 1985. Darwin's reading and the fictions of development. In *The Darwinian Heritage*. Edited by D. Kohn, 543–588. Princeton, NJ: Princeton University Press.

———. 2000. Rhyming as resurrection. In *Memory and Memorials, 1784–1914*. Edited by M. Lappe, J. M. Shuttleworth, and S. Campbell, 189–207. London: Routledge.

Bender, B. 1996. *The Descent of Love: Darwin and the Theory of Sexual Selection in American Fiction, 1871–1926*. Philadelphia: University of Pennsylvania Press.

———. 2004. *Evolution and "The Sex Problem": American Narratives During the Eclipse of Darwinism*. Kent, OH: Kent State University Press.

Bennett, A. [1905] 1906. *Sacred and Profane Love*. Leipzig: Tauchnitz.

Bergson, H. 1907. *L'évolution créatrice*. Paris: Alcan.

———. 1911. *Creative Evolution*. New York: Holt.

Berkove, L. I. 2004. Jack London and evolution: From Spencer to Huxley. *American Literary Realism* 36: 243–255.

Blake, D. H. 2010. Whitman's Ecclesiastes: The 1860 "Leaves of Grass" cluster. *Huntington Library Quarterly* 73: 613–627.

Blind, M. 1899. *The Ascent of Man*. London: Fisher Unwin.

Bloom, H. 2005. Introduction. *Edwardian and Georgian Fiction*. Edited by H. Bloom, 1–40. New York: Chelsea House.

Blunt, W. S. 1914. The Canon at Aughrim. *The Poetical Works of William Scarwen Blunt*. W. S. Blunt, 236–253. Vol. 2. London: Macmillan.

Bowler, P. J. 1984. *Evolution: The History of an Idea*. Berkeley: University of California Press.

———. 1988. *The non-Darwinian Revolution: Reinterpreting a Historical Myth*. Baltimore, MD: Johns Hopkins University Press.

———. 1996. *Life's Splendid Drama*. Chicago: University of Chicago Press.

Bown, N. 2010. What the alligator didn't know: natural selection and love in *Our Mutual Friend*. 19: *Interdisciplinary Studies in the Long Nineteenth Century*. (10). DOI: http://doi.org/10.16995/ntn.567

Bradley, A. 2009. The New Atheist novel: Literature, religion, and terror in Amis and McEwan. *Yearbook of English Studies*, 39: 20–38.

Bradley, I. C. 1988. *The Annotated Gilbert and Sullivan: Trial by Jury, The Sorcerer, Patience, Princess Ida, Ruddigore, The Yeomen of the Guard*. London: Penguin.

Brantlinger, P. 1988. *Rule of Darkness: British Literature and Imperialism, 1830–1914*. Ithaca, NY: Cornell University Press.

———. 2012. Race and the Victorian novel. In *The Cambridge Companion to the Victorian Novel* (2nd ed.). Edited by D. David, 129–147. Cambridge: Cambridge University Press.

Bridges, R. 1953. *Poetical Works of Robert Bridges*. Oxford: Oxford University Press.

Browne, J. 1995. *Charles Darwin: Voyaging. Volume I of a Biography*. New York: Knopf.

———. 2002. *Charles Darwin: The Power of Place. Volume II of a Biography*. New York: Knopf.

Browning, R. 1981. *The Poems, I*. London: Penguin.

Buchan, J. 1910. *Prester John*. Edinburgh: Blackwood.

———. [1916] 1992. *Greenmantle*. In *The Complete Richard Hannay*. 105–347. London: Penguin.

Buckland, A. 2008. Thomas Hardy, provincial geology and the material imagination. *Interdisciplinary Studies in the Long Nineteenth Century* 19 (6): DOI: http://dx.doi.org/10.16995/ntn.469.

Buckland, W. 1823. *Reliquiae Diluvianae*. London: John Murray.

Bud, R. 2013. Life, DNA and the model. *British Journal for the History of Science* 46: 311–334.

Bulwer Lytton, E. 1859. *What Will He Do with It?* Edinburgh: Blackwood.

Burchfield, J. D. 1975. *Lord Kelvin and the Age of the Earth.* New York: Science History Publications.

Burnett, J. 1773–1792. *On the Origin and Progress of Language.* Edinburgh and London: Balfour and Cadell.

Burroughs, E. R. [1912] 2008. *Tarzan of the Apes.* London: Penguin.

Bury, J. B. [1920] 1924. *The Idea of Progress: An Inquiry into Its Origin and Growth.* London: Macmillan.

Bush, S. G. 1996. *A History of Modern Planetary Physics: Nebulous Earth.* Cambridge: Cambridge University Press.

Butler, S. 1872. *Erewhon, or Over the Range.* London: Trubner.

———. [1887] 1920. *Luck or Cunning?* London: Fifield.

———. 1903. *The Way of All Flesh.* London: Grant Richards.

———. 1935. *Letters Between Samuel Butler and E.M.A. Savage 1871–1885.* London: Jonathan Cape.

Byatt, A. S. [1992] 1994. *Angels and Insects.* New York: Random House.

Byron, G. G. Lord. 1847. *The Works of Lord Byron.* London: John Murray.

Canales, J. 2015. *The Physicist and the Philosopher: Einstein, Bergson, and the Debate That Changed Our Understanding of Time.* Princeton, NJ: Princeton University Press.

Canning, G., H. Frere, and G. Ellis. [1798] 1854. *The Loves of the Triangles.* London: Willis.

Cannon, W. F. 1961. The impact of uniformitarianism. Two letters from John Herschel to Charles Lyell, 1836–1837. *Proceedings of the American Philosophical Society* 105: 301–314.

Canton, W. 1927. Through the ages: The legend of a stone axe. *The Poems of William Canton,* 50–58. London: George G. Harrap.

Carey, J. 2009. *William Golding: The Man Who Wrote Lord of the Flies.* New York: Free Press.

Carlyle, T. 1829. Signs of the Times. *Edinburgh Review,* XCVIII. Reprinted in T. Carlyle, *Critical and Miscellaneous Essays,* New York: Appleton, 1864, 187–196.

———. [1834] 1987. *Sartor Resartus: The Life and Opinions of Herr Teufelsdröckh.* Oxford: Oxford University Press.

———. 1993. *On Heroes, Hero-Worship, and the Heroic in History.* Berkeley: University of California Press.

Carroll, L. 1871. *Through the Looking-Glass, and What Alice Found There.* London: Macmillan.

Chambers, R. 1844. *Vestiges of the Natural History of Creation.* London: Churchill.

———. 1846. *Vestiges of the Natural History of Creation* (5th ed.). London: Churchill.

Chopin, K. [1899] 1994. *The Awakening.* New York: Norton.

Clark, R. and A. Gordon. 2003. *Ian McEwan's "Enduring Love": A Reader's Guide.* New York and London: Continuum.

Cleto, F. 1992. The biological drama: Darwinian ethics in George Gissing's fiction. *The Gissing Journal,* 28: (3) 1–13, (4) 11–21.

Clough, A. H. 2003. *Arthur Hugh Clough: Selected Poems.* Edited by S. Chew. London: Routledge.

Conan Doyle, A. [1887] 2003. *The Complete Sherlock Holmes, Volume 1.* New York: Barnes and Noble.

———. [1912] 1995. *The Lost World.* Oxford: Oxford University Press.

Condorcet, A. N. [1795] 1956. *Sketch for a Historical Picture of the Progress of the Human Mind.* New York: The Noonday Press.

Conner, F. W. [1949] 1973. *Cosmic Optimism: A Study of the Interpretation of Evolution by American Poets from Emerson to Robinson.* New York: Farrar, Straus and Giroux.

Conrad, J. [1899] 1990. *The Heart of Darkness.* New York: Dover.

Cotter, J. F. 1995. Hopkins and Job. *Victorian Poetry* 33: 283–293.

Curwen, H. 1886. Zit and Xoe: Their early experiences. *Blackwood's Magazine* 139: 457–478, 612–634.

Cuvier, G. 1813. *Essay on the Theory of the Earth.* Translated by Robert Kerr. Edinburgh: W. Blackwood.

———. 1817. *Le règne animal distribué d'aprés son organisation, pour servir de base à l'histoire naturelle des animaux et d'introduction à l'anatomie comparée.* Paris: Déterville.

Dalziel, P. 2000. Religion. *Oxford Reader's Companion to Hardy.* Edited by N. Page, 368–374. Oxford: Oxford University Press.

Darwin, C. 1839. *Journal of Researches into the Geology and Natural History of the Various Countries Visited by HMS Beagle.* London: Henry Colburn.

———. 1859. *On the Origin of Species by Means of Natural Selection, or the Preservation of Favoured Races in the Struggle for Life.* London: John Murray.

———. 1861. *Origin of Species* (3rd ed.). London: John Murray.

———. 1868. *The Variation of Animals and Plants Under Domestication.* London: John Murray.

———. 1871. *The Descent of Man, and Selection in Relation to Sex.* London: John Murray.

———. 1872. *The Expression of the Emotions in Man and Animals.* London: John Murray.

———. 1958. *The Autobiography of Charles Darwin 1809–1882* (With the original omissions restored. Edited and with appendix and notes by his granddaughter Nora Barlow). London: Collins.

———. 1985–. *The Correspondence of Charles Darwin.* Cambridge: Cambridge University Press.

Darwin, C., and A. R. Wallace. 1858. On the tendency of species to form varieties; and on the perpetuation of varieties and species by means of selection. *Proceedings of the Linnaean Society, Zoological Journal* 3: 46–62.

Darwin, E. 1789. *The Botanic Garden* (Part II, *The Loves of the Plants*). London: J. Johnson.

———. 1794–1796. *Zoonomia; or, The Laws of Organic Life.* London: J. Johnson.

———. 1803. *The Temple of Nature.* London: J. Johnson.

Darwin, F. 1887. *The Life and Letters of Charles Darwin, Including an Autobiographical Chapter.* London: John Murray.

Dawkins, R. 1976. *The Selfish Gene.* Oxford: Oxford University Press.

———. 1986. *The Blind Watchmaker.* New York: Norton.

———. 1995. *A River Out of Eden.* New York: Basic Books.

———. 1998. *Unweaving the Rainbow: Science, Delusion and the Appetite for Wonder.* New York: Houghton Mifflin.

———. 2006. *The God Delusion.* New York: Houghton, Mifflin, Harcourt.

Dean, S. 1977. *Hardy's Poetic Vision in* The Dynasts: *The Diorama of a Dream.* Princeton, NJ: Princeton University Press.

Debrabant, M. 2002. Birds, bees and Darwinian survival strategies in *Wives and Daughters. Gaskell Society Journal* 16: 14–29.

Dennett, D. C. 2006. *Breaking the Spell: Religion as a Natural Phenomenon.* New York: Viking.

Deresiewicz, W. 1998. Heroism and organicism in the case of Lydgate. *Studies in English Literature: 1500–1900* 38: 723–740.

Desmond, A. 1984. Robert E. Grant: The social predicament of a pre-Darwinian transmutationist. *Journal of the History of Biology* 17: 189–223.

———. 1997. *Huxley: From Devil's Disciple to Evolution's High Priest.* New York: Basic Books.

Desmond, A., and J. Moore. 2009. *Darwin's Sacred Cause: How a Hatred of Slavery Shaped Darwin's Views on Human Evolution.* New York: Houghton Mifflin Harcourt.

DeWitt, A. 2013. *Moral Authority, Men of Science, and the Victorian Novel.* Cambridge: Cambridge University Press.

Dickens, C. [1837] 1948. *The Pickwick Papers.* Oxford: Oxford University Press.

———. [1838] 1948. *Oliver Twist.* Oxford: Oxford University Press.

———. [1853] 1948. *Bleak House.* Oxford: Oxford University Press.

———. [1854] 1948. *Hard Times.* Oxford: Oxford University Press.

———. [1857] 1948. *Little Dorrit.* Oxford: Oxford University Press.

———. [1860] 1948. *Great Expectations.* Oxford: Oxford University Press.

———. [1865] 1948. *Our Mutual Friend.* Oxford: Oxford University Press.

Dickinson, E. 1960. *The Complete Poems of Emily Dickinson.* Edited by Thomas H. Johnson. New York: Little, Brown.

Diderot, D. 1943. *Diderot: Interpreter of Nature.* New York: International Publishers.

———. [1796] 1972. *The Nun*. London: Penguin.

Dijksterhuis, E. J. 1961. *The Mechanization of the World Picture*. Oxford: Oxford University Press.

Disraeli, B. [1847] 1871. *Tancred*. New York: Appleton.

———. [1870] 1894. *Lothair*. London: Longmans.

Dixon, E. S. 1862. A vision of animal existences. *Cornhill Magazine* 5 (27): 311–318.

Dolin, T. 2008. *George Eliot*. Oxford: Oxford University Press.

Dostoevsky, F. [1880] 1983. *The Brothers Karamazov*. Translator, A. R. MacAndrew. New York, NY: Bantam Books.

Dreiser, T. [1900] 1991. *Sister Carrie*. New York: Norton.

Eagleton, T. [1974] 1998. Thomas Hardy and *Jude the Obscure*. *The Eagleton Reader*. Edited by S. Regan, 36–48. Oxford: Blackwell.

Ebbatson, R. 1982. *The Evolutionary Self: Hardy, Forster, Lawrence*. Brighton, Sussex: Harvester.

Eberwein, J. D. 2013. Outgrowing Genesis? Dickinson, Darwin, and the higher criticism. In *Emily Dickinson and Philosophy*. Edited by J. Deppman, M. Noble, and G. L. Stonum, 47–66. Cambridge: Cambridge University Press.

Eliot, G. 1861. *Silas Marner*. Edinburgh and London: William Blackwood and Sons.

———. [1874] 2011. *Middlemarch: A Study of Provincial Life*. London: Collins.

———. [1876] 1967. *Daniel Deronda*. London: Penguin.

———. [1879] 2016. *The Impressions of Theophrastus Such*. NP: Printed by CreateSpace, for the Freeriver Community.

Ellegård, A. 1958. *Darwin and the General Reader: The Reception of Darwin's Theory of Evolution in the British Periodical Press, 1859–1872*. Gothenburg: Acta Universitatis Gothoburgensis, LXIV.

Emerson, R. W. [1841]. The Over-Soul. In *Self-Reliance, the Over-Soul and Other Essays*. Claremont, CA: Coyote Canyon Press, 55–68.

———. [1844] 1920. Surface. In *A Treasury of English Prose*. Edited by L. P. Smith, 196–198. Boston: Houghton Mifflin.

Evans, E. J. 2001. *The Forging of the Modern State: Early Industrial Britain, 1783–1870* (3rd ed.). Harlow, Essex: Longman.

Faggen, R. 1997. *Robert Frost and the Challenge of Darwin*. Ann Arbor: University of Michigan Press.

Faulkner, W. [1936]1986. *Absalom! Absalom!* New York: Vintage.

Fielding, K. J. 1996. Dickens and science? *Dickens Quarterly* 13: 200–16.

Fisher, P. 2003. Silas Marner. *George Eliot's* Silas Marner. Edited by H. Bloom, 5–14. New York: Chelsea House Books.

Fontana, E. 2005. Darwinian sexual selection and Dickens's "Our Mutual Friend." *Dickens Quarterly* 22: 36–42.

Fowles, J. [1969] 1998. *The French Lieutenant's Woman*. New York: Little, Brown.

Frangsmyr, T., ed. 1983. *Linnaeus: The Man and His Work*. Berkeley: University of California Press.

Frost, R. 1969. *The Poetry of Robert Frost*. Edited by E. D. Lathem. New York: Henry Holt.

Froude, J. A. 1849. *The Nemesis of Faith*. London: John Chapman.

Fulweiler, J. 1994. "A Dismal Swamp": Darwin, design and evolution in *Our Mutual Friend*. *Nineteenth-Century Literature* 49: 50–74.

Gaskell, E. [1855] 2011. *North and South*. London: Collins.

———. [1866] 1996. *Wives and Daughters*. London: Penguin.

Gatty, Mrs. A. 1862. Inferior animals. *Red Snow and Other Parables from Nature*. Mrs. A. Gatty. London: Bell and Daldy.

Gissing, G. [1891] 1976. *New Grub Street*. London: Penguin.

Glendening, J. 2013. *Science and Religion in Neo-Victorian Novels: Eye of the Ichthyosaur*. London: Routledge.

Godwin, W. [1793] 1976. *An Enquiry Concerning Political Justice, and Its Influence on General Virtue and Happiness*. Penguin: Harmondsworth, Middlesex.

———. [1794] 1982. *Things as They Are; or, The Adventures of Caleb Williams*. Oxford: Oxford University Press.

Goldberg, M. K. 1972. *Carlyle and Dickens*. Athens, GA: University of Georgia Press.

Golding, W. 1954. *Lord of the Flies*. London: Faber and Faber.

———. [1955] 1962. *The Inheritors*. New York: Harcourt.

———. 1956. *Pincher Martin*. London: Faber and Faber.

Gould, S. J. 1980. The Piltdown conspiracy. *Natural History* 89 (August): 8–28.

———. 1999. *Rocks of Ages: Science and Religion in the Fullness of Life*. New York: Ballantine.

Graham, K. W. 1990. *The Politics of Narrative: Ideology and Social Change in William Godwin's Caleb Williams*. New York: AMS Press.

Granofsky, R. 2003. *D. H. Lawrence and Survival: Darwinism in the Fiction of the Transitional Period*. Montreal: McGill-Queen's University Press.

Graver, S. 1984. *George Eliot and Community: A Study of Social Theory and Fictional Form*. Berkeley: University of California Press.

Gray, A. 1876. *Darwiniana*. New York: D. Appleton.

Greene, G. [1938] 1991. *Brighton Rock*. London: Penguin.

———. [1973] 1974. *The Honorary Consul*. New York: Simon and Schuster.

Greenslade, W. 1994. *Degeneration, Culture and the Novel 1880–1940*. Cambridge: Cambridge University Press.

Haggard, H. R. [1885] 2006. *King Solomon's Mines*. Oxford: Oxford University Press.

———. [1886] 1991. *She*. Oxford: Oxford University Press.

Halberstam, J. 1993. Technologies of monstrosity: Bram Stoker's *Dracula*. *Victorian Studies* 36: 333–352.

Hale, P. 2013. Monkeys into men and men into monkeys: chance and contingency in the evolution of man, mind and morals in Charles Kingsley's *Water Babies*. *Journal of the History of Biology* 46: 551–597.

Hamilton, W. D. 1964. The genetical evolution of social behaviour. *Journal of Theoretical Biology* 7: 1–52.

Hardy, T. 1873. *A Pair of Blue Eyes*. London: Tinsley Brothers.

———. [1878] 1999. *The Return of the Native*. London: Penguin.

———. [1892] 2010. *Tess of the D'Urbervilles*. London: Collins.

———. [1895] 1960. *Jude the Obscure*. London: Macmillan.

———. [1903–1906–1908] 2013. *The Dynasts*. CreateSpace Independent Publishing Platform.

———. 1987. *The Collected Letters of Thomas Hardy: Volume 6: 1920–1925*. Oxford: Oxford University Press.

———. 1994. *Collected Poems*. Ware, Hertfordshire: Wordsworth Poetry Library.

Harris, M., and J. Johnson, eds. 1998. *The Journals of George Eliot*. Cambridge: Cambridge University Press.

Harris, S. 2004. *The End of Faith: Religion, Terror, and the Future of Reason*. New York: Free Press.

Haught, J. F. 2008. *God and the New Atheism: A Critical Response to Dawkins, Harris, and Hitchens*. Louisville, KY: Westminster John Knox Press.

Hegel, G. W. F. [1817] 1970. *Philosophy of Nature*. Oxford: Oxford University Press.

Henson, L. 2003. History, science and social change: Elizabeth Gaskell's 'evolutionary' narratives. *Gaskell Society Journal* 17: 12–33.

Herschel, J. F. W. 1830. *Preliminary Discourse on the Study of Natural Philosophy*. London: Longman, Rees, Orme, Brown, Green, and Longman.

———. 1841. Review of Whewell's *History* and *Philosophy*. *Quarterly Review* 135: 177–238.

Higginson, T. W. 1891. Emily Dickinson's letters. *The Atlantic* 68: 444–456.

Hilton, B. 2006. *A Mad, Bad and Dangerous People? England 1783–1846*. (The New Oxford History of England.) Oxford: Oxford University Press.

Himmelfarb, G. 2009. *The Jewish Odyssey of George Eliot*. New York: Encounter Books.

Hitchens, C. 2007. *God Is Not Great: How Religion Poisons Everything*. New York: Hachette.

Holmes, J. R. 2009. *Darwin's Bards: British and American Poetry in the Age of Evolution*. Edinburgh: Edinburgh University Press.

———. 2012. Literature and science vs history of science. *Journal of Literature and Science* 5: 67–71.

Hughes, L. K. 2007. *Cousin Phyllis, Wives and Daughters,* and modernity. In *The Cambridge Companion to Elizabeth Gaskell.* Edited by J. L. Matus, 90–107. Cambridge: Cambridge University Press.

Hughes, T. 1971. *Crow.* New York: Harper.

Hughes, W. R. 1890. *Constance Naden: A Memoir.* London: Bickers.

Hull, D. L., ed. 1973. *Darwin and His Critics: The Reception of Darwin's Theory of Evolution by the Scientific Community.* Cambridge, MA: Harvard University Press.

Hume, D. [1757] 1963. A natural history of religion. In *Hume on Religion.* Edited by R Wollheim. London: Fontana, 31–98.

Hunter, A. 1983. *Joseph Conrad and the Ethics of Darwinism.* London: Croom Helm.

Hutton, J. 1788. Theory of the Earth; or an investigation of the laws observable in the composition, dissolution, and restoration of land upon the Globe. *Transactions of the Royal Society of Edinburgh* 1 (2): 209–304.

Huxley, J. S. 1912. *The Individual in the Animal Kingdom.* Cambridge: Cambridge University Press.

Huxley, T. H. [1859] 1893. The Darwinian hypothesis. *Times,* December 26. Reprinted in T. H. Huxley, *Collected Essays: Darwiniana.* London: Macmillan, 1–21.

———. [1860] 1893. The Origin of Species. In *Collected Essays: Darwiniana.* London: Macmillan, 22–79.

———. [1893] 2009. *Evolution and Ethics, edited with an introduction by Michael Ruse.* Princeton, NJ: Princeton University Press.

Ingham, P. 2003. *Thomas Hardy (Authors in Context).* Oxford: Oxford University Press.

James, H. 1865. "Our Mutual Friend." *The Nation* 786–7.

———. 1873. "Middlemarch." *Galaxy* 15: 424–428.

———. [1881] 2011. *The Portrait of a Lady.* London: Penguin.

James, W. 1880a. Great men, great thoughts, and the environment. *Atlantic Monthly* 46 (276): 441–59.

———. 1880b. *The Principles of Psychology.* New York: Henry Holt.

———. 1907. *Pragmatism: A New Name for Some Old Ways of Thinking.* New York: Longmans, Green.

Jones, H. F. 1919. *Samuel Butler, Author of Erewhon (1835–1902): A Memoir.* London: Macmillan.

Kant, I. [1787] 1998. Preface to the Second Edition. In I. Kant, *Critique of Pure Reason.* Translated and edited by P. Guyer and A. W. Wood, 106–124. Cambridge: Cambridge University Press.

Keane, P. J. 2008. *Emily Dickinson's Approving God: Divine Design and the Problem of Suffering.* Columbia: University of Missouri Press.

Kendall, M. 1887. *Dreams to Sell.* London: Longmans, Green.

Kenny, A. 2005. *Arthur Hugh Clough: A Poet's Life.* London: Continuum.

Killham, J. 1958. *Tennyson and "The Princess": Reflections of an Age.* London: Athlone Press.

Kimler, W., and M. Ruse. 2013. Mimicry and camouflage. In *The Cambridge Encyclopedia of Darwin and Evolutionary Thought.* Edited by M. Ruse, 139–145. Cambridge: Cambridge University Press.

Kingsley, C. [1848] 1983. *Alton Locke: Tailor and Poet.* Oxford: Oxford University Press.

———. 1855. *Glaucus, or The Wonders of the Shore.* Cambridge: Macmillan.

———. [1863] 2008. *The Water-Babies: A Fairy Tale for a Land-Baby.* London: Penguin.

Kipling, R. [1895] 2000. *The Jungle Books.* New York: Bantam.

———. [1901] 1994. *Kim.* London: Penguin.

———. 2001. *Collected Poems.* Ware, Hertfordshire: Wordsworth Poetry Library.

———. 2009. *Writings on Writing.* Cambridge: Cambridge University Press.

Kirkby, J. 2010. "[W]e thought Darwin had thrown 'the Redeemer' away": Darwinizing with Emily Dickinson. *The Emily Dickinson Journal* 19: 1–29.

Knowles, S. D. G. 1998. "Then You Wink the Other Eye": T. S. Eliot and the Music Hall. *ANQ: A Quarterly Journal of Short Articles, Notes and Reviews* 11: 20–32.

Kuhn, T. 1962. *The Structure of Scientific Revolutions.* Chicago: University of Chicago Press.

LaHaye, T., and J. B. Jenkins. 1995. *Left Behind: A Novel of the Earth's Last Days.* Wheaton, IL: Tyndale House.

Lamarck, J-B. 1809. *Philosophie zoologique*. Paris: Dentu.

Lankester, E. R. 1880. *Degeneration: A Chapter in Darwinism*. London: Macmillan.

Larson, E. J. 1997. *Summer for the Gods: The Scopes Trial and America's Continuing Debate over Science and Religion*. New York: Basic Books.

Larson, E. J., and M. Ruse. 2017. *The Story of Science and Religion: Dialogue Concerning Two Chief Ways of Knowing*. New Haven: Yale University Press.

Larson, J. L. 1985. *Dickens and the Broken Scripture*. Athens: University of Georgia Press.

Lawrence, D. H. [1915] 1949. *The Rainbow*. London: Penguin.

———. [1921] 1960. *Women in Love*. London: Penguin.

———. [1927] 1974. *Mornings in Mexico and Etruscan Places*. London: Penguin.

———. 1979. *The Letters of D. H. Lawrence: Volume I, September 1901–May 1913*. Edited by J. T. Boulton. Cambridge: Cambridge University Press.

Le Conte, J. 1891. *Evolution: Its Nature, Its Evidences, and Its Relation to Religious Thought*. New York: Appleton.

Lehan, R. 2005. *Realism and Naturalism: The Novel in an Age of Transition*. Madison: University of Wisconsin Press.

Lennox, J. 2009. *God's Undertaker: Has Science Buried God?* Oxford: Lion Hudson.

Levine, G. 1963. Isabel, Gwendolen, and Dorothea. *ELH* 30: 244–257.

———. 1988. *Darwin and the Novelists: Patterns of Science in Victorian Fiction*. Cambridge, MA: Harvard University Press.

Lewis, C. S. [1945] 1996. *That Hideous Strength*. New York: Simon and Schuster.

Lewis, M. [1796] 2008. *The Monk: A Romance*. Oxford: Oxford University Press.

Lewontin, R. C. 1974. *The Genetic Basis of Evolutionary Change*. New York: Columbia University Press.

Lightman, B. 2009. *Evolutionary Naturalism in Victorian Britain: The "Darwinians" and Their Critics*. Farnham, Surrey: Ashgate.

———. 2010. Darwin and the popularization of evolution. *Notes and Records of the Royal Society* 64: 5–24.

Litvack, L. 2004. Outposts of Empire: Scientific discovery and colonial displacement in Gaskell's "Wives and Daughters." *Review of English Studies* 55: 727–758.

Livingstone, D. N. 2008. *Adam's Ancestors: Race, Religion, and the Politics of Human Origins*. Baltimore: Johns Hopkins University Press.

Loesberg, J. 2008. Darwin, natural theology, and slavery: a justification of Browning's Caliban. *ELH* 75: 871–897.

London, J. [1903] 1990. *The Call of the Wild*. New York: Dover.

———. 1912. "The Scarlet Plague." In *London Magazine*, 513–540. New York: Macmillan.

Lundin, R. 2004. *Emily Dickinson and the Art of Belief*. Grand Rapids, MI: Eerdmans.

Lyell, C. 1830–1833. *Principles of Geology: Being an Attempt to Explain the Former Changes in the Earth's Surface by Reference to Causes Now in Operation*. London: John Murray.

MacDuffie, A. 2014. *The Jungle Books*: Rudyard Kipling's Lamarckian fantasy. *PMLA* 129: 18–34.

Mallet, P. 2009. Hardy and philosophy. *A Companion to Thomas Hardy*. Edited by K. Wilson, 21–35. Chichester: Wiley Blackwell.

Malthus, T. R. [1798] 1959. *Population: The First Essay*. Ann Arbor: University of Michigan Press.

Martin, C. A. 1983. Gaskell, Darwin, and *North and South*. *Studies in the Novel* 15: 91–107.

Mayhew, R. J. 2014. *Malthus: The Life and Legacies of an Untimely Prophet*. Cambridge, MA: Harvard University Press.

McDonald, R. 2012. "Accidental variations": Darwinian traces in Yeats's poetry. *Science in Modern Poetry: New Directions*. Edited by J. R. Holmes, 151–166. Liverpool: Liverpool University Press.

McElrath, J. R., and J. Crisler. 2010. *Frank Norris: A Life*. Champaign: University of Illinois Press.

McEwan, I. 1997. *Enduring Love*. London: Cape.

———. [2005] 2006. *Saturday*. London: Vintage.

———. 2006, April 1. A parallel tradition. *The Guardian*.

McGrath, A. 2013. *C. S. Lewis—A Life: Eccentric Genius, Reluctant Prophet.* Carol Stream, IL: Tyndall House.

McGrath, A., and J. C. McGrath. 2007. *The Dawkins Delusion: Atheist Fundamentalism and the Denial of the Divine.* Downers Grove, IL: InterVarsity Press.

McIntosh, J. 2000. *Nimble Believing: Dickinson and the Unknown.* Ann Arbor: University of Michigan Press.

Medawar, P. B. 1961. Review of the *Phenomenon of Man. Mind* 70: 99–105.

Meredith, G. 1870. "In the woods." *Fortnightly Review,* 8, 179–183.

———. [1879] 1968. *The Egoist.* London: Penguin.

Meyers, J. 1990. *D. H. Lawrence: A Biography.* New York: Knopf.

Millay, E. St. V. 1922. *A Few Figs from Thistles: Poems and Sonnets.* New York: Harper.

———. 1956. *Collected Poems.* New York: Harper.

Milton, J. [1667] 2000. *Paradise Lost.* London: Penguin.

Mivart, St. G. 1871. *Genesis of Species.* London: Macmillan.

Moore, A. 1890. The Christian doctrine of God. In *Lux Mundi.* Edited by C. Gore. London: John Murray, 57–109.

Moore, G. 1898. *Evelyn Innes.* London: T. Fisher Unwin.

———. 1901. *Sister Teresa.* London: T. Fisher Unwin.

———. [1909] 1929. *Sister Teresa.* Second edition. London: Ernest Benn.

Moore, G. E. 1903. *Principia Ethica.* Cambridge: Cambridge University Press.

Morton, P. 1984. *The Vital Science: Biology and the Literary Imagination, 1860–1900.* London: Allen and Unwin.

Müller, F. 1869. *Facts and Arguments for Darwin.* Translated by W. S. Dallas. London: John Murray.

Murphy, P. 2002. Fated marginalization: Women and science in the poetry of Constance Naden. *Victorian Poetry* 40: 107–130.

Myers, F. W. H. 1881. George Eliot. *The Century Magazine* November.

Naden, C. 1999. *Poetical Works of Constance Naden.* Kernville, CA: High Sierra Books.

Nagel, T. 2012. *Mind and Cosmos: Why the Materialist Neo-Darwinian Conception of Nature Is Almost Certainly False.* New York: Oxford University Press.

Najder, Z. 2007. *Joseph Conrad: A Life.* London: Camden House.

Naso, A. 1981. Jack London and Herbert Spencer. *Jack London Newsletter,* 14: 13–34.

Newman, J. H. 1864. *Apologia Pro Vita Sua.* London: Longman, Green, Longman, Roberts, and Green.

Newton, K. M. 1974. George Eliot, George Henry Lewes, and Darwinism. *Durham University Journal* 66: 278–293.

Noll, M. 2002. *America's God: From Jonathan Edwards to Abraham Lincoln.* New York: Oxford University Press.

Norris, F. 1899. *McTeague: A Story of San Francisco.* New York: Grosset and Dunlap.

Numbers, R. L. 2006. *The Creationists: From Scientific Creationism to Intelligent Design.* Second Edition. Cambridge, MA: Harvard University Press.

Obama, B., and M. Robinson. 2015. President Obama and Marilynne Robinson: A conversation. *New York Review of Books.* LXII (17): 4–8, LXII (18): 6–8.

Olby, R. C. 1963. Charles Darwin's manuscript of pangenesis. *The British Journal for the History of Science,* 1: 251–263.

Owen, R. 1849. *On the Nature of Limbs.* London: Voorst.

———. 1860. *Paleontology or A Systematic Summary of Extinct Animals and their Geological Relations.* Edinburgh: Adam and Charles Black.

Paley, W. [1794] 1819. *Evidences of Christianity (Collected Works: III).* London: Rivington.

———. [1802] 1819. *Natural Theology (Collected Works: IV).* London: Rivington.

Parrett, A. 2004. Introduction. *The Martian Tales Trilogy.* Edited by E. R. Burroughs, xiii–xix. New York: Barnes and Noble.

Paterson, J. 1959. *The Return of the Native* as antichristian document. *Nineteenth-Century Fiction.* 14: 111–127.

Peacock, T. L. [1817] 1891. *Melincourt*. London: Dent.

Pearson, K. 1900. *The Grammar of Science* (2nd ed.). London: Black.

Peel, R. 2010. *Emily Dickinson and the Hill of Science*. Cranbury, NJ: Fairleigh Dickinson University Press.

Perry, C., and W. Zade. 2012. Interview with Pattiann Rogers. *Missouri Review*. 32 (4), 76–95.

Peterson, W. S. 1970. Gladstone's review of *Robert Elsmere*: Some unpublished correspondence. *The Review of English Studies* 21: 442–461.

———. 1976. *Victorian Heretic: Mrs Humphry Ward's* Robert Elsmere. Leicester: Leicester University Press.

Pizer, D. 1961. Evolutionary ethical dualism in Frank Norris' *Vandover and the Brute* and *McTeague*. *PMLA* 76: 552–560.

Plantinga, A. 2011. *Where the Conflict Really Lies: Science, Religion, and Naturalism*. New York: Oxford University Press.

Najder, Z. 2007. *Joseph Conrad: A Life*. London: Camden House.

Poirier, R. 1990. *Robert Frost: The Work of Knowing*. Redwood City, CA: Stanford University Press.

Popper, K. R. 1974. Intellectual autobiography. In *The Philosophy of Karl Popper*. Edited by Paul A. Schilpp, 1:3–181. LaSalle, IL: Open Court.

Poulton, E. B. 1890. *The Colours of Animals*. London: Kegan Paul, Trench, Truebner.

———. 1908. *Essays on Evolution, 1889–1907*. Oxford: Oxford University Press.

Provine, W. B. 1971. *The Origins of Theoretical Population Genetics*. Chicago: University of Chicago Press.

Railsback, B. E. 1995. *Parallel Expeditions: Charles Darwin and the Art of John Steinbeck*. Moscow, Idaho: University of Idaho Press.

Reade, W. W. [1875] 2012. *The Outcast*. Los Angeles: IndoEuropean.

Richards, R. J. 1987. *Darwin and the Emergence of Evolutionary Theories of Mind and Behavior*. Chicago: University of Chicago Press.

———. 2008. *The Tragic Sense of Life: Ernst Haeckel and the Struggle over Evolutionary Thought*. Chicago: University of Chicago Press.

Richards, R. J., and M. Ruse. 2016. *Debating Darwin*. Chicago: University of Chicago Press.

Richardson, A. 1998. 'Some science underlies all art': The dramatization of sexual selection and racial biology in Thomas Hardy's *A Pair of Blue Eyes* and *The Well-Beloved*. *Journal of Victorian Culture* 3: 302–338.

Riquelme, J. P. 1999. The modernity of Thomas Hardy's poetry. In *The Cambridge Companion to Thomas Hardy*. Edited by D. Kramer, 204–223. Cambridge: Cambridge University Press.

Roberts, J. H. 1988. *Darwinism and the Divine in America: Protestant Intellectuals and Organic Evolution, 1859–1900*. Madison: University of Wisconsin Press.

Robinson, M. [1998] 2005. *The Death of Adam: Essays on Modern Thought*. New York: Picador.

———. [2004] 2005. *Gilead*. London: Virago.

———. 2008. *Home*. New York: Farrar, Straus, and Giroux.

———. 2014. *Lila*. London: Virago.

———. 2015. *The Givenness of Things: Essays*. New York: Farrar, Straus and Giroux.

Robinson, R. 1980. Hardy and Darwin. In *Thomas Hardy: The Writer and His Background*. Edited by N. Page, 128–15. New York: St. Martin's.

Roger, J. 1997. *Buffon: A Life in Natural History*. Translated by S. L. Bonnefoi. Ithaca, NY: Cornell University Press.

Rogers, P. 2001. *Song of the World Becoming: New and Collected Poems 1981–2001*. Minneapolis, MN: Milkweed.

Roppen, G. 1956. *Evolution and Poetic Belief: A Study in Some Victorian and Modern Writers*. Oslo: Oslo University Press.

Rossetti, C. G. 1904. Later life: A double sonnet of sonnets. In *The Poetical Works of Christina Georgina Rossetti: With Memoir and Notes &c.* Edited by W. M. Rossetti. London: Macmillan.

Roth, P. [1969] 1994. *Portnoy's Complaint*. New York: Random House.

Ruddick, N. 2007. The fantastic fiction of fin de siècle. *The Cambridge Companion to the Fin de Siècle*. Edited by G. Marshall, 189–206. Cambridge: Cambridge University Press.

Rudolph, J. L. 2015. Myth 23. That the Soviet launch of Sputnik caused the revamping of American science education. In *Newton's Apple and Other Myths about Science*. Edited by R. L. Numbers and K. Kampourakis, 186–192. Cambridge, MA: Harvard University Press.

Rudwick, M. J. S. 2005. *Bursting the Limits of Time*. Chicago: University of Chicago Press.

Rupke, N. A. 1994. *Richard Owen: Victorian Naturalist*. New Haven: Yale University Press.

Ruse, M. 1975a. Charles Darwin's theory of evolution: an analysis. *Journal of the History of Biology* 8: 219–241.

———. 1975b. Darwin's debt to philosophy: an examination of the influence of the philosophical ideas of John F.W. Herschel and William Whewell on the development of Charles Darwin's theory of evolution. *Studies in History and Philosophy of Science* 6: 159–181.

———. 1979. *The Darwinian Revolution: Science Red in Tooth and Claw*. Chicago: University of Chicago Press.

———. 1982. *Darwinism Defended: A Guide to the Evolution Controversies*. Reading, MA: Benjamin/ Cummings.

———. 1986. *Taking Darwin Seriously: A Naturalistic Approach to Philosophy*. Oxford: Blackwell.

———, editor. 1988a. *But Is It Science? The Philosophical Question in the Creation/Evolution Controversy*. Buffalo, NY: Prometheus.

———. 1988b. *Homosexuality: A Philosophical Inquiry*. Oxford: Blackwell.

———. 1996. *Monad to Man: The Concept of Progress in Evolutionary Biology*. Cambridge, MA: Harvard University Press.

———. 1999. *Mystery of Mysteries: Is Evolution a Social Construction?* Cambridge, MA: Harvard University Press.

———. 2003. *Darwin and Design: Does Evolution Have a Purpose?* Cambridge, MA: Harvard University Press.

———. 2005. *The Evolution-Creation Struggle*. Cambridge, MA: Harvard University Press.

———. 2006. *Darwinism and Its Discontents*. Cambridge: Cambridge University Press.

———, ed. 2009. *Philosophy After Darwin: Classic and Contemporary Readings*. Princeton, NJ: Princeton University Press.

———. 2012. *The Philosophy of Human Evolution*. Cambridge: Cambridge University Press.

———. 2013. *The Gaia Hypothesis: Science on a Pagan Planet*. Chicago: University of Chicago Press.

———. 2015a. *Atheism: What Everyone Needs to Know*. Oxford: Oxford University Press.

———. 2015b. Sexual selection: Why does it play such a large role in the *Descent of Man*? In *Current Perspectives on Sexual Selection: What's Left After Darwin?* Edited by T. Hoquet, 3–17. New York: Springer.

Sage, V. 1999. Dickens and Professor Owen: Portrait of a friendship. In *Le Portrait*. Edited by P. Arnaud, 87–101. Paris: Presses Universitaires Paris-Sorbonne.

Salmon, M. A. 2000. *The Aurelian Legacy: British Butterflies and Their Collectors*. Berkeley: University of California Press.

Salter, M. J. 1997. Foreword. In *The Collected Poems of Amy Clampitt*. A. Clampitt, xiii–xxv. New York: Knopf.

Saunders, J. P. 2009. *Reading Edith Wharton Through a Darwinian Lens: Evolutionary Biological Issues in Her Fiction*. Jefferson, NC: McFarland.

Schmitt, C. 2014. Evolution and Victorian fiction. In *Evolution and Victorian Culture*. Edited by B. Lightman, and B. Zon, 17–38. Cambridge: Cambridge University Press.

Schweik, R. 1999. The influence of religion, science, and philosophy on Hardy's writings. In *The Cambridge Companion to Thomas Hardy*. Edited by D. Kramer, 54–72. Cambridge: Cambridge University Press.

Secord, J. A. 2000. *Victorian Sensation: The Extraordinary Publication, Reception, and Secret Authorship of* Vestiges of the Natural History of Creation. Chicago: University of Chicago Press.

Sepkoski, D. 2012. *Rereading the Fossil Record: The Growth of Paleobiology as an Evolutionary Discipline*. Chicago: Chicago University Press.

Sepkoski, J. J. Jr 1994. What I did with my research career: or how research on biodiversity yielded data on extinction. In *The Mass Extinction Debates: How Science Works in a Crisis*. Edited by W. Glen, 132–44. Stanford, CA: Stanford University Press.

Shatto, S. 1976. Byron, Dickens, Tennyson, and the Monstrous Efts. *The Yearbook of English Studies* 6: 144–155.

Shaw, G. B. 1921. *Back to Methuselah: A Metabiological Pentateuch*. London: Constable.

Shelley, P. B. 1821. *Queen Mab*. London: Clark.

Showalter, E. 1990. *Sexual Anarchy: Gender and Culture at the Fin de Siècle*. New York: Viking.

Shuttleworth, S. 1984. *George Eliot and Nineteenth-century Science: The Make-believe of a Beginning*. Cambridge: Cambridge University Press.

Sidgwick, H. 1876. The theory of evolution in its application to practice. *Mind* 1: 52–67.

Sinclair, U. [1906] 2001. *The Jungle*. New York: Dover.

Singer, R. E. 1963. *Job's Encounter*. New York: Bookman.

Singley, C. J. 1995. *Edith Wharton: Matters of Mind and Spirit*. Cambridge: Cambridge University Press.

Smith, A. [1776] 1994. *An Inquiry into the Nature and Causes of the Wealth of Nations*. New York: The Modern Library.

Smith, J. 1995. "The Cock of Lordly Plume": Sexual selection and *The Egoist*. *Nineteenth-Century Literature* 50: 51–77.

———. 1999. Darwin's barnacles, Dickens's *Little Dorrit*, and the social uses of Victorian seaside studies. *LIT: Literature Interpretation Theory* 10: 327–347.

Smuts, J. C. 1926. *Holism and Evolution*. London: Macmillan.

Spencer, H. 1851. *Social Statics; Or the Conditions Essential to Human Happiness Specified and the First of Them Developed*. London: J. Chapman.

———. 1852. A theory of population, deduced from the general law of animal fertility. *Westminster Review* 1: 468–501.

———. 1857. Progress: Its law and cause. *Westminster Review* LXVII: 244–267.

———. 1860. The social organism. *Westminster Review*. LXXIII: 90–121.

———. 1862. *First Principles*. London: Williams and Norgate.

———. 1867. *First Principles* (2nd ed.). London: Williams and Norgate.

———. [1873] 1889. *The Study of Sociology*. New York: Appleton.

———. 1879. *The Data of Ethics*. London: Williams and Norgate.

Stapledon, W. O. 1930. *Last and First Men: A Story of the Near and Far Future*. London: Methuen.

Steinbeck, J. [1939] 2006. *The Grapes of Wrath*. London: Penguin.

———. [1942] 1962. *The Log from the Sea of Cortez*. New York: Viking.

Steiner, R. [1914] 2005. *Occult Science: An Outline*. Forest Row, Sussex: Rudolf Steiner Press.

Stevenson, L. 1932. *Darwin Among the Poets*. Chicago: University of Chicago Press.

Stevenson, R. L. [1886] 2003. *Dr. Jekyll and Mr. Hyde*. New York: Norton.

Stoker, B. [1897] 1993. *Dracula*. London: Penguin.

Strachey, L. 1918. *Eminent Victorians*. London: Chatto and Windus.

Straley, J. 2007. Of beasts and boys: Kingsley, Spencer, and the theory of recapitulation. *Victorian Studies* 49: 583–609.

Sulloway, F. J. 1979. *Freud: Biologist of the Mind*. New York: Basic Books.

Sumner, W. G. 1914. *The Challenge of Facts and Other Essays*. New Haven: Yale University Press.

Swinburne, A. C. 1904. *The Poems of Algernon Charles Swinburne*. London: Chatto and Windus.

Taylor, E. 1989. *The Poems of Edward Taylor*. Chapel Hill: University of North Carolina Press.

Teilhard de Chardin, P. [1955] 1959. *The Phenomenon of Man*. London: Collins.

Tennyson, A. 1850. *In Memoriam*. London: Edward Moxon.

———. 1870. *The Holy Grail and Other Poems*. London: Strahan.

———. 1886. *Locksley Hall: Sixty Years After Etc*. London: Macmillan.

———. 1892. *The Death of Œnone, Akbar's Dream, and Other Poems*. London: Macmillan

———. 1994. *The Works of Alfred Lord Tennyson*. London: Wordsworth.

Tennyson, G. B. 1965. *Sartor Called Resartus: The Genesis, Structure and Style of Thomas Carlyle's First Major Work*. Princeton, NJ: Princeton University Press.

Thain, M. 2003. "Scientific Wooing": Constance Naden's marriage of science and poetry. *Victorian Poetry* 41: 151–169.

Thompson, J. [1874] 2003. *The City of the Dreadful Night*. London: Agraphia.

Tredell, N. 1998. *Joseph Conrad: Heart of Darkness*. New York: Columbia University Press.

Tutt, J. W. 1890. Melanism and melanochromism in British lepidoptera. *The Entomologist's Record, and Journal of Variation* 1 (3): 49–56.

Twain, M. [1884] 1985. *The Adventures of Huckleberry Finn*. London: Penguin.

———. [1903] 2004. Was the world made for man? In *Letters from the Earth: Uncensored Writings*. Edited by B. DeVoto, 221–226. New York: First Perennial Classics.

Uglow, J. 1993. *Elizabeth Gaskell: A Habit of Stories*. London: Faber and Faber.

Vendler, H. 2010. *Dickinson: Selected Poems and Commentaries*. Cambridge, MA: Harvard University Press.

Vogeler, M. S. 2008. *Austin Harrison and the English Review*. Columbia: University of Missouri Press.

Voltaire. [1759] 1947. *Candide*. Harmondsworth, MDX: Penguin.

Vonnegut, K. [1985] 1999. *Galapagos*. New York: Random House.

Wallace, A. R. 1866. On the phenomena of variation and geographical distribution as illustrated by the Papilionidae of the Malayan region. *Transactions of the Linnean Society of London* 25: 1–27.

———. 1889. *Darwinism: An Exposition of the Theory of Natural Selection with Some of its Applications*. London: Macmillan.

———. 1891. *Natural Selection and Tropical Nature*. London: Macmillan.

Ward, Mrs. H. 1888. *Robert Elsmere*. London: Macmillan.

———. 1909. Introduction. In *The Writings of Mrs. Humphry Ward: Robert Elsmere. Volume I*. Boston and New York: Houghton Mifflin, xiii–xliv.

Weismann, A. 1882. *Studies in the Theory of Descent*. Translator R. Meldola. London: Sampson Low, Marston, Searle, and Rivington.

Weldon, W. F. R. 1898. Presidential Address to the Zoological Section of the British Association. *Transactions of the British Association*. 887–902. Bristol.

Wells, H. G. [1895] 2005. *The Time Machine*. London: Penguin.

———. [1897] 1938. A Story of the Stone Age. *The Famous Short Stories of H. G. Wells*. New York: Garden City Publishing.

Wharton, E. 1904. *The Descent of Man and Other Stories*. New York: Charles Scribner's Sons.

———. [1905] 2002. *The House of Mirth*. New York: Dover.

Whewell, W. 1837. *The History of the Inductive Sciences*. London: Parker.

———. 1840. *The Philosophy of the Inductive Sciences*. London: Parker.

White, G. D. V. 2006. *Jane Austen in the Context of Abolition: "A Fling at the Slave Trade."* London: Palgrave-Macmillan.

Whitehead, A. N. 1929. *Process and Reality: An Essay in Cosmology*. New York: Macmillan.

Whitman, W. 1892. Darwinism—(then furthermore). In *Complete Prose Works*. W. Whitman, 326–327. Philadelphia: McKay.

———. 2004. *The Complete Poems*. London: Penguin.

Williams, C. 1983. Natural selection and narrative form in "The Egoist." *Victorian Studies* 27: 53–79.

Wilson, A. 1956. *Anglo-Saxon Attitudes*. London: Secker and Warburg.

Wilson, E. O. 1975. *Sociobiology: The New Synthesis*. Cambridge, MA: Harvard University Press.

———. 1978. *On Human Nature*. Cambridge, MA: Harvard University Press.

Wolosky, S. 1988. Rhetoric or not: Hymnal tropes in Emily Dickinson and Isaac Watts. *New England Quarterly* 61: 214–232.

Wordsworth, W. 1994. *The Works of William Wordsworth*. Ware, Hertsfordshire: The Wordsworth Poetry Library.

Yeats, W. B. 1996. *The Collected Poems of W. B. Yeats*. Edited by R. J. Finneran. New York: Scribner.

Zaniello, T. 1988. *Hopkins in the Age of Darwin*. Iowa City: University of Iowa Press.

Zapedowska, M. 2006. Wrestling with silence: Emily Dickinson's Calvinist God. *American Transcendental Quarterly* 20: 379–398.

INDEX